D1360747

Final Cut Pro Workflows

The Art Institute of San Antonio
10,000 IH 10 West
San Antonio, TX 78230

Final Cut Pro Workflows
The Independent Studio Handbook

Jason Osder
Robbie Carman

ELSEVIER

Amsterdam • Boston • Heidelberg • London • New York
Oxford • Paris • San Diego • San Francisco • Singapore
Sydney • Tokyo
Focal Press is an imprint of Elsevier

Publisher: Joanne Tracy
Acquisitions Editor: Dennis McGonagle
Assistant Editor: Chris Simpson
Marketing Manager: Christine Degon
Publishing Services Manager: George Morrison
Project Manager: Marilyn E. Rash
Copyeditor: Dave Buskus
Proofreader: Dianne Wood
Indexer: Ted Laux
Cover Design: Maria Mann
Typesetting: Amigo Media
Text Printing: Sheridan Books
Cover Printing: Phoenix Color Corp.

Focal Press is an imprint of Elsevier
30 Corporate Drive, Suite 400, Burlington, MA 01803-4255, USA
Linacre House, Jordan Hill, Oxford OX2 8DP, UK

Copyright © 2008 by Elsevier Inc. All rights reserved.

No part of this publication may be reproduced, stored in a retrieval system, or transmitted in any form or by any means, electronic, mechanical, photocopying, recording, or otherwise, without the prior written permission of the publisher.

Permissions may be sought directly from Elsevier's Science & Technology Rights Department in Oxford, UK: phone: (+44) 1865 843830, fax: (+44) 1865 853333, e-mail: permissions@elsevier.com. You may also complete your request on-line via the Elsevier homepage (*http://elsevier.com*), by selecting "Support & Contact" then "Copyright and Permission" and then "Obtaining Permissions."

Recognizing the importance of preserving what has been written, Elsevier prints its books on acid-free paper whenever possible.

Library of Congress Cataloging-in-Publication Data
Osder, Jason.
  Final Cut Pro workflows : the independent studio handbook / Jason Osder,
  Robbie Carman.
      p. cm.
Includes index.
ISBN 978-0-240-81005-8 (alk. paper)
1. Digital video—Editing—Data processing. 2. Final cut (Electronic resource)
  3. Workflow. I. Carman, Robbie. II. Title.
TR899.O84 2007
778.59'3—dc22   2007038743

British Library Cataloguing-in-Publication Data
A catalogue record for this book is available from the British Library.

For information on all Focal Press publications visit our website at
www.books.elsevier.com.

07 08 09 10 11   10 9 8 7 6 5 4 3 2 1

Working together to grow
libraries in developing countries

www.elsevier.com | www.bookaid.org | www.sabre.org

ELSEVIER   BOOK AID International   Sabre Foundation

To my grandfather, Benjamin Klein.

To all of my teachers and collaborators,
especially those whose voices echo
in the pages of this book.

– Jason Osder

To my parents, John and Marcia,
for supporting me in my dream to do what I do.

To my beautiful wife, Catherine.
Without her love and support, this book
would not have been possible.

Finally, to John Woody, my mentor,
who showed me the power and beauty
of teaching and learning.

– Robbie Carman

About the Authors

Jason Osder is adjunct assistant professor in the School of Media and Public Affairs at The George Washington University. He is an Apple-certified Final Cut Pro instructor and an experienced producer and information architect.

Robbie Carman is part of the first generation of certified Apple Final Cut Pro instructors. Currently, he is certified to teach Final Cut Pro, DVD Studio Pro, Aperture, Motion, and Color. Robbie specializes in online editing and color correction on standard- and high-definition projects.

Jason Osder and Robbie Carman are partners at Amigo Media, a consultancy with the motto *Relate, Educate, Create*. Learn more at *www.amigomediallc.com*.

Contents

Acknowledgments

Many people have helped us in the creation of this book and deserve special thanks.

Alexis Van Hurkman's technical knowledge and professional guidance were invaluable. Tom Steinfeldt and Jill Ralph provided early help in getting the writing of this book off the ground.

Thank you to Luke Lindjhem, Catherine Carman, and Blaine Graboyes for donating their time to review the manuscript and provide comments—your real-world perspectives were very valuable.

Thanks to Paul Temme and Dennis McGonagle at Focal Press for shepherding through our first book.

Thanks to Megan Drygas for being our releif production artist in the final inning and to Amos Gelb, Director of the Semester in Washington Journalism program at the School of Media and Public Affairs at The George Washington University for the conversation that became the opening of Chapter 12.

We would also like to acknowledge several individuals and organizations that have helped by allowing us to take pictures and use other resources.

- Sam Crawford, chief engineer, and Rob Henninger, president and CEO, Henninger Media Services in Arlington, Virginia (*www.henninger.com*)

- Arjun Rao, Sean Gallagher, and Abby Greensfelder at Halfyard Productions in Bethesda, Maryland (*www.halfyardproductions.com*)

- Ben Howard, director of postproduction, NAHB Production Group in Washington, D.C. (*www.nahbprods.com*)

- Wendy Harmic, chief engineer at the School of Media and Public Affairs at The George Washington University (*www.gwu.edu/~smpa/*)

Foreword

So you need to make a movie. Or a documentary. Or a corporate communications video. Or an episodic web-delivered serial adventure show, for that matter.

You've done a very good thing by picking up this book.

Video and film programs have always been made or broken by the amount of preparation that was done before even a single frame was recorded. At every step of preproduction, production, and postproduction, choices that affect both time and money (and usually both) assail you from every direction. Some are purely a matter of aesthetic preference, while others might be life or death decisions for your budget—and by extension your project. However, it can be difficult to know which pennies saved today will turn into pounds spent tomorrow.

Veterans of the postproduction process themselves, Robbie Carman and Jason Osder have navigated this minefield for various professional clients for years. In this book, they've undertaken the herculean task of cataloging and organizing just about every workflow you might reasonably undertake as you work your way from choosing which format to shoot your project in, through figuring out how best to put the finishing touches on the audio and color of your soon-to-be-complete masterpiece.

Production and postproduction aren't easy, and the technologies that we all rely on to do our work are constantly evolving, making possible new and creative solutions to the corners that we're constantly backed into. If you want my advice, take a slow morning off, sit down in a comfortable chair with a nice cup of coffee, and read this book from cover to cover. Dog-ear the pages that might apply to your particular project, and take plenty of notes. The project you save will likely be your own.

Alexis Van Hurkman
Writer, Director, Colorist

How to Get the Most From This Book

Final Cut Pro Workflows can be read cover to cover, but it is really designed to be a studio handbook—a quick reference used to put concepts into action. Like a good travel guide, this book combines useful practical instruction with historical context and anecdotal examples.

To organize this material, *Final Cut Pro Workflows* is presented in the following three parts:

Part 1: Final Cut Pro in Context is the most theoretical and historical section. Its goal is to bring all readers up to speed with some basic history about motion picture editing and Final Cut Pro, and also to define the idea of the workflow.

Parts 2 and 3 are more specific, but they rest on the principles explored in this part. Readers who are already familiar with Final Cut Pro, or have a long history with postproduction in general, will probably be familiar with some of this information. However, readers who come to this book with postproduction knowledge based mostly on FCP (or the opposite: old postproduction hands new to this software) will find Part 1 especially useful to fill in the gaps in their knowledge and put everything into context.

Part 2: Roles, Technologies, and Techniques is the guts of the book: the practical instruction. Each chapter in this part breaks apart a particular stage of the postproduction process, offering specific information and instruction on FCP techniques and workflow methods.

The chapters can be read as a refresher, or used in the studio as a problem-solving guide. Some of them give instruction on advanced techniques that often fall outside the scope of a manual or even a traditional software book: how to upload video files for online review, how to work with a vendor for finishing work, or how to decide whether it is reasonable to do that work on your own with Final Cut Pro.

Part 3: Real-World Workflows takes the ideas from Part 1 and the techniques from Part 2 and shows how they really play out in projects. These case studies highlight the importance (and, ultimately, the limitations) of workflow thinking and of good planning in general.

Part 3 has a unique perspective. In the real world, sometimes the best-laid plans go awry. Often we plan our workflows concentrating on the technical aspects, but then it is the creative or managerial aspects that turn out to be the real challenges. The real world is also made up of real people, and sometimes (actually, almost all of the time) interpersonal issues are challenges too.

With all of this potential for drama, we hope that the case studies in Part 3 are entertaining as well as informative.

Iconography

Final Cut Pro Workflows is also organized around three themes that are represented as icons and serve as a guide to the book's content. These categories are not seen as mutually exclusive, but more as overlapping areas of concern or modes of thinking.

Figure P.1   Managment icon.

Management issues revolve around budgets, schedules, staffing, and executive decisions. Although such issues don't always involve finances and money, these concerns are never far away.

Management issues are also workflow issues. The type of thinking and planning that goes into making detailed workflows is part of this category.

In addition, management issues are not separate from technical and creative issues. Often major management roles, such as the executive producer, have oversight of the larger creative and technical concerns.

Figure P.2   Technical icon.

Technical issues involve equipment—hardware and software. They may include production issues such as format choice, shooting ratio, and timecode. In post-production, they include tape formats, hard drives, capture cards, new storage media, and codecs.

Technical issues touch creative issues in the way that all artists use their tools. Technical issues and management issues are interdependent at all stages of planning and executing a project.

Figure P.3 Creativity Icon.

Creative issues are the ones most central to telling the story and painting the picture. This includes writing the script, making the editorial decisions in the editing room, and aesthetic choices such as pacing, music, tone, graphics, and color correction. Creative goals are dependent on both technical and managerial support.

You will see these icons on the outer edge of every page of the book, and occasionally in other places as a helpful cross-reference. They will help you see the threads that run through different aspects of applying workflow thinking to Final Cut Pro postproduction projects.

Final Cut Server and Web Content

A funny thing happened while we were writing this book. Apple announced the software Final Cut Server—a product made to facilitate Final Cut Pro workflows. Because this is an important advance, we wanted to write about it, but unfortunately, Apple was not ready to actually release the software by the time this book went to press.

To learn more about Final Cut Server, check this book's Web site for additional content: *http://booksite.focalpress.com/Osder/finalcut/*. While there, you'll find some more auxiliary content: additional case studies and a color appendix meant to accompany Chapter 10.

Address Your Needs

In the end, how to get the most from *Final Cut Pro Workflows: The Independent Studio Handbook* depends a lot on you and what you are trying to do:

- If you are relatively new to FCP and beginning to use it as a professional for the first time, a complete reading would be a good investment of time.

- If you have been a Final Cut Pro editor, but are taking on management or budget responsibilities for a postproduction project, you may want to concentrate on the chapters and parts marked with the management icon.

- Or, if you are experienced in postproduction, but starting a project of a type that is new to you, you might skip to Part 3 and look for a case study that is similar to your present goals.

Finally, all of the book rests on a simple philosophy: Final Cut Pro and related technologies have put professional postproduction in the hands of a much wider range of people. The ratio between technical quality and cost is continually shrinking. This is not to say that owning the equipment is the same as being able to do the work, and the difference lies in the knowledge of postproduction principles. The purpose of *Final Cut Pro Workflows* is to provide the instruction and proper context for all users to become more professional in their use of Final Cut Pro.

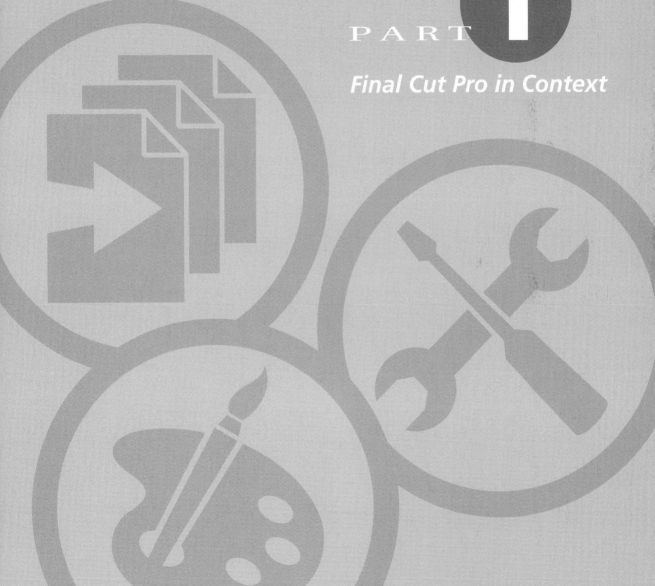

PART **1**

Final Cut Pro in Context

1 What Makes Final Cut Pro Special?

When it was released in 1999, Final Cut Pro (FCP) was a revolutionary piece of nonlinear editing software. Since then, the software (and the hardware that runs it) has matured substantially—adding features and spawning a complete suite of postproduction tools, Final Cut Studio.

Most people who were already working in postproduction knew they were seeing something special the first time they saw Final Cut Pro. To people who have entered the business since then, FCP is an industry standard.

Why is that? Why did seasoned professionals sense a sea change in the first few clicks? How has this software thoroughly changed the industry in a few short years? What makes Final Cut Pro so special?

There is a simple answer to that question: *money.*

Final Cut Pro has consistently done more things effectively, intuitively, and inexpensively than any of its competitors. From the program's first release and through its subsequent improvements, FCP has lowered the financial ceiling on professional-quality postproduction. This chapter is about how and why this has happened.

To fully understand what makes Final Cut Pro special, why it has had such an effect on the industry, and ultimately how to get the most out of it in your own projects, we must take a brief step back and look at FCP in context.

A Brief History of Editing the Motion Picture

The invention of motion picture technology preceded the invention of editing by several years. The first "films" by pioneers such as Thomas Edison and the Lumière brothers were single shots—a passionate kiss or a parade of royalty. *The Great Train Robbery* (1903) is widely considered to be the first use of motion picture editing, as well as the first narrative film.

Cutting together, or editing, footage to tell a story is a concept and a process that is largely distinct from simply capturing the moving image. As with all art forms, the aesthetics and technology of editing have changed and will continue to change, but many of the base concepts remain the same.

The evolution of editing technology has followed a predictable path from film, to magnetic analog tape, to digital media, and finally to ever less expensive digital media and higher resolutions. Final Cut Pro represents a key link in this evolution, but mostly because it does well (and inexpensively) what editors have always been doing.

Originally, film editing was performed as a physical process—pieces of film were taped together. The resulting assembled piece of film was played back, and this was essentially the finished product. Fast-forward to the age of video, and the analogous process becomes known as linear editing. Linear editing is done with a system that consists of two videotape recorders (VTRs) and two video monitors. Like cutting film, this was a straightforward process of playing the desired clip on one VTR (the source deck) and recording it on the other (the record deck).

Over time, these linear editing systems became more sophisticated. They worked with high-quality video formats, were controlled by computers, and integrated with graphics systems (Chyron) to overlay titling on video. Still, the basic principles of linear editing had not changed: two VTRs (one to play, the other to record).

There was one basic limitation to this system, and it was a frequent frustration for editors. The problem with linear editing is that once you lay down a piece of video on the record tape, you can record over it, but you cannot move it or change its length (at least not in a single pass).

In the early 1980s, with the power of computers on the rise, a new way to edit was invented: nonlinear, or digital, editing. Nonlinear editing is based on a completely different concept: convert the video into digital files (digitize). Then, instead of editing videotape to videotape, edit with these digital files that allow nonlinear access (you can jump to any point at any time with no cuing of the tape).

Putting a new shot at the beginning of a sequence (an insert edit) was no longer a problem. With all of the video existing as digital bits, and not on a linear tape, an insert edit was merely a matter of giving the computer a different instruction or pushing a different button on the keyboard. If linear editing is like writing on a typewriter, then nonlinear editing is like a word processor.

The Big Three: DV, FireWire, and FCP

By the mid-1990s, digital nonlinear editing was common but expensive. Three related pieces of technology were introduced that together drastically changed the face of postproduction.

The first is prosumer digital video (generally referred to as DV, this implies the encoding format DV-25 and the tape formats miniDV, DVCAM, and DVCPRO that work with it). These new formats were smaller and cheaper than existing broadcast formats such as Betacam SP, but with nearly the same quality. DV is also a digital format, meaning that the camera replaced the traditional tubes with new digital chips, and the video signal that is laid down onto the tape is also digital: information encoded as bits, rather than the analog information. To really understand DV, one must realize that it refers to both a tape format (a new type of physical videotape and cassette) and a codec. "Codec" is short for compression/decompression or code/decode. It refers to any algorithm used to create and play back video and audio files. Chapter 5 is all about codecs, but the important thing to realize at this point is that the DV-25 specification that appeared in the mid-nineties had both a tape and codec component, and both were of a higher quality in a smaller size than had previously been possible.

The second technological advance was FireWire, or IEEE 1394, a new type of digital protocol used for data transfer. Somewhat similar to USB, FireWire allows faster communications with external devices than was previously possible. In fact, FireWire is

Input/Output Protocol Basics

An input/output protocol, or I/O, is more than just a cable. An I/O is really made up of three components:

1. *The Cable.* There is a lot to a cable. Besides being the right type (FireWire, component, SDI), other considerations include the length of the cable, its flexibility, strength, and price. Considerations include maximum length, signal loss, and power use.

2. *The Connections.* Once you have the proper cable type, it is important that this cable is actually able to plug in to the hardware you are using. Many I/O protocols allow various types of device connections. In the case of FireWire, there are actually three device connection types—four-pin, six-pin, and nine-pin connectors—and three matching cable connections. Before buying a cable, make sure to check which type your device uses.

3. *Transfer Methodology.* This is how the devices "talk" to each other. Transfer methodology is a necessary component of any I/O protocol, even if it may go unnoticed by many users because it is usually hardwired into the circuitry of the device you are using. In the case of FireWire, it is built right into the port and is a three-layer system:

   a. *The Physical Layer* is the hardware component of the protocol that presents the signal from the device.

   b. *The Link Layer* translates the data into packets that can be transferred through the FireWire cable.

   c. *The Transaction Layer* presents the data to the software on the device that is receiving it.

fast enough to allow video capture directly from a DV camera into a computer without any additional hardware.

This brings up another example of changing terminology. In the previous section, we described "digitizing"—the process of loading video into a computer (making it digital). The process of loading DV into a computer through FireWire is essentially the same, but it cannot properly be called digitizing because the video is already digital! (Of course, many people have continued to call this process digitizing, because that was the accepted term.) More on this process can be found in Chapter 6: Preparation.

With DV cameras and FireWire devices already becoming popular, Apple Computer released Final Cut Pro in 1999. I remember sitting in a friend's basement, with a borrowed camcorder, capturing digital video through FireWire into Final Cut Pro for the first time. Prior to that, I had used only "professional" systems, and I was amazed to see video captured onto a sub-$10,000 system (including the camera).

By the eve of the millennium, all three of these advances had been established:

- An inexpensive, high-quality video format (DV)
- A high-bandwidth data-transfer protocol fast enough to capture video directly (FireWire)
- An inexpensive but robust nonlinear video-editing program (Final Cut Pro)

This trio created the technical and market conditions for unprecedented changes in the creation of video projects at all levels.

It should be made clear that Final Cut Pro was not (and is not) the only nonlinear editing program available. However, from the beginning, certain things made FCP special. Indeed, it is FCP, and not any of its competitors, that is quickly becoming the industry standard.

The QuickTime Video Architecture

QuickTime has been around since 1991, when it was introduced as an add-on to the Mac operating system that was used for playing video. At the time, this was a major advance and there was nothing comparable. Essentially, QuickTime is a video architecture, an infrastructure that allows video to be played on a computer. The codec is the algorithm used to encode and decode the digital video; the architecture is the virtual machine that does the decoding.

Final Cut Pro utilizes the QuickTime video architecture for driving video playback while editing. Final Cut Pro is the tool; QuickTime video is the material that the tool works on. This is why the media files you use in FCP have the .mov extension—the native extension of QuickTime files. FCP is not the only Apple program that utilizes the QuickTime architecture; iMovie and iTunes work in much the same way.

Going back to the old days of film, the individual snippets of film are QuickTime files, and the machine used to cut, tape, and play back is Final Cut Pro. As we said, many of the essential principles of editing have not changed very much. If you need further examples of this, notice the language that Final Cut Pro uses (such as "clip" and "bins") and the iconography (such as the symbols in the browser and the shape of the tools), and you will realize that the very design of the program is meant to recall traditional film methods.

What Is a Codec?

Codec means code/decode, compression/decompression, or compressor/decompressor, and is the name given to the specific algorithm used to compress a piece of audio or video. There is an extended discussion of codecs in Chapter 5. For now, it is enough to know that within the QuickTime architecture, multiple codecs are supported for different media types.

Resolution Independence

If you have used QuickTime to view video on the Web, you may have noticed that it can play back video of various sizes. This ability to work with video of different sizes is known as resolution independence, and it is something that Final Cut Pro shares with QuickTime.

This means that FCP can work with standard- and high-definition footage, and even the higher-definition resolutions used for film and digital intermediate process. It is a very versatile program in this way, and we have seen it used for off-sized video pieces as small as a Flash banner and as large as the JumboTron at the local football stadium.

This is unusual in nonlinear editing solutions, both within and outside Final Cut Pro's price range. With other editing product lines, there is often one piece of software

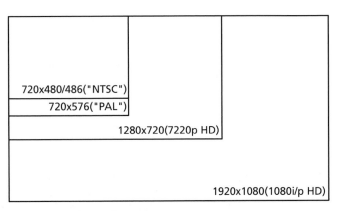

720x480/486("NTSC")
720x576("PAL")
1280x720(7220p HD)
1920x1080(1080i/p HD)

Figure 1.1 Common video frame dimensions.

for DV, another for uncompressed video, and yet another that handles HD. In Final Cut Pro, you may need different hardware to effectively work with different sizes and resolutions, but the software stays consistent.

Resolution independence is not only a benefit for working with different types of video. It also makes for a more flexible postproduction process at any resolution. The reason for this is that Final Cut Pro can mix resolutions and work at a lower resolution for speed and to conserve disk space (higher resolutions often have larger file sizes), and then return to the higher resolution for finishing.

This way of thinking is known as an offline/online workflow, and we will talk much more about it. Originally, it came about in the early days of nonlinear editing, before computers were robust enough to handle full-resolution footage digitally. The solution was to edit with low-resolution proxies or "offline" clips, and then assemble the final piece in a traditional tape-to-tape room based on the decisions that were made nonlinearly.

Final Cut Pro has added a lot more flexibility to this method. Resolution independence means that an HD piece can be rough cut at DV resolution, then reconformed to HD, or that a long piece can be assembled as a low-quality proxy to save drive space. The case studies in Part 3 have several permutations of this.

The resolution-independent nature of Final Cut Pro has gotten more robust in version 6 of the software. Two new features—the Open Format Timeline and the ProRes 422 codec—both expand the flexibility of the system in working with different formats and resolutions. Briefly, the ProRes 422 codec allows users to work with

Resolution and Screen Size

Resolution should not be confused with screen size. Resolution refers to the number of pixels that make up the video frame. A standard-definition (SD) video image is 720x486, and is the same whether you are watching a 13-inch or a 72-inch television. (The difference is that each individual pixel is larger on the larger set.)

Figure 1.1 shows the pixel resolutions, aspect ratios, and relative sizes of some common video formats. For more information on video formats, see Chapter 7.

near-uncompressed-quality video at approximately one-quarter of the bitrate. The Open Format Timeline option will support mixed-format playback on a Timeline with no rendering. These are both very sexy new features, and have the potential to cause another mini-revolution in the postproduction industry, as that financial ceiling for uncompressed and HD work again collapses.

The Democratization of the Form and the Rise of the Prosumer

Prior to the introduction of the Big Three technologies, cost was a huge barrier to entry for any video production even approaching the professional level. There were low-end formats, such as 8mm tape, but their quality was suspect. There were few good inexpensive solutions for editing.

This lower price combined with user-friendly products that were easier to learn made video available to the masses. This leveling applied to aspiring filmmakers, as well as to students, and also moms and dads who wanted to film softball games and birthday parties. The field now was wide open, as an art form, a hobby, and a business.

Alvin Toffler coined the term "prosumer" in his 1980 book *The Third Wave*. The word, a combination of *producer* or *professional* and *consumer*, denoted a blurring of the line that separated a professional producer and an amateur hobbyist. This is an apt description of many of the people who benefited from the democratization of video technologies. Moreover, a line (between professional and amateur) that had once seemed rigid has now been irrevocably breached.

The democratization of the form and the rise of the prosumer is actually a much broader phenomenon. The popularity of do-it-yourself home improvement and the user-made Internet are two more examples.

These changes in video technology allowed higher quality at a lower price and a new degree of creative freedom for professionals and aspiring filmmakers alike. Consider the film *Timecode*, which has simultaneous action filmed with four DV cameras, and the TV series *K Street*, which used a raw documentary style to depict the behind-the-scenes action in Washington, DC. Consider the rise of documentary in general—the genre has changed from a fringe academic form to popular entertainment.

There is a downside to this new availability of technology, this democratization: there are a lot of people who know just enough to be dangerous. This part of the phenomenon runs the gamut from a well-meaning relative who gets over his head with a wedding video to expensive corporate debacles where money is invested in new equipment without the necessary time, planning, and talent to accomplish the real goals.

In the old days, there was a hard line between those who could produce video and those who could not. Only a few could afford the investment in equipment it would take to create video at all. With the new low-priced gear, anyone could do it, so the difference became true practical knowledge and experience—that is, the difference between owning the equipment and knowing how to use it. With the prevalence of Final Cut Pro, we have independent filmmakers doing more and better work than ever before, but we also have hacks selling services from Apple's marketing material that they don't really have the ability to perform. With great power comes great responsibility—learn the craft; don't be a hack!

This is the production/business environment that we now operate in. There is a lot of opportunity here, and greater creative freedom than ever before. To properly navigate this new environment, our most valuable assets are practical and theoretical knowledge. Only by understanding the production process at a conceptual level can you efficiently communicate with clients and vendors to get the best product at the best price.

In the new arsenal of equipment, Final Cut Pro is both a scalpel and a bazooka. It is special because of its power, flexibility, and price point. Understanding FCP's strengths and weaknesses, and how to build intelligent workflows, will allow you to more effectively plan and execute projects.

Plays Well with Others

One more thing that is special about Final Cut Pro is the software's connectivity and sociability. Admittedly, it is strange to talk about a program being "sociable," but there are actually three interrelated concepts here:

1. Final Cut Pro has a lot of tools that make it useful in team workflows. Projects can be organized, planned, and executed by small and large groups effectively. This is a broad concept that includes the sharing of media, effective methods for reviews of work-in-progress cuts, and working with people of diverse technical abilities.

2. Final Cut Pro works well with other software. This holds true for preparing assets before ingesting into FCP, and also for doing finishing work after the editing is done. Because Final Cut Pro now exists within the larger Final Cut Studio, which includes other postproduction tools, the integration with these programs is particularly tight. Photoshop also works especially well with FCP. Transfer formats such as OMF and XML allow a wide range of data translation to other programs. Lastly, many other companies create plug-ins for Final Cut Pro to create new special effects.

3. Final Cut Pro works well with third-party hardware. Many companies produce hardware specifically to integrate with Final Cut Pro. Probably the most important type of third-party hardware is capture cards, which allow ingestion from a wider range of videotape formats.

Final Cut Pro is uniquely situated as a hub in many current postproduction processes, in large part because of how well it works with other software and hardware, and in team environments.

Getting the Most from Final Cut Pro with Workflows

Because Final Cut Pro is a central piece in many video projects, it is important to plan how this tool will be used by the people on the team and with the other tools in play. Users come to FCP with diverse skill sets and expectations. This sometimes creates the potential for misunderstanding.

Detailed planning of the stages of the process is the best way to get everyone on the same page for an efficient project. We call these plans workflows, and they are the subject of the next chapter.

2 What Is a Workflow?

A workflow is a plan.

If every postproduction project is a journey (and most are), then the workflow is a map with your intended route highlighted. Like any journey, it is sometimes permissible to take a detour, or to alter your route on the way, but the workflow is the plan you make before you embark.

There are certain steps in every postproduction project, and therefore a generic workflow that is adapted to fit the needs of each particular project (see Figure 2.1). In addition, workflows extend both before and after the editing process, and are applicable to the production and delivery aspects of a project (for instance, DVD interactivity).

The focus of this book is using Final Cut Pro as a versatile and robust tool that fits centrally into many different postproduction workflows. However, the ideas here can (and, if possible, *should*) be implemented before any footage is shot, through final delivery of a project.

Understanding workflows and workflow thinking will help your projects be much more efficient regardless of what role you have. It will make communication within your team and with outside vendors clearer. Ultimately, good workflows will save you time and money.

We use a specific set of symbols and icons to show workflows, but boxes and arrows are not what make the workflow. It is more a matter of telegraphing each step of the process in detail. This can be done on paper or computer, in writing or with diagrams, or any combination. It is important to document your workflow so that it can clearly be shared with other members of the team.

The Generic Postproduction Workflow

The Ingest Stage of the project covers the process of getting media into the Final Cut Pro environment so that you can edit with it. Often, when we talk about ingest, we will be talking about Log and Capture (see Chapter 7). However, these terms are not always synonymous.

Log and Capture refers specifically to ingestion from tape formats (usually a large part of the content for a video project). Ingest is a broader term that includes preparing all assets for use in Final Cut Pro, including scanning and adjusting photographic elements, preparing and importing audio assets, and graphics.

Figure 2.1   Generic postproduction workflow.

Postproduction technology changes just as fast as other areas of computer technology. Recently, these developments have led to the term "ingest," incorporating new and exciting hard-drive, solid-state, and optical acquisition formats such as P2 and XDCAM. These IT-friendly formats offer exciting new possibilities in the postproduction workflow, offering the ability not only to save time and money, but also to open the door to new resolutions and frame rates previously not found in one acquisition format.

Whether the initial source is film, printed material, recorded audio, digital videotape, or solid state, all of your media need to be converted to a digital file that can be saved or transferred to a hard drive that is accessible to FCP, and imported into an FCP project, where it is represented in the browser to then be used in your project.

As you might expect, the ingest stage is key in workflow thinking and media management. Along with "sucking in" media, the ingest stage is also your first and best opportunity to apply organizational thinking. You can rarely have too much organization in the early stages of a project.

For the purposes of the generic workflow, we define *The Editing Phase* broadly, as everything between ingesting the footage and making the final outputs. This includes assembly and editorial, as well as graphics, compositing, audio mix, and color correction. Of course, these are distinct steps, and they are treated as such, but in the simplified generic workflow, the edit phase is just the wide middle where you do all the stuff with your media.

Many of the individual steps in this category can be performed within the Final Cut Pro interface. However, this is not always the case. Indeed, the interaction between different postproduction tools is an important aspect of workflow thinking. This interaction involves various types of outputs and exports. These small outputs that occur at key stages of the project are also very important to workflow thinking.

We could have chosen to include a finishing stage of the generic workflow. This would logically denote steps such as audio mix and color correction. However, we chose to combine all of this work under one large step to make a point: the distinctions between these steps are no longer as clear as they once were. There are two reasons for this, and both are creatively empowering:

1. It has become possible to do high-quality finishing work on the desktop, both with Final Cut Studio and other software. When more steps are done in the same environment, it can be less clear what the specific steps are. For instance, where color correction used to be something that happened in a separate room and only once a project had been editorially completed and outputted to tape, it now can take place in downtime of the editorial process. (Though this is not always a good idea!)

2. Aesthetically, what was traditionally considered finishing work has become a more creative endeavor, contributing to the emotive storytelling power of the medium. Thus, specialties such as sound effects and color grading (tinting the image for a visual effect), which were once considered elements of technical finishing, are also now considered creative storytelling tools.

We choose to group all of this work under one large category in the generic structure, but deal with each individual step in detail in the chapters that follow because we embrace these ambiguities. Part of the power of Final Cut Pro, and the accessibility of professional-quality postproduction tools, is being able to do more of the traditional finishing steps, and to use them creatively.

The Output Stage is taking a project from Final Cut Pro to its final distribution medium. Like the ingest phase, this is particularly important when it comes to workflow thinking. And again, this is an instance where considerations about the final product should enter into the planning throughout the process.

Outputting may involve recording to tape, making digital files or compressions, or some combination. It is not uncommon for output stages to involve interactivity, alternative versions, and intricate organizational schemes. When video content has more than one intended output, we talk about a workflow being "branched," indicating that at some point, the path of the workflow will split into two to provide for the alternate outputs (Figure 2.2).

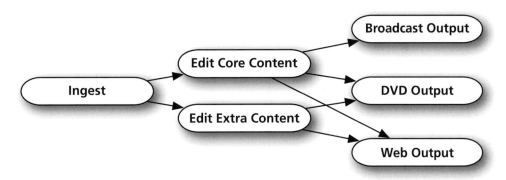

Figure 2.2 Branched workflow.

Workflow Documents

Although there is no strict way to design or document workflows, it is important that these plans are committed to paper and that a good record of your workflow thinking is made for all who are involved with the project. The definition of a workflow document can be looked at broadly. Workflows are represented not only with flowchart diagrams. Is a schedule a workflow document? Yes. How about a paper edit with timecode references for an assembly in FCP? Sure. Documenting your plans and workflow concepts is something that producers have always done, whether they called it that or not.

Documenting your workflows—as diagrams, schedules, job descriptions, and so on—serves at least three interrelated functions:

1. It gets everyone on the same page. It is relatively easy to sit with people on a team and verbally agree to the direction or plan for a project. However, when everyone looks at the same sheet of paper and endorses it, it is more likely that they are actually in agreement as to the plan.

2. These documents become stakes in time. Meaning that even as workflows adjust in the course of the projects, people can go back to earlier documents as a record of what was planned by the team and when.

Document Versioning

Because your workflow documents will evolve over time and may be used and contributed to by many people, it is important to name them carefully and to have a system of version numbers and dates. At a minimum, any production document should have a "last updated" date on it. In some cases, it pays to have a more robust system with version numbers and tags for what a given version represents or who last contributed to it.

3. Sometimes new people join the project, and workflow documents are a quick way to get them up to speed.

If you choose to make a visual diagram of your workflow, here are some tips:

- Draw it on paper first. There is a great advantage to drawing your workflow on paper before you try to make it pretty on the computer. Graph paper is your friend, and don't be afraid to trash a lot of sheets—but please recycle!

- Use a vector-based drawing program. Adobe Illustrator is a common vector-based drawing program. OmniGraffle is a more pared-down tool, made for diagramming. Both tools are vector based, which means that items are inherently scalable and resizable.

Sometimes these visual representations are the best way to express the entire workflow on one page. Remember, they are generally only good as an overview, and more-traditional schedule and specification documents are also needed.

The Power of Workflow Thinking

The power of workflow thinking is not much different from the power of good planning. A workflow is a plan that focuses on the technical process of a project and the roles needed at each stage to accomplish the final goal. You could easily make a workflow for starting a new business or moving to a new apartment.

The more complicated a project, the more that detailed planning and workflow thinking are necessary. Although media projects have gotten more affordable, and Final Cut Pro is a key tool making this possible, they are no less complicated. Without good planning, FCP is a powerful tool that is often not fully utilized. With a good workflow, FCP can be part of an integrated, cost-effective solution.

PART 2

Roles, Technologies, and Techniques

3 Traditional and New Postproduction Roles

Postproduction joke, circa 1998:

Question: What do you call a producer who edits?
Answer: A predator.

Fast-forward ten years, and it is not even clear anymore why this is funny. Today, it is completely normal to see job postings for a producer/editor, but back in the late 1990s, it was still the norm for one person to produce (make the decisions) and another to edit (push the buttons). Therefore, just being a producer who edits was an affront to some people: you are breaking the rules; you are taking someone's job; you are a carnivore.

With the emergence of tools such as Final Cut Pro, many professionals are asked to play the role of jack-of-all-trades. Generalists have become as common as specialists (if not more so). It's important, however, to take a look at traditional roles in the postproduction process, how they have changed over the years, and where they are heading in the future.

In this chapter, we will explore the traditional postproduction roles and their metamorphosis during the period that Final Cut Pro has come into prominence. This is not merely academic. Understanding these different roles sheds light on the responsibilities of all team members and aids in the design of workflows. Even when the roles have morphed and recombined—*especially* when the roles have morphed and recombined—it is important to know who is responsible for what part of the process.

The following descriptions are by no means absolute, nor are they mutually exclusive. As we will see in Part 3, it is the blending of these roles that actually makes most workflows work!

Executive Producer

Even with the changes in technology, there has always been a tried-and-true (if slightly tongue-in-cheek) way to define the executive producer. It's the person who signs the checks. This may not be literally true in all cases, but rest assured, every EP that ever was, was more than a little bit concerned about the money.

Because the executive producer position is defined as a management role (with a particular attention to financial issues), the role has stayed relatively stable even as the industry has changed. A postproduction budget using Final Cut Pro may be smaller than one using previous methods, but developing and managing that budget is still much the same.

All this talk about budgets is not meant to imply that an EP spends all of his or her time analyzing a budget line by line. (The person who does this is generally called a line producer.) The key to the role is the "executive" part. An executive producer green-lights projects (i.e., okays the money to fund a production). They may also hire some of the other key people, such as producers, actors, and the director. In any case, the EP sits at the top of the organizational hierarchy. As the name implies, the executive producer is the CEO of a production.

There are different kinds of executive producers for different types of productions. For instance, when multiple large companies are involved in a single project (maybe a studio, a network, and a sponsor), sometimes each one will assign their own executive to look out for their particular priorities.

An executive producer for a typical Hollywood film is generally someone that the studio has assigned to the project with no real creative input in the project. Their role is one of an overseer, ensuring that the film is on schedule and, most importantly, on budget. This person will interact primarily with the director or other producers.

In recent years, it has been common for directors who want total control over their project to also be executive producers; generally, this also means that the director is monetarily vested in the project. Some successful actors have also made a transition to the role of executive producer. Again, there is often a money connection. It is also true on smaller film projects that the executive producer or producers often have a personal financial stake in the film.

A television executive producer is more often an employee of a network, rather than some sort of personal investor. Television EPs may have creative input, especially regarding a show's big picture. Aspects such as time slots, marketing, show titles, and promotions are all the domain of the television EP.

Sometimes an executive producer is hired for the money they can raise, sometimes to lend clout to a project (often a name can bring the money), and sometimes for the actual managerial and creative oversight.

An executive producer needs to be a strong leader with an eye for the big picture: organized, forward thinking, and strong willed.

Producer

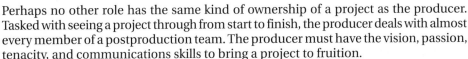

Perhaps no other role has the same kind of ownership of a project as the producer. Tasked with seeing a project through from start to finish, the producer deals with almost every member of a postproduction team. The producer must have the vision, passion, tenacity, and communications skills to bring a project to fruition.

The producer is often one of the first people on a project after it has passed the conceptual or development stage, and thus he or she should have a feel for the greater context of the production: the goals, budget and schedule parameters, the team roles, and so on. If the executive producer is the CEO of a production, then the producer would be a vice president or managing partner.

It is the vision and creativity that fuel new ideas. It steers the path and efforts of the rest of the team members. A producer is the answer person. Whether approving a script or brainstorming for the next episode, major decisions and new ideas all go through the producer.

Most of all, he or she takes responsibility for the project. If there are problems, the producer is the first one to get the call. It could be the EP at 10:00 p.m. or the assistant editor at 2:00 a.m.; when you are the one with the answers, expect to leave your phone on.

If a project stalls or otherwise runs into creative or technical problems, the producer is often the first person who catches the blame. It is easy for almost anyone else on the team to point the finger at the producer, and claim that they lacked sufficient direction.

Organization, versatility, and strong interpersonal skills are traits of a good producer.

Associate Producer

An associate producer may do quite literally anything on a project: review scripts, log footage, wrangle talent, negotiate million-dollar deals, get coffee. . . . Working as an AP, I once had to drive a shark-bite victim to the hospital—and wait while he was stitched up!

Like the roles of assistant editor, production assistant, and assistant producer, the role of the associate producer has an element of apprenticeship. The AP is seen as being at about the middle on this totem pole. It is a good place to develop the communications and leadership skills needed to take on the responsibility of producer.

It should not be surprising that in this journeyman position, associate producers often shoulder the brunt of the work without receiving much appreciation. In this way, it is akin to being a graduate research assistant or a medical resident. You may feel you have all of the skills, but you lack the experience to get the title.

Although much of the work assigned to an associate producer is often menial (reviewing scripts, research, vendor research), it frequently has a tangible effect on the development of a production and is one reason strong associate producers are in high demand.

With the growth of Final Cut Pro, ambitious associate producers, perhaps like no other role in a postproduction workflow, have been able to become editors and Motion Graphics Designers and achieve other postproduction roles. This is because they are dedicated to getting the job done—and now the equipment is not price-prohibitive for them to learn.

Good associate producers are hardworking, motivated, and possess strong communications skills.

Writer

A good writer puts the vision of the producer on paper. The writer's script serves as a road map for editors, mixers, colorists, and others involved in the postproduction process. In the traditional sense, a writer also writes lines for talent, and in a broader sense writes a story. Although the central role of the writer has remained the same, new technology has assisted him or her in producing and editing scripts. New technology in postproduction has also given the writer new horizons for what is possible. For example, writers with more hands-on knowledge about visual/special effects will often include these in their scripts.

The role of the writer is radically different in fictional projects (feature films, episodic television, and so forth) compared to nonfiction projects (for example, documentaries, natural history, reality TV). In a fictional piece, the writer is responsible for the story in the traditional sense—in other words, they make it up. In documentaries and other nonfiction projects, the writer's task is to structure the story based on the footage, interviews, and archival materials.

Being highly organized and having strong language skills are typical traits of a writer.

Assistant Editor

Ask any assistant editor, and they will tell you that they have the most underappreciated (but most important) role in the postproduction process. Like others, this critical role has changed considerably over the years. One thing, however, has remained the same—although assistant editors gain valuable experience, they still get stuck doing a lot of grunt work!

From the golden era of Hollywood to million-dollar linear editing suites to sleek nonlinear setups, the assistant editor (AE) has always played a support role. The AE has also always been seen as an apprenticeship and an opportunity to learn the craft of editing—the aesthetic, creative, and technical aspects.

Many of today's best editors began their careers as assistant editors, developing their craft by watching and supporting master editors. Although theirs is assuredly a position that receives little fanfare, assistant editors play a vital role in many postproduction workflows.

In the old days of film editing, the role of the AE was to find reels; load them onto the Moviola, Steenbeck, or other such device; queue shots for the editor; sometimes splice shots; run errands; and get coffee for the editor.

As technology progressed, the assistant editor found new tasks in linear editing suites—such as queuing videotapes, running title generators (Chyron), loading edit decision lists (EDLs), and of course getting coffee for the editor. Often linear edit rooms were quite large, with a sea of knobs and buttons to keep track of. Here, the AE was quite literally an extension of the editor—a second set of hands for controlling these large systems.

From the early to the mid-1990s, the role of the assistant editor started to change in a more substantial way. No longer just an extra set of hands, assistant editors often worked independently. With the growth of nonlinear editing, the AE was often tasked with digitizing and logging footage, doing assembly edits, and performing other technical tasks such as media management.

Today, the role of the assistant editor has become rather technical. Mainly responsible for digitizing and ingest, the typical AE also performs graphics prep, compressions, media management, and dubs. In a modern postproduction workflow, the AE is often a critical role in the success of a project.

Hardworking, eager to learn, and technically savvy are all traits of an assistant editor.

Editor

Francis Ford Coppola said, "The essence of cinema is editing. It's the combination of what can be extraordinary images of people during emotional moments, or images in a general sense, put together in a kind of alchemy."

The role of the editor has always been key in the postproduction process. Often the editor provides visual expertise to help the producer decide which shots to use and how to use them. Moreover, the editor uses his or her strong sense of aesthetics to make choices that can evoke joy, sadness, confusion, or intrigue. If you're reading this book, you probably consider yourself an editor on some level.

Technology has not necessarily changed the core role of the editor, but it has most definitely changed the execution of the process.

In the early part of the twentieth century, the tools of the trade allowed the editor to make edits to picture and sound. However, specialty work such as visual effects, motion graphics, titling, and sound design were reserved for specialists on specialized (and expensive) equipment.

In the heyday of linear editing, sophistication of edit systems was often measured in visual-effects capabilities, and the editor found new creative possibilities. Nonlinear editing brought even more new capabilities for the editor. These creative possibilities, however, were often tempered by strong-minded producers who now knew what was creatively possible (and thought they knew best), thus forcing the editor into an operator role.

In recent times, more technology has been placed in the hands of the editor—be it the latest and greatest switcher or the first nonlinear edit system in the area. In many cases, aesthetic decisions have been placed in the hands of the producer. The editor has become a button pusher and a technical problem solver.

Now tools such as Final Cut Pro have allowed more people to actually become editors. At one end of the spectrum, this means that "amateurs" can now try their hand at professional techniques and storytelling. At the other end, Walter Murch and many other editors at the top of their game have been able to transcend the role that technology plays in the editing process. In so doing, they have been able to affirm the classic aesthetic role of the true editor.

Changes in technology have been the biggest influence on the role of the editor and have solidified the editor's role as central in a postproduction workflow.

Creative, patient, and technologically savvy are typical traits of the editor.

Online Editor

During the emergence and evolution of digital nonlinear editing, the role of the online editor has gone through some major adjustments. There are actually three distinct methods of online editing that have come to be during this relatively short period of time.

In the early days of nonlinear editing, the role of the online editor was clear. He or she was the person who worked in the online room—a linear editing suite that was configured to work at the highest possible quality. Because early nonlinear systems were not capable of digitizing or displaying video in a high-quality, or "uncompressed" (1:1), fashion, the online process consisted of reassembling the proper clips based on the editing decisions made on the nonlinear system.

The online editor was also responsible for final tweaks to the program. These were things such as performing complex video effects that the offline editor and or offline system could not perform, basic color correction, or editing the show into segments to fit specific broadcast requirements such as show length, slates, and versions.

The next technical advance to affect online editing was the uncompressed nonlinear editing system. Increased computer power, drive speed, and throughput allowed these systems to ingest, display, and output video while preserving its highest possible quality. At first (and before FCP), all of these advances were expensive.

The second online editing method replaced the linear online room with one of these new uncompressed nonlinear systems. The first step for the online editor was to redigitize the clips used in the show at their highest possible uncompressed quality. This process became known as conforming a show. It was similar to reassembling a show in the linear room, but provided the flexibility of nonlinear editing combined with the quality of uncompressed video.

Once the show was redigitized, the online editor performed most of same tasks as their linear predecessor. However, nonlinear online edit systems opened up a whole new world of possibilities for effects work, color correction, and audio. Online editors who had come from a linear background quickly had to learn new skills that previously had been reserved for specialists.

The reason for reconforming a show is that the offline stage allowed massive amounts of video to be captured at a lower quality. Because drive space was generally a limitation of nonlinear systems, this method allowed drive space to be conserved in the offline stage. Then only the clips that were actually chosen in the offline stage ever needed to be captured at full quality.

For short pieces such as TV commercials, some workflows started to skip the offline phase entirely, and ingest the small amount of needed footage at uncompressed quality from the beginning. As media storage space has gotten less expensive, uncompressed, or 1:1, editing has become more common, even for longer pieces.

This represents the final online editing method. The idea is that the entire traditional offline/online process is thrown out in favor of just capturing the footage you need at its full quality. In this scenario, the online editor's role has evolved again. The final tweaks and preparation for broadcast are still important tasks, but without the elements of reassembly or reconforming, the online editor's job has become less clear to many observers. Add to this the fact that many offline editors and offline systems can now do sophisticated graphics, image treatment, and color work, and this has become a complicated professional landscape.

Today, although "online editor" still has the same general meaning that it always had, different shops and projects can be quite dissimilar in terms of what steps are actually performed at the online stage. An online editor's duties may include any number of the steps needed to prepare a show for broadcast (see sidebar, Preparing a Show for Broadcast), and can be done in any of the three methods mentioned. In any case, the online editor is expected to be a technical expert, the "final eyes" on a project.

The increased complexity of this role is due largely to an expanded toolset. In addition to performing work such as conforming, blurring, masking, titling, and adhering to other specific broadcast requirements, the online editor is now frequently tasked with performing final color correction and ensuring broadcast legality, audio mix, and sound design. Toolsets such as Final Cut Studio have made this work easier for the online editor to perform. In smaller projects, the online editor is often the final step in quality control.

Attention to detail and thoroughness, and being technically knowledgeable are typical qualities of the online editor.

Preparing a Show for Broadcast

The online editor's life can sometime be, well . . . boring. This boring life is often made up of technical tasks. Most of these fall under the category of broadcast packaging. This means making sure that the show is cut to time—different networks have different specifications for segment length. It also means blurring and masking logos and objectionable content—no network wants to get sued. Lastly, this means creating clean scenes. Anytime a shot appears with a title or graphic, or there is a blurred shot, these appear at the end of a master tape "clean," or without the graphics and blurs. If the show ever needs to be distributed for other purposes, such as for international distribution, the shot that had the lower third can be replaced with clean original.

Audio Mixer

Many larger post houses have dedicated mixing services. There are also many companies dedicated solely to audio work and mixing. One of the largest roles in this field is the audio mixer. The audio mixer plays a large but seldom glorified role in the postproduction process.

It is often said that sound can play a larger role then picture in a project. Indeed, many people either do not notice or are willing to forgive problems in picture, attributing them to the purposeful intentions of a editor or producer, or just not noticing. However, audio issues are much more noticeable and distracting to the viewer at large. They tend to instantly break the suspension of disbelief, and quickly remind a person that they are watching—and listening to—a (flawed) manufactured product.

Each one of us has probably changed the channel to find large volume changes between shows or commercials, or found it hard to hear narration because the music in the program is too loud. For most, these issues take away from the dramatic, comedic, or other intentions that the producer originally had. Thus, the role of the audio mixer is of utmost importance.

Like the role of the editor, that of the audio mixer has remained essentially the same over the years, but technology has greatly influenced what is possible and how it is done. The audio mixer is responsible for balancing levels of dialogue, music, and sound effects. He or she is also generally responsible for editing audio for things such as removing breaths and adding equalization.

In the early days of production, the audio mixer was often also the recording engineer, making sure that things got recorded properly. Of course there was basic audio mixing and editing, but, like the editor, most of this editing was done in a linear way with crude editing tools.

Soon thereafter, as technology began to develop at an ever-quickening pace, stereo and four-track recorders were replaced with multitrack recorders, sophisticated mixing boards capable of handling multiple submixes were developed, and outboard effects processing gear was developed, which gave the audio mixer even greater control and lent creativity to the mix. New thinking in speaker designs and room design led to increasingly better-sounding mixes.

Just as with advances in picture editing, the real boom came with the development of nonlinear audio editing. By the mid-1990s, although many facilities and audio mixers were still using analog linear equipment, a few were starting to use nonlinear editing. This allowed the audio mixer to make faster changes to what once were arduous tasks—removing breaths, for example. Racks of outboard gear were now software plug-ins—allowing a more self-contained solution and, in most cases, saving a facility or audio mixer thousands of dollars.

Cross-development of audio- and video-editing software allowed for new interoperability between the two disciplines. Technologies such as Avid's OMF allowed a video editor to export a file to the audio mixer. Once this file was opened up on the nonlinear audio system, the audio mixer could look at the timings and track layout in exactly the same way the video editor could on their system.

Today, the audio mixer is a master of nonlinear technique. Like video editors, the audio mixer often has mastery of multiple systems.

Technically creative and musically oriented are typical traits of the audio mixer.

Sound Designer

Sound design is its own discipline: putting in sound effects to match on-screen action (and sometimes mood). However, the sound designer is not always a separate role from the audio mixer, or even the editor. In many facilities, the sound designer is a special and creative discipline.

Using many of the same tools as the audio mixer, the sound designer's role is to seamlessly add in Foley sounds such as city noise, footsteps, punch sounds, clothes ruffling, and so on. In doing so, the sound designer often uses a large library of pre-recorded sounds. When these are not available, the sound designer might also employ the use of a Foley stage to create and record sounds.

The sound designer is often a middle step between the editor and the audio mixer. By using their skill to add sounds, designers are able to contribute volumes to a program. As viewers, we are able to subconsciously process these sounds as part of a more complete picture of the scene before us.

If you are curious about sound design, listen carefully and pay attention to the sound when you watch television, and especially film. Have you ever been watching a historical documentary and heard gunshots or hoofbeats when watching archival footage that was clearly done before the advent of sync sound recording? Have you ever noticed the background sounds in a well-produced horror movie? *The Sixth Sense*, for instance, uses low breathing sounds in the background *during the entire film!* Sound design can be a fascinating mix of wild creativity and also subtlety and restraint. Often you are adding depth and emotional resonance to a piece in a way that most viewers will not consciously notice.

Creativity and attention to detail are typical traits of the sound designer.

Video Engineer

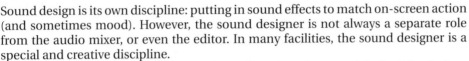

Many assistant editors will tell you that they are the most underappreciated members of a typical postproduction workflow. Any video engineer can tell you that opinion is dead wrong!

The video engineer has always played a support role, rarely getting the credit when an edit system or deck performs flawlessly after a major meltdown, but always carrying the blame when then there is a problem.

In many large facilities, the video engineer is responsible for making recommendations about what technology should be acquired, and how to implement that technology into existing infrastructure and maintenance (updates, repairs, etc.) after the technology has been acquired. The engineer usually plays a large role in the design of edit suites, machine rooms, and other IT systems such as a SAN (shared area network). (More on SANs can be found in Chapter 5: Compression and Storage.)

The video engineer is often tasked with developing systems for media management and tape handling (dubbing, storage libraries, and backup), as well as ensuring that operators of systems have a set of guidelines as to what they are allowed to do and not allowed to do on a particular system.

> ## To Update or Not to Update?
>
> It seems like a regular morning as Bob the engineer walks into the office. Today is Thursday, and Bob and the staff of Best Video Ever Productions are in the midst of a huge production. The end is near, though—next Monday, they are set to deliver their soon-to-be award-winning production. But this Thursday is different. There are a few editors in one of the edit suites scratching their heads, there is an account manager pacing the hallway, and Bob is wondering why his cell phone has been going off every few minutes. As it turns out, a freelance editor who was hired to help with the project updated software overnight—and this has caused some major problems. Bob loves being an engineer, but today he wishes that he were not an engineer.
>
> It is always a debate about when to update software (and hardware). The pros of early updating are to stay current with technology and to take advantage of the most up-to-date features. The cons of early updating are that the bugs are not always worked out of the newest software. This can be a particular problem in a complex postproduction environment where a lot of hardware and software needs to function together.
>
> This is the situation Bob found himself in—a situation he would have preferred to avoid.

In smaller facilities, the video engineer often has to play the roles listed above, but generally this not a dedicated position. In many cases, the most technically minded editor or designer ends up playing the role of engineer. In our democratized postproduction reality, this is both a blessing and a curse. A blessing because the facility does not need to hire an additional staff member to fill the role, but a curse because most of the time, that technically minded editor or designer gets sucked into a constant barrage of maintenance and/or answering questions. As a result, their work suffers.

Being extremely technically savvy, having gifted problem-solving abilities, and possessing stick-to-itiveness are all common traits found in a video engineer.

Motion Graphics Designer

The role of Motion Graphics Designer is not a new one, but it is one that has evolved drastically as technology has changed. Traditional animation artists have always designed while putting their designs or drawings into motion. Early on, this was much the same as cell-based animation, but technology has played a large role in the development of the modern motion graphic artist.

Motion Graphics Designers were originally traditional graphic designers who every once in a while happened to do work for film and TV. Early on, this meant a big emphasis on typography. As technology progressed, designers who longed to have their designs in motion were able to do so more easily.

During the 1980s and the first half of the 1990s, motion graphics were difficult to produce and were typically tied to expensive pieces of hardware and software. By the late 1990s, less expensive and faster software packages were available. This development led to more people wanting motion graphics in their programs—the graphics were many times easier to produce, and more people were exploring motion graphics design.

Today, the true Motion Graphics Designer often produces motion graphics for a variety of media such as the Web, DVD, and video projects. Applications such as Motion 3 have expanded the ability of the designer to create in real time.

A keen design sense, being technically savvy, and the unique ability to put designs into motion are common traits found in a Motion Graphics Designer.

Compressionist

The role of the compressionist did not really exist until the introduction of the compact disc and its use as an interactive medium. For a time, the compressionist was a specific and dedicated role, but now almost anyone who works in video plays the compressionist at least occasionally.

With video technologies such as Apple's QuickTime, it was relatively easy to get your video compressed to fit on an interactive CD; however, getting it to look good was another thing. It was in this balance of video/audio quality and space limitations on a medium that the role of the compressionist was born.

With knowledge of video architectures such as QuickTime, Windows Media Player, RealPlayer, and their corresponding codecs, the compressionist was a computer magician. Typically using dedicated hardware and software, the compressionist was able to take high-resolution video and audio and convert it into a small package that could fit on a CD (and soon after, the Web and DVDs as well).

This role was vital in larger postproduction houses because it coincided with a larger change in roles for people such as editors, who were already being taxed with having to learn new skill sets. By the mid- to late 1990s, the compressionist was also being called on to compress audio and video for the Internet and DVD.

Today, the role of the compressionist has waned considerably because assistant editors, editors, and other specialists such as DVD designers and Web designers are often responsible for compression for various media. It helps that improvements in software have made it much easier to get acceptably good compressions without needing as much time or skill. Compression is now often used in postproduction workflows to review works in progress. In larger facilities and projects, there is sometimes still a dedicated compressionist. If there is enough demand, this can be vital in streamlining workflows.

Attention to detail and vast technical knowledge of video and audio are typical qualities of a compressionist.

Compositor

"In visual effects post-production, compositing refers to creating new images or moving images by combining images from different sources—such as real-world digital video, film, synthetic 3-D imagery, 2-D animations, painted backdrops, digital still photographs, and text." (Wikipedia)

Most compositors are actually editors or Motion Graphics Designers. We make a point of noting that this is a separate position for the purpose of explaining a role that is often overlooked or misunderstood. Although many editors and designers by virtue of the toolsets that are available to them could be called compositors, compositing has become a unique discipline.

The goal of the compositor is to get separate items to seamlessly work together. Examples of such work would be shooting a subject on a green or blue screen and placing that subject on a background.

Although Final Cut Pro has some compositing ability, very sophisticated compositing projects (think *Lord of the Rings*) use dedicated compositing software such as Shake.

The most important skills for a compositor are technical know-how (often with very complicated software packages) and an extremely good eye for detail. Although some editors and Motion Graphics Designers perform this task, again, the most complicated projects usually have a person (or many people) who specializes in this work.

Colorist

"Wow, that looks great!" These are words a colorist loves to hear, even though a viewer may not associate the colorist's work with the final quality of the piece. The colorist never gets much glory because (much like the audio mixer and sound designer) their contribution is subtle, working primarily on the viewer's subconscious.

The goal of the colorist is to balance the hue, saturation, and brightness of each shot of the piece so that they blend seamlessly. The colorist also sometimes has the opportunity to affect the mood or emotional tone of the piece. When color adjustments are used just to make the footage look "natural," this is called "color correction"; when used for stylistic or emotive effect, this is referred to as "color grading." The films *Traffic* and *The Matrix* are two early examples of this stylistic trend. Another trend is using color (and other effects) to give an entire film a nostalgic feel (think *O Brother, Where Art Thou?*).

The role of colorist is a prime example of how the changes in technology have pushed creative boundaries.

Originally, the colorist was called a color timer. With film-based projects, the color timer would work with the director of photography and the director to chemically alter the film during the developing and printing process in order to give a desired look or to accurately reproduce a scene. Until recently, with the introduction of digital color correction systems, the color timer had a critical role.

For television projects acquired on film, the telecine system was invented. Early on, these machines altered colors via voltage changes as the film was being scanned, allowing the colorist to control the balance of colors as the image was transferred from film to videotape.

By the mid-1980s, the first digital color correction systems appeared. Originally, these systems allowed the colorist to control the telecine, but later they were morphed into the tape-to-tape video color correction systems that many post facilities use today. It was during this time that the colorist took on a more specialized role. Although at the time the colorist toolset was really no more than a time base corrector (TBC), the colorist became responsible for scene-to-scene contrast and color continuity, as well as, in some cases, developing stylized looks.

Today, colorists use varying toolsets—from high-end tape-to-tape systems to software-based systems such as Final Cut Pro and Color. No matter the toolset, the colorist still has one important role—make it look good!

Attention to detail, creativity, and keen perception are all traits a typical colorist has.

Postproduction Supervisor

In a typical project, there are people, equipment, rooms, egos, deadlines, and deliverables to deal with. If managing all of this sounds like lots of fun, then you're probably a postproduction supervisor!

The postproduction supervisor plays a vital role in the workflow, and is often yet another unsung hero. Mainly a managerial position, the postproduction supervisor must also be aware of current trends in postproduction technology. It is common for postproduction supervisors to have formerly been editors, mixers, or in another creative role.

The postproduction supervisor is a master of workflows. They will work with other key members of the team in designing the initial plan, and may be largely responsible for making and maintaining the documentation. As a project progresses, the postproduction supervisor manages the execution of that workflow, and is continuously refining the workflow as he or she goes along. This process of refining eventually means adding resources and time estimates to the workflow tasks, and this becomes the schedule.

One of the largest roles that the postproduction supervisor plays is keeping to a postproduction schedule and managing costs associated with the postproduction process. The role is often a go-between for different team members and vendors—a communication hub. Much of the responsibility for budgeting time and money lies directly with the postproduction supervisor. The tools for this role are spreadsheets, address books, and every kind of communication device imaginable.

Organized, technically minded, and hardworking are typical traits of the postproduction supervisor.

Media Architect

The media architect is a new role that has come to postproduction because of the increasing prevalence of interactivity. When video is being produced for use as an element in an interactive piece, there is a whole new set of concerns around how these video clips are going to fit together in the final piece. Partly this involves the user's experience—in what order, and through what set of actions, will each piece of video be played? The media architect also has technical concerns—what is the best way to produce the video for the desired media? And what technologies will support the user interaction and display of video?

The media architect is also familiar with workflow thinking. Often there are additional workflow steps, even entire additional workflows, once the video is finished. This may involve the design of (many) animations and menus, plus encoding the video and authoring a disc. Figure 2.2 shows a generic branched workflow, used when video assets are being produced that will ultimately be used in different distribution formats. The media architect keeps up-to-date on all emerging and evolving media technologies.

Somewhat new as a role unto itself, media architecture has been going on in some form since the advent of interactive media (a very early example being video kiosks). Often producers, maybe working with techs and designers, did this conceptualization. Producers who were good at it may have branded themselves interactive producers, and, ultimately media architects.

Media architecture is also closely related to information architecture. The distinction between the two is that information architecture is generally thought to focus on textual and photographic "information," whereas media architecture focuses more on videocentric applications. To look at the state of the Web in 2007, it seems clear that these architectures will continue to evolve. Five years ago, information architecture was in its infancy. Now the role has become a Web industry standard. It is a logical prediction that as interactive video applications mature, the media architect will follow suit.

Lastly the media architect does not limit himself or herself to interactive video, but rather, is multidisciplinary by nature—able to work in gaming, social networking, VR (virtual reality) applications, museum installations, and so on.

Good media architects possess superior imagination and communications skills and are familiar with a wide range of interactive technologies and user-experience theory.

Dual Roles, Hybrid Roles, and Evolving Roles

What is a producer/director? A producer/editor? A postproduction executive? These are fairly familiar dual or hybrid roles. They are new roles contracted from the original roles to denote a dual responsibility and/or a responsibility that has elements of two or more traditional roles.

When performing these mixed functions, it is important to understand your specific tasks and how they affect other team members. For instance, someone hired as a producer/editor might not be expected to have ALL of the technical knowledge of a dedicated editor. A common solution in current workflows is to have an online editor who receives the work of the producer/editor and then improves upon it and prepares it for distribution. In a scenario like this, strong communication between the team members is necessary for a smooth workflow.

Evolving roles are those that change over time, either by design or necessity. Sometimes people with roles in the production phase change duties in postproduction so they can follow a project through. So a production assistant might become an assistant editor. Also, things just happen in the course of a project. So an assistant editor maybe becomes an online editor (yikes!) when the online editor quits two days before the deadline.

Having a role change in an unplanned way is a double-edged sword. On one side, you may find yourself getting paid as an intern, but taking on the responsibilities of a postproduction supervisor. However, those situations are some of the best ways to gain experience to move up the food chain.

Jack-of-All-Trades, the One-Man Band, and the Kitchen-Sink Syndrome

The jack-of-all-trades and the one-man band are both forms of generalist—those of us who base our careers on a rounded knowledge of many techniques and technologies. The jack-of-all-trades version tends to play different roles on different projects— versatile and agile, he or she likes to latch onto a project by providing useful services at multiple stages. I once did the information architecture for a large Web site, and then stayed on to produce and edit the video elements. The one-man band is similar, but less team oriented. This type of generalist wants to find projects where he or she can do most (or, ideally, absolutely all) of the necessary work, and therefore make the best profit margin.

In the democratized video-production environment, both of these are potential options. However, one must beware of what we call the kitchen-sink syndrome. Just because you know how to do a lot of things doesn't mean you know how to do *everything*. It is important to know what you don't know. And some specialization is a good thing.

We knew a company that started as a small graphic-design studio. Quickly, it added video postproduction, Web sites, and DVDs to its services. Pretty soon the studio was into events management and distribution deals for cell-phone content. The company lost its way badly and went out of business. Don't be a victim of the kitchen-sink syndrome. Know who you are.

Roles and Responsibilities in Workflows

When planning workflows, it is best to start by thinking of the tasks that need to be performed, rather than the titles or the people who are going to do them. This will lead to areas of responsibility, and ultimately to defining the roles needed to complete the project.

By starting with responsibilities, you can develop roles as you conceive the workflow, project plan, schedule, and budget. Production teams are inherently fluid. People are leaving for work or personal reasons. New people are coming on, and others are taking on new responsibilities and changing roles. A good workflow supports this fluidity by clearly defining the steps or tasks in your particular production.

4 Video Standards and Formats

We tend to like to draw postproduction workflows as flowcharts, boxes, and arrows to represent stages and resources and tasks. We imagine our project flowing through these paths and processes, but what exactly is this stuff? For that matter, what do the lines and arrows and boxes really represent in terms of real-world equipment? While we are at it, what about all those acronyms and numbers: DV-25, XLR, BNC, 720p?

Let's put it this way—video technology and the associated terminology are complex.

Unless you like to read manuals as bedtime reading or can quote format bandwidth down to the megabit, you're probably confused about a lot of things. This chapter is by no means the end-all of technical literature. It is a quick resource for some common questions and answers about formats, connectors, and other video and audio terminology.

To really develop a postproduction workflow, it is necessary to understand some principles of video technology. It is helpful to be familiar with the different types of video formats and the physical media and cables that store and transfer these signals. It's great if you occasionally know what the acronyms you are using actually stand for, and it is particularly helpful if you understand a bit about the relative strengths and weaknesses of various video formats and how they are traditionally used.

A Brief History of Videotape Formats

From the time the first motion images were recorded onto a piece of film, a debate—or, as some would say, a war—broke out. The format war has raged while advances in technology have changed the front on which this war has been fought. For over half a century, the war was about film stocks and which were best for any given situation. By the late 1950s through today, the front has shifted to videotape, and now tapeless acquisition formats.

This war, driven by large marketing budgets of manufacturers and consumers who want the best quality at the cheapest price, is something that doesn't look to have an end. To fully understand the plethora of current videotape and tapeless acquisition formats, it will be helpful to take a brief look at the history of videotape formats (for simplicity's sake, we will not be looking at the many film stocks available).

Figure 4.1 Ampex Quadruplex machine.

The need for videotape was driven largely by the major networks in the 1950s. Because the dominant acquisition format at the time was film, there were often delays in developing the film. Other technical concerns, such as time-delay broadcasts for the West Coast, were reasons the networks looked for an alternative to film. In 1956, Ampex released a magnetic-tape format known as Quadruplex. Quad for short, this format got its name from how the recordings were made using four spinning heads. Quadruplex ran 2-inch-wide tape on very large open-reel VTRs such as the Ampex VR-1000. This original Quad VTR was monochrome. Updated releases over the next decade expanded the format's capability. Early versions of this format needed to be physically spliced for editing.

By the mid-1970s, Quad had been trumped by another reel-to-reel format known as 1-inch Type C (yes, there were other types; for example, Type B was used in Europe). Co-developed by Ampex and Sony, the Type C format had advantages over Quadruplex: smaller reels, smaller VTRs that consumed less power, and new features such as slow

Figure 4.2 Sony 1-inch reel-to-reel machine.

motion. Machines in the 1-inch format also typically required less maintenance than did Quad machines. This was important because it was during this time that the video postproduction industry was growing, and dependability in large facilities was a must.

One of the drawbacks of formats such as Quad and 1 inch was that they were reel to reel. Because of this, the tape was often subject to damage from such things as heat, the elements, and liquids. In addition, these reels were large and bulky, making them difficult to transport and store.

In 1969, Sony introduced a format called U-matic. This system used a videotape cassette containing ¾-inch tape, commonly referred to as ¾. A composite format (composite is explained later in this chapter) like 1 inch, ¾ became a dominant standard for much of the 1970s and 1980s, thanks to its small form, ease of use, and robustness in edit facilities. The success of U-matic in large part paved the way for the success of videotape cassettes for the next 35 years.

In 1976, JVC launched a new format called Video Home System. You probably know this better as VHS. A ½-inch magnetic tape, VHS quickly became the standard for home recording as well as for duplication.

Originally, VHS players and recorders used mono audio. By the mid-1980s, hi-fi and stereo technologies improved audio performance. VHS also improved its visual performance when S-VHS, or Super VHS, was brought to market. VHS also came to the home camcorder market with VHS-C. These compact tapes could be played back in a standard VHS player using an adapter. VHS-C competed with Video 8 and, later, Hi8 from Sony.

VHS was one player in an infamous war of formats. During the late seventies and early eighties, JVC's VHS went to war with Sony's Betamax. Although in some regards technically superior to VHS, Betamax eventually lost the format war. Many think this was due mainly to the initial limitations of Betamax—the format could record only one hour, whereas VHS could record about two hours. The battle between VHS and Betamax has become legendary in marketing and business circles. Recently, VHS and its derivatives have had a small resurgence with formats such as D-VHS, capable of recording HD. Digital-S (also known as D-9) is another variant.

In 1982, Sony upped the ante with a new format called Betacam. This analog component (component is explained later in this chapter) format was a large leap forward in quality from the composite formats such as U-matic and 1 inch. Small tapes and portability led to large use and acceptance of the format by news organizations.

Figure 4.3 Sony ¾-inch U-matic deck.

Betamax Lives?

Betamax was actually the same tape as the professional Betacam format, but used composite recording instead of the higher-quality component recording of the Betacam format. Betacam also ran at a higher speed, thus increasing its quality over Betamax.

In 1985, Sony released the Video 8 format. Video 8's main claim to fame was that it was very small in size. Using 8mm magnetic tape housed in a small cassette, Video 8 was more practical for camcorders than full-size VHS and Betamax were. In fact, Sony went on to market small handheld camcorders.

A few years later, in 1989, Sony released Hi8 to be a direct competitor to S-VHS for the camcorder. Hi8 improved visual quality over Video 8. Audio quality was also sometimes improved by using two channels of digital audio. (Digital 8 is the ultimate descendant of all the 8mm formats. Released by Sony in 1999, it used the same cassettes, but recorded with the DV codec.)

Video formats had a busy year in 1986. Sony released another landmark format called Betacam SP (BetaSP—the SP stands for "superior performance"). Improvements included increased resolution of 340 horizontal lines, 90-minute cassettes, and metal formulated tape (Betacam used oxide tape). Added together, these features, along with dramatic improvements in deck technology, made Betacam SP a standard for acquisition and mastering from the mid-1980s until recently. Indeed, SP is still a common format for news and lower-end productions.

In 1986, Panasonic also introduced a format called MII to compete directly with Betacam SP. (The original M format, introduced by RCA in 1982, was defunct.) MII was technically similar to BetaSP and enjoyed some initial success in news gathering, but ultimately failed.

Also in 1986, an exciting format was introduced called D-1. This is generally considered to be the first major digital videotape format. Unlike analog formats such as Betacam, Betacam SP, and MII, D-1 recorded uncompressed digital component video. Because the video was uncompressed, the digital video took enormous amounts of

Figure 4.4 Sony Betacam SP deck.

Figure 4.5 Sony D-1 deck.

bandwidth. Tapes and decks were very large compared to other formats. The D-1 format was also tremendously expensive, possibly preventing its widespread adoption.

D-1 required facilities that had been designed around composite formats such as ¾ to invest even more money in the adoption of this digital component mastering format. D-1, however, was considered by many as the Holy Grail for image quality for quite some time. D-1 also refers to a video standard developed by SMPTE (Society of Motion Picture and Television Engineers). In fact, SMPTE was instrumental in the introduction of the D-1 tape format utilizing their specification. D-1 today is primarily an archival format, and is not used for postproduction purposes.

At the 1988 installment of the NAB (National Association of Broadcasters) convention, a new, less expensive digital composite format called D-2 was introduced. Although still recording a digital uncompressed signal, D-2 was able to save bandwidth by recording in composite. This had the added benefit of better integrating into the composite model of many postproduction facilities. Of note, D-3 was a competing digital composite format from Panasonic. The D-2 format and its competitors were short lived.

Figure 4.6 Sony D-2 deck.

There have been many more videotape formats over the years—some more obscure than others—but one thing is an absolute: videotape (and now tapeless) formats will continue to change, and keeping up with the technical aspects of these formats will always be challenging. Understanding where video has been, as well as the terminology involved, will help you be prepared to understand where video is going.

Near the end of this chapter, there are descriptions of the digital and (a few) analog formats that are common today. Currently, there is an explosion in the number, quality, and versatility of new digital formats. This trend has been ongoing for at least five years, and it will continue. Because video technology is changing so rapidly in the digital age, it is best to understand concepts that are transferable, if not immutable.

Cost vs. Quality

Let's face it—postproduction is a business. As much as it is about art and design, one of the major questions that goes through the head of every owner, CTO (chief technology officer), or engineer in a post house is: "What is the balancing act between cost and quality?"

The same question runs thought the mind of a producer, postproduction supervisor, or EP when he or she is planning the workflow for a new project. The issue may be acquisition format, color correction, or mix, but the analysis is often cost versus quality. This has been the case from 35mm and 16mm, through analog and digital video mastering formats, to HD and HDV, and it will continue.

Broadcast decks can be very expensive; the list price as of May 2007 for the HDCAM SRW-5500 dual-format (HDCAM and HDCAM SR) deck is $98,000! To put things in perspective—that same amount of money could buy you a new Porsche GT3!

Renting vs. Purchasing Decks

One of the biggest decisions when setting up a new facility or edit suite is whether to invest in decks or not. Decks are often one of the most expensive pieces of equipment in a postproduction workflow. Choosing whether to purchase decks or to rent them when you need them can be easy if you look at a few criteria.

Consider purchasing if:

1. You use the deck on a daily basis.
2. The deck can be used over multiple projects.
3. The new deck will pay for itself quickly with new project fees.
4. Your finances can support the outlay of cash.

Consider renting if:

1. You require the deck for only a few days, such as for loading or doing outputs.
2. The format is specific to only the project you're working on now.
3. You can bill rental fees into general project fees.
4. Your finances cannot support a large outlay of cash.

In the postproduction world, quality is tied directly to cost.

This does not mean that acceptable quality cannot be attained at lower costs. After all, Final Cut Pro owes much of its success to the explosion of the DV-25 format. There is a special type of psychology in play when it comes to technology. We like to refer to it as techno-lust. Just because a higher-quality format or device exists does not mean that it will mean any more to you. Just because a format is out there that is technically superior does not mean that the format you're currently working in is inferior. When making decisions about decks and devices, you must look not just at the quality that the equipment will provide you, but also at how the cost involved will be made up or disbursed with the work that you are doing.

One problem with techno-lust is that it puts the emphasis on equipment and format, and not on skill and creativity. We like to teach our students that regardless of what format you are working with, you should strive to use the best technique and the most originality you can. In the democratized video-production environment, it is less often your equipment that will differentiate you, and more often your skill in using it.

In this sense, Final Cut Pro has contributed to dramatically redefining the cost-versus-quality equation.

Video Technology

Making sense of decks and formats can certainly be challenging. In the next few sections, we will discuss some of the terminology and technical aspects of audio and video. However, this is not an engineering manual. There are a number of great books on the subject, including the following: *How Video Works,* 2nd ed., by Marcus Weise and Diana Weynand (Focal Press); *Digital Video and HDTV Algorithms and Interfaces* by Charles Poynton (Morgan Kaufmann); *A Technical Introduction to Digital Video* by Charles Poynton (John Wiley & Sons); and *Optimizing Your Final Cut Pro System* by Sean Cullen, Matthew Geller, Charles Roberts, and Adam Wilt (Peachpit Press).

Color Encoding Demystified

As you start researching such things as video-capture devices, decks, cabling, and connections, there is a lot of terminology that looks as though it belongs in algebra class. Some of that terminology has to do with the color space of video.

You've probably heard of the RGB color model. In the RGB model, combining various values of red, green, and blue makes colors. Those values also determine the brightness of the color. The RGB model is inherently how computer monitors work. This model is a large color space allowing for a great number of colors in varying levels of brightness.

Y'UV has traditionally described how analog video was recorded on tape. Y'UV is a sort of catchall that is often used interchangeably for a number of similar color models such as composite, Y/C, $Y'P_BP_R$, $Y'P_{B-Y}P_{R-Y}$, and $Y'C_BC_R$. Technically (the math part), these terms are not all the same thing. Applications such as Final Cut Pro use the term Y'UV in this generic way, whereas technically, $Y'C_BC_R$ would be more appropriate for how FCP handles component digital video.

Y'UV is the standard way of processing, or encoding to video, from the RGB model. In this model, Y' is the "lightness," or luma, portion of the signal; the color, or chrominance, portion of the signal is represented by U and V (these are called color-difference channels). The U channel is made by subtracting Y' from blue in the RGB model, and the V channel is made by subtracting Y' from red in the RGB model. Compared to the

What's with the Prime?
(the Difference between Luma and Luminance)

Throughout this book when discussing color, and specifically color space, we use the sign ' (prime) quite a bit. This symbol is supposed to clear up (yeah right!) the difference between luma in a video signal and luminance as a scientific term defined by a group called CIE (International Commission on Illumination, abbreviated as CIE from its French title: Commission Internationale de l'Eclairage).

In a 2001 paper on this subject, Charles Poynton states that *"true CIE luminance denoted Y is formed as weighted sum of linear RGB,"* whereas for video *"to form luma, denoted Y' as a weighted sum of nonlinear (gamma-corrected) R'G'B'."*

Still with us?

In simpler terms, Y refers to luminance as a component of color science and unaltered RGB (which approximates how the eye perceives "lightness"). Y' refers to luma; luma being the adaptation of *luminance for video,* and built from gamma-corrected RGB denoted as R'G'B'. So it can be said that the ' symbol refers to nonlinear treatment, or gamma correction.

Whereas, in practical terms, not a whole lot of people use this distinction, it is technically incorrect to refer to luma as Y in video, and it is technically incorrect to call Y' luminance in video systems.

Remember that, and you might someday win *Jeopardy!*

RGB model, the Y'UV system is more efficient for things such as broadcasting. Because our eyes are more sensitive to the brightness portion of the signal (Y') than to the color portion of the signal (U, V), color information can actually be discarded, making for a less bandwidth-intensive signal. This is impossible to do in the RGB model because the RGB values store combined color and brightness information. We'll talk more about this later in the chapter, when we discuss color sampling and subsampling.

Composite describes Y'UV video transmitted down one wire on one cable. Because the different parts of the signal are combined on one wire, it is prone to noise and degradation.

Y/C describes analog S-Video. This improves on composite by separating the luma and chroma portions of the signal onto two separate wires in the same cable. This cuts down on noise and degradation.

$Y'P_BP_R$ describes analog component video. This is an analog signal where the separate channels are transported on three separate cables.

$Y'C_BC_R$ describes digital component video. This is a digital signal where the separate channels are transported on separate cables like analog component, or a single digital cable such as SDI, which is described later in the chapter.

A wonderful development in recent years is that of true R'G'B' formats. Sony's HDCAM SR is one such format capable of recording true R'G'B' video. Much more bandwidth intensive than $Y'UV/Y'C_BC_R$ video, R'G'B' video can use the full gamut of the RGB model for stunning color and quality. True R'G'B' formats are ideal for high-end applications such as feature or nature films, as well as for finishing, such as color grading.

Chroma Subsampling

Now that we have a pretty good working knowledge of video color space, let's examine another frequently confusing subject of chroma subsampling. Perhaps you've heard of formats that are 4:2:1, or capture devices that can capture 4:2:2. These are both examples of chroma subsampling.

Before we decode the ratio, it should be noted that chroma subsampling is handled differently in the analog domain. Therefore, when referring to different parts of the digital signal only, it is correct to use $Y'C_BC_R$, not Y'UV.

Remember that $Y'C_BC_R$—and, in general, the Y'UV color model—allow for separate encoding of the luma and chroma portions of the signal. One benefit of this system is that because our eyes are much more sensitive to brightness in a signal, we can actually get rid of some color information and not sample color as frequently as we do luma. This could be thought of as a form of compression, because in doing so, we can save bandwidth—and, for practical purposes, disk space (more about this in the next chapter).

Lets look at the ratio.

The first number, 4, refers to the horizontal sampling of luma. The second number refers to the horizontal subsampling of C_B and C_R. The third number can describe two things. If it is the same as the second number, it means that the chroma channels were sampled equally. If the third number is 0, it means that every other scan line is sampled at 4:2:2. The alternate lines are actually sampled at 4:0:0—no chroma at all. Every other line is black and white, and shares color information with its neighbor. There can actually be a fourth number, and it will always be the same as the luma sampling. This fourth number refers to the alpha, or transparency component, of a signal.

Common Sampling Ratios

4:4:4—Generally refers to R'G'B' in which there is actually no chroma subsampling, but can also refer to a lesser used 4:4:4 $Y'C_BC_R$. HDCAM SR is a tape format that is capable of recording 4:4:4 R'G'B'.

4:2:2—In this ratio, color (C_BC_R) is sampled only half as often as the luma portion of the signal. Although it might seem like a lot of tossed-out information, 4:2:2 is considered professional quality, and has been defined as such by the ITU-R.BT601 standard. Panasonic's DVCPRO50 and DVCPRO HD, Sony's Digital Betacam, and new versions of their XDCAM system are all examples of 4:2:2 formats.

4:1:1—In this ratio, color (C_BC_R) is sampled only a quarter as often as the luma portion of the signal. The 4:1:1 ratio is used for DV-25 formats such as miniDV, DVCAM, and DVCPRO. Although many still consider 4:1:1 nonprofessional for lots of reasons, 4:1:1 recording has become acceptable for broadcast.

4:2:0—In this ratio, color (C_BC_R) is sampled alternately at 4:2:2 and 4:0:0 every other line. The 4:2:0 ratio is used for MPEG-1 and MPEG-2, JPEG images, and DV-25 PAL.

3:1:1—This ratio is used for Sony's HDCAM format. In 3:1:1, color (C_BC_R) is sampled a third as often as the luma portion of the image. Note, though, that luma is sampled less than that of other standard subsampling types—this is to reduce bandwidth and storage requirements of high-definition video.

A Ratio Based on What?

A ratio describes the relationship between numbers. The numbers themselves are not important; it is their relationship to one another that matters. Thus, 2:1:1 is the same ratio as 4:2:2. So the question arises: Why is the first number, the one on which the ratio is based, always 4?

According to Charles Poynton, this number is 4 because it is "*a historical reference to a sample rate roughly four times the NTSC or PAL color subcarrier frequency, when subcarrier-locked sampling was under discussion for component video.*"

Aren't you glad you asked?

Bit Depth

Like other video semantics, bit depth has been debated and discussed greatly. However, it is not nearly as complicated as other areas of video. Although there is some math involved, bit depth can be understood after some explanation.

Video that is 8-bit $Y'C_BC_R$ uses 220 values to represent luma and chroma. Because of the way $Y'C_BC_R$ video is encoded, this is different from graphics applications that use a full 256 values. In video formats such as DV, 8-bit color space is common, and can be preferable when digitizing video—8-bit files take up less space than do other bit depths. However, 8-bit color space can be limiting due to the range of colors that it can display. An example of this is 8-bit color gradients where banding is visible.

Video that is 10-bit $Y'C_BC_R$ allows for 876 values to represent luma and chroma. Again, because of the way it is encoded, 10-bit $Y'C_BC_R$ video does not use the full 1024 levels of 10-bit encoding. Digital Betacam and D-5 are 10-bit formats, and this is also the preferred bit depth for digitizing and creating digital files—10-bit video allows for a large color range in the image. Although 10-bit color depth will create larger files, banding in graphics will be reduced.

It is possible now with R'G'B' formats such as HDCAM SR and compatible codecs (more on codecs in the next chapter) to work with full-range 10-bit (0–1023) video.

Bit depth is not only an important discussion to have when talking about graphics or gradients. When working with a medium that has a larger bit depth, techniques such as keying and color correction have a larger range for their corrections and alterations.

A new and exciting development is floating-point bit depth. This uses fractional values of color. In other words, there can be values that are in between whole values. This allows for a much larger range of values than can be used in 8- or 10-bit video, but only certain file formats support floating-point bit depth. This is often used when working with film projects, but floating space can be used to preserve the most color information in any image. Although floating-point bit depth is not yet used on an actual tape or tapeless format, many motion graphics programs (for example, Motion 3) support 16-bit and 32-bit floating color space.

Alexis Van Hurkman's *Encyclopedia of Color Correction: Field Techniques Using Final Cut Pro* is an excellent resource for more information on color space and bit depth.

Resolution

Perhaps you've heard of this new thing called high-definition (HD) video?

All joking aside, HD is high definition because of its increased resolution. A relatively easy way to think about resolution is in megapixels—a value of 1 million actual pixels. This

480, 486, or 525 Lines?

Almost always when discussing resolution, the question is asked: "What's the difference between NTSC 720 x 480 and 720 x 486? And why do I hear that NTSC is really 525 lines of resolution?"

NTSC does have a total of 525 lines in the image. Some of these lines actually appear outside the viewable area of the TV; this known as overscan. The lines outside the viewable area carry information such as closed-captioning and sync data.

So then what is the difference? The spec calls for 486 lines, but many digital video-acquisition compression schemes and transmission formats often use 480 lines because the math is easier.

When encoding into a digital format, many encoders use a 16 x 16 section (macroblock) of the image to encode (486 ÷ 16 = 30.375 and 480 ÷ 16 = 30). Using whole numbers allows computers and associated hardware to be more efficient and faster when making calculations about encoding video.

has become a standard measurement of resolution for still cameras, and many people are familiar with the concept of megapixels. And like a lot of things in life, bigger is better!

NTSC video is 720 x 486 pixels, or roughly 0.3 megapixel. Not so good when you consider that even cell phones can take higher-resolution images than that these days.

PAL video is 720 x 576 pixels, which, at 0.4 megapixel, is only marginally better.

High-definition video comes in two flavors: 1280 x 720 pixels and 1920 x 1080. The former is roughly 0.9 megapixel; the latter works out to a more respectable 2.1 megapixels.

Beyond HD, new digital acquisition tools such as the RED ONE camera can record 2K and 4K resolution, or 4520 x 2540—a stunning 11.5 megapixels for 4K! There are different standards in place for 2K and 4K, such as the Academy standard and the Digital Cinema Initiative. DCI states that 2K is 2048 x 1080 (or 2.2 megapixels), and 4K is 4096 x 2160 (or 8.8 megapixels).

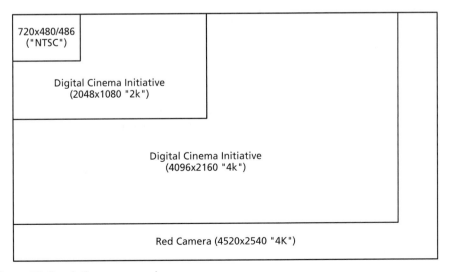

Figure 4.7 Resolutions compared.

Pixel Aspect and Aspect Ratio

In standard-definition PAL and NTSC video, the pixels are not square. They are rectangular—a little taller than they are wide, resulting in a pixel aspect ratio of 0.9 to 1.

Most high-definition formats use square pixels. However, there are a few anamorphic HD formats that use nonsquare pixels to create their widescreen aspect ratio (for example, Panasonic's DVCPRO HD).

Computer monitors use square pixels.

These distinctions are especially important when designing graphics for video or displaying graphics or square-pixel video on nonsquare devices such as NTSC television. For more information about designing graphics for video and how to compensate between square and rectangular pixels, check out the previous chapter. For much more information, see Richard Harrington's excellent book *Photoshop for Video,* 3rd ed. (Focal Press).

If pixel aspect describes the ratio of width to height of an actual pixel, aspect ratio describes the ratio of width to height of the entire image. This ratio is often described with numbers such as 4 x 3 and 16 x 9, or in decimals such as 1.33:1 or 1.78:1. HD formats are 16 x 9; SD formats are most often 4 x 3.

Progressive vs. Interlaced

There has been quite a bit of discussion over the past few years about progressive scan and interlacing. This is because extended-def formats such as 480p (think progressive-scan DVD players) and high-def formats such as 720p and 1080i have come to the foreground.

If you've ever loaded film into a projector, you know that the motion picture is actually made up of still images projected at speed to produce motion. This works great for projecting film, but when TV was invented, limitations of technology and the need to conserve transmission bandwidth led in the 1930s to the development of interlacing.

We already know that an NTSC image is made up of 525 lines, of which we see about 486 or 480 in the active image area. In a CRT (cathode-ray tube), these lines are

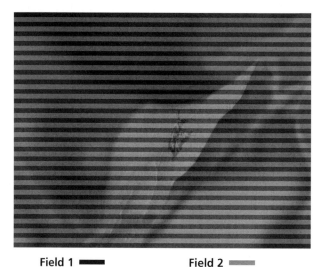

Field 1 ▬   Field 2 ▬

Figure 4.8 Interlaced image.

Ah, More Math! 29.97 and 59.94

Originally, the field rate of NTSC was $\frac{1}{60}$ of a second. This number was chosen to match AC power-line frequencies of 60Hz in North America ($\frac{1}{50}$, or 50Hz, in PAL). Unfortunately, the engineers who designed the specification did so for a black-and-white video signal, and they did not plan ahead for color. So when color television arrived, they had to make a change in the signal. For technical reasons, this turned out to be a 0.1 percent slowdown in the frame rate. This worked out to 29.97fps, leading to a field rate of 59.94fps. (The actual calculation for frames per second is 30×1000/1001, which equals 29.97002997003. For fields, the calculation is 60×1000/1001, which equals 59.940059944006.)

drawn on-screen using an electron beam inside the monitor. In interlaced television, these lines are not drawn onto the screen all at once, but alternately, as two separate images called fields. Put these two pictures together, and you have one frame of video. In NTSC interlaced video, each field happens in about $\frac{1}{60}$ of a second. Adding two fields happens in about $\frac{1}{30}$ of a second, or one frame of video (30fps). In NTSC, the even (or lower) fields are drawn first, then the odd (or upper) fields.

Interlaced video has been the standard for over 50 years, but with the growth of display devices such as LCD, plasma, and DLP over the past ten years, progressive-scan video has come to the forefront. Early in their development, these devices had a very difficult time displaying interlaced video and making it look good. Because there is no electron beam drawing the image on-screen, but rather pixels that are on or off, these devices often show a problem of the interlace system: interlacing artifacts (though CRT devices can also show these problems). These artifacts include interline twitter (a flickering when vertical details in the image appear to shake or move, like fine lines on a shirt) and interlace combing (a "feathering" of the image); they are annoying and ugly. To get around problems with interlaced video, modern displays de-interlace, or remove a field to display the video as progressive.

In progressive video, instead of fields being drawn separately, the image is drawn all at once. Most of us are already familiar with progressive-video devices such as our computer monitors. Progressive scan is much more akin to a roll of film, with each frame being displayed as one whole piece rather than as two separate ones.

Although interlaced video has been given a bad rap recently, there are several benefits to this technology. For one thing, it saves on bandwidth. For another, interlaced images tend to be sharper.

Progressive-scan video is more bandwidth intensive at an equal scan rate. Nonetheless, many viewers feel that progressive-scan images are generally more pleasing and in general have a more filmic quality about them.

Another phrase or concept that has developed with the advent of HD video is PsF, or progressive segmented frames. PsF is a recording scheme in which progressive images are recorded as two separate fields. Hold on a second. . . . You are asking yourself: "What, then, is the difference between PsF and interlaced?" As previously mentioned, a good way of thinking about interlaced video is that it is really two separate images being displayed alternately. In PsF, there are two fields that are really the SAME image being displayed in alternate fashion. A good use of segmented frames would be HDCAM material shot progressive.

Frame Rate

While the discussion of progressive and interlace formats has been going strong, perhaps no other area has spawned as much discussion and confusion as frame rate. Is it 24 or 23.98? Is 59.94 frame rate or field rate? We admit that this is confusing, and so some further explanation is in order.

If you look at a piece of 8mm film (or even 16mm or 35mm), you will notice that the film is really a series of images When run at speed, these images convey motion. How fast the film moves is known as the frame rate.

Perhaps you've seen an early movie from around the turn of the 20th century and noticed choppy motion—for example, people making erratic movements. This is caused by the film's slower frame rate. If you look closely, you will see what appears to be a lot of flicker in the image. Believe it or not, there actually has been quite a bit of study regarding the physiological effects of frame rate. When film is projected or displayed at a slow enough speed, the viewer can actually detect individual frames and notice flicker. When the film is projected or displayed fast enough, however, the viewer sees the motion as constant (persistence of vision) and without flicker (flicker fusion threshold). Although each person has a different persistence of vision and flicker fusion threshold, these phenomena do exist, and understanding different frame rates is important.

Film is displayed and projected at 24fps (frames per second).

NTSC television is displayed at 29.97fps (originally 30fps—see the earlier discussion for why the frame rate changed).

PAL television is displayed at 25fps.

Okay, so that was pretty easy to understand—but like most things in life, it's not that simple.

With HD formats, the concept of frame rate has become confusing. These formats are often noted by descriptions such as 720p60 or 1080i50. The first part of these equations describes the resolution of the image; the second tells us whether the image is progressive or interlaced; the last part is the image frame rate or field rate. It should be noted that all of the frame rates that we are about to discuss actually describe acquisition and mastering. For all intents and purposes, everything in the NTSC countries is broadcast at 29.97; in PAL countries, this is 25fps.

24—We know that film has a native frame rate of 24. In recent years, there has been a large emphasis placed on 24 frames per second acquisition and recording. This acquisition always takes place as progressive, hence 24p. Whereas some digital cameras and edit systems these days are capable of recording at true 24fps, most record at 23.98fps. This is to maintain compatibility with NTSC broadcasting (trust us, the math works). In the past few years, there has been an explosion of 24p, especially as it relates to DV 24p. This raises some issues (see the sidebar, Understanding Pulldown and 24p).

25—The standard PAL frame rate.

29.97—The standard NTSC frame rate. As previously described, the original frame rate of NTSC was an even 30fps, but due to the introduction of color, this frame rate had to be slowed by 0.1 percent ($30 \times 1000/1001$) to 29.97fps.

30—Originally the frame rate of NTSC video, 30fps is often used for progressive standard-definition video, a.k.a. 30p. And 30p is really 29.97; however, it is progressive rather than interlaced. This is often done to give a "film look."

Understanding Pulldown and 24p

Everyone likes film! The true 24 frames per second is pleasing to the eye, and in many ways is idolized as the ideal frame rate. The problem has always been trying to get 24 progressive frames per second to work with 29.97 interlaced frames per second for broadcast. The math can be complicated, but not if you understand pulldown.

To get 24 progressive frames into 29.97 interlaced frames, pulldown is applied. This refers to the resequencing of frames from one frame rate to another. This added pulldown was originally developed to aid in the telecine process of transferring film to video. Known as 3:2 or 2:3 pulldown (or 2:3:2:3 to be more technically accurate), all refer to the same process, albeit in slightly different patterns. Let's take, for example, four frames of film. In the 2:3 pattern, the first frame (or A frame) is pulled down to one full frame of video (two fields). The B frame is pulled down to the second frame of video (two fields) and to the first field of the third frame of video. The C frame is pulled down to the second field of video frame 3, and to the first field of video frame 4. The D frame is pulled down to the second field of video frame 4, and as both fields in video frame 5. So, by using this pattern, we actually get five frames of interlaced video for every four frames of progressive video.

This all results in the pattern AA BB BC CD DD for a 2:3 pattern, and AA AB BC CC DD for a 3:2 pattern.

Generally speaking, when people say they are using 3:2 pulldown, they are referring to the 2:3 pattern.

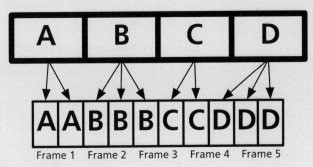

Figure 4.9   3:2 pulldown cadence.

Some cameras, such as the very popular Panasonic DVX100, have a unique take on 24p. In that camera, for example, there are two recording modes. First, 24p Normal, which adds 2:3 pulldown in-camera to give the look of 24fps, but can be captured and outputted as 29.97fps. Then there is 24p Advanced, which has a 2:3:3:2 pattern. When capturing via FireWire, Final Cut Pro can remove this pulldown, getting the video back to true 24p.

Cinema Tools, which is included with Final Cut Studio 2, is also a useful tool for adding or removing pulldown, depending on your workflow.

50—Here is where the confusion between frame rate and field rate starts. PAL has a frame rate of 25fps, yet it has a field rate (how often each field is drawn on-screen) of $\frac{1}{50}$ second, or 50Hz (50 fields per second = 25fps interlaced). When discussing high-def formats, 50 can refer to 50 frames per second or to 50 fields per second. Here is how to tell the difference: When a format is interlaced, 50 generally refers to fields per second (e.g., 1080i50). Because there are 50 fields per second, this still equals 25 frames per second. When progressive, 50 generally refers to 50 frames per second. In the case of 720p high def, the resolution is roughly half that of 1080 high def, so frame rate can be increased and fill about the same bandwidth—for example, to 720p50 (note that 720p50 is not actually supported in FCP).

59.94—The same as 60. Due to the need to keep compatibility with 29.97, field and frame rates that are noted as 60 are really 59.94. For example, 720p60 would more accurately be described as 720p59.94; however, it's easier just to use a whole number.

60—NTSC has a frame rate of 30fps, and has a field rate (how often each field is drawn on-screen) of $\frac{1}{60}$ second, or 60Hz (60 fields per second = 30 frames per second interlaced). When discussing high-def formats, 60 can refer to 60 frames per second or to 60 fields per second. Here is how to tell the difference: When a format is interlaced, 60 generally refers to fields per second—that is, 1080i60. Because there are 60 fields per second, this still equals 30 frames per second. When progressive, 60 generally refers to 60 frames per second. In the case of 720p high def, the resolution is roughly half that of 1080 high def, so frame rate can be increased and fill about the same bandwidth—for example, to 720p60. An exception to this general rule is 1080p60, which is the best of the best when it comes to HD. It is full resolution and has a superhigh frame rate of 60fps. Please note that when discussing any 60i or 60p format, the actual frame rate/field rate is 59.94 in order to be compatible with NTSC's frame rate of 29.97.

Timecode

Put simply, timecode is a way of identifying frames on a tape. Standardized by SMPTE in the late 1960s, timecode comes in two flavors—dropframe and non-dropframe, which we will look at momentarily. First, let's look at a typical timecode—01:24:41:12 is an example of a typical timecode readout. Read from left to right, it means 1 hour, 24 minutes, 41 seconds, and 12 frames. The pattern is HH:MM:SS:FF, where the FF number will always be the highest frame for a given frame rate. In NTSC, for example, this would be 29 frames; in PAL, 24 frames. The counting is always zero based, meaning that the 30th frame in NTSC or the 25th frame in PAL is the next whole second.

Timecode is occasionally seen with a semicolon prior to the frames (for example, 01:23:14;16). This distinction is to identify dropframe (with the semicolon) and non-dropframe (with a colon). Let's look at the difference.

NTSC video operates at 29.97 frames per second, but we count it at 30 frames per second. This discrepancy means that over the course of an hour, timecode would actually be 3.6 seconds longer then the actual time! To fix this, engineers came up with dropframe. By "dropping" the first two timecode numbers every minute, except for each tenth minute (10, 20, 30, etc.), timecode will match real time. One thing that dropframe *does not* do is actually drop real video frames. It is simply a method of counting.

One last area to understand about timecode is how it is actually recorded on tape. There are two methods. Why two, you might ask? In the early days of video, there was no timecode, so the following methods were created as an afterthought and had to be added to the signal.

LTC—Longitudinal timecode (LTC is pronounced "LIT-see") is added to the video as an audio signal on a dedicated audio track. LTC can be read while the tape is playing or fast-forwarding; when playing very slowly or while paused, LTC cannot be read.

VITC—Vertical interval timecode (VITC is pronounced "VIT-see") is embedded as part of the video signal itself at the top of the image (outside the normal 480 or 486 lines). Because it is part of the video signal, VITC can be read when playing very slowly or while paused, but often cannot be read while fast-forwarding or rewinding.

When logging and capturing footage, Final Cut Pro uses either LTC or VITC to read timecode from the video device and to populate timecode metadata for your clips. FCP can read both LTC and VITC, and you can actually choose which one to read, or if both are read, in the device-control tab of Audio/Video Settings. Not all video formats have timecode, though. Formats such as VHS do not have timecode, and therefore Final Cut Pro cannot control the device (more on device control below). You will have to capture from those devices using the noncontrollable-device option.

It is also important to note that film has a system of identifying frames called Keycode, and a related system called ink numbers.

Audio Sample Rate and Bit Depth

We've talked a lot about video, but after all, audio is half of the equation, so let's discuss two areas of the audio signal: sample rate and bit depth.

You have probably seen common sample rates for digital audio in manuals, on the Internet, and elsewhere. Numbers such as 44.1kHz or 48kHz refer to audio sample rate. As a general rule of thumb, the larger the number, the better sounding (especially in the higher end) and larger the file will be. Also, like many of the things we've discussed so far, there is a little math involved!

Human hearing ranges from about 20Hz to 20kHz, although in reality these numbers are less for most people. Our range of hearing is important to understanding sample rate. The highest frequency that can be recorded or reproduced by any device is half that of the sampling frequency (the Nyquist-Shannon sampling theorem). For example, if a CD has a sample rate of 44.1kHz, that means the maximum frequency it can produce is 22.05kHz. Most digital video samples audio at 48kHz, for a maximum reproducible frequency of 24kHz! Another common sample rate is 32kHz, with a maximum frequency of 16kHz. For practical purposes, this means that two of these sample rates—44.1 and 48—can reproduce frequencies beyond that of human hearing!

For video purposes, all of these sample rates (32, 44.1, and 48kHz) exceed the maximum reproducible frequency of an NTSC broadcast.

With the appropriate equipment, Final Cut Pro can work with sample rates ranging from 32 to 96kHz.

Audio bit depth is similar to that of video bit depth. Just like a higher video bit depth, where gradients become smoother and there is a larger range of colors that can be used, high bit depth in audio leads to a larger dynamic range and smoother blending between frequencies. Probably the most common bit depth is 16 bit, but some formats are capable of recording 20 bit, or even 24 bit. Again, as a general rule of thumb, the larger the number, the better. FCP can work with bit depths of 8, 16, and 24 bits.

Video and Audio Signal Paths and Deck Control

If you have ever looked a bird's nest of cables and said to yourself, "Wow! This is a great opportunity to rewire the studio," perhaps you should skip to the next section. But if

SDI, HDMI, TRS, and the like sound like acronyms you see on the back of a luxury car while sitting in traffic, please read on.

In this section, we'll take a brief look at common types of connections and their uses.

Video

Analog

Composite—Composite video these days is the lowest common denominator when it comes to video signals—pretty much anything has a composite connection on it. Composite video was the standard type of connection for early video devices such as 1 inch and ¾ inch and even Betacam. This video is called composite because the brightness (Y', or luma) and the color channels (U and V, or chrominance) are carried as a "composite" down a single pair on a single cable. Composite is the de facto connection on consumer equipment such as VHS players—that is, the yellow jack. In the professional environment, composite connections are often used for low-quality dubbing and low-end monitoring. Composite video connections carry only analog standard-definition video.

S-Video—S-Video (or separate video or Y/C) is the next step up from composite video. Commonly using a four-pin connector, this connection carries video down two separate pairs—one that carries (Y'), or luma, and another that that carries (C), or the chrominance portion of the signal (U,V in the Y'UV model). Because they are carried down separate pairs, the signals benefit from reduced interference between their color and brightness portions. In the professional environment, S-Video connections are often used for dubbing and low-end monitoring. S-Video connections carry only analog standard-definition video.

Component—Component video is the king of analog video. This type of connection carries luma (brightness) on one cable, and than splits chrominance onto two separate cables. Component video allows for much higher quality than composite video or Y/C because it splits the signal into three separate cables, thus eliminating much of the cross talk, or interference, that is inherent to composite and S-Video signals. The first cable, green (Y'), carries the luma portion of the video; red (P_R) and blue (P_B) carry the color portion of the image. In the professional environment, component video is often used for analog input and output from edit systems and decks, as well as for monitoring.

Digital

FireWire—Pioneered by Apple in the mid-1990s and subsequently adopted by the Institute of Electrical and Electronics Engineers as the IEEE 1394 standard,

Figure 4.10 *Left to right:* FireWire 400, FireWire 800, DVI, and HDMI connections.

Connections and Cables

When discussing audio and video signal paths, it gets a little confusing—are we talking about the connection, the part on the end of the cable, or are we talking about the actual cable?

Most professional video cables, such as component and SDI, use 75-ohm coaxial cable. This cable is standardized using a simple protocol: RG-X, with X being the category of cable. Professional video cables most often use RG-6 and RG-59 type 75-ohm coax.

For the actual connectors, there are numerous types. Some of the most common are:

RCA—This is a standard connection type for consumer equipment. RCA connectors are used for audio and for video. These connections are typically color coded: yellow for composite video, red for the right channel in stereo audio, white for the left channel in stereo audio. In analog component bundles, red is for P_R, blue is for for P_B, and green is for Y'. Orange is for digital coaxial audio S/PDIF.

BNC—Bayonet Neill-Concelman; or, if you really want to impress your friends, British Naval Connector. The Bayonet Neill-Concelman connector, so named for its inventors, is the standard type for professional video connections. BNC connections are also sometimes used with AES/EBU digital audio signal paths. A defining characteristic of the BNC connector is a twisting lock that prevents accidental unplugging.

XLR—most commonly found in professional audio devices as well as microphones, the three-pin XLR connection carries balanced audio. Two of the pins carry the signal—one of these is the normal-polarity, or "hot," signal; the other is the inverted-polarity, or "cold," signal. Combined with the third pin, or "ground," a balanced connection is created.

Figure 4.11   *Left to right:* RCA, BNC, and XLR connectors.

FireWire has become a standard connection between miniDV, DVCAM, and DVCPRO decks. It has also been adopted as an option on some DVCPRO50 and DVCPRO HD decks from Panasonic, and on some Sony professional decks such as the J3. FireWire is also referred to as i.Link, which is Sony's name for the technology.

FireWire comes in two varieties: 400Mbps and 800Mbps. FireWire 400 is the connection most often found on decks and computers, and has two different connectors—a six-pin (generally found on computers) and a four-pin connector (generally found on decks). FireWire 800 and its nine-pin connectors are not as widespread for video purposes as FireWire 400 is, but FireWire 800 is starting to be found on HD video interfaces such as AJA's Io HD. FireWire carries digital audio, video signals, and device control.

DVI—Originally designed for the computing industry, Digital Visual Interface became a standard connection in home theaters for connecting displays to sources such as cable boxes (using the DVI-D variant). In professional video, DVI is sometimes used for connecting display devices such as LCD and plasma monitors, as well as projectors. DVI is being superseded by HDMI.

HDMI—High-Definition Multimedia Interface. HDMI has become a standard digital connection on display devices. HDMI supports uncompressed high-definition video and digital audio, and even device-control signals. Compared to FireWire, HDMI allows for larger bit depths and full-color resolution. Although still used mainly as a connection type for display devices, it is also being adopted in the industry as a connection type to nonlinear editors from decks and cameras.

SDI—Serial Digital Interface. SDI is the de facto standard connection type for higher-end digital decks such as Digital Betacam and DVCPRO50, and for high-definition formats such as HDCAM and DVCPRO HD. SDI carries uncompressed 4:2:2 digital component video. This connection type comes in two flavors. The first, SD-SDI, which is covered under the SMPTE 259M standard, transmits 270Mbps of component digital video and can also carry audio, all along one cable. The second type is HD-SDI. As the name suggests, HD-SDI can carry higher-bandwidth (1.485Gbps) component video with audio; it is covered under the SMPTE 292M standard. It should be noted that although there are specific cables geared to transmission of HD-SDI signals, in most cases—especially for shorter runs—the same actual coaxial cable can be used for SD-SDI and HD-SDI. Transmission differences take place on the decks and capture devices.

Dual-Link SDI—As its name suggests, dual-link SDI uses two HD-SDI connections to transmit ultrahigh-resolution HD video. This standard, also known as SMPTE 372M, supports 10-bit 1080p formats, and is capable of supporting true 4:4:4 R'G'B' video. Sony's HDCAM SR, for example, can record and transmit 4:4:4 R'G'B' video over a dual-link connection.

3-Gig SDI—A relatively new standard (SMPTE 424M) can technically do the same thing as dual-Link SDI; however, it simplifies the connection process by eliminating the second cable. Thus, 3-gig SDI can transfer the same 2.97Gbps that dual-link SDI can, but does so along one cable. There are not that many devices currently that use this connection, but it is only a matter of time before 3-gig SDI becomes widespread.

Audio

Unbalanced—An unbalanced audio connection is standard for consumer devices. Often an unbalanced audio connection uses RCA connections. In an unbalanced connection, the signal travels down the cable and there is only one connector. These connections are prone to hum and other interference. Unbalanced audio connections usually carry consumer "low- level" line-level audio (–10dBm). This number is calculated by comparing it to a reference signal. The connections you use to hook up your headphones and stereo speakers are of this type.

Balanced—Balanced audio is a standard for professional audio devices. The most common connection for balanced audio devices is the XLR, although another type, called TRS (tip-ring sleeve), is also sometimes used for balanced connections. Balanced audio is made up of three parts: the normal-polarity, or "hot," part of the signal; the inverted-polarity, or "cold," part of the signal; and the ground. In an XLR connection, this is done with three pins. In a TRS connection, it is done using the tip, which is "hot"; the ring, which is "cold"; and the sleeve, which is the ground. This construction resists outside interference, or noise. Balanced audio connections usually carry professional "high-level" line-level audio (+4dBm). Like low-level audio, this number is calculated by comparing it to a reference signal.

AES/EBU—A digital audio connection developed by the Audio Engineering Society and the European Broadcasting Union. In addition to describing a connection, this also represents a standard (officially AES3). AES/EBU audio can stand for a method of combining two channels of 48kHz audio onto one signal, but more broadly it simply describes a protocol of transferring digital audio. AES/EBU is found most often on professional-level equipment. AES/EBU connections come in more than one flavor, and are most commonly found using an XLR connection, although they can also use a BNC connection.

S/PDIF—Sony/Philips Digital Interface Format. This digital audio connection carries AES/EBU audio on either RCA cables or TOSLINK optical cables. Although found on some professional gear, S/PDIF is more commonly used in the world of home theater.

SDI—As noted previously, SDI can carry video along with audio. Known as embedded audio (AES/EBU audio is embedded in the signal), SDI can carry up to eight channels of uncompressed audio.

HDMI—Like SDI, HDMI can also carry an audio signal. The new HDMI 1.3 standard has expanded audio support.

Deck Control

As we will see in Chapter 5, a key concept for nonlinear editing is deck control, which allows the computer to control the deck as a peripheral. This means that you can play, stop, fast-forward, and so forth, using the computer interface and without touching the deck. The following is a list of common deck-control protocols.

RS-422—A standard communication protocol for professional video decks. RS-422 uses a nine-pin connector to attach a deck to a video-capture device. Standard deck-control operations (fast-forward, rewind, shuttle, jog, etc.) can be sent via this protocol. RS-422 is frame accurate and is supported by Final Cut Pro.

RS-232—A relative of RS-422, this is a standard protocol. Often used on lower-end or older decks, RS-232 is supported by Final Cut Pro.

FireWire—Besides being able to transfer video and audio, FireWire can also transfer device-control instructions. However, FireWire is not a dependable frame-accurate device-control protocol.

HDMI—Much like FireWire, High-Definition Multimedia Interface can carry video, audio, and device control. New devices—such as Blackmagic's Intensity Pro, Sony's HDR-HC3, and Panasonic's HDC-SD1—are all capable of HDMI device control, along with high-resolution video and audio.

Figure 4.12 RS-422 connector.

Common Digital Formats

For your reference, let's take a look at some common digital and analog formats. Of course there are other formats on the market, but this list represents some of the most popular. Prior to starting a production or postproduction project, it is recommended that you discuss with all of those involved which format best suits a given project.

DV-25

What it is: The format that started the revolution! DV-25 has become synonymous with desktop editing. It is the encoding algorithm frequently used for miniDV, DVCAM, and even DVCPRO tape formats. DVCAM, marketed by Sony, runs at a slightly faster speed and uses locked audio (where each frame of audio is locked to a frame of video). DV and DVCAM are both shooting and studio recording formats.

Tech specs: DV-25 records a 4:1:1 (for NTSC; 4:2:0 for PAL) 8-bit signal with 5:1 compression at 25Mbps. DV-25 includes two channels of 48kHz 16-bit audio, or four channels of 32kHz 16-bit audio on small or large cassettes. Recording time depends on which tape speed you are using.

Interfacing with FCP: FireWire is the simplest method of transferring DV-25 video and audio. FireWire can also be used to provide deck control. Some higher-end DV-25 decks, such as the Sony DSR-1800, can also use SDI with RS-422 deck control.

DVCPRO

What it is: A variation of DV-25, DVCPRO is marketed by Panasonic and is often touted as having better dropout resistance than DV or DVCAM. Although not as common as DV and DVCAM, DVCPRO decks can play both of those formats. DVCPRO is a shooting and a studio recording format.

Tech specs: DVCPRO records a 4:1:1 8-bit signal with 5:1 compression at 25Mbps for both NTSC and PAL, as well as two channels of 48kHz 16-bit audio to small or large cassettes that use 6.35mm tape.

Interfacing with FCP: FireWire is the simplest method of transferring DVCPRO video and audio. FireWire can also be used to provide deck control. However, many DVCPRO decks do not have FireWire, so SDI is the best method of transfer. Device control is through RS-422.

DVCPRO50

What it is: DVCPRO50 is a professional video format from Panasonic. Although only an 8-bit format, it is sometimes compared to the 10-bit Digital Betacam format

Figure 4.13 Panasonic DVCPRO deck.

in terms of overall visual quality. DVCPRO is a very popular format for television, corporate, and indie filmmaking because it delivers great results—and usually for a lower price than Digital Betacam. DVCPRO50 is both a shooting and a studio recording format.

Tech specs: DVCPRO50 records a 4:2:2 8-bit signal at 50Mbps (hence the name), with a mild 3.3:1 compression and up to four channels of 48kHz 16-bit audio onto both small and large cassettes that use 6.35mm tape.

Interfacing with FCP: Through a digital capture device, FCP can capture SD video and embedded audio through SD-SDI. With FireWire-equipped DVCPRO50 decks such as the AJ-SD930B from Panasonic, FCP can capture DVCPRO50 through FireWire, and can also remove advanced 2:3:3:2 pulldown via Firewire. If desired, many digital capture devices also support AES/EBU digital audio capture. Device control is through RS-422.

Digital Betacam

What it is: Digital Betacam is the de facto standard for SD recording. Along with D-5 (described next), it is the only other 10-bit SD format. Digital Betacam is a shooting and a studio recording format and is less expensive than D-5.

Figure 4.14 Sony Digital Betacam deck.

Tech specs: Digital Betacam records a 4:2:2 10-bit signal with a very light 2.5:1 compression at 90Mbps, with up to four channels of 48kHz 20-bit audio onto both small and large ½-inch Betacam-based tapes.

Interfacing with FCP: Through a digital capture device, FCP can capture SD video and embedded audio through SD-SDI. If desired, many digital capture devices also support AES/EBU digital audio capture. Device control is through RS-422.

D-5 SD

What it is: D-5 SD's claim to fame is that it is the only 10-bit truly uncompressed studio recording format on the market. D-5 is not an acquisition format.

Tech specs: D-5 SD records a 4:2:2 10-bit uncompressed (170Mbps) signal with up to four channels of 48kHz 16-bit audio onto a medium or large D-5 ½-inch tape cassette.

Interfacing with FCP: Through a digital capture device, FCP can capture uncompressed SD video and embedded audio through SD-SDI. If desired, many digital capture devices also support AES/EBU digital audio capture from a D-5 SD deck. Device control is through RS-422.

Betacam SX

What it is: Although not very common in many postproduction workflows, Betacam SX is still relatively common in the news. Betacam SX is a shooting and a studio recording format. Betacam SX was replaced by Sony's MPEG IMX, and more recently has been transplanted into other formats such as XDCAM and P2.

Tech specs: BetaSX records a 4:2:2 8-bit signal with MPEG-2 compression at 19Mbps and four channels of 48kHz 16-bit audio onto small and large ½-inch Betacam-based cassettes.

Interfacing with FCP: Through a digital capture device, FCP can capture SD video and embedded audio through SD-SDI. If desired, many digital capture devices also support AES/EBU digital audio capture from a BetaSX deck. Device control is through RS-422.

MPEG IMX

What it is: MPEG IMX, as the name suggests, is an MPEG-2 recording format. The interesting thing about MPEG IMX is Sony's push to make the decks more of a piece of network hardware than a simple video deck. Using a special card in the IMX deck with the proper software, the deck itself becomes visible on the network as an e-VTR. IMX media can be transferred over a network rather than using traditional video infrastructure. IMX is also at the core of systems such as Sony's XDCAM.

Tech specs: MPEG IMX records a 4:2:2 8-bit signal of I-frame-only MPEG-2 (discussed in the next chapter) at 30, 40, or 50Mbps with either four channels of 48kHz 24-bit or eight channels of 48kHz 16-bit audio.

Interfacing with FCP: Through a digital capture device, FCP can capture SD video and embedded audio through SD-SDI. Media can be imported (from an e-VTR or an existing file on disk) into FCP using Telestream's MXF component plug-in that "unwraps" the IMX file into a .mov file (more on this in the next chapter). If desired, many digital capture devices also support AES/EBU digital audio capture from an MPEG IMX deck. Device control is through RS-422.

Figure 4.15 Sony MPEG IMX deck.

HDV

What it is: HDV has done for high definition what DV did for standard definition. HDV is considered by some to be a consumer format, but its use is widespread in professional circles as well. In recent years, HDV has exploded—it is now available in 1080 and 720 variants at various frame rates, including 24p (ProHD from JVC).

Tech specs: HDV records a 4:2:0 8-bit signal using MPEG-2 compression at 25Mbps for 1080, and at 19.7Mbps for 720. The 1080 images are spatially subsampled, This means that a 1920 x 1080 image is recorded 1440 x 1080, but displayed at 1920 x 1080 in FCP and on a monitor. "Squeezing" a video image to record a widescreen frame onto a format that is not widescreen is known as *anamorphic*. The 720 images are not subsampled. HDV records two channels of 48kHz 16-bit MPEG-1 Layer II compressed audio onto miniDV tape.

Interfacing with FCP: The easiest method for interfacing HDV with FCP is with FireWire. Using FireWire is limiting in some situations, such as dubbing to other HD formats and with some facilities infrastructure. Devices such as the Miranda HD-Bridge DEC+ can convert HDV over FireWire to SD/HD SDI with embedded audio, and can convert FireWire device control to RS-422 to be used with a digital capture device.

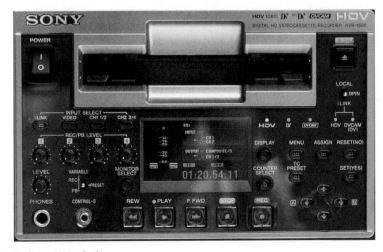

Figure 4.16 Sony HDV deck.

DVCPRO HD

What it is: Also known as DV100, DVCPRO HD is a professional format that is very popular for high-definition acquisition. DVCPRO HD is both a shooting and a studio recording format, and both cameras and decks can record in 720 or 1080 lines. The Panasonic AJ-HDC27, also known as the VariCam, is a very popular DVCPRO HD camcorder capable of recording various speeds from 4fps all the way to 60fps.

Tech specs: DVCPRO HD records a spatially subsampled (720 and 1080) 4:2:2 8-bit signal at 100Mbps with 6.7:1 compression onto small or large cassettes that use 6.35mm tape with up to eight channels of 48kHz 16-bit audio. Spatially subsampling the material works in the following method: A 1920 x 1080/60 (NTSC) image is subsampled to 1280 x 1080, a 1920 x 1080/50 (PAL) image is subsampled to 1440 x 1080, and both a 1280 x 720/60 and a 1280 x 720/50 image are subsampled to 960 x 720 (note that FCP doesn't currently support 1280 x 720/50 images). Another way to think of subsampling is that the image is recorded as nonsquare pixels. Once digitized, FCP and other apps in the FCP Studio can compensate for this and display the image correctly as square pixels.

Interfacing with FCP: Through a digital capture device, FCP can capture HD video and embedded audio through HD-SDI. With a FireWire-equipped deck such as the Panasonic AJ-HD1400, FCP can capture DVCPRO HD through FireWire. In the case of VariCam footage using FireWire, FCP can remove pulldown to get back to the overcranked or undercranked frame rate. Cinema Tools can also be used. If desired, many digital capture devices also support AES/EBU digital audio capture. In most applications, device control is through RS-422, but can be FireWire.

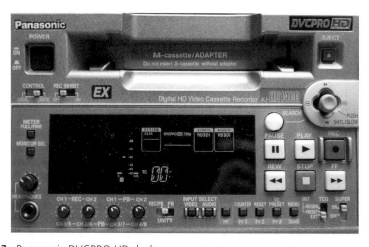

Figure 4.17   Panasonic DVCPRO HD deck.

HDCAM

What it is: HDCAM is generally considered the Betacam SP of high definition. It's everywhere! HDCAM is a shooting and a studio recording format. Although solely a 1080-line shooting format, some studio decks are capable of outputting 720. In

Figure 4.18 Sony HDCAM deck.

some applications, HDCAM is being supplanted by HDCAM SR, but the former is still a very popular format for shooting and studio recording.

Tech specs: HDCAM records a 3:1:1 8-bit signal with 4.4:1 compression at 144Mbps and four channels of 48kHz 20-bit audio onto ½-inch Betacam-derived tape. Like DVCPRO HD, HDCAM subsamples the 1920 x 1080 image to 1440 x 1080. HDCAM can shoot and record at a variety of 1080 frame rates, including 24p.

Interfacing with FCP: Through a digital capture device, FCP can capture HD video and embedded audio through HD-SDI. If desired many digital capture devices also support AES/EBU digital audio capture. Device control is through RS-422.

HDCAM SR

What it is: The latest and the greatest from Sony. HDCAM SR is a new format, but is already being proclaimed the top dog in the HD market. HDCAM SR is capable of both 1080- and 720-line recording (only 720p60), and is both a shooting and a studio recording format.

Tech specs: HDCAM SR records either a 4:2:2 $Y'C_BC_R$ or a 4:4:4 R'G'B' 10-bit signal with MPEG-4 compression. When recording in standard quality of 440Mbps in 4:2:2 mode, it uses 2.7:1 compression; in 4:4:4 R'G'B', it uses 4.2:1. Some HDCAM

Figure 4.19 Sony HDCAM SR deck.

SR decks, such as the portable SRW-1 from Sony, can record 4:4:4 R'G'B' video at 880Mbps with a lighter 2:1 compression. This is known as 2x, or HQ, mode. HDCAM SR records up to 12 channels of 48kHz 24-bit audio.

Interfacing with FCP: Through a digital capture device, FCP can capture 4:2:2 Y'C$_B$C$_R$ uncompressed HD video and embedded audio through HD-SDI. Because HDCAM SR supports 4:4:4 R'G'B', video can be captured through dual-link HD-SDI. If desired many digital capture devices also support AES/EBU digital audio capture. Device control is through RS-422.

D-5 HD

What it is: Until recently, D-5 HD has been considered the de facto standard for HD studio recording. Its main competitor is HDCAM SR, but D-5 still remains a viable format simply because it provides amazing picture quality that is less expensive than the HDCAM SR (as of May 2007). D-5 HD is capable of recording all of the 720 and 1080 variants, but is only a studio recording format.

Tech specs: D-5 HD records a 4:2:2 8-bit signal with 4:1 compression, or a 4:2:2 10-bit signal with 5:1 compression at 269-323Mbps, depending on format. D-5 HD records up to four channels of 24-bit audio, or eight channels of 20-bit audio, onto a ½-inch D-5 cassette.

Interfacing with FCP: Through a digital capture device, FCP can capture HD video and embedded audio through HD-SDI. If desired, many digital capture devices also support AES/EBU digital audio capture. Device control is through RS-422.

Figure 4.20   Panasonic D-5 HD deck.

Common Analog Formats

Although there are a multitude of analog formats still to be found in the dark alleys of postproduction, the world in which we now find ourselves is a digital one. So, rather than detail a lot of analog formats, let's take a look at the two most common analog formats that we encounter on a daily basis.

VHS/S-VHS

What it is: VHS is the format we have all come to hate. . . . I mean love! The winner of the format war with Sony's Betamax, VHS has been largely supplanted by DVD in almost every consumer respect. VHS/S-VHS will most likely remain a format that has to be dealt with from time to time in the postproduction world.

Tech specs: VHS uses ½-inch cassettes with composite recording. VHS can have one or two channels of linear audio (audio that runs on the edge of a tape), or two channels of AFM (audio frequency modulation) stereo audio—better known as hi-fi. This is recorded in the same path as the video. S-VHS improved the overall visual quality of VHS, and in most cases also provided S-Video (Y/C connectors) for improved visual quality when connected to a compatible display device.

Interfacing with FCP: Using an analog capture device, FCP can capture analog composite or Y/C video and unbalanced analog audio. There is no deck control available for VHS/S-VHS, so FCP must use Capture Now in order to capture (more about this in Chapter 7: Ingest).

Betacam SP

What it is: Probably one of the most popular professional formats of all time. This analog format was a standard broadcast format for almost 30 years. Finding a home in production and postproduction, Betacam SP is still in use today. However, BetaSP machinery is no longer made by Sony, due largely to proliferation of DV and other digital formats.

Tech specs: Betacam SP uses ½-inch metal tape and analog component recording. BetaSP is available in small (maximum length: 30 minutes) and large (maximum length: 90 minutes) cassettes.

Interfacing with FCP: Using an analog capture device, FCP can capture analog $Y'P_BP_R$ component video and balanced analog audio. Deck control is RS-422. Equipment such as the J Series and other higher-end Sony decks can play Betacam SP because they are based on the same transport system.

Other Digital Acquisition and Recording Formats

For years, the postproduction market has been dominated by tape. Recently, the market has seen the next force in acquisition and recording formats: tapeless. Instead of recording to tapes, these new formats record sound and images to optical, disk-drive, or solid-state media. Tapeless formats have several advantages over tape:

1. Not being tape-based, these formats do not have the inherent problems that tape does—for example, tape hits, slow rewind and fast-forward times, and tape jams.

2. Tapeless formats tend to be more flexible than tape-based formats are. For example, Panasonic's P2 format is capable of recording anything from DV up to DVCPRO HD at multiple frame rates.

3. The time benefits of tapeless acquisition are undeniable. Transferring footage without having to digitize allows for streamlined postproduction workflows.

Our main focus is the two most popular tapeless formats: P2 and XDCAM. This is because these two are the most solidified in the marketplace. It is important to note that there are other tapeless formats available.

Formats such as Thomson Grass Valley's Infinity and Ikegami's Editcam systems are just as exciting as P2 and XDCAM, but have not gained widespread commercial appeal. Just like P2 and XDCAM, both Infinity and Editcam use MXF wrappers. However, there is no native support of these formats directly in FCP. Via USB 2.0, Telestream's

MXF components can extract the DV, DV-50, or IMX media from these formats for use in FCP.

AVCHD, developed by Sony and Panasonic, employs the MPEG-4 AVC (MPEG-4 Part 10), better known as the H.264 codec, to greatly improve image quality and decrease storage requirements compared to the MPEG-2 system that many HD systems currently use. AVCHD will also allow for the recording of up to 7.1 digital audio. The neat thing about this format is that it can use many different types of media, such as miniDV, hard disk, and solid state. Although some products currently exist, there is as of yet no widespread adoption of AVCHD.

Also on the horizon for late 2007 is XDCAM EX, which is Sony's first solid-state recording system. Employing 34mm express cards dubbed SxS cards, the format will shoot 1080 and 720 at multiple frame rates, including 24, and is seen as a direct competitor to P2.

Although not technically a format, Focus Enhancements' FireStore allows cameras with FireWire ports to record directly to disk, and to have media directly available for FCP.

Lastly, let's not forget about the digital cinema market. A number of high-end tapeless acquisition products exist, but price and lack of commercial appeal have limited their widespread adoption.

One thing is for sure: tapeless acquisition marks a sign of things to come.

P2

What it is: P2 (Professional Plug-in) is a solid-state recording medium from Panasonic. It allows for recording of DV-25, DVCPRO, DV-50, and DVCPRO HD in multiple frame rates onto the P2 card. P2 is a shooting and a studio recording format, although it is commonly used only to shoot.

Tech specs: P2 records DV-25, DVCPRO, DVCPRO50, and DVCPRO HD with multiple frame rates, with media contained inside an MXF wrapper. Technical specifications are the same as those formats. Cameras, readers, and decks typically have two to five card slots, thus allowing for spanning of footage over multiple cards.

Interfacing with FCP: The first step to transferring P2 footage is to mount the P2 card(s). This can be done in several ways: (1) Because a P2 card is essentially a PC

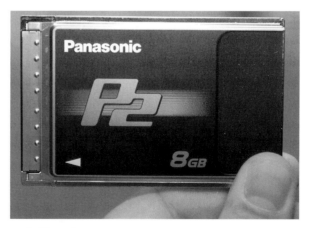

Figure 4.21 Panasonic P2 card.

card, one can use a PC card reader, or even the internal PC card slot found on an Apple PowerBook (note: you must download and install the P2 driver software from Panasonic's web site). (2) Use any of the Panasonic P2 card readers or the P2 store unit. (3) Configure a P2 camera as the card reader. With any of these methods, use the Log and Transfer utility inside FCP to transfer the footage. You can also use a P2 camera as a traditional VTR, and capture the material via FireWire using Log and Capture in FCP (more on this in Chapter 7: Ingest). Lastly, you can also use a P2 deck such as Panasonic's AJ-SPD850 to capture P2 footage via SDI with RS-422 deck control.

XDCAM SD and HD

What it is: XDCAM is a tapeless format that uses Sony's blue-laser technology (similar to that of Blu-ray DVD) to record SD (XDCAM SD) or HD (XDCAM HD) images onto 23.3GB media dubbed Professional Disc (there is also a 50GB dual-layer version). XDCAM has grown quite considerably over the past few years, with exceptional growth in news and sports.

Tech specs: XDCAM uses either DVCAM or IMX recording for XDCAM SD, and therefore the tech specs are the same as for those formats. XDCAM HD uses 4:2:0 MPEG-2 in three modes: 18Mbps (LP), 25Mbps (SP, essentially HDV), and 35Mbps (HQ). Both XDCAM SD and XDCAM HD wrap media in an MXF container. XDCAM HD, like HDCAM and DVCPRO HD, subsamples the image down to 1440 x 1080. XDCAM supports up to four channels of 48kHz 16-bit audio. At NAB 2007, Sony announced the next generation of XDCAM HD, which will shoot 4:2:2 at 50Mbps! This camera will be accompanied by a deck with matching specs. As of May 2007, these devices were not yet commercially available.

Interfacing with FCP: Here is how to interface XDCAM material in FCP: (1) Transfer XDCAM material via FireWire using Sony's XDCAM transfer software (available from Sony's web site). This software will unwrap MXF containers and deliver compatible QuickTime files to FCP. (2) Use Telestream's MXF components to browse, unwrap, and import XDCAM footage from an Ethernet-equipped XDCAM or XDCAM HD deck. Lastly, much like P2, XDCAM footage can be digitized via SDI with RS-422 control.

Figure 4.22 Sony XDCAM HD deck.

Capture Cards and Boxes

Now that we have a good working knowledge of the history of video formats, connection types, and stats for common modern video formats, there are a few more pieces of the hardware puzzle: capture cards and hard drives. First, we take a look at capture cards. We save drives until the next chapter.

The purpose of the capture card is to interpret the video signal for the computer.

Whether you realize it or not, all Apple computers have a built-in capture card: your FireWire port! That's right—Apple has been nice enough to provide a high-quality digital interface to decks. Although most often used for mini and DVCAM decks, as previously mentioned, some higher-end decks are now using FireWire as an option.

FireWire is often a nice, convenient option, but it doesn't work in all situations. For one thing, it does not have a high enough transfer rate for some video formats. Secondly, it is strictly a digital-to-digital device, so additional hardware will be needed for any analog decks. Many third-party manufacturers make the cards and devices that support video capture.

Over the past few years, two major players have dominated the Mac market for capture cards and devices: AJA and Blackmagic Design.

Both companies offer a range of products for standard-definition, high-definition, and analog and digital connections. You can check them out on the Internet at *www.aja.com* and *www.decklink.com*

The Next Step

For the workflow designer, decisions regarding video standards and formats are important, but they are intimately related to another set of concerns. In the next chapter, we will discuss the technical aspects of video compression and storage.

5 Compression and Storage

Now that we have taken a look at video terminology and formats, there are two more topics that are important to helping build a successful postproduction workflow: codecs and storage.

Understanding codecs and storage is essential when discussing postproduction workflows for two reasons:

1. Choice of codec(s) directly influences image quality, color depth, and storage requirements.
2. Choice of storage and its deployment directly influences how much media can be stored, if those media can be successfully played back (high data rates), and what sort of redundancy is available.

Codecs and storage are, of course, in a constant state of flux. We can remember the first FireWire drives we used in the early days of Final Cut Pro. Those drives were 20GB, and we were thinking, "Wow! What are we ever going to do with that much storage!" Of course, these days, 500GB, 750GB, and even 1TB drives are available as single-drive solutions!

In the same time period that computer power has been increasing, so has the sophistication of compression. MPEG-4 codecs used in formats such as HDCAM SR or H.264, sometimes used for web compressions and high-definition DVDs, would not be possible if it were not for ever-quickening computer processors and graphics cards.

In this chapter, we will take a look at compression and storage strategies as they apply to workflows.

What Is a Codec?

A codec can be understood in three ways.

The first is that of a system that compresses an image, video, or audio into a smaller form. This can be desired for several reasons:

1. You want to save disk space.

2. Your hard drives are not fast enough to play back uncompressed or high-data-rate video.

3. To allow for faster and easier transmission on the Web, DVD, or even broadcast and satellite. In this regard, a codec can be understood as a *co*mpressor/*de*compressor.

The second way to think of a codec is as a system that accesses and carries digital information. This is when you want to maintain the original format compression in postproduction (DV, DVCPRO, DVCPRO50, or DVCPRO HD). Whether it is tape based or tapeless, recording almost always uses a compression scheme. In this way, you're not making the data smaller, but rather moving it in its original form. In fact, the term "codec" is often used in this way to describe sequences and even files. For example, questions such as "What kind of sequence are you using?" or "What type of file is it?" often are answered with "Oh, it's a DVCPRO50 sequence" or "It's an uncompressed 10-bit file." In this regard, codec can be understood as a *co*der/*de*coder.

The third way to think about a codec is as a transportation medium for analog video. Because analog video is obviously not digital, when digitized, there must be a system in place that organizes and structures the information on disk. This is where once again a codec comes into play.

One area to clarify is that encoding video doesn't always make it smaller. In fact, sometimes this is not the goal at all. Final Cut Pro is in many ways format and codec agnostic. Because of this, you can use a third-party capture card. For example, DV footage could be captured as uncompressed, or DVCPRO HD footage could be captured as ProRes 422. In the past, this has often been done to match other footage in a project and/or sequence settings so as not to have to render. Now, in Final Cut Pro 6, the Open Format Timeline has made this much less necessary, although you still may want to use this method to obtain the best overall performance.

The Codec Conundrum

Before we get into the technical specifics of codecs, we need to look at something we call the "codec conundrum."

Codecs often make a trade-off between quality, data rate, and efficiency. Generally, a good-looking codec will take up a lot of disk space, and a good-quality small file will take a long time to compress. However, this is not always the case. Just because something has a very low data rate does not mean that it can't look good. If footage looks amazing, it might use a very inefficient codec that takes a long time to render.

This conundrum is constantly present in postproduction. It wasn't all that long ago that digital video codec formats such as DVCAM, DVCPRO, and DV—which are heavily compressed and have very low data rates—were thought to be completely unacceptable for broadcast. Flash forward a few years, and the conundrum is still a source of debate. Now the same debate happens in the wild world of high def. HDCAM, with its high data rate, was once thought to be the cream of the crop in the HD world. Today, HDCAM is now snubbed in some circles in favor of the MPEG-4 codec of HDCAM SR, which is more efficient, has an even higher data rate, and is better looking.

Even armed with technical knowledge of formats and codecs, the codec conundrum always finds a way of creeping into a postproduction workflow. This is not necessarily a bad thing—it allows for a larger discussion on the meaning of quality. As a rule of thumb, this discussion generally leads to higher data rates and codecs delivering the best quality with greater efficiency. But only you can decide what is best for your particular workflow.

Data Rate

So far in this book, we have been referring to data rates, using terms such as megabits per second (Mbps) and gigabits per second (Gbps). Sometimes data rate is referred to in bytes rather then bits: megabytes per second (MBps) or gigabytes per second (GBps). We explain below how bytes are larger chunks of data than bits are, but *all* of these things refer to data rate.

So, what is a bit, and what is a byte, and how does bitrate relate to data rate? Let's first start with the basics.

A *bit* is the smallest piece of digital information represented by a 1 or a 0, and is abbreviated with a lowercase *b*.

A *byte* is collection of 8 bits, and is abbreviated with an uppercase *B*.

Kilo means "thousand" and is abbreviated as *K. Mega* means "million," and is abbreviated as *M. Giga* means "billon," and is abbreviated as *G. Tera* means "trillion," and is abbreviated as *T*.

Generally speaking, bits describe flow of data or transmission speed. For example, HD-SDI has a bandwidth of 1.485Gbps, meaning that 1.485 billon bits can flow down the cable in this way. It is common to use the word *bitrate*, but more generally, this can still be referred to as "data rate."

Bytes generally describe storage requirements. For example, we have all seen hard drives with the notation 200GB. This means the drive is capable of storing 200 billon bytes of information. Here is where things get tricky. It is common to also use bytes when referring to data rate—in the digital world, data rate is inherently linked to storage requirements. For example, DV at 29.97fps has a data rate of 3.6MBps.

Using bytes instead of bits is done mainly to keep the math easier when describing or discussing data rates. Take, for example, our DV file. If we were to refer to it in small notation (megabits), it would be 28.8Mbps, which can add up to some very large numbers quickly. The opposite of this is equally hard math. If we were to refer to this same file using the larger notation of gigabits, it would be 0.028125Gbps.

As a general rule of thumb, the higher the data rate, the better looking the image—although this is not always true because it is highly dependent on the method of encoding. As we will see, one of the goals of compression is to lower the overall data rate while losing only a minimal amount of quality.

Term/Prefix	Letter	Value
Bit	b	1
Byte	B	8
Kilo	K	1,000
Mega	M	1,000,000
Tera	T	1,000,000,000

Figure 5.1 Common data abbreviations.

How Codecs Work

Codec development is driven partly by technology, partly by quality aesthetics, and partly by consumer demand. Some codecs—such as DV—have seen universal success, whereas others have failed, and still others—such as ProRes 422—appear very

Constant and Variable Bitrate

We already know that bitrate can refer to the "flow" of information down a cable, for example. This flow could also happen on a DVD in a DVD player to produce an image on your screen, or from a camera's CCD (charge-coupled device) to its recording medium. In this way, bitrate can mean how fast data must flow to reproduce an image. However, not all parts of the image are equal—there are always going to be parts of an image that do not move as much as others, and parts of images that are more detailed then others. To deal with this, there are two methods for transmitting bits: constant bitrate and variable bitrate.

A good way to think of constant bitrate (CBR) is that the same quality (bitrate or data rate) is applied to the entire piece of video regardless of whether it is moving fast from frame to frame or whether each frame has a high level of detail. This often leads to differences in quality throughout the piece of video. Most production video codecs use a constant-bitrate method.

Variable bitrates (often abbreviated VBR), on the other hand, take into account changes from frame to frame and detail in each frame, and can apply a variable bitrate (data rate). In other words, parts of the image that are not moving can get compressed more (lower bitrate) than those that are moving quite a bit (higher bitrate). The same is true for detailed portions of the image—low levels of detail can be compressed quite a bit, whereas high levels of detail will not be compressed as much. Some video codecs, such as MPEG, can use the variable-bitrate method.

promising. This section is not intended to be a manual on the engineering of a codec, but rather is meant to help you further your understanding of how video codecs and other compression schemes (MPEG, for example) work. The goal is to apply this knowledge to your workflow thinking, and to help you choose an appropriate codec and compression scheme for your work.

Lowering the Data Rate

Generally speaking, the goal of compression is to lower the data rate of an image or footage, thus reducing its overall storage requirements. Acquisition formats use compression to fit data onto a storage medium, and offline editing involves fitting large quantities of footage onto media drives.

Video compression is complicated. Our goal is to give you some principles and concepts to help understand it so you can make more informed decisions for production and postproduction. Later in this chapter, there are detailed descriptions of the technical principles of compression. First, we go over four concepts (sometime overlooked) that can be used for additional compression with any of the principles.

1. *Chroma Subsampling*—As we have previously mentioned, chroma subsampling is a fundamental method of reducing data rate. In a 4:4:4 image, there is no subsampling taking place, and the color should be identical to that of the original image. When chroma subsampling (for example, 4:2:2) is applied, color information is lost, thus reducing data rate and file size.

2. *Reducing Image Size*—A high-definition image has more pixels then does a standard-definition image. Because of this, the data rate for the SD image is lower

than that of the HD image. Another way of looking at this is that images that are digitized smaller will have a lower data rate, and thus less in the way of storage requirements, than the original image. This is a common technique used for workflows that have both offline and online phases—where, for example, an HD image is captured at half size, thus reducing its data rate.

3. *Reducing Bit Depth*—We already know that bit depth refers to the number of values possible to represent luma and chroma in an image. The larger the bit depth, the greater the range of information that can be stored by each pixel—and the more information for each pixel, the higher the data rate. So by reducing bitrate from 10 bits to 8 bits, you reduce the file size by more than 20 percent.

4. *Reducing Frame Rate*—By reducing frame rate, we can effectively lower the data rate for a piece of video even if it uses the same codec. Because there are fewer frames to process, the data rate is reduced. This method is most commonly used for web compression.

Compression Ratios

Throughout this book, as well as in technical literature or on the Web you might read about a concept called compression ratios. Although this concept is not technically difficult, let's take a moment to look at what a compression ratio means.

The larger a compression ratio, the more compression is applied. For example, DV has a compression ratio of 5:1, whereas DVCPRO HD has a compression ratio of 6.7:1. This ratio can be looked at in two different ways:

1. Uncompressed Size/Compressed Size

2. Uncompressed Data Rate/Compressed Data Rate

So in the case of our DV file with a compression ratio of 5:1, this means that the uncompressed file would be five times the size of the compressed file. Or, looked at another way, the uncompressed file would have five times the data rate of the compressed file.

Of course, compression ratios aren't everything. Codecs continue to get better, which means ever-higher quality at ever-lower date rates.

$$\text{Compression Ratio} = \frac{\text{Uncompressed Size}}{\text{Compressed Size}}$$

$$\text{Compression Ratio} = \frac{\text{Uncompressed Data Rate}}{\text{Compressed Data Rate}}$$

Figure 5.2 Two ways to look at compression ratios.

Lossless Compression

On a recent trip to Las Vegas for the NAB (National Association of Broadcasters) annual meeting, I was reminded of lossless compression as I sat at the blackjack table. While playing the game, I thought to myself, "Wouldn't it be nice if every dollar I bet, I got back?" Of course, Las Vegas doesn't work like this—but video compression can.

Lossless compression works on a simple principle: what you put in is what you get out. In other words, an image or video that uses lossless compression will be exactly the same *after* the compression as it was before. Lossless compression typically uses a scheme called run-length encoding.

In any given image, there are thousands—if not millions—of pixels, and each pixel in the image has information that describes its color and brightness (Y'UV, Y'C$_B$C$_R$, RGB, etc.). Each pixel has 3 bytes of information to describe its pixel (in 8-bit encoding).

To compress the image, run-length encoding uses lines of pixels, or sections of those lines, that are identical, instead of using the values of each pixel. For example, a line of video might have 50 pixels of the same value. In run-length encoding, this section would be calculated as 50, X,X,X, where X equals the value of the pixel. This takes up only 4 bytes of information—in the original image, the calculation for the same section would have been 50 pixels × 3 bytes = 150 bytes (remember that each pixel has 3 bytes to describe it). You can see that this is a gigantic space savings over the calculation of millions of pixels. The best part is that it's just good math, and you are left with the original image.

Lossless compression does particularly well with images or video that have large areas of repeating pixels. Lossless compression does have its downsides, though. Lossless codecs typically don't compress more than 2:1. Also, lossless codecs—in part due to run-length encoding—are very processor intensive.

In the computer world, lossless codecs such as Apple's Animation are generally used as "transfer" and archiving codecs—"transfer," as in moving video files and images from one application to another without losing any information. An example of this might be rendering out of Motion for use in FCP or another application. Lossless codecs are also a good choice for archiving of material because the footage is not "stuck" in a particular lossy compression scheme (discussed in the next section).

One limitation of the Animation codec is that it is an 8-bit RGB codec. This means that when you use the file in Y'C$_B$C$_R$ color space, a conversion takes place. Also, an 8-bit codec has less of a range of information than does a 10-bit codec.

Lossy Compression

If lossless compression outputs what is inputted, then lossy compression—you can probably guess—"loses" something along the way. In general, the goal is to make this loss acceptable—and even imperceptible—to most people.

Lossy compression works on the idea that parts of the image can be compressed or even discarded more then others. For example, in the previous chapter, we discussed chroma subsampling. Chroma subsampling works on the idea that our eyes are much more sensitive to luma (brightness) then to chroma (color). Therefore, a common way of compressing an image is by chroma subsampling, where color is sampled half, or even a quarter, as frequently as luma is.

Lossy compression is always a balancing act between image quality, data rate, motion fluidity, and color depth. New methods and techniques (such as ProRes 422) are being developed all the time to try to bring this balancing act into equilibrium. Although no lossy codec is perfect, many do an exceptional job. Perhaps the biggest advantage of lossy codecs, especially when compared to their lossless cousins, is their ability to drastically reduce data rate and file size. Compression ratios of 100:1 are not uncommon with lossy codecs. This drastic reduction of data rate is what makes formats such as DV and MPEG so exceptional—you can get acceptable quality with a relatively low data rate.

Spatial Compression

Spatial compression—also known as intraframe compression because it looks solely within each frame to make compression choices—is used in schemes such as DV and in many other, if not most, video codecs.

In spatial compression, repetitive information in each frame can be discarded to obtain compression. Depending on the codec, there are several techniques used to decide what information is repetitive. These techniques as a whole are referred to as basis transformations, and are complex mathematical formulas to "transform" spatial data into another form so that repetitive information can be analyzed and eliminated.

The most common technique is called DCT (discrete cosine transform), which turns pixels into frequency blocks (8 pixels x 8 pixels). Once the pixels have been converted into frequency blocks, those that are zero or close to zero are discarded. By effectively eliminating pixels, compression is achieved. What happens to areas where pixels were eliminated, you might ask? The pixels that were left behind are increased in size to fill in the gaps.

Have you ever watched digital television and noticed a big area of blue sky that was filled with a blue square? This is spatial video compression.

Another basis transformation that is sometimes used is called wavelet. Apple's Pixlet codec developed with Pixar is an example of a codec that uses wavelet basis transformation. This compression method has not yet achieved wide use.

Temporal Compression

Temporal compression, also known as interframe compression, is a method of compressing that works based on portions of the image that do not change from frame to frame. What characterizes interframe compression is the comparison of changes between adjacent frames instead of on a single-frame basis like spatial compression.

The beauty of temporal compression is that these changes are stored as instructions rather than actual images. As you can imagine, these instructions take up a lot less space than an actual image would. Like spatial compression, there are many techniques possible for temporal compression, but one of the most common (although it uses spatial as well) is MPEG, which is described next.

Temporal compression was originally used solely for distribution—DVDs, digital television, and so on. However, temporaral compression has gradually worked its way into acquisition and postproduction with formats such as HDV and XDCAM.

MPEG

Moving Picture Experts Group (MPEG) compression is a compression scheme that by this point anyone reading this book is probably familiar with from use on the Web and maybe even DVDs. MPEG is a committee of the International Organization for Standardization. MPEG codecs are a dominant force in video today. MPEG comes in a few varieties named for the version of the specification: MPEG-1, MPEG-2, MPEG-4. These varieties all improve on each other, and further improvement is undoubtedly in the future of this scheme.

MPEG first uses spatial compression to eliminate redundant information in the footage, then uses temporal compression to compare frames to compress the image even more. Before discussing the individual schemes of MPEG compression, we need to talk about some of the basics of MPEG. With MPEG variants being used in acquisition and postproduction as well as distribution, learning the technical underpinnings is useful in designing workflows.

GOP

A Group of Pictures (GOP) is the pattern in which IPB frames are used (these frames are described next). A GOP must always start with an I-frame, and can have a com-

Figure 5.3   A GOP.

bination of B- and P-frames in between. Typically, these patterns are I-frame only, IP, IBP, or IBBP. The more P- and B-frames in the GOP the longer the GOP. The longer the GOP, generally the better the compression—but this leaves potentially larger room for image degradation. GOPs tend to be either 7 or 15 frames for NTSC, and 7 or 12 for PAL, but different lengths are possible. GOPs can also be open or closed. In an open GOP, there are frames in one GOP that can "talk" to frames in another GOP. This generally allows for greater compression versus closed GOPs, in which one GOP cannot "talk" to another.

I-Frame

I-frame stands for intrapicture, intraframe, or even keyframe. The I-frame is the only complete, or self-contained, frame in a GOP, although it is broken down into 16 x 16 pixel segments called macroblocks. In common GOP lengths such as 15, 12, or 7 frames, the I-frame would be the first frame in the GOP. Because I-frames are the only complete picture, they take up more space in the final video file. Some codecs and formats that use MPEG use an I-frame-only scheme (IMX). This delivers outstanding video quality, but sacrifices compression efficiency.

P-Frame

P-frame stands for predicted pictures, or simply predicted frame. P-frames contain information called motion vectors, which tell how the previous frame (which can be an I or P) has changed to arrive at the current frame. Motion vectors are created by comparing macroblocks on the previous frame. Motion vectors can include information about what has moved in the frame and how it has moved, but also luma and chrominance changes. Depending on the change, P-frames create new macroblocks to make the change. P-frames are not self-contained and cannot be accessed in editing or in DVD design. Substantially smaller than I-frames, P-frames help to achieve the high compression of MPEG.

B-Frame

B-frame stands for bidirectional pictures or bidirectional frame. B-frames are like P-frames, but can look both ways (toward I- or P-frames) in a GOP—unlike P-frames, which can look only backward.

Profiles/Levels

All varieties of MPEG can use what are called profiles and levels. Put simply, profiles refer to the combination of IPB frames that are used along with color encoding. Levels refer to image size (SD, HD, etc.), frame rate, and bitrate (data rate). This is a way of defining standard methods for encoding MPEG. For example, MPEG-2, which is used for many formats—including DVD, digital broadcasting, and HDV—has six profiles and four levels (see below) The most common implementations of this combination are Main Profile/Main Level (or MP@ML), used for DVD and digital broadcasting, and MP@H-14, used for HDV (Main Profile/High 1440). Other formats, such as Sony's XDCAM HD, use 422P@H-14 (4:2:2 Profile/High 1440).

MPEG-2 Profiles

Name (abbr)	Color Subsampling	Types of Frames
Simple Profile (SP)	4:2:0	I, P
Main Profile (MP)	4:2:0	I, P, B
4:2:2 Profile (422P)	4:2:2	I, P, B
SNR Profile (SNR)	4:2:0	I, P, B
Spatial Profile (SP)	4:2:0	I, P, B
High Profile (HP)	4:2:2	I, P, B

MPEG-2 Levels

Name (abbr)	Max Size	Max FPS	Max Bitrate
Low Level (LL)	352 x 288	30	4 Mb/sec
Main Level (ML)	720 x 576	30	15 Mb/sec
High 1440 (H-14)	1440 x 1152	60	60 Mb/sec
High Level (HL)	1920 x 1152	60	80 Mb/sec

Figure 5.4   MPEG-2 profiles and levels.

Now that we know a little more about some of the basics of MPEG, let's briefly take a look at some of the common varieties of MPEG. For more technical information on MPEG compression, profiles, and levels, check out *http:// www.mpeg.org* and *http:// www.chiariglione.org/mpeg/*

MPEG-1
This has become a ubiquitous file type on the Internet for video and audio delivery. MPEG-1 Layer 3 (better known as MP3) is an industry-standard file type for delivery and distribution of high-quality audio on the Web, and for devices such as portable MP3 players. MPEG-1 was also the file format of choice for VCDs (video compact discs), a popular format prior to the widespread adoption of MPEG-2 (described next) and DVDs. MPEG-1 is typically encoded at roughly half the resolution of an NTSC D-1 frame. Although capable of pretty good quality, MPEG-1 has been mostly replaced on the Web by other MPEG variants such as MPEG-4. For all intents and purposes, MPEG-1 has been supplanted by MPEG-2 for optical media such as DVDs.

MPEG-2
This is the standard file type for DVD, as well as for digital cable and satellite broadcasts. MPEG-2 is generally seen as the replacement for MPEG-1, and typically is used as such (DVDs versus VCDs). MPEG-2 is usually encoded at full-frame 720 x 480 and, unlike MPEG-1, is capable of supporting interlaced footage.

MPEG-4
This takes many of the compression techniques found in MPEG-1 and 2 and improves upon them *greatly*. MPEG-4 is used for delivery and distribution for cable and satellite (although this is currently in the early stages), the Internet, cell phones, and other devices, including recording formats such as HDCAM SR. MPEG-4 variations include

popular codecs such as H.264 (AVC). Probably the biggest feature of MPEG-4 over its predecessors is the use of what are called objects and how those are encoded.

In MPEG-4, an object can be video, audio, or even text. Because all of these are different elements, MPEG-4 can use different techniques to compress them. MPEG-4 also uses a much more sophisticated take on the IPB frames of GOPs to increase compression efficiency. Like the profiles and levels described above for MPEG-2, MPEG-4 has its own profiles and levels for different uses.

JPEG

Because JPEG compression has become a ubiquitous format, especially for images, we discuss it here. JPEG stands for the Joint Photographic Experts Group. This type of compression uses many techniques we've already discussed, such as chroma subsampling and basis transformations—namely, DCT (discrete cosine transform) to convert the image into frequency blocks (8 pixels x 8 pixels) to remove redundant data.

There are some variants on JPEG compression—for example, Motion-JPEG (M-JPEG), which essentially applies to moving images the same spatial-compression techniques used for still images. JPEG 2000 is a more refined version of JPEG compression that specifically can use much higher compression ratios than does the regular version. JPEG tends to fall apart at high compression ratios, whereas JPEG 2000 does not.

The OfflineRT settings in Final Cut Pro use Photo-JPEG compression to provide a highly compressed file for offline editing. This was an update to the offline/online concept, opening the door to laptop editing. Some people use OfflineRT (essentially a brand name) interchangeably with Photo-JPEG.

Compression Artifacts

As we've mentioned, no compression scheme is perfect. One of the issues that is constantly at hand with compression is that of compression artifacts. Compression artifacts are parts of the image that in some way have been messed up due to compression. Every compression scheme has its own inherent artifacts. For example, DV, which achieves some of its compression from chroma subsampling and is an 8-bit format, often suffers from "stair-stepping" (also called "aliasing"). This occurs on the edges of objects, where subtle color gradations cannot be rendered, and takes the form of what appear to literally be steps.

Compression artifacts often have a domino effect through postproduction. Because of their bit depths and chroma subsampling, DV and HDV, for example, are not particularly suited for tasks such as chroma keying. The person trying to pull the key has an exceedingly difficult task because the artifacts in the image make it that much harder to pull a clean key.

Some common artifacts include:

Mosquito Noise—generally due to DCT basis conversion used in spatial compression. Mosquito noise looks like blurry and scattered dots throughout the image, particularly on things that have neatly defined edges (text, for example).

Chroma Smearing—generally due to chroma levels that are too high. Chroma smearing looks like colors bleeding into one another, taking on a smudged appearance.

Image Blocking—generally due to images moving very fast. This is especially noticeable in compression schemes such as MPEG and others that use macroblocks. During fast motion, the macroblocks are sometimes visible.

Media Architecture

So far in our discussion of codecs, we have assumed (because FCP is a Mac application) that all codecs are QuickTime codecs. Although all of the codecs that we discuss *are* QuickTime codecs, this brings up a bigger point about media architecture and file wrappers.

QuickTime is a media architecture, Windows Media is a media architecture, and RealPlayer is a media architecture. These architectures are also referred to as file wrappers. We use the term "wrappers" because they literally wrap the media with metadata about the clip. A media architecture can be thought of as having three parts:

1. The architecture, which acts like a governing body, keeping track of files, codecs, and even interactivity that it supports.

2. The files themselves—that is, .mov, .tiff, .jpeg, .mpeg.

3. The codec at work to play or view the file. Sometimes, as in the case of a JPEG image, the file type is the same as the codec, but this not always the case. In video, a .mov file, for example, can use multiple types of compression. One file might use the DV codec, whereas another uses the DVCPRO HD codec.

Exploring different media architectures could be the topic of another book—or even books! So let's keep it simple. QuickTime, the architecture that FCP and Macs use, supports dozens of different file types, with dozens of different types of compressions. For more information about supported file types and codecs, check out *http://www.apple.com/quicktime/player/specs.html*

With that said, let's take a look at one more increasingly important aspect of media architectures.

MXF and AAF

The world is increasingly moving toward open source—meaning standards and technology that are not owned by any one person or company. The open-source movement does not apply just to the world of IT—video technology is also jumping on the open-source bandwagon. MXF and AAF are a big stride into the world of open source for video.

MXF—Stands for Material eXchange Format. MXF files contain video and audio formats such as DV, DVCPRO HD, and IMX. Final Cut Pro natively supports MXF depending on the format. For example, using the Log and Transfer window, FCP can "unwrap" MXF files on a P2 card for logging and transferring to your machine and FCP project. Other MXF wrapped formats—such as Sony's XDCAM and XDCAM HD, Grass Valley's Infinity, and Ikegami's Editcam—can be used in Final Cut Pro with a little work, using Telestream's MXF components, as described in Chapter 4.

AAF—Stands for Advanced Authoring Format. AAF is billed as a "universal" wrapper for almost everything in postproduction, including text documents used for scripts, camera information such as aperture and shutter speed, and video and audio files, along with dozens of other pieces of information. AAF support is still in its infancy in Final Cut Studio.

Common Codecs

OfflineRT (Photo-JPEG)—The OfflineRT settings in FCP are based on Photo-JPEG compression. This is a great offline (hence the name) choice for standard-definition and high-definition projects. The advantage of OfflineRT is its space savings. Hours of footage can be captured using extremely little disk space. The downside of OfflineRT is its relatively poor image quality. The case study in Chapter 15 utilizes the OfflineRT codec to provide reference to a large amount of footage on one small drive.

Specs—OfflineRT uses JPEG compression with a 40:1 compression ratio, bit rates of less then 500KBps, 8 bit, with 4:2:0 chroma subsampling.

DV-25—The DV-25 codec, or simply the DV codec, is partly responsible for the DV revolution. The DV codec is the native codec of DV, DVCPRO, and DVCAM devices. The DV codec provides a good balance between image quality and compression for standard-definition video. DV is often the best choice of codec for footage that originated as DV. DV can suffer from poor color rendering due to its chroma subsampling and 8-bit color depth. The DV codec is a standard-definition codec.

Specs—DV uses spatial DCT compression with a 5:1 compression ratio, a CBR of 25Mbps, 8 bit, with 4:1:1 chroma subsampling for NTSC, 4:2:0 for DV and DVCAM PAL.

DVCPRO50—DVCPRO50 improves greatly upon the quality of DV. DVCPRO50 is the native codec of DVCPRO50 devices. DVCPRO50 provides excellent image quality and is often the next-best choice (after uncompressed codecs) for standard-definition footage. DVCPRO50 is a standard-definition codec.

Specs—DVCPRO50 uses spatial DCT compression with a 3.3:1 compression ratio, a CBR of 50Mbps, 8 bit, with 4:2:2 chroma subsampling.

IMX—A high-quality I-frame-only MPEG-2 codec, IMX is the native codec of Sony's IMX tape format. It can also be used for other formats, such as Sony's XDCAM, Grass Valley's Infinity, and Ikegami's Editcam. IMX provides very good image quality, but suffers from MPEG-2 artifacts such as image blocking. IMX is a standard-definition codec.

Specs—IMX uses spatial-compression I-frame-only MPEG-2 with a CBR of 30, 40, or 50Mbps, 8 bit, with 4:2:2 chroma subsampling (422P@ML).

DVCPRO HD—A high-quality, low-data-rate HD codec. DVCPRO HD is the native codec of DVCPRO HD devices. DVCPRO HD provides high-quality HD images at a very low data rate (for HD). DVCPRO HD is a good alternative codec for other HD formats thanks to its excellent image quality and low data rate. DVCPRO HD is a high-definition codec.

Specs—DVCPRO HD uses spatial DCT compression and image subsampling with a 6.7:1 compression ratio, a CBR of 100Mbps, 8 bit, with 4:2:2 chroma subsampling.

Apple Uncompressed 8-Bit 4:2:2—Developed by Apple, the uncompressed 8-bit 4:2:2 codec delivers excellent image quality for both standard-definition and high-definition projects. The uncompressed 8-bit codec is one of the best codec choices for projects that require the best SD and HD image quality. The 8-bit codec saves disk space compared to the 10-bit codec, but has fewer color gradations. The Apple uncompressed 8-bit 4:2:2 codec is both an SD and an HD codec.

Specs—The uncompressed 8-bit 4:2:2 codec uses spatial DCT compression with a 1:1 compression ratio, a CBR of 168Mbps, 8 bit, with 4:2:2 chroma subsampling.

Apple Uncompressed 10-Bit 4:2:2—Also developed by Apple, this is the 10-bit equivalent of the uncompressed 8-bit 4:2:2 codec. The Apple uncompressed 10-bit 4:2:2 codec is both a standard- and a high-definition codec. This is a good choice for mastering and short-form archiving.

Specs—The uncompressed 10-bit 4:2:2 codec uses spatial DCT compression with a 1:1 compression ratio, a CBR of 224Mbps, 10 bit, with 4:2:2 chroma subsampling.

HDV—The HDV codec uses a long GOP MPEG-2 compression scheme. Like DV, it suffers from poor color fidelity due to its chroma subsampling. The HDV codec does provide very usable high-definition images. Sony's XDCAM HD format also uses the HDV codec for CBR footage. The HDV codec is a high-definition codec. Although convenient for acquisition, HDV is not a favored postproduction or mastering codec.

Specs—The HDV codec uses spatial compression to eliminate redundant data, and then temporal compression to compare frames with a 27:1 or 47:1 compression ratio, depending on line variant. HDV uses image subsampling (1440 x 1080) for 1080-line variants, a CBR of 19Mbps for 720-line variants, and 25Mbps for 1080-line variants, 8 bit, with 4:2:0 chroma subsampling (MP@H-14).

Apple Intermediate—Although native HDV can be edited directly in Final Cut Pro, because it has a long GOP frame structure, performance may suffer. The Apple Intermediate codec fixes this by providing an I-frame-only solution for HDV footage. Because it is I-frame only, using this codec will increase storage requirements by three to four times over the storage requirements for native HDV. The Apple Intermediate codec is a high-definition codec.

Specs—The Apple Intermediate codec uses I-frame-only spatial compression with variable compression ratios and data rates from approximately 56Mbps to 96Mbps, depending on image complexity. This codec is 8 bit, with 4:20 chroma subsampling, matching HDV.

XDCAM HD—Although standard-definition XDCAM uses DV or IMX codecs, XDCAM HD in Final Cut Pro uses either the HDV codec for 25Mbps CBR footage or the XDCAM HD codec for 18Mbps and 35Mbps VBR footage. The XDCAM HD codec is sometimes called MPEG HD by Sony. This is a high-definition codec.

Specs—The XDCAM HD codec uses spatial compression to remove redundant data, and temporal compression to compare frames. XDCAM HD has data rates of 18Mbps VBR, 25Mbps CBR, and 35Mbps VBR. XDCAM uses image subsampling (1440 x 1080), 8 bit, with 4:2:0 chroma subsampling (MP@HL). Final Cut Pro does not yet have a 4:2:2 50Mbps XDCAM HD codec (422P@H-14) to support new cameras from Sony.

ProRes 422—This is a brand-new codec announced by Apple at NAB2007. The ProRes 422 codec allows standard-definition data rates for high-definition material. This codec is available in two modes: the standard ProRes 422 and ProRes 422 (HQ). This codec can be used for both SD and HD footage, though most users will probably use it solely for HD. ProRes 422 is currently one of the best alternatives to an uncompressed SD or HD workflow. The ProRes 422 codec is both a standard- and a high-definition codec.

Specs—ProRes 422 uses spatial DCT compression and proprietary Apple technology with variable compression ratios, VBR 145Mbps for SD, VBR 220Mbps for HQ with HD footage, VBR 42Mbps for SD, VBR 63Mbps for HQ with SD footage, 8 or 10 bit, with 4:2:2 chroma subsampling.

Both AJA and Blackmagic (DeckLink) have their own 8- and 10-bit codecs. In many cases, though, both companies default to codecs that ship with Final Cut Pro. Of note, there are a couple of third-party codecs worth mentioning.

AJA 10-Bit RGB and 10-Bit Log RGB—Intended for high-end postproduction workflows, including 2K film digital intermediate postproduction, these are R'G'B' codecs, not $Y'C_BC_R$. As such, they offer a wider range of usable color information. The difference between the two codecs is that 10-bit RGB is a linear codec, and as such uses a range of color values—64–940 (876 values)—often referred to as SMPTE range. And now for the cool part: this codec offers full-range encoding of 0-1023 (1024 values) for true 10-bit color. The 10-bit Log RGB codec uses a logarithmic scale to assign color values. This is done in an attempt to better reproduce film's range of latitude.

Installing and Removing Codecs

Most installers for codecs are smart enough to place the codecs where QuickTime and Final Cut Pro can use them. It is important, however, to know where on your system these codecs live. That way, you can delete them or add them as necessary—for example, for troubleshooting purposes.

Codecs live in *System Drive/Library/QuickTime*.

Storage

So you've found the best format for your needs, purchased a deck and capture card or interface, chosen your codec, and are ready to start your project—only to realize that you've forgotten one critical thing: Where are you going to store all the media? It's time to talk storage.

Understanding Drive Interfaces

There have been major developments over the years in hard-drive technology. Drives have become faster, smaller, and able to store more. Although most of these changes have taken place inside the drive itself in terms of how data is written, and so on, we would need a lot more pages to describe these improvements. In general, faster rotational times and seek times, larger buffers, and large sustained read and write numbers all make for a better drive. Let's discuss what most people think about in terms of different types of hard drives: the drive interface—in other words, how the drive connects to the computer.

IDE, EIDE, ATA, and PATA—All of these acronyms refer to the same type of interface, which is the most common type of drive on the market these days. These drives can be found in personal computers, inside external USB and FireWire drives (although those drives often contain a separate card that bridges to USB or FireWire), as well as RAID solutions such as Apple's Xserve RAID (although bridged to Fibre Channel). Over the years, different names have been used, but in general they refer to the same interface. IDE stands for Integrated Drive Electronics, EIDE stands for Enhanced Integrated Drive Electronics, ATA stands for AT Attachment, and PATA stands for Parallel ATA—to distinguish it from Serial ATA, or SATA (see below). These drives are often noted with the bus type and speed—for example, Ultra ATA/133 (shorthand: ATA/133). The bigger the number, the faster the interface can run. There are, however, two components to this system: the drive and the controller. The controller is often a card or is built into the computer, and is what is responsible

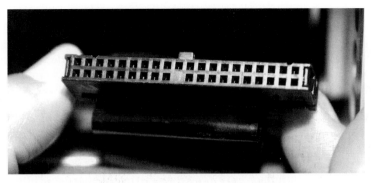

Figure 5.5 ATA ribbon cable.

for communicating with the drive. This is important because if you attach a faster drive to a slower controller, the drive will operate at the slower speed.

These drives use a 2-inch-wide, 40-pin ribbon cable and a 4-pin power cable. These cables often make it difficult to use drives in tight spaces—namely, the inside of a computer case. Limited to two drives per cable, these drives also have configuration jumpers to mark which is the "master" drive and which one is the "slave." Somes types of controllers can choose master or slave by placing the jumpers into "cable select" mode. These drives come in capacities up to 1TB in size (as of July 2007).

SATA—Serial ATA is quickly replacing ATA as the de facto standard in computers, external drives, and RAID units. One advantage of SATA is that the large and cumbersome interface cable of ATA has been replaced with a small seven-pin ¼-inch-wide cable. Of course, drives using SATA connections are also faster. The original spec (SATA I) ran at 150MBps. SATA II runs at 300MBps and is backward compatible with SATA I. However, when a SATA II device is connected to a SATA I controller, the device will run at the slower speed. Originally designed for internal (inside a computer) applications, SATA in recent years has also found a place in external drives and RAIDS. With cabling, it is known as eSATA (external SATA). G-Technology, for example, makes an excellent product known as G-SATA, which is a great solution for external SATA.

SATA RAIDs have become very popular for those who need huge amounts of storage that is exceptionally fast but does not require a large cash investment. It

Figure 5.6 SATA connector.

should be noted that there is a little bit of magic going on when RAIDs or multiple SATA drives are being used externally. SATA is a point-to-point protocol. This means that each drive connects via a single cable to the controller. Until recently, this involved inserting a multiport interface card into the computer and connecting each drive or channel of a RAID to the card. Now most manufactures use what is called a port multiplier. Each drive in the external unit connects to the port multiplier. Externally, one or two ports connect to the host controller, depending on the number of drives in the unit. The port multiplier does translation to decide which drive to use for reading and writing data.

SCSI—Small Computer System Interface is something that many are glad that they are not subject to using in their daily work anymore! SCSI for quite some time was a standard device interface until it was replaced by cheaper—and often simpler—interfaces. This of course doesn't mean that SCSI is dead; the interface is still used quite a bit in RAID arrays.

The nomenclature for SCSI is a little bit of an alphabet soup. There are narrow and wide data units (describing how large the data path is: 8 bit or 16 bit). There are different speeds of the units—for example, Ultra, Ultra2, Ultra160, Ultra 320. There are different signal types (how the data flows down the cable), such as HVD (high-voltage differential) and LVD (low-voltage differential). SCSI also has an identification system for the devices on the bus. SCSI supports up to 16 devices (on a wide data path), but each device must have its own unique identifier. If two devices share the same ID, you can have lots of problems.

The SCSI chain of devices must also be terminated—either with a jumper found on some devices, or with an external terminator pack that plugs into the last device on the chain. That's a lot of stuff to remember! These days, though, most SCSI units typically use either Ultra160 or Ultra320 SCSI, both of which are wide (16-bit) low-voltage differential (LVD). The SCSI Trade Association (*http://www.scsita.org/aboutscsi/termsTermin.html*) has more information on the different types of SCSI.

Fibre Channel—These days, the Holy Grail of interfaces is Fibre Channel. If you've ever looked at purchasing a Fibre Channel device, you might think these things were made of gold! Available in throughputs of 100, 200, or 400 MBps, Fibre Channel devices are very fast. Often they are used in superhigh-performance RAIDs such as Apple's Xserve RAID, and in SAN setups such as Apple's Xsan. Although the simplest Fibre Channel connection is directly to the host computer via an interface card called a host bus adapter (HBA), which is a point-to-point connection, most applications of Fibre Channel tend to be used in either "loop" or "switched fabric" modes.

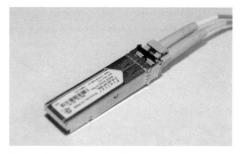

Figure 5.7 Fibre Channel optical connector with transceiver.

In the loop mode, Fibre Channel devices are attached to a Fibre Channel switch. In this setup, only one Fibre Channel device can talk to only one computer on the hub at a time. Switched fabric connects Fibre Channel devices to a Fibre Channel switch. Unlike loop mode, however, all devices on the switch can talk to each other. The switched-fabric mode is the most common setup in SAN solutions.

True Fibre Channel hard drives do exist, but they are SUPER expensive. Many Fibre Channel setups—for example, Apple's Xserve RAID—actually use cheaper ATA or SATA drives, and bridge inside the unit to convert to Fibre Channel. One other interesting thing about Fibre Channel interfaces is the cables they use. For short distances, copper cables can be used. For long distances—which are likely to be found in SAN setups—more expensive and very delicate fiber-optic cabling with optical transceivers must be used.

FireWire—This has become probably the most common type of interface for connecting drives and other devices (such as decks and cameras) to the Mac. FireWire is also known as i.Link (Sony's moniker) and, more generically, IEEE 1394.

FireWire comes in two varieties: 400 and 800 (IEEE 1394b). There are three types of connectors: four pin, six pin, and nine pin. Six-pin and nine-pin connectors can also carry power, a nice feature for smaller 2.5-inch portable drives. FireWire supports up to 63 devices at the same time on the bus; however, it will operate only as fast as the slowest device on the bus.

This is particularly important to understand because not all devices that use FireWire are created equal. FireWire can actually run at 100, 200, 400, or 800 Mbps (S100, S200, S400, S800), allowing for actual throughputs up to about 80MBps. When connecting, say, a DV deck and a FireWire hard drive on the same bus, you might get really slow performance and symptoms such as dropped frames. This is because most DV decks run at the slowest speed of S100, or just about 8MBps, severely limiting overall performance of the bus.

There is no such thing as a true FireWire drive. Whether they are FW400, FW800, or part of a combo, FireWire drives are really ATA or SATA drives internally, using an FW bridge for external connections.

Figure 5.8 *Left to right:* FireWire 400 (six pin), FireWire 400 (four pin), FireWire 800 (nine pin).

USB—Universal Serial Bus comes in two varieties: 1.0 (or 1.1) and 2.0 (Hi-Speed USB). USB 1.0 or 1.1 has a transfer speed of 1.5 MBps (12 Mbps in the spec), which is okay for computer mice and if you want to wait all day for something to transfer. Hi-Speed USB 2.0 has a much more respectable transfer rate of 30-40MBps (480 Mbps in the spec). In practice, USB 1.0 and USB 2.0 are not as fast as FireWire, due mainly to the fact that with USB, the speed of the host machine has a lot to do with how fast a transfer is going to happen. Like FireWire, USB is subject to slowing down if there is a slower device on the bus. As with FireWire, most external drives use a USB 1.0/USB 2.0 bridge connected internally to an ATA or SATA drive.

Media and Their Requirements

At the end of the day, hard-drive technology comes down to two questions: How much stuff can I get on a given drive volume? And will it play back without dropping?

To get a better grasp on this, one must understand that different formats are going to have different requirements for storage and performance. An important factor is data rate (discussed in detail above). In video, it is common to see data rates in megabytes per second (MBps). For example, DV has a data rate of 3.6MBps. This means that to play back this file, a hard drive must be able to spit out at least 3.6 megabytes per second. Data rate can also be used to figure out storage requirements. Take our DV file. If it has a data rate of 3.6MBps, then every minute it needs 217MB of storage space, and every hour it needs 13GB.

Data rate—and therefore the speed requirements of the disk and how much storage you will need—can be impacted by frame rate and whether the file includes audio.

Other bandwidth concerns include how many streams (layers or tracks) of video you need to play. If you have a Final Cut Pro Timeline with four tracks of DV video all playing at the same time, then you have just increased your bandwidth requirements by a factor of 4. This can get exceptionally complicated when discussing SAN systems—where you might have one person trying to work with HD video, and another person using, say, DV video. However, calculating each person's bandwidth requirements will help you get in the ballpark for figuring out SAN bandwidth requirements.

AJA has a great tool called the AJA Data Rate Calculator (*http://www.aja.com/html/ support_kona3_swd.html*). This is useful for calculating the data rate and storage requirements of various common formats.

Storage Strategies

Now that we understand a little more about interface technologies, data rates, and bandwidth, you're actually going to have to use the drives. Let's take a look at three common drive applications.

Single-Drive Solutions

In recent years, with the increase in speed and capacity of drives, single-drive solutions have become common. The biggest factors that influence single-drive solutions are rotational speed of the drive (rpm), buffer size, and interface. It is common to use single FireWire drives for DV, DVCPRO50, and other compressed formats, or to have a separate "media" drive or drives internally in your Mac.

There comes a time, however, when every single-drive solution will meet its limits. Typically, when a drive starts to get full, it becomes less efficient, and throughputs go down. Also, a MAJOR limitation of single-drive solutions is lack of redundancy. This means that if all of your media, project files, and other assets are all on one drive, if that drive dies, you've lost everything! Implementing a backup strategy is especially important for single-drive solutions, even if this means backing things up to another single drive. Having multiple single drives has its advantages as well. Typically, this means having a system drive, or a drive that contains nothing but applications and associated files, in addition to other (single) drives that are your media drives. In the professional world, redundancy and speed are paramount. That doesn't mean that single-drive solutions are not used, but there may be better options out there, depending on your situation.

RAID Solutions

Although single-drive solutions are a viable strategy, and often the easiest to set up and purchase, RAID units provide two major improvements over single-drive units: speed and redundancy. RAID stands for Redundant Array of Independent (or Inexpensive) Disks (or Drives). Put more simply, a RAID is a method of grouping together multiple drives to act as one volume.

As simple as it sounds, there are some key concepts to take a look at when discussing a RAID. Just because you have a bunch of disks in an enclosure does not mean they know how to work together! Let's take a look at a few methods for creating a RAID.

Striping—If you have experience with RAIDs, you are probably familiar with striping. This is the easiest way to improve overall performance. When drives are striped together, data is written across the drives in the stripe instead of to just an individual drive. The management of how this data is written across the drives is done either by software such as the Mac OS X disk utility or by a hardware controller built into the RAID unit. The nice thing about striping is that the more drives you add to the striped set, the larger performance gains you get. Another positive about striping is that your striped volume capacity is the sum of the capacity of the drives involved. On the downside, striping provides NO redundancy. Because data is being written across drives, if one of the drives fails, all the data is lost. A pure striped set is also known as RAID level 0.

Mirroring—If striping is the best performance scheme, then mirroring provides the best redundancy. In a mirrored volume, data is written to drives at the same time. For example, if two drives were put in a RAID using mirroring, the data would be written to both of those drives simultaneously. If one drive were to die, you would still have all of the data on the second drive. Like striping, you can set up mirroring with the Mac OS X disk utility or by using a hardware controller on some units. Although this method is great for redundancy, it does nothing for speed. Another limiting factor of a mirrored RAID is that available capacity of the created volume is half of the sum of the contributing drives. A true mirrored set is also known as RAID level 1.

Striping with Parity—Have you ever heard the phrase, "you can't have your cake and eat it too"? Well, that is true with striped and mirrored sets. With striped sets, you get performance gains; with mirrored sets, you get redundancy. Wouldn't it be nice if you could have both? You can! The answer is striping with parity.

Although traditional striping and mirroring can have their advantages, almost every IT or pro video deployment will use a striping-with-parity scheme. Here is how it works.

Unlike striping or mirroring, striping with parity uses *parity bits* to help maintain data redundancy while at the same time keeping speed improvements. In striping with parity, only the important bits are remembered; this is done by using something called a truth table. The truth table employs fancy math to decide which bits are kept. After you do the math, any of the drives can be used to restore another drive if any should fail. A downside of striping over parity is that the created volume has reduced capacity.

Striping with parity can take on different methods—what are referred to as RAID levels. We already know that level 0 is striping, and that level 1 is mirroring. Here are some other common schemes.

RAID 3—This adds a dedicated parity drive to a striped set. On the plus side, RAID 3 does not lose much performance, even if a drive fails. Raid 3 can be slow because the parity drive is sometimes a source of a data bottleneck, especially when files

Figure 5.9 A pair of Apple Xserve RAIDs.

are constantly being written to the RAID. This scheme requires a minimum of three drives and a hardware RAID controller.

RAID 5—Instead of using a single drive for parity information, RAID 5 distributes parity information over all of the drives in the set. This effectively reduces the data bottleneck of RAID. This scheme requires a minimum of three drives and a hardware RAID controller.

RAID 50—This scheme uses two RAID 5 sets striped together. RAID 50 is often thought to be the best balance of performance and redundancy. RAID 50 setups tend to be expensive because they generally use lots of drives, a hardware RAID controller, and quite often drive interfaces such as Fibre Channel. RAID systems such as Apple's Xserve RAID can use RAID 50.

There are a number of other RAID schemes that are available and worth researching—for example, RAID 0+1, RAID 10, and RAID 30. These are less common, however. Although setting up a simple RAID 0 or RAID 1 is very easy to do for the average user, complex schemes such as RAID 50—especially when they occur in a larger storage pool such as a SAN (discussed below)—can be complex to set up and manage. Because of that complexity, we highly suggest either learning more about storage and RAID setups (there are lots of great resources for this on the Web and in print) or hiring an IT professional to assist you.

SAN Solutions

In its basic form, a SAN (storage area network) is a method of using a shared-storage pool so that all members of a workgroup can gain access to the same data. This can be very helpful in many workflows. There is an example of this in the case study in Chapter 18.

SANs represent a major leap forward in the way that storage is designed and thought of. Although, in principle, all SANs do the same thing, there are differences in deployment, software, hardware, and management. This section is not intended to be a guide to setting up a SAN such as Apple's Xsan. For more information about setting up an Xsan environment, check out *Xsan Quick-Reference Guide,* 2nd ed. by Adam Green and Matthew Geller (Peachpit Press) and *Optimizing Your Final Cut Pro System* by Sean Cullen, Matthew Geller, Charles Roberts, and Adam Wilt. (Peachpit Press). Let's take a look at some of the SAN components, using an Xsan environment as a guide.

Hardware—Hardware for an Xsan can be broken down into a few separate components:

1. *Xserve RAIDs*—For shared storage. These are the drives that store media files for the SAN. Xserve RAIDs connect to the SAN via Fibre Channel (built into an Xserve RAID).

2. *Metadata Controllers (MDCs)*—Computer processors, usually Xserves. The metadata controllers (there are usually two with one for backup) control the traffic to the shared storage on the SAN. The metadata controllers must have a Fibre Channel host adapter installed to connect to the SAN via Fibre Channel.

3. *Open Directory*—As part of OS X Server software, usually running on a separate Xserve, although it can run on one of the metadata controllers. Open Directory centralizes user authentication to machines and the SAN. This helps the SAN by identifying each user and the group to which that user belongs. This is key to setting up parameters for determining which users or groups can access what shared storage. This can run either inside the SAN (on one of the metadata controllers) or outside the SAN (more on this later).

4. *Client Computers*—Up to 64 (including any MDCs) via Fibre Channel. These computers—for example, a Mac Pro G5 or G4 (dual 800 MHz or faster)—request media from the shared storage. The client computers also must have Fibre Channel host bus adapters installed to connect to the SAN via Fibre Channel. Additionally, the client computers should have two Ethernet ports: one dedicated to the metadata network, and one dedicated to the outside network (i.e., the Internet). More on this later.

5. *Fibre Channel and Ethernet Switches*—The Fibre Channel switch is the device that all Fibre Channel traffic goes through. As mentioned above, switches run in two modes: loop (where only two ports on the switch can talk at the same time) and fabric (where all ports can talk to each other at the same time). A

Figure 5.10 An Xsan deployment.

fabric Fibre Channel switch is generally recommended. All metadata traffic goes through an Ethernet switch to and from the MDCs. This should be a gigabit Ethernet switch.

Networks—There are generally three separate networks for an Xsan:

1. *The Fibre Channel Network* carries all of the media requested by client computers from the shared storage through the Fibre Channel switch to the host bus adapter on the client computer, or vice versa (i.e., media being written to shared storage).

2. *The Metadata Network* carries all the information about traffic on the SAN between the metadata controllers and client computers via an Ethernet switch.

3. *The Outside Network* is independent of the SAN, and is usually used to gain access to the Internet and other file servers.

Software—Software is required to run an Xsan:

1. *Xsan Software*, available from Apple, is $999 per seat.

2. *OS X or OS X Server* running on metadata controllers and clients. It is possible to allow other operating systems—such as Windows and Linux—to access the Xsan by using StorNext, from Quantum Corp.

An Xsan network can be an absolute blessing, but if not set up and managed correctly, it can also be a disaster waiting to happen. Although implementation of an Xsan environment is generally easier and certainly more cost effective than competing solutions, setup and maintenance can be daunting, especially in a large deployment. As we discussed in Chapter 3, a dedicated engineer or IT person is often overlooked, or thought of as an unnecessary role, especially in smaller shops. Instead, responsibilities for setting up and managing an Xsan fall on an editor, a designer, or—heaven forbid!—an executive producer. This can be very dangerous.

We have been involved in some large television shows that have successfully used an Xsan environment; one of these shows is described in Chapter 18. However, things do not always go smoothly. A friend working in New York City recently told us a story about an Xsan disaster on a cable-television series (the show will go unnamed because it was such a disaster!). This is a great example of the importance of really learning Xsan and OS X Server.

In the story, the IT person in charge of managing the SAN left for another company three or four days before the start of postproduction on the series. Due in part to the great initial setup of the SAN, everything was flawless at first. As time went on, though, and users had to be added or deleted from the SAN, or when other maintenance had to be done, things QUICKLY went downhill. In this particular case, an enterprising assistant editor, who honestly was probably trying to go the extra mile, thought he could do the maintenance himself. Long story short: corrupted media, lost users, and over 300 hours of footage lost!

Do yourself a favor, and really learn about Xsan and associated topics such as Open Directory and OS X Server prior to finding yourself in one of these situations. Better yet, if the budget will allow, hire an Xsan expert. Trust us: it's worth it.

Next Steps

Over the past two chapters, we have covered many of the technical aspects of video, codecs, and storage. Now, armed with this technical information, it is time to start putting this knowledge into action. The next seven chapters put practical information more in context with workflows and, indeed, with Final Cut Pro.

6 Preparation

Everything that you do on a project before you actually start to ingest media into Final Cut Pro contributes to having a successful and efficient editing experience. Decisions that you make all along the way—script, location, lighting, audio recording, and shooting format—each have a part in defining what happens in post. Mistakes made in the preproduction and production phases have a way of rippling through the postproduction process, sometimes combining or compounding to make bigger headaches.

As mentioned in Chapter 2, workflows should be thought of as extending both before and after the postproduction process—before, as in preproduction and shooting; and after, in terms of compression, interactivity, and distribution concerns.

This book is about applying workflow thinking to Final Cut Pro, but part of this is FCP's extensibility—the ability to "play well with others," as mentioned in Chapter 1. FCP's ability to play well with others also depends on others playing well with it. This chapter is about producing and preparing assets that will work well in FCP and throughout the postproduction process.

Because this is potentially a rather large topic (worthy of a whole book or two, not just one chapter), we have focused on three areas:

- Issues beginning in the preproduction and production phases that are particularly important to Final Cut Pro and postproduction; specifically, issues that often cause problems, especially for the inexperienced.

- The preparation of assets: techniques that occur between actual acquisition (shooting, recording, scanning, etc.) and ingest into Final Cut Pro.

- Organization and metadata, always a workflow concern.

The theme of the chapter is preparation. In the literal sense, this is learning things such as how to use Photoshop to create and save the best type of still-image file to use in FCP. This chapter is also about preparation writ large—learning to identify issues during earlier phases of the process, and to foresee how they will affect you in postproduction.

We hope that this chapter helps you avoid problems before they happen. There is also a fair amount here about how to fix the problems you fail to avoid.

Timecode Issues

Perhaps the most common production mistake that has ill effect on the postproduction process is broken or messed-up timecode. The technology of timecode is discussed in detail in Chapter 4: Video Standards and Formats. If you have not read Chapter 4, for now it is sufficient to understand timecode as an addressing system for video.

Each frame of a videotape or clip has (or should have) a unique timecode number. The machines we use to work with video have no way of recognizing what is on the video or audio tracks of a tape. They rely on the timecode. This means that having consistent timecode and unique reel numbers for all of your sources is going to be important for a smooth workflow. A lot of the discussion that follows is based on tape-based acquisition, and a lot of the problems are more common with subprofessional equipment. Some of the same principles can be applied to professional tape-based equipment as well as to newer tapeless cameras and devices.

There are two classic problems with timecode, and both are fairly easy to understand and avoid:

1. *Broken Timecode*—When the timecode is discontinuous on the tape. This generally occurs when timecode resets or starts over on a source tape. So the timecode on the tape starts at 0:00:00;00, and starts counting frames. But then, at some point, for some reason, in the middle of the tape, the timecode starts over at zero. Now one tape has two frames number 0:00:00;00, 0:00:00;01, and so on. That is a problem because the timecode numbers are no longer unique. There are two frames with the same number—how can the computer tell the difference between the two?

2. *Nonunique Reel Names*—When multiple sources have the same reel name/number in FCP. Along with continuous timecode, for this system to work, the other requirement is for each tape to have a unique name expressed in the Reel field (more on how to do this in the next chapter). If all of your tapes start with a timecode of 0:00:00;00, it is important that each tape have its own name or number—or else, again, the computer has two frames of video (this time on two different tapes) that it has no way of distinguishing between.

Though these two problems are similar in a sense, you handle them differently. The second one is easy to avoid, so let's deal with that first.

A system for naming and/or numbering your tapes should be instituted during preproduction, before the first frame is ever shot. Like many aspects of media management, the larger the project is, and the more people who are involved, the more sophisticated the organizational scheme needs to be and the more important it is that you stick to it. If you are shooting a ten-minute interview on one tape, and it is the only shoot for the project, tape naming is no big deal. On the other hand, if you have a dozen videographers covering an event for several days, a tape-naming convention is an absolute necessity.

This idea should be carried over from tapes to any tapeless shooting format. The media cards, disks, and devices (hardware) associated with tapeless acquisition should be clearly labeled, and the media files created on these devices should follow naming conventions, just like all media-management aspects of a project.

On a complex shoot, we recommend a simple and rigid system for naming tapes and storage devices. For instance, every videographer writes on the tape the following: their initials, the date, and a sequential tape number for each tape they use in the course of the project. It doesn't really matter what the system is (want to use last names instead of initials? . . . fine). It does matter that you start the system from the beginning and that everyone on the project adhere to it religiously.

If this system has been implemented correctly during production, then avoiding the problem in FCP is exceedingly simple. Just make the Reel field exactly match what is written on the tape. Bingo—unique reel numbers.

Of course, there are levels of complexity. What about a project with hundreds of archival tapes, maybe originally belonging to different stations with the schemes of different organizations? You may need to devise your own naming scheme, perhaps using abbreviations for the original source of the tape instead of the initials of the shooter. At any level of complexity, the same principles apply:

1. Invent a simple and rigid naming system for tapes before shooting/research begins.

2. Stick to this system throughout production.

3. Whatever your system calls for your shooters to write on the tapes, use the exact same thing in the Reel field.

Some larger postproduction operations have gone even more sophisticated with tape identification—creating a bar-code system for all tapes in their facility, and a library database. In effect, this means that every tape in their facility has a unique number associated with it. Later in this chapter, there is more discussion about using databases for organizing assets. Also, the new Final Cut Server is an Apple product designed to facilitate these types of systems.

Now that we have tape and reel naming under control, we have to deal with the more pernicious issue of broken timecode. This causes numerous problems in post. First, let's look at some techniques for avoiding timecode breaks in the first place, and then some tricks and tips to deal with timecode breaks in post.

Every shooter should have, as a goal, avoding timecode breaks when shooting. However, the methods for achieving this goal are dependent largely on the type of equipment the shooter is using. Specifically, one of the things that set truly professional video cameras apart from their prosumer cousins is the control over timecode. Also, strategies for timecode with tapeless devices sometimes follow these principles, but they can also be quite different.

Professional cameras traditionally have very robust control over timecode. You can set precisely what number the timecode should start on, or set it to always read the time of day, or to sync multiple cameras so they all lay down the same timecode. Learning how to use these professional camera controls is outside the scope of this book, but once you master them, it should be no problem to avoid timecode breaks with your professional camera.

Prosumer cameras create their own set of problems when it comes to timecode because they do not have as extensive a set of tools for controlling timecode while shooting. Instead, the camera does some things with timecode that are not always helpful. Compounding the problem is the fact that there is no set of rules for how these cameras operate when it comes to timecode, so different cameras might do slightly different things.

The biggest problem seems to be caused by the inaccuracy of the tape mechanism in prosumer cameras. These cameras will generally take any timecode that is already started on the tape and continue with it. However, often when the camera is turned off, it will slip a few frames forward. (Some cameras will even do this when they automatically go into a "standby" mode.) When the tape slips forward, it goes to a part of the tape that has no timecode. A common result for inexperienced shooters is tapes with timecode breaks (timecode starting again from zero), as described above.

If this seems like a mess, it is. However, we already have the solution, which is that the camera will generally continue with timecode that has already been established. This feature gives us two different ways to avoid timecode breaks:

1. "Blacking" tapes. The idea of blacking tapes is simply to lay down a blank signal (i.e., record onto the tape with the lens cap on and no microphone plugged in) for the length of the tape before you take it out for the shoot. The result is that you get continuous timecode from beginning to end, and most prosumer cameras will just keep this timecode.

2. A method with a similar effect, but one that is somewhat less foolproof, is this: whenever you are done shooting for a moment, let the camera record an extra three to five seconds before stopping it. Then, before you start shooting again, rewind the tape just a bit so that you start recording over that little bit of pad that you left. Because you are starting recording where there is already established timecode, the timecode will continue unbroken.

The main difference between the two methods is that with the pad method, you need to remember each time you start and stop the camera, but with blacking, you do it all at the beginning and then you can forget about it.

So, by remembering these tips, you can avoid timecode breaks by practicing good shooting habits. It is inevitable that you will have to deal with this problem at some point, however, so here are a few suggestions on how to fix timecode problems:

1. If the problem is really bad, you can consider dubbing to new master tapes. The idea is that you record the source tapes with the messed-up timecode onto a new tape. In this process, you ensure that the new tape has consistent timecode from beginning to end. The new tape now becomes your master, and there is no need to ever go back to the tape with the broken timecode.

2. There are some techniques associated with Log and Capture that can help with timecode breaks. These are discussed in the next chapter.

3. If you have to work with only source footage that has timecode breaks, it is best to try to treat each discrete timecode section of a tape as its own tape. So, when that timecode starts over in the middle of the tape, you would name the reel "Tape 1 After TC Break," or something along those lines. Now, if you ever need to go back to that tape and find that footage, you have a good clue as to how the broken timecode has been sorted out.

Working with timecode, there are only two fundamental things to keep in mind:

1. If at all possible, get good, unbroken timecode when you shoot.

2. The computer is stupid. It can't look at the images, and it can't hear the audio, so all it has to go on is the timecode. Consequently, if your shooter messes up that timecode, you may have to do something inefficient or inelegant to deal with the computer's stupidity, such as dub your source tapes or have crazy reel names (for example, "Tape 1 After Break").

Audio Issues

Problems with audio can be as bad as timecode issues in post—maybe worse. There are few things more frustrating than having an interview that looks good, with great content, but the audio is too low to be usable, or it has interference. Bad audio (whether due to mistakes made on the shoot or in post) tends to be much more distracting to a viewer than technical problems in the video would be.

This is not a book about field audio techniques, so we have limited this chapter to a few tips that you can use in the field to try to ensure good audio, as well as some ideas of how to evaluate audio and make judgment calls about it before you start editing.

Basic tips for ensuring good field audio:

1. *Pay attention to audio levels and quality while shooting.* Sounds obvious, doesn't it? It is surprising how many newbies, and even experienced producers, allow poor audio to be recorded simply because no one is paying attention.

    If at all possible, we recommend having a dedicated audio person on any shoot. In a professional environment, this person usually controls his or her own equipment—including microphones and, in some cases, a standalone audio recording device such as a hard-disk recorder.

    Even if you are not using sophisticated audio equipment, it stills pays to have someone listening to headphones and watching the audio meters. Although it is not always possible with a small crew, we prefer that the crew member doing this is dedicated to audio rather than just having the person running the camera also wear the headphones.

    The more attention you pay to audio during the shoot (including having someone on location who is dedicated to audio concerns), the better chance you have of avoiding audio problems.

2. *Isolate separate microphones to separate audio tracks.* When using more than one microphone (for instance, maybe you have a lavaliere mic on your interview subject, and a high-quality shotgun mic mounted on the camera), record these signals separately so that they can be isolated in post later.

    When recording audio onto videotape, this is usually accomplished by taking advantage of the two separate audio tracks on the tape (DV tapes generally record two audio tracks; some professional formats, such as DVCPRO50, actually have four). Traditionally, these two tracks can be used for stereo audio, but when shooting, you can utilize them to isolate microphones.

    Normally, this is done by plugging the microphones into separate ports, and then setting the camera so that the signals remain isolated on the tracks. (These controls are slightly different on different cameras.) If you use this technique, it is important when you capture the material into FCP that you capture it as separate mono tracks, and not as stereo pairs (more on this in Chapter 7: Ingest).

    If you are using more sophisticated equipment, you may be able to record more than two microphones separately. The beauty of recording the different microphones separately is that if one has a problem (say, for example, that your lavaliere mic runs out of batteries midway through a shoot, and no one notices), you have a separate backup.

3. *Make wise decisions on microphones.* Microphones are designed differently for specific reasons. Before using a mic for any given situation, make sure it is the correct microphone or mic setup for the situation. For example, using an omnidirectional mic on a camera is going to pick up a lot more sound then using a unidirectional microphone. Similarly, using a boom mic in a noisy situation to record an interview is probably not as good a choice as using a lav.

Just as with timecode problems (like many things in this chapter), avoiding audio problems on the shoot has a lot to do with simply being aware of things that could go wrong and guarding against them. So, what to do if you have failed to avoid problems? (Or maybe you weren't even there, and a bunch of tapes with bad audio just landed on your desk. . . .) What can you do to deal with this situation before editing?

Unfortunately, not much.

Some audio problems can be fixed in post; others cannot. Some can be fixed only with major time and expense. Preparing for your edit is not the stage in the process to try to fix bad audio (this should come later, when you know what audio you actually need for your piece). What is worthwhile to do at this stage is to evaluate your audio to see which of these categories to put it in: usable, unusable, or usable only with additional time and/or budget.

Before starting to work with material that has problematic audio, you should first determine whether this audio is ever going to work in your final piece. If not, it might be time to plan a reshoot or ADR (automated dialogue replacement) session. If you do think that the audio is fixable, how will it be fixed, and how long will this take? It might be worth running some tests at this stage.

Another set of questions you might ask concern the tolerance your project has for audio glitches. The type of distribution the piece is going to have, along with the budget, will provide the answers to your questions. A broadcast-television piece has little tolerance for bad audio, and typically the budget will allow for fixing the problems in post or will permit reshooting. On a student film, the tolerance for mistakes is probably higher (and the budget is less).

Lastly, it is worth considering at this stage who is going to make these audio fixes, and on what equipment. Final Cut Pro contains some audio tools, but audio tweaking is not in the core of its functionality. Soundtrack Pro, part of Final Cut Studio, contains more sophisticated audio tools such as background-noise sampling. Tools that are even more robust are included in desktop audio programs such as Pro Tools. At the high end, there are dedicated audio suites that can perform the most detailed work most quickly. If you need to spend a lot of time in a dedicated audio suite, it will be expensive.

When bad audio hits your desk, it is a good idea to evaluate what level of equipment will be needed to fix it (if, indeed, the audio is fixable at all). If you are already planning to use a dedicated audio mixer, it might be a good idea to send that person a sample of the trouble audio and get an evaluation and time estimate on fixing it. Remember, if you are planning on doing audio tweaking in Final Cut Pro, some editors are better at this than others. It is not really part of the traditional editor's role to be able to do sophisticated work on audio. However, as we described in the previous chapter, roles are blurring and expanding (due largely to the availability of tools such as FCP, Soundtrack Pro, and Pro Tools). More editors are able to do basic audio tweaking these days, but this should not be assumed.

Sometimes the best thing you can do with bad audio when beginning an edit project is be honest. There are times when an editor must deliver the unpleasant news that a reshoot is needed, or that the budget is busted. All too often, the issue that prompts this call is bad audio.

Continuity Issues

Concerns that are more relevant to the fiction-film world include continuity issues. The problem is that fiction films are generally not shot in script order (neither the scenes that make up the film nor the shots that make up a particular scene).

So someone needs to worry about continuity: Is the actor's hair longer in this scene than in another scene that comes later in the chronology? In the course of a meal, is an actor's drinking glass progressing from full to empty, or is it fluctuating wildly? In the movie *Fletch*, there is a scene where Chevy Chase shoots a basketball. In the next shot, he is holding the basketball again, but there is no shot (indeed, not even any elapsed time) showing when he picks it back up. This is a classic continuity issue.

On a fiction-film shoot, generally there is a person whose job it is to worry about such things. This person spends most of his or her time on set making detailed notes in a continuity log. This log ultimately forms a continuity report for a given scene. As the project moves into postproduction, these responsibilities come to rest (at least partially) on the editor.

As you can imagine, good continuity work on set helps an editor's job immensely. If things were not shot with continuity in mind (for example, if the main actor were to get a radical haircut midway through shooting), there might be little that the editor could do to fix the problem.

But the editor was not on the set, so how does he or she get the continuity information? If this information is only in the form of a log, the editor must wade though this, thus slowing down the editing process, or else have an assistant on hand to constantly be looking for continuity problems.

However, there is a process where the continuity information can be imported into FCP as metadata. Using this method, this crucial continuity information is available to the editor with each clip and is generally very helpful.

Continuity information can be populated in Final Cut Pro via custom software (XML interchange), text files, and manual labor (the last being the most time consuming).

Often on fiction films, continuity information feeds into a larger database about the footage. This continuity information can then be exported as a part of an Excel log or an XML file where the comments and or log notes populate appropriate columns in Final Cut Pro. Continuity information can also be added as metadata with applications such as Final Cut Server.

Most of the time, this continuity information is applied directly inside Final Cut Pro by editing the Comment and Log Note columns. Generally an assistant editor enters this information, but, depending on the size of the facility, you might not have that luxury.

Review Screeners

One of the most important things that happens after shooting and prior to editing is that some form of screeners, or copies of the raw footage, are created. This enables various team members to view the footage, comment on it, start thinking about editorial decisions, and make decisions about further shooting. Making and distributing these screeners is a crucial part of the process.

A lot of the techniques described in this section are applicable both to screening raw footage before the editing process and to reviewing work-in-progress cuts (the topic of Chapter 9). These activities are similar in that the goal is to review material and take good notes, but different in the type of material and the purpose of the review. Chapter 9 has more hands-on instruction for making and posting web-ready video files. These techniques can also be used for screeners.

VHS Screeners

The old way of screening footage is quite simple: dub the master tape onto VHS with "burn-in" timecode windows. "Burn-in" refers to the timecode numbers being visually represented as an on-screen counter. This is useful anytime you want to take detailed notes while watching any footage or work in progress. Screeners are probably one of the only places that VHS tapes are still a little bit popular. For a long time, VHS has been a cheap and dirty way to view footage, and there is really nothing wrong with it (that is, if the person screening still has a VHS player). Of course, with the advances in technology, some new ways to view raw footage have come to the forefront.

QuickTime Screeners

We know that FCP is based on the QuickTime video architecture, and we know that QuickTime is also a consumer video format that can play with free software. It seems logical, then, that QuickTime has potential for screening purposes, and it does. The advantages in using QuickTime to screen footage include:

1. Has built-in timecode that displays in the player.
2. Can display markers as comments.
3. Can be used on the Web, on disk, and through an internal network.
4. Can have nonlinear access to clips.

Disadvantages include:

1. You need to take the time and have the disk space to capture all of the material you want to screen and in many cases, compress it.
2. Everyone on your team might not be comfortable yet with a digital review process if they have been doing it with tape for 20 years.
3. Some people might have technical problems, such as not having the software.

Creating QuickTime outputs from Final Cut Pro is quite easy. The menu File > Export gives you three relevant choices for this sort of thing. Please skip ahead to Chapter 9 for more hands-on instruction in this area.

DVD Screeners

DVD screeners are becoming more popular. This is probably because DVD has supplanted VHS as the most ubiquitous consumer video format. Like QuickTime screeners, using an FCP system to create DVD screeners is very time consuming. There are also hardware products available that create a DVD from a tape in a "one-step" process (there is actually always more than one step involved in making a DVD, but these machines make it appear seamless to the user). Normally, we are not big fans of these all-in-one black boxes, but for the purpose of making quick DVD screeners, they can be a decent solution.

Timecode Filters

Final Cut Pro is able to add burn-in timecode to any footage by using the timecode reader filter (Effects > Video Filters > Video > Timecode Reader). This filter reads the timecode that is on the clip, and displays it right on the video. This is very similar to what professional decks do when you add burn-in timecode to VHS screeners, but this burn-in can be used in QuickTime compressions, DVD screeners—or, indeed, just to have timecode on-screen when a group is reviewing footage inside the FCP interface.

Not everyone knows about the timecode reader filter, but it comes in very handy sometimes. Unlike adding burn-in on a tape, the timecode reader filter does take some time to render. One new feature in Compressor 3 is a timecode filter that can be added onto a compression. If your review screeners are on the Web or DVD, this new feature can save you a step and some time.

Managed Media and Database Solutions for Screening Footage

Some of the newest thinking on screening footage (especially for large productions or in team environments) is to make it an integrated part of media-management systems. This frequently involves a database, and often this database supports a web application that facilitates screening footage (among other things).

There are several layers to this onion, and at this point, we are tearing off just the papery skin. This discussion of media-management considerations starts earlier in this chapter with reel naming, but it is a theme that runs throughout the book, including:

- A section later in this chapter on media management in general and how it relates to preparing for post.
- Chapter 12 is all about sharing and managing media, and contains a lot of detail on the Media Manager. This is a tool inside Final Cut Pro that is used for the large-scale manipulation (or management) of media files.
- Chapters 14 and 16 are both case studies that demonstrate innovative solutions to screening raw footage by taking advantage of Final Cut Pro.
- Final Cut Server is a new piece of software by Apple that adds a whole new set of tools for reviewing footage (and much more). This is covered in a web-only chapter because the software was not available at the time of writing.

Generally, incorporating the screening process into your greater media-management scheme has the advantages of consolidating the data and the process, and allowing efficient communication and collaboration (including online). As we said before, it is on a large project with a large team where these innovations make the biggest difference.

Logging and Transcribing

Logging and transcribing are another important part of the process (though not a whole lot of fun). For many projects, an accurate transcription (a written document of everything that is said on the tape) and a shot log (a list of everything that happens visually on the tape) are absolute necessities. It used to be that this step was done almost all of the time, but a lot of projects move forward into editing these days without this (admittedly time-consuming and tedious) step.

Maybe the reason that logging and transcribing are sometimes skipped is that with new, inexpensive edit equipment, the temptation is to say: "We can look at that footage anytime in a nonlinear way, so do we need a transcript?" The answer is that the transcript helps the producer and/or writer get a handle on the entirety of the content and find the best bites to tell the story. It also helps the editor quickly jump to the right part of a clip.

If you find yourself doubting that last statement, just try taking a piece that has two or more interviews that are each at least an hour long, and cutting that piece without a transcription. We bet you'll wish you had one!

Here are some tips if you find that the responsibility to transcribe and/or log tapes has fallen to you:

1. *Be detailed.* If the bite looks good on paper, but in the shot the boom is in frame, note that this will have an effect on if the shot gets used. Remember that a writer might use your transcript for scriptwriting without actually looking at the footage, so he or she will need as many contextual clues as you can provide.

2. *Use timecode as much as possible.* Every new bite should start with a timecode reference. If something happens mid-bit—the subject coughs, let's say—it doesn't hurt to put another timecode notation right where it happens. This might help the writer decide whether to use the bite, or the editor might work around the cough and make it usable.

3. *Note reel numbers.* Many interviews span multiple tapes. In case different timecode wasn't used for each tape (tape 1 starting with hour 1, tape 2 starting with hour 2, etc.), it is important to note the reel. Nothing is more frustrating to a producer or editor than having a great bite, and even having the timecode for that bite, but not being able to find it.

Transcription and logs are most valuable for the scripting and "paper editing" process that traditionally comes next. This is another thing that sometimes gets short-changed these days. And again, this is probably a mistake.

Scripts as Workflow Documents

In the days of linear editing, it was practically a necessity to arrive at an edit session with a very detailed script. With linear editing, there was some room to make adjustments during the process, but it was limited and time consuming. Consequently, creative decisions in the editing room tended toward things that were more purely aesthetic—for example, does one B-roll shot look better than another? (And even these comparisons were time consuming.) Being prepared for the edit session meant having a script that very clearly outlined your story and how it was to unfold.

So most of the creative storytelling process actually took place before the editing began. This was by necessity, but it also provided a useful division of labor. Because it was inefficient to let editorial storytelling (or writing) bleed too much into the edit session, it was clear-cut how the job of the writer or writer/producer was different from that of the editor.

Of course, nonlinear editing—and particularly Final Cut Pro—changed this for a lot of people. Just as with transcribing and logging, the temptation now is to skip careful scripting because it is cheaper to just mess around in the editing room. In keeping with our theme, this section describes the traditional workflow for scripts and paper edits. Our intention is to help FCP users understand the constituent parts of the process as they have always existed. In this way, users can design better workflows for the new postproduction environment.

The information that follows is slanted toward nonfiction filmmaking, but inferences can certainly be made to the narrative-filmmaking world. Also, as much as anywhere else in this book, these are not hard-and-fast rules. Every project is different, and thus each one requires a slightly different approach to scripting (and to editing, and to media management . . . it is these differences that make your workflow).

To a workflow planner, the purpose of the script is to provide a document that is most useful at any given phase of the process to represent the objectives of the final product. In the following sections, we discuss the script techniques and script types we find particularly useful on most independent-studio projects.

Two-Column Scripts

This is a technique that is simple and works. The idea is to use one column (usually the left) for visuals, and the other (usually the right) for audio content.

That's pretty much it: separate the audio from the video so that you can simultaneously write what happens and indicate synchronization and juxtaposition between the eyes and ears. This technique is analogous to the video and audio tracks in FCP, and is symbolic of the way we think about audio/video production in general. Nearly every video or audio program incorporates the concept of tracks. The two-column format is just a convention to put this concept on paper.

Shooting Script

This is a version of the script that you create to take out into the field on the shoot. Depending on the variables of your project, the shooting script could take any form. It might be one of the two-column scripts described above, but it might also be more of a schedule format, with times and call lists for specific scenes. One of the big variables in how you format your shooting script is the degree to which you are shooting scripted or spontaneous content. With content that is more scripted, the shooting script needs to have everyone's lines (duh!). For an interview, the script might roughly outline the areas to be covered and/or the questions for the interviewer. If the producer intends to change angles at some point during the interview (for instance, to move to a tighter shot for the more emotional questions), that information would be on a good shooting script. The shooting script should telegraph the whole shooting day.

Voice-over Script

A specialized script prepared specifically for the recording session, the voice-over script contains several key features:

1. A VERY clear and readable script for the talent—big, bold letters, well-spaced lines, and often ALL CAPS.

2. Any unusual pronunciation explained in detail (often this is not enough, so it pays to have an expert if there are challenges in this area).

3. A clear area for note taking.

One thing we like to do in creating VO scripts is to adapt the two-column script by erasing the visuals from the right column and making this a place for notes.

Editing Scripts

This is the one that matters most to the editor. Let's say I am working as an editor in a more traditional workflow. It is the start of a new project, and I know little about it in advance. I am really hoping that the producer that I am about to start working with has done a good job preparing his or her editing script.

What I don't want is for that producer to throw a bunch of tapes onto the table, then describe to me in emotive terms and wild hand gesticulations what is expected from the piece. The purpose of the editing script is (still) to make concrete, as much as possible, the intended structure of the piece. Traditionally, this was one of the most important postproduction workflow documents—and it still is.

In a lot of new postproduction workflows, the line between the producer and the editor has been blurred. The temptation is to think that if the storyteller is now the same as the person pushing the buttons, then the editing script is not as important. We think that is wrong in most cases. When roles are consolidated and the person making editorial decisions is the same as the person pushing the buttons, we think it may be even more important to create an editing script.

Another function of the editing script is to provide some level of instruction for the editor as to where to get the shots that are needed. Often this is a clear notation of time-code and tape number, and this information comes from the screeners and transcripts. When an editing script reaches a level of detail where it basically has all of the information needed to assemble a piece, this is sometimes referred to as a paper edit.

Paper Edits

In the current environment of desktop editing, paper edits are certainly not in vogue. Further advances promise to make this term seem even more archaic. There are actually two senses in which we think the concept is still valuable, and plenty of projects and workflows where it remains a useful step.

The two meanings for *paper edit* are related but different, and neither one is very clearly differentiated from the previous description of the editing script.

1. When an editing script is very detailed, and in particular when it has complete timecode information for both A-roll and B-roll shots, it is said to be a paper edit (i.e., all the information you need for the edit, but on paper). Paper edits of this sort are particularly useful in workflows where the editor is going to be making the first assembly with little or no supervision.

2. What Michael Rabiger calls "the first conceptual blueprint." The idea here is that one of the most effective ways to structure your story is to break up its constituent parts, then write them on pieces of paper (think 3×5 cards). Then you can shuffle these cards around, trying different story-structure ideas (e.g., chronological, topical, etc.). This would usually happen before the editing script and is a classic screenwriting technique.

Sure, these methods may have largely gone out of style, and maybe we can achieve the same objectives today aided by databases and online collaborative environments (and we like these things and talk about them a lot in this book). But as Rabiger points out, sometimes there is a benefit to being on paper with your ideas, to stepping way from the technology—and, indeed, the footage—and to looking at things more purely as a storyteller. We have even seen the 3×5 card method used as a diagnostic tool for a film that had already been cut, but where the story wasn't working.

The lesson here is that just because technology is more available does not mean that it is actually helpful at absolutely every stage of a project. Recognize that the traditional steps of the process became tradition because they work. Sometimes these more traditional approaches can help the modern team step away a bit and look at things in a new (yet classic) way.

Preparing an Excel Batch List

Another variation on this theme is to use Microsoft Excel to create a batch list to be imported into Final Cut Pro. This has some clear advantages over the traditional paper edit because:

1. You get all of the advantages of a spreadsheet, such as sortability and organization.

2. You can save your Excel file as a tab-delimited text file, and FCP can turn it into a batch list to be captured. Other metadata, such as log notes and comments, can come along too.

The biggest rule of thumb when using an Excel batch list is to make sure that your columns match exactly the field names in the Browser window of Final Cut Pro. In other words, if you want to populate the Log Note column in FCP, you need to make sure you name the column (the first row) "Log Note." Another thing to keep in mind is that if you want to designate dropframe timecode, use a semicolon for the last divider (HH:MM:SS;FF); if you want non-dropframe, use all colons.

For instructions on how use this file as a batch list in Final Cut Pro, see Chapter 7: Ingest.

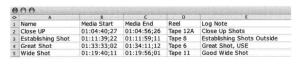

	A	B	C	D	E
1	Name	Media Start	Media End	Reel	Log Note
2	Close UP	01:04:40;27	01:04:56;26	Tape 12A	Close Up Shots
3	Establishing Shot	01:11:39;22	01:11:59;11	Tape 8	Establishing Shots Outside
4	Great Shot	01:33:33;02	01:34:11;12	Tape 6	Great Shot, USE
5	Wide Shot	01:19:40;11	01:19:56;01	Tape 11	Good Wide Shot

Figure 6.1 You can use Microsoft Excel to make batch lists that can be imported directly into Final Cut Pro.

Preparing Still Images

Of course, not all of our source media start as videotapes. Many projects require that still images (of various types and from various sources) be incorporated into Final Cut Pro. This is another area where playing well with others is key.

And again, this is a topic that could really have a whole book written about it. In fact, there is a great book that focuses on just this topic: Richard Harrington's classic *PhotoShop for Video*, now in its third edition from Focal Press.

Rich's book goes deep into creating graphics for video—definitely outside the scope of this volume. Our purpose, rather, is to provide some concepts, terminology, and tips for preparing still images to be imported into Final Cut Pro.

Resolution and Size

Probably the most important things to be aware of when preparing images for video are resolution and image size. This can be a little tricky because FCP will allow you to work with images that are not prepared ideally for the video environment. Usually this will just slow things down because the computer needs to do more processing.

Video-format resolution is described in brief in Chapter 1, and in detail in Chapters 4 and 5. We know already that the resolution of standard-definition video is 720 by 486. When preparing still images, the resolution of your video frame is known as the raster size (as in, that photo is two times raster). This is important, because a photo or image that is the size of raster, used at 100 percent, will fill the screen entirely. However, if you want to move around on the image—what we sometimes call scan and pan, or the Ken Burns effect—you will need to prepare your image larger than raster because it is best to avoid using images at over 100 percent of their natural size.

We recommend that all images be saved at 72ppi (pixels per inch), and in RGB color. Again, Final Cut Pro will take images that are an accepted file type, but are not prepared exactly to this specification, and will allow these images to be imported. This might bog down your system, however. As we will see, frame size (pixel dimensions) is the key factor to pay attention to.

(For a quick-and-dirty, step-by-step process for preparing photos for video, please see the following sidebar, Using Photoshop to Prepare Photographs for FCP.)

File Formats

As we said with resolution, Final Cut Pro will actually allow file formats to be imported that are less than ideal. Sometimes this will have an effect on quality, or on system performance while editing, or on both.

For still photographs, an uncompressed bitmap format is preferred. TIFF and TARGA are both industry standards. Generally, a JPEG might work okay, but this format should be avoided because of compression issues. Often stock photographs are supplied at low-compression JPEG to more quickly download. This is acceptable, but not technically ideal.

Using Photoshop to Prepare Photographs for FCP

There is a lot that can be said on the topic of preparing photos for video, but this tutorial is strictly basic: a few steps that, if done in order, will help you use Photoshop to quickly prepare photographs so that they are technically suited for your needs in Final Cut Pro. Now, there are a lot more things you can do in Photoshop, and these steps could be streamlined, automated, or augmented, but this process will get the job done with minimal time and effort.

With a photograph (say, from a digital camera or a raw scan) open in Photoshop, here are the minimal steps we like to do to prepare it for video:

1. *Check the image size and resolution.* Open the Image Size window with the menu Image > Image Size. Take note of the pixel dimensions and how they compare to the raster size of your video project. Is the image as large as, or larger than, raster? If not, you may consider trying to find a higher resolution or a larger image, or perhaps think of a creative way to use this photo so it does not take up the whole screen. (The rest of this tutorial assumes that you are working with a photo that is larger than raster. This is usually true if you acquired your photo with a digital still camera or a scanner.)

   • *Check the Resolution field in the Image Size window.* If this is anything other than 72ppi, we recommend changing the number in the Resolution field to 72, with the Resample Image box unchecked. We are not actually adjusting the size of the photo at this time. That will come later.

2. *Check the color space of the image* with the Image > Mode menu. There will be a check by the current working space of your photo. You want RGB for color pictures. Grayscale will also work, but definitely convert anything that is CMYK.

3. *Crop the photo.* If the image is already close to raster size, or larger than raster but already roughly in the aspect ratio that you want to use, you may want

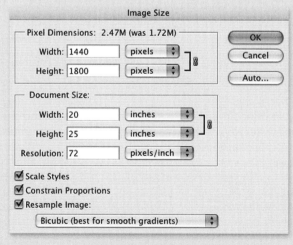

Figure 6.2 The Image Size window in Photoshop.

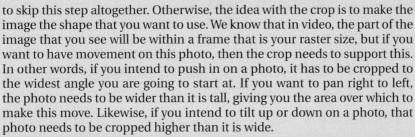

Figure 6.2 The Image Mode window in Photoshop.

to skip this step altogether. Otherwise, the idea with the crop is to make the image the shape that you want to use. We know that in video, the part of the image that you see will be within a frame that is your raster size, but if you want to have movement on this photo, then the crop needs to support this. In other words, if you intend to push in on a photo, it has to be cropped to the widest angle you are going to start at. If you want to pan right to left, the photo needs to be wider than it is tall, giving you the area over which to make this move. Likewise, if you intend to tilt up or down on a photo, that photo needs to be cropped higher than it is wide.

- (At this point, you might do some other steps such as color correcting your photo, but this is a bare-bones tutorial.)

4. *Size the image (set its pixel dimensions).* Now, back to Image > Image Size one last time. At this point, the image is at the correct resolution, correct color space, and correct aspect ratio, so we just need to adjust its size. Do this with the Pixel Dimension field in the top half of the window, and make sure that both the Resample Image box and the Constrain Properties box are checked. This will ensure that you do not "stretch" your image.

- To choose exactly what these numbers should be, you have to again consider your raster size and the way you plan to use the photo. Take the example of a photo used for a left-to-right pan. You have already cropped the image to the correct aspect ratio for this movement. Now, if you set the height to be a little taller than raster (say, 25 percent taller), your photo will be large enough to do what you want, and you can do the final position and the animation inside FCP.

- (One other thing that you might want to consider at this point is pixel aspect ratio, described later in this chapter.)

5. *Save as an uncompressed file type.* At this point, all you have left to do is save the image. Accomplish this with menu File > Save As. With the Format pull-down, choose a file type that does not use any visual compression (lossless), such as TIFF or TARGA. FCP supports other still-image file types, but these are two of the best to use for photographs. Remember, on a larger project, you should have already worked out some naming conventions for images, as well as how the files should be organized on your media drive.

Bit Depth

There is a complete discussion of bit depth in Chapter 4. The same principles apply to still images as well. Just as with video, an image at a lower bit depth might look okay, but when you start to composite with it, the lower bit depth might not work as well as an image with higher bit depth.

Color Mapping

One thing about working with digital nonlinear editing systems is that the image you see on the computer's RGB monitor is not the same as the image you see on the NTSC screen. This is true for several reasons, but one is the way color is created in video (discussed in detail in Chapter 4). Because digital color is created differently in the two systems, and because your photographs exist natively in the RGB system, the colors need to be transposed. This is called color mapping.

RGB is generally represented in video as $Y'UV$—or, more specifically, as $Y'P_BP_R$ for analog video and $Y'C_BC_R$ for digital video. This conversion process is not one to one. RGB is represented as 0–255 (8 bit), with black being 0 and 255 being white—but in video color space, black is 16 and white is 235. The extra values above 0 and below 255 allow for superblack and superwhite values.

This color mapping and the relationship of video color space and RGB color are in play anytime you bring a digital still image into Final Cut Pro, but these factors are particularly important for designing graphics and images for video—and are vital to ensuring legal chroma and luma values.

Transparency and Alpha Channels

Still images that have transparent areas (think of a graphic title that needs to sit on top of a video shot) need to "carry" that transparency with them from the image-editing program to Final Cut Pro. In the video world, the most common way to save and transfer transparency information is with an alpha channel.

An alpha channel works much like a color channel (red, green, and blue), except that it carries transparency information instead of color information. Alpha channels have bit depth as well. In an image with a 1-bit alpha channel, each pixel is either on (opaque) or off (transparent). An 8-bit alpha channel supports 256 gradations of transparency.

Some types of still-image files support alpha channels, and some do not. Luckily, two of the uncompressed file formats that Final Cut Pro favors (TIFF and PSD) both support alpha. In Photoshop, you may have a choice to save with or without the alpha channel, and you can actually view and edit the alpha channel by using the Channels pallet. Once imported into FCP, there is a column in the Browser that describes the alpha channel (if any) that accompanies each piece of media (video files can have alpha channels too).

There is an awful lot more to learn about alpha channels, and about preparing still images for video generally. There is no more comprehensive resource than *Photoshop for Video*.

Square and Nonsquare Pixels

As described in Chapter 4, many video formats (including DV) use nonsquare pixels. The pixels in a digital still image and the native pixels in Photoshop are square. When you introduce this square-pixel material into the nonsquare-pixel environment, this can cause distortion. This was once something that motion graphics designers spent a lot of time worrying about. Today, it is still something to be aware of, but both Final Cut Pro and Photoshop have features that make this easier to deal with.

1. FCP will automatically account for the difference in pixel aspect ratios when you place a still image on a Timeline that uses nonsquare pixels. FCP will automatically account for this discrepancy by "stretching" the image (or by giving it an aspect ratio in the Distort section of the Motion tab).
2. Photoshop has the option of working with nonsquare pixels. You can access this with the pulldown menu Pixel Aspect Ratio when you start a new document, or with the menu Image > Pixel Aspect Ratio once a file is already begun. Be aware that the document does not *really* have nonsquare pixels; it just displays as if it did inside Photoshop. Then, when Final Cut Pro adjusts to account for the pixel shift, the image looks the same as it did inside Photoshop.

The long and the short of this is that this problem is less complicated than it used to be because the tools have gotten better. It is still good to be aware of square and nonsquare pixels when working with stills for video. There is much more about this in *Photoshop for Video*, including the traditional mathematical way that motion graphics designers have traditionally dealt with this.

Preparing Motion Graphics Files

When we talk about motion graphics files, we are talking about animated graphics that are created outside the FCP interface, and therefore need to be prepared properly for ingest. In some ways, this preparation is like preparing still-image files. We are using a different set of tools, but many of the same principles apply. In another sense, working with motion graphics is like working with video sources because the files themselves are video, and usually QuickTime.

Again, books upon books have been written about motion graphics, and this little section is not going to replace them. For books on motion graphics, and particularly After Effects, check out anything by Chris and Trish Meyers. For a great book on Motion, check out *Apple Pro Training Series: Motion 3* (Peachpit Press 2007) by Damian Allen, Mark Spencer, Bryce Button, and Tony Huet .

The following is a list of concepts and terms that should help you understand this part of the workflow.

Motion Graphics Software

Just as with nonlinear editing software, there are quite a number of desktop motion graphics applications on the market. Three of the most popular are Adobe After Effects, Autodesk Combustion, and Apple Motion.

The common workflow for motion graphics involves outputting from a motion graphics program (this is analogous to Save As in PhotoShop, and the file type is usually QuickTime). Most, if not all, motion graphics programs are capable of exporting QuickTime. Motion, which is part of Final Cut Studio, also has tighter integration with Final Cut Pro; Apple calls this integration "round-tripping." It is discussed later in this section.

Size and Quality

Generally motion graphics files should be created and exported at exactly the size of raster. There is rarely a reason to do it any other way.

When it comes to making the QuickTime file that is going to be composited, the highest possible quality is desired. The logic of this is that when compositing the motion graphics with video elements, all of the information (higher bit depth, uncompressed data) will be taken into account in the math of the composite. Or, to put it another way, working with the highest possible quality of file will just look better in the final piece. (Or at least the designer will think so!)

Transparency and Alpha Channel

Alpha channels work pretty much the same way in motion graphics files as they do in still-image files—it's just that they are in motion. If your motion graphics have portions that "show through" to video content, then you need to have an alpha channel. Including an alpha channel is usually a choice when exporting from motion graphics programs. The animation codec is valued for its ability to carry an alpha channel.

Most motion graphics programs will also allow you to export an alpha channel *only*. This used to be more common when a lot of compositing programs needed to deal with the alpha channel separately from the video. Today, most compositing programs deal with an included or embedded alpha channel.

If you are working with motion graphics files in FCP, and they seem to have black background associated with them, you probably have a problem with your alpha channel.

Round-tripping

With the program Motion, Apple streamlined a way to deal with incorporating motion graphics into Final Cut Pro. Called "round-tripping," the idea is that you can move back and forth between the FCP (editing) environment and the Motion (motion graphics/animation) environment without ever needing to render QuickTime files. With round-tripping, the actual file that is imported into the Browser to create the clip used on the FCP Timeline is not a video file (.mov); it is a Motion project file (.motn). This is referred to as a Motion clip in FCP, and represents a whole different approach to integrating motion graphics.

The two benefits to this are (1) that you don't need to render in two places, and (2) that changes to your motion graphics will automatically be updated in FCP. There is a lot more on round-tripping in Chapter 11: The Power of Final Cut Studio.

Preparing Audio Files

As with other file types, Final Cut Pro also has a certain way that it likes audio files. On the whole, it is probably less complicated to prepare audio files for import than to prepare video files. This is because audio files have fewer important variables to worry about. Also, as with still-image files, FCP can work with a wide range of audio files, but it will work most efficiently if they are prepared perfectly. Generally this means two things:

1. The file is saved in the AIFF or WAV file format, although many others will also work. AIFF is just an Apple standard format for audio files. Broadcast Wave Format (BWF) files are now supported, and carry timecode.

2. The file has a sample rate and a bit depth that are the same as the sequence in which you are using it. Very often this is 48kHz, 16 bit. Final Cut Pro will play audio that does not match the sample rate of the sequence, but this will cause a small drop in performance—FCP needs to convert these files on the fly for playback. For an explanation of audio sample rates and bit depth, see Chapter 4.

One area that we get a lot of questions about is how to import audio from a CD and do so easily. Many people simply drag audio files from a CD to their scratch disk, but let's take a look at an easy and efficient method for importing audio from a CD using iTunes.

Unless you've been under a rock for the past few years, chances are that you've heard about iTunes. The proliferation of the iPod has, of course, popularized iTunes. What a lot of people don't realize is that iTunes can also be a powerful tool for batch converting and transferring audio from CDs for use in your project. In a few steps, you can easily import audio files from a CD into Final Cut Pro with help from iTunes:

Playback Controls   Volume   Song List   Display   Search Fields

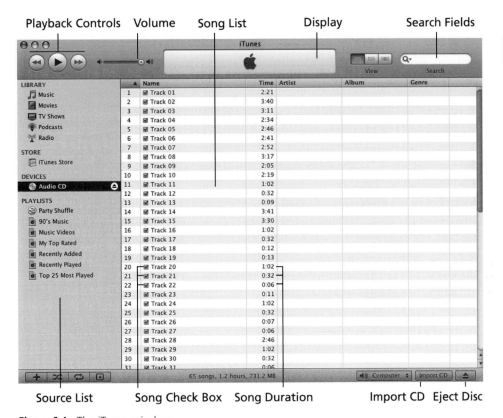

Source List   Song Check Box   Song Duration   Import CD   Eject Disc

Figure 6.4 The iTunes window.

1. Insert your audio CD into your machine, and iTunes will launch.

2. The CD will appear as a source on the left side of the interface. If you click on the CD, its contents will be displayed in the main part of the iTunes interface. The cool thing is that if you are connected to the Internet, iTunes can populate song names (depending on the disc).

3. Next to each song on the disc, there is a check box. If the box is checked, the song will be imported; if it is unchecked, the song will not be imported. This is a way to selectively choose which files will take part in the import operation.

4. Before importing, you need make sure the files are appropriate for use in FCP. In general, this means importing an AIFF at 48kHz, 16 bit. To check this, go to the File Menu > Preferences. Once the Preferences window has opened, click on the Advanced button (the cog icon).

5. Next, click on the Import button in the middle of the window below the cog. There are a few things we want to change here.

6. Change the Import Using pulldown to AIFF Encoder.

7. Change the Setting pulldown to Custom.

8. A new window pops up. Switch the Sample Rate, Sample Size, and Channels to the following: 48.000kHz, 16 bit, Stereo. Then click OK.

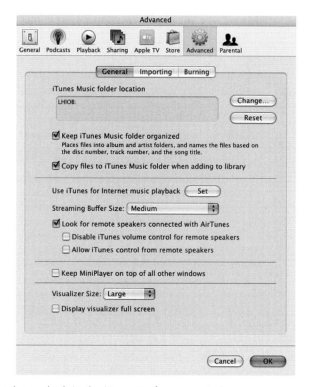

Figure 6.5   The Advanced tab in the iTunes Preferences window.

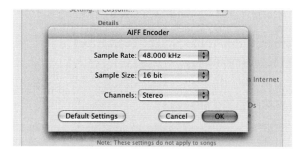

Figure 6.6   48kHz, 16 bit, Stereo settings for the AIFF Encoder.

Figure 6.7   Click here to choose iTunes folder location.

9. You should now be back in the Import area of Advanced Preferences.

10. The last thing to change/check is that the check boxes for "Automatically retrieve CD track names from the Internet" and "Use error correction when reading Audio CDs" are checked.

11. iTunes by default imports to /username/Music/iTunes. It would make sense, though, to import music for use in an FCP project to your scratch disk. To do this, make sure that Advanced Preferences is still active (the cog), and then click the General button below. Here, you can choose to change your iTunes Music folder location to the same place as your FCP scratch disk. You will want to create a subfolder in your scratch disk location called Audio or something similar. Just remember, if you also use iTunes to manage music for your iPod, you'll probably want to change this back to your Music folder.

12. After you have set up your preferences, click OK. Back in the main iTunes window, click the Import button in the lower right corner of the interface to import the songs you have checked.

Back in Final Cut Pro, go to the File Menu > Import > Folder, and navigate to the location where you imported the music. Click on the folder, then click Choose. Congrats: you now have all your music.

Media Management Part 1

This chapter just starts to touch on a large area of concern that can be generally lumped together under the heading "Media Management." This topic touches many aspects of using Final Cut Pro professionally, and of workflow thinking in general. Chapter 12: Sharing and Managing Media expands on the ideas in this section, and covers methods and strategies for scaling FCP to meet the needs of larger and more-complex projects and teams. Also, a number of the case studies have media-management aspects.

We would argue that "media management" is most properly defined as a loose category used to describe a certain mode of thinking that includes concerns such as:

- File-naming conventions
- Storage space and the organization of hard drives
- Duplicates and master copies
- The transfer of media from one resource to another and through the phases of a project
- Archiving of media and projects

These are concerns that are present throughout a project, and good media management is an integral part of any workflow, helping to provide the scaffolding and organizational schema for a project.

We believe that there are really only a couple of rules when it comes to media management, and almost everything else comes down to the conventions you choose for a particular project. Here are the rules:

1. *It is easier to stop using organizing conventions than it is to add them later.* It doesn't matter so much exactly what your naming conventions are, or how you choose to organize your scratch disk. What matters is that you choose a system, and that everyone on the project sticks with it as much as possible.

2. *The larger the project, the more sources, and the more people who are working on it, the more important it is to have tight media management.* Sometimes we talk

about this media-management stuff as though, if you were to mess it up, the sky would fall. The truth is that on a very small project, with one editor and only one or two sources, media management is really no big deal. Which is to say that Final Cut Pro is smart enough that, even if you just wing it, you probably won't have a problem. If you are working on a large project—say, a two-hour historical documentary, as in the case study in Chapter 15—with hundreds of separate video and archival sources, media management is crucial to your sanity.

It is logical that the preparation for postproduction is an important stage for media management. This is the stage where many of the organizing principles of the project are set. Of course, some media assets will have their own inherent information—such as tape names and timecode, as described above. As you prepare your media (this chapter) and ingest your media into Final Cut Pro (the next chapter), you are taking this information, plus any you choose to add, and turning it into the metadata that will appear in your Browser and allow you to find and manipulate your media in FCP.

The media-management questions you should ask (and, if all goes well, answer) as you prepare for your edit include:

1. *What are the file-naming conventions for the project?* This includes how captured video and audio will be named on the hard drive, as well as still images and graphic files. It is worth asking also how revisions to files will be named. Also, how will versions of your Final Cut Pro project be named? How will sequences and bins inside the Browser be named? This is all part of setting naming conventions, and again, it is all much more important on a bigger project.

2. *How are the media drives organized for this project?* This includes questions such as, Do photographs have their own directory on the media drive, or are they grouped together with graphics? In networked postproduction environments (discussed in Chapter 12), you need to ask questions about logins, network organization, and permissions. See Chapter 18 for a case study of a shared-storage Xsan environment.

3. *What are the steps in the workflow where media needs to move from one resource to another, and how will this be accomplished?* We generally call these moves handoffs, and they include a designer handing off files to an editor, as well as an offline editor handing off to an online editor and a mixer. Handoffs are always key points in workflows. The Media Manager (discussed in Chapter 12) is a powerful tool for facilitating certain kinds of handoffs.

Database Systems

We mentioned above that some large post houses incorporate a bar-code system for their tape library, and then have a database system to keep track of the tapes. The case study in Chapter 16 is about a web database of QuickTime screener clips accessed by producers and editors around the country. And in fact, the Browser is in essence a powerful database full of the metadata for an editing project.

So, on one level or another, we are always talking about databases when we are talking about media management, but the idea here is still extensibility. Just as it does in other areas, Final Cut Pro also plays nicely with other databases.

In Chapter 16, we see how XML (eXtensible Markup Language) allows media metadata to be exported along with QuickTime compressions to create web content. This sort of extensibility has been available for some time, as have digital asset management (DAM) systems—external databases that store media and metadata and make it searchable and accessible. Although some of these solutions were considered scalable, conventional wisdom remains that real DAM requires some substantial investment.

Although a robust database system, beyond just the FCP Browser, might facilitate a lot of medium-sized projects, it has only been on some of the largest FCP projects we have participated in that the investment was made in an additional DAM. However, there is a new piece of software right on the horizon that promises to bring robust database support simply and economically to all stages of the postproduction process.

Final Cut Server

Final Cut Server is a new piece of software that has been announced, but, as of this writing, has yet to hit the market. The idea is to make sophisticated database media management for all stages of a project available and fully integrated into Final Cut Pro through an inexpensive piece of software.

Billed as "media asset management and workflow automation software," Final Cut Server could potentially integrate into and facilitate almost all of the things discussed in this chapter. Final Cut Server also touches many other aspects of workflow thinking. In particular:

- Screeners, log lists, and paper edits, as described before
- Online reviews, discussed in Chapter 9
- Sharing and managing media, discussed in Chapter 12
- The case study in Chapter 16, which was custom coded using XML and Perl, would almost certainly be done as a Final Cut Server implementation today.

We are very excited that Apple is addressing some of the aspects of the postproduction process that really interest us—aspects that are sometimes lacking in the democratized postproduction world. At the same time—as with all evolutionary change—the goals, ideas, and concepts stay largely static, but the tools get better and more affordable. Because the software is so new, specific information did not make it into this book. Please check *http://booksite.focalpress.com/Osder/finalcut/* for two exciting chapters about Final Cut Server.

Preparation and Workflows

In one sense, creating the workflow for a postproduction project is itself part of the preparation stage of that project. At the same time, workflow thinking, preparation, and long-sightedness (and let's add media management) are activities and modes of thinking that occur (or should) at many stages of a project.

This chapter, all of these concepts, and this entire book should all imply a holistic way of doing projects. The relative importance and methods of preparation on a given project depend on many variables, but most of all on the overall size and complexity of that project.

We hope that this chapter gives you many specific things to think about when moving into the postproduction phase. Moreover, preparation is an important element of workflow thinking, learning to be precise in your planning and actions and to foresee the likely consequences.

7 Ingest

A crucial step in any workflow is ingesting footage into the nonlinear editing system. Traditionally, this process has referred to solely tape-based sources. In this regard, the process was known simply as "digitizing," and, in Final Cut Pro, as "Log and Capture." As technology changes, these terms themselves can sometimes be misnomers.

Traditionally, the Log and Capture process has been referred to as "digitizing" because shooting formats were analog. The process of getting your footage into a nonlinear editing system was literally "digitizing" because you were making an analog, linear format into a digital, nonlinear one. Today—with digital formats such as DV, DVCPRO50, Digital Betacam, HDV, and HDCAM—we are only "capturing" digital information from linear sources, and putting it on a hard drive where it can be accessed nonlinearly by Final Cut Pro.

The Log part, or "logging," refers to adding metadata (see the sidebar, Metadata), and the Capture part refers to creating digital files on a hard drive from the video on the tapes.

Although traditional tape-based ingest is still the norm for the vast majority of projects, tape has many limitations, as discussed in Chapter 4. Tapeless acquisition and postproduction are quickly developing into the standard method for working on any given project. Therefore, the traditional idea of digitizing and Log and Capture has morphed to include these tapeless formats. In addition to tape and tapeless formats, ingest also includes other files that may be needed for a project—for example, audio, images, and motion graphics. In Final Cut Pro, ingest can be broken down into four different actions:

1. Log and Capture from a tape-based source.
2. Log and Transfer from Panasonic's P2 format.
3. Transfer from other tapeless sources—such as Sony's XDCAM and XDCAM HD, Grass Valley's Infinity, and Ikegami's Editcam—using third-party components.
4. Importing other files from disk, such as audio, images, and motion graphics.

No matter the method of ingest, ideas and strategies employed at the ingest stage are integral to successfully executing workflows. Errors made at this stage have a way of rippling through the rest of a project. Choosing an incorrect codec or not paying attention to your scratch disks can make for big headaches later. It is vitally important to log properly so people involved in the project can find footage easily within Final Cut Pro.

> ## Metadata
>
> Metadata (the prefix *meta* meaning "after" or "about," and *data* meaning "information") is literally data about data. For Final Cut Pro purposes, the metadata is information such as reel number, timecode, and logging notes. The data is the video and audio itself that is being captured to the hard drive.

The ingest stage is different in different projects. In general, the larger a project and the more people who are involved, the more important it is to be organized during every stage. Remember, although in many cases we can redo or change work done in the ingest stage, it pays (literally) to be careful and diligent. The power of good ingest practices is illustrated in Part 3: Real-World Workflows, where each project utilizes a different scheme.

None of the methods of ingest that we will break down in this chapter are mutually exclusive—meaning that in any given project, there might be tape-based and tapeless sources, as well as media that are already on disk (audio, graphics, etc.), all of them needing to be used in the project. All you need to do is choose the appropriate method of ingest.

Prior to breaking down all of the methods of ingest in FCP, let's first take a look at a few topics that are common to all methods of ingest.

Scratch Disks

Scratch disks are the hard drives (or parts of hard drives) assigned to Final Cut Pro when it needs to write new files. Scratch disks can be set by going to the FCP menu and choosing System Settings (note that scratch disks can be set in other ways, such as from the Capture Settings tab in the Log and Capture window).

There are at least two very good reasons to pay attention to what is set as the scratch disk:

1. In most circumstances, you want to avoid using your system drive as your scratch disks. There are several reasons for this, but the biggest is that scratch disks sometimes get large amounts of data written to them quickly, and you never want to risk filling your system drive to capacity.

2. For more sophisticated media-managements techniques (discussed in Chapter 12, as well as in the case studies), you will want to know where your media files are being written to, so that you can stay organized.

When you assign a scratch disk, Final Cut Pro automatically makes a directory structure in that location. This includes new folders for Capture Scratch, as well as folders for Audio Render and Video Render files. If you assign different scratch disks for different types of files, this will change slightly.

This opens up two main approaches to scratch disks. Some users leave their scratch disk settings alone almost all of the time (usually assigning the root level of their media drive as the permanent scratch disk). The other scenario is to create a project-based directory that contains your scratch disks, as well as your projects and all related media. You can find more information and strategies for setting up scratch disks in Chapter 12: Sharing and Managing Media.

Strategies for Ingest

Every project has its own strategy for ingest. The exact strategies and controlled vocabularies used in this stage will differ depending on the specifics of the footage, the final product, and the workflow.

Some editors like to capture whole source tapes and/or cards/discs, and then break these apart into more manageable pieces of video inside Final Cut Pro. Using subclips and markers to do this is discussed in the next chapter. Other workflows require that detailed decisions are made at the time of ingest, and that consistent metadata is entered.

Here are some factors that will help you devise an ingest strategy:

Drive Space—When drive space was more expensive, it was often a major limiting factor in capturing video. In those days, it was important to make choices about what was really worth capturing, because you might not have room to capture extra. Even today, depending on the length of your project, and how much drive space you have available, drive space may still be a limiting factor.

Shooting Ratio—This refers to the amount of footage shot compared to the total running time (TRT) of the final piece. A shooting ratio of 60:1 means shooting 60 hours of footage for a 1-hour final piece (and some documentaries have shooting ratios this high). With a high shooting ratio, you are almost certainly not going to capture all of your footage, so choices will need to be made.

Roles and Responsibilities—As with many things we discuss, it is important to know who is doing what. If someone other than the editor is responsible for ingest (say, an assistant editor), then good instructions on what to ingest and how to log become very important, because the metadata (In and Out points, etc.) might be the only reference the editor has about a project when he or she begins. (Planning these "handoffs" is at the heart of workflow thinking.)

Offline/Online Workflow—Another important factor that plays into your ingest strategy is whether you are working offline, or working at the final quality for your project. There is much more about this in the case studies in Part 3. In general, one reason for an offline stage is to ingest much more video than will be in the actual project at offline quality, and then come back at a later stage and recapture at a higher quality only the video you are actually using.

Hardware—Finally, we should note that ingest can be a hardware-intensive part of the process. At a minimum, you will need to connect your machine to a FireWire device (to capture many broadcast formats, you will need a deck, a capture card, and/or tapeless media and accessories), and you may have to adjust your ingest strategy based on the access you have to hardware. For instance, if you can use a deck free at work, but do not have the time there to log footage in detail, you may want to capture whole tapes and worry about finding specific shots later.

There are many factors that go into making good strategic decisions about the ingest stage. Understanding the flexibility of the program, and designing a workflow that fits your specific project, will help make strategic ingest decisions simple and logical.

Log and Capture

The Log and Capture window is our primary interface to tape-based footage. The Log and Capture window can be opened with menu File > Log and Capture, or by pressing

Figure 7.1 The Log and Capture window.

Command-8. If you do not have a camera or deck attached to your machine (with deck control), you may get a warning message that says: "Unable to initialize video deck. You may still log offline clips or use Capture Now." For the full functionality of the Log and Capture window, you'll need a controllable video device.

Overview of the Log and Capture Window

Once opened, the Log and Capture window (Command-8 or File > Log and Capture) operates in some ways like a standalone tool. It also has a close link to the Browser, which is where your media and your metadata will be accessible to you in the FCP interface.

The window has two distinct sides. On the left is an area used to preview your source and to mark In and Out points (where you would like the clip to start and end). On the right is an area with three tabs across the top; this area is used to set various parameters about the capture and to enter the metadata. The Log and Capture window will look a little different when capturing HDV footage using an HDV capture preset; however, functionality of options that appear is the same as the normal Log and Capture window.

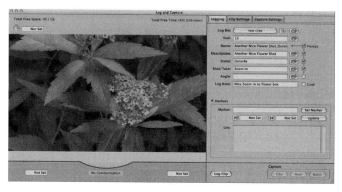

Figure 7.2 The HDV Log and Capture window.

Timecode Duration   Current Timecode

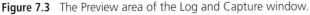

Mark In   Device Status   Mark Out
Controls   Controls

Transport Controls

Figure 7.3 The Preview area of the Log and Capture window.

Preview Area

The first thing to notice about the Log and Capture window is the large Preview area that takes up the left side of the window. This is where you will see your source—that is, the footage on your tape.

Below this, you will usually see basic VCR-style controls. However, these will not be present if you do not have a controllable device (deck or camera) attached to your system. In its place you will see "No Communication." On either side of the VCR controls are jog and shuttle wheels that let you quickly navigate your source and are meant to resemble the jog/shuttle wheel on professional video decks.

You can also use keyboard shortcuts to navigate to different parts of your source tape. These keyboard controls are the same as you use inside the editing application: Space bar to play, K to stop, J to reverse, and L for fast-forward. J and L work much like the shuttle control, in that hitting L multiple times makes the tape go faster with each click (up to four strokes). Also, if you are already on fast-forward, J will reduce the speed with each click—down to normal, and then into reverse.

Underneath the tape controls are two timecode boxes, each flanked by a button. These windows show your In and Out points (the beginning and end of a clip you want to capture), and initially they will say "Not Set." The buttons are used to set these points.

Up top, there are two more timecode boxes. On the left, you see the duration of the clip. This means that if we have marked an In point at 1:00 on the source tape and an Out point at 1:30, this box would read 00:00:30;00 (hh:mm:ss;ff). The timecode box on the top right is the source timecode—this will always show the current location on the tape.

Logging Tab

Of the three tabs on the right side of the Log and Capture window, the Logging tab is where you will spend the majority of your time. It is here that you enter information about the clips you are capturing (metadata). This information will become a part of the clip as it is viewed in FCP's Browser window and will enable you to quickly find and reference your video clips.

There is a surprising amount of control available in this one tab, and the choices that you make here are important to good workflow and media-management execution. The following is a detailed description of each aspect of the Logging tab.

Log Bin—If you have not already assigned a logging bin when you open the Log and Capture window, you will notice that the gray button to the right of Log Bin will have the name of your project. What this really means is that when you log and capture a clip, it is going into the main level of your Browser.

The idea of setting the logging bin is that you can log clips directly into a specific

Figure 7.4   The Logging tab of the Log and Capture window.

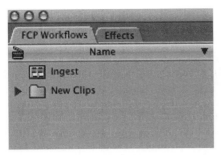
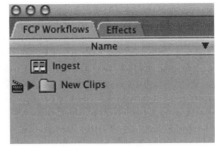

Figure 7.5 Logging bin set to main level *(left)*; logging bin set to a bin called New Clips *(right)*.

bin in the Browser, and begin your media management from the get-go.

Notice the small clapboard icon in the Browser. This is how Final Cut Pro indicates the current logging bin. Figure 7.5 shows the logging bin set to the main level of the Browser *(left)*, and to a new bin called New Clips *(right)*.

The logging bin can be set in the Browser with a contextual menu (Control-click or right-click on bin) or under the File > Set Logging Bin. In the Logging tab, the button to the far right of Log Bin makes a new bin in the Browser and automatically sets this new bin as the logging bin. (You can rename this bin later.) The button with the folder icon and an up arrow provides a simple way to navigate or change the logging bin to the level directly above the current one.

Reel—This is where you enter the name of the "reel" (or tape). As a general rule, what you enter here should match the label on your actual tape. (For why this is important, see the sidebar, Why Reel Numbers Are Important.)

The small clapboard next to the reel number lets you sequentially change the reel. For example, if you enter "Tape 1" in the field and then click the clapboard, it's automatically changed to Tape 2 without needing to enter the number. Also, when you insert a new tape into the VTR, Final Cut Pro will prompt you and ask if you want to change the reel number.

Why Reel Numbers Are Important

Although it is true that logging footage and entering metadata is important, and that accuracy and detail matter on most projects, the reel numbers are particularly important.

The idea is that every source tape or device that you are capturing from should have a unique reel number that has a one-to-one link with a physical videotape or media storage device. The reason for this is straightforward: if, in the course of your workflow, or because of a drive failure, you need to recapture, how will FCP know one source tape from another? With unique reel numbers, Final Cut Pro will be able to automate this process. Without proper reel numbers, this process will be arduously done by hand.

Reel numbers are an especially important piece of metadata, because they make the connection between the media file and the original source.

Name (Description, Scene, Shot/Take, Angle)—The next four fields in the Logging tab all work together. The first thing you should notice is that Name is grayed out, not letting you enter anything. The reason for this is that the clip name is determined by the information in the other four fields and the small check boxes to the right of each field.

To see how this works, let's start by checking all of the boxes. If you enter "Waterfalls" into the Description box, "Brazil" into the Scene box, "Pan" into the Shot/Take box, and "b camera" into the Angle box, you'll notice that the name of the clip is now "Waterfalls_Brazil_Pan_b camera."

Now, experiment with unchecking one of the boxes—say, Scene. Notice that "Brazil" has now been dropped from the Name field. So the clip name is determined by the metadata entered into the four other fields, as filtered through the check boxes that you select.

Like the reel number, you can also use the clapboards to sequentially change each parameter.

You'll notice one more big check box that says Prompt. When this box is unchecked, Final Cut Pro will take the metadata exactly as it is in the fields. When the Prompt box is checked, FCP pops up a dialogue box giving you another chance to check over and change the name and log note. This overrides the auto-naming of the clip.

Log Note—This field is used to add longer, more descriptive notes on your clip. Unlike the fields above it, the log note is never included in the clip name.

Markers—This area is used to add markers—like bookmarks—in the clip. Markers can have names, and they may be used to mark specific lines of dialogue or action in the clip. However, markers cannot be added while Final Cut Pro is actually capturing, only while previewing the tape.

All of the preceding tools are used to enter metadata; however, we have not yet seen how to actually capture the video. There are several options for this, and they are found in the row of buttons at the bottom of the Logging tab.

Log Clip—Enters the logging information into the Browser to be captured later (probably in a batch). You will notice that when you log a clip, a new icon appears in the Browser. It is a clip with a red line through it (Figure 7.6). This red line indicates that the clip is "offline"—meaning that Final Cut Pro is aware of a clip, but does not have a link to the actual video file. (This is a totally different meaning of "offline," and has nothing to do with the quality of the video.)

Capture Clip—Captures a single clip that you have marked and logged. Using Capture Clip means capturing each clip of video immediately after logging it.

Capture Now—Captures any incoming signal and makes it into a media file. We call this "dumb capture," but it is actually useful when you have tricky timecode situations (such as source with no timecode—for example, VHS or a satellite feed) or a device where no device control is available. You can add metadata into the Logging fields when using Capture Now, but you are not marking an exact clip or controlling a deck.

Capture Batch—Captures multiple clips that have been marked and logged. Using this button will prompt you with another window that allows you to choose exactly what to capture in the batch: Selected Clips, Offline Clips, or All Clips. In a normal logging scenario, it is the offline (logged but not captured) clips that you will want, but this pulldown can be useful at other points in the project. This window also allows you to check or change the codec you are using to capture.

Using an Excel Spreadsheet as a Batch List

As we mentioned in Chapter 6, creating a batch list is an easy way to prepare our clips for capture in Final Cut Pro. After you have created the list, it's quite easy to use in FCP.

1. Go to the File Menu > Import > Batch List.

2. Following the batch list, there will be a frame rate displayed. This number is based on the frame rate of your current sequence preset.

3. Navigate to the location where you saved the batch list and click Choose.

4. Your clips will come in as offline clips (the red slash through their names); they are now ready to be captured.

Clip Settings Tab

The Clip Settings tab (see Figure 7.6) is where you tell FCP exactly what it is supposed to capture in a given clip. Often this is a simple matter of just choosing what combination of audio and video you want.

The Clip Settings tab also has video scopes that allow you to take a look at the video signal as it is coming into the computer. If you are working with an analog capture card (and thus, again, literally digitizing), the Clip Settings tab allows some adjustment of this signal in the way it is converted to digital.

One of the most interesting aspect in the Clip Settings tab from a workflow point of view is the control of audio tracks. Final Cut Pro supports up to 24 audio tracks, although it is not often that you have this many tracks to capture. For instance, DV tapes support 4 tracks, but most people use only 2. It is more common to see 4 audio tracks utilized in a higher-end format such as DVCPRO50.

The Clip Settings tab gives you control over which audio tracks to capture and how. The small round button to the left of each track is the Capture button. If the button is green, you will be capturing this audio track; if it is grayed out, you will not.

There is one more possibility here. The button to the left of each pair of tracks is the Toggle Stereo/Mono button. When this button is light gray and showing two separate circles (left side of Figure 7.8), each audio track will be captured as a separate mono track. When dark gray, showing intersecting circles (right side of Figure 7.8), the tracks will be captured as a stereo pair.

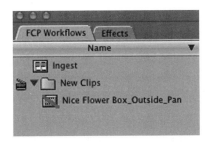

Figure 7.6   Offline clip in the Browser.

Figure 7.7 The Clip Settings tab.

Figure 7.8 Toggle set to two mono tracks *(left)*; toggle set to stereo *(right)*.

There are two tried-and-true examples of how this is used in the real world. The first is to use separate microphones isolated to separate tracks. With this method, if one of your microphones is distorted, you can just turn off the track during capture and use only the good mic.

Second, most broadcast master tapes have different types of audio on different tracks (i.e., voice isolated from natural sound and music). If you have a project that involves capturing from a master to reuse for something new, this is very useful. (If you don't immediately see why, think about how difficult it is to cut a voice track if it is already mixed with music.)

Thinking about how to use the audio tracks available to you on capture (and when shooting) is an important aspect of workflows. Remember, problems with audio are often more noticeable to a viewer than video problems are.

Capture Settings Tab

The Capture Settings tab (Figure 7.9) is where you tell FCP how to capture your clips. Settings here include Device Control (how FCP communicates with and controls your

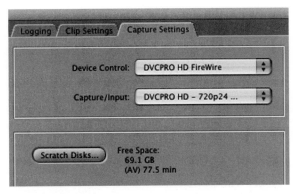

Figure 7.9 The Capture Settings tab.

deck), Capture/Input (where you set the codec your clip will be captured as—much more on codecs in Chapter 5), and a button that brings up the Scratch Disks window.

One important time that Final Cut Pro writes new media files is during capture. The scratch disks can be set through the rightmost tab in the Log and Capture window, and using the Scratch Disk button.

The Scratch Disks window (Figure 7.10) is reachable in other ways in Final Cut Pro. This is logical because initial captures are not the only kind of file that FCP writes. Indeed, if you look at this window, you will see that it allows you to set scratch disks not only for video and audio captures, but also for video and audio render files, the audio waveform and thumbnail images, and the automatically saved copies of a project.

Figure 7.10 The Scratch Disks window.

Log and Transfer

As we've already discussed, the proliferation of tapeless formats over the past few years has been amazing. One of those formats, Panasonic's P2, has seen widespread acclaim for its flexibility. Cameras such as the AG-HVX200 can shoot anything from DV up to 1080i HD at various frame rates!

Apple has recognized the importance of this format and has developed the Log and Transfer window. (This feature can also be used with Sony Video Disk Units (VDUs) and AVCHD formats.) Although we can capture footage from a P2 camera as we would with the Log and Capture window, why would we? That is a linear process, and more time consuming than it should be. P2 is a tapeless format, and data is written directly to the P2 card. Because this data can be accessed nonlinearly, we can simply transfer the data from the card to our scratch disks.

The P2 cards contain data in the MXF format, which is an open-source "wrapper" for various types of video codecs. It is these MXF files that need to be "unwrapped" to ingest this type of media into FCP. There is more on MXF in Chapter 5. The beauty of the Log and Transfer window is that even though Final Cut Pro cannot use MXF files directly, it can extract the media contained inside the MXF structure.

Let's look at the process.

Mounting a P2 Card and Folders

Prior to actually using the Log and Transfer window, we need to mount the P2 card (and/or folders) to our computer to be able to read data off it. There are several methods for doing this:

1. Using a Panasonic P2 card reader or store drive connected to your machine via FireWire or USB.

Figure 7.11 The Log and Transfer window.

2. Using the PCMIA card slot on a PowerBook (note that this requires a driver from Panasonic (*https://eww.pavc.panasonic.co.jp/proav/support/cs/csregistp2m/ep2main/soft_e.htm*). Newer MacBook Pros do not have this capability natively because they use the newer and faster ExpressCard/34 slot. However, adapters are available (*see http://www.duel-systemsadapters.com/*).

3. Using a P2-equipped camera, such as the AG-HVX200, as a card reader connected via FireWire.

4. Mounting P2 archived disk images (more on this later).

5. Via a folder on a local or networked disk (more on this later).

Once you have mounted your P2 card or archived image or found the folder that contains the P2 file structure, it's time to ingest the media. Inside Final Cut Pro, go to the File Menu > Log and Transfer or Command-Shift-8. A new window will open up. Don't let the window scare you—it's really not that complicated. Let's break it down into its separate parts.

The Browse Area

The Browse area of the Log and Transfer window is where you can see the separate media files that are contained on P2 volumes or in folders.

The top bar of the Browse area contains a number of controls.

Add Folder Button—Opens a dialogue box to choose a folder with the valid P2 folder structure.

Eject Button—Ejects the selected folder, P2 card, or disk image. If you have a P2 card selected, this button will also unmount the card in the Finder.

Search Box—Using this box, you can search for clip names and timecode. Unlike the search function in the Browser of Final Cut Pro, which returns items in a separate

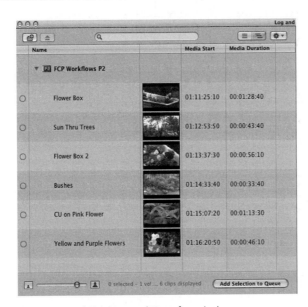

Figure 7.12 The Browse area of the Log and Transfer window.

Figure 7.13 Action menu with nothing selected *(left)*; Action menu with P2 card selected *(center)*; Action menu with clip selected *(right)*.

window, the search function in the Log and Transfer window simply limits which clips are displayed below.

View Buttons—There are two options here: the Flat List view (the one with the parallel lines) and the Hierarchical List view (the one with stair-stepped lines). In the Flat List view, clips are listed without regard to the card or folder they are in. This view is much like the List view in the Final Cut Pro Browser, with one big difference: spanned clips are grouped together as one item. Spanned clips are clips that "span" across multiple P2 cards or have reached a file size of 4GB. In the Hierarchical List view, clips are grouped by their volume or folder.

Action Pop-up—The Action pop-up menu contents will change depending on what you have selected. With nothing selected, your options are to add a custom path (same as the Add Folder button) and preferences for the Log and Transfer window. With a P2 card selected, you can choose to add all of the clips on that volume to the Transfer Queue, to archive the contents of the card to a disk image or a folder, or to unmount the card. With a clip selected, you can choose to add that individual clip to the Transfer Queue, to delete or rename the clip, or to revert to the original metadata (more on this later).

The middle part of the Browse area contains folders and volumes you have mounted (P2 cards will mount here automatically), and will look slightly different depending on your selected view. There is one icon here to pay attention to. On the left-hand side is a circle called the media map indictor. If the clip has not been transferred, the indictor will be blank. If you have transferred only part of the clip (using In and Out points), the icon will be split in half like a pie chart. If you have transferred a clip in its entirety, the circle will be full.

The bottom of the Browse area has a slider to resize thumbnails, as well as an info section in the middle. The info section tells you how many clips you have selected, how many volumes are mounted, and how many clips are being displayed. Lastly, there is a button to add the currently selected clip(s) to the queue (more on the Transfer Queue in another section).

Archiving and Valid Folders

Before we move on to the other parts of the Log and Transfer window, let's take a look at the concepts of archiving to disk your images and folders. Prior to transferring your footage and reformatting your cards is the time to consider archiving.

Unlike tape, P2 is meant to be reused, and unlike tape, this can present some problems. If you ever lose the media (for example, deleting it from your drive), most

Figure 7.14 A valid P2 folder.

likely you will have already formatted the P2 card for reuse. For redundancy, many workflows archive the contents of the card. Many workflows first transfer the clips (which go to your scratch disk), and then archive the original structure of the P2 card onto a different drive. Using the Log and Transfer window, we can archive the contents of the card two ways: as a disk image (.dmg) or as a folder.

A disk image is a .dmg file that is the same size as the card you archived, even if it's not full. If you were ever to accidentally wipe from this card the media you had transferred, you could mount the disk image and transfer the footage again.

Archiving to a folder creates a valid P2 archive folder that transfers only the contents on the card to a location of your choice. This brings up an interesting issue. Many people make archives manually by simply dragging items off a mounted P2 card onto the drive of their choice. It's okay to do this (although FCP makes it more elegant), but you *must* make sure that you copy the whole contents folder, not just subfolders, for Log and Transfer to recognize the items as part of a valid P2 folder. So, what is a valid P2 folder?

A valid P2 Folder contains:

Contents—The main parent folder that all subfolders live in.

Audio—As the name implies, this folder contains audio for your clips as MXF files.

Clip—Contains XML files for each clip. These XML files contain metadata and instructions about what MXF files belong to each clip.

Icon—Contains thumbnails of each clip.

Proxy—Contains low-resolution video clips for each full-resolution clip. Not all P2 cameras create these.

Video—Contains all of the video for your clips as MXF files. These files correspond to the codec you shot with—DV, DVCPRO HD, and so on.

Voice—Contains voice notes for each clip. Not all cameras support this feature.

The Preview Area
The Preview area is very similar to that of the Log and Capture window. In fact, there are only a few differences in terms of overall functionality.

Clips are loaded into the Preview area when you select them in the Browse area. So if you select a single clip in the Browse area, it's automatically loaded into the Preview area. What's neat about this is that if you select multiple clips, the Log and Transfer window will bridge them automatically for you—meaning that when you reach the end of clip 1, clip 2 will start playing.

Once a clip is loaded into the Preview area, you can set In and Out points and navigate (JKL, jog/shuttle, etc.) just as you would in the Log and Capture window.

Timecode Duration | Clip Name | Current Timecode

In Point Controls | Prev/Next Clip Buttons | Out Point Controls

Transport Controls | Scrubber Bar

Figure 7.15 The Preview area of the Log and Transfer window.

There are, however, a number of things to be aware of:

Clip Name—You'll notice when you load a clip into the Preview area between the duration and current timecode box that the name of your clip is displayed. By default (or prior to naming it), this will display something like 000126. This number is the clip ID. Every clip will have a unique clip ID. Even if you rename the clip, this ID will come along as part of the clip. This is important if you ever need to retransfer or find offline media.

Next Clip and Previous Clip Buttons—Because we aren't dealing with a linear format such as tape, we can easily choose to navigate to the next or previous clip in the Browse area. We do this by using the Next Clip and Previous Clip buttons at the bottom of the Preview area.

Add Clip to Queue Button—Similar to the button found at the bottom of the Browse area, this will take the clip that you're working with and, based on In and Out points and logging and import settings (discussed next), add that clip to the Transfer Queue.

Audio Preview—Another difference between the Preview area and the Log and Transfer window is that in the Preview area, you can hear your audio only when you are playing at normal speed (backward or forward)—you cannot hear audio while scrubbing.

Poor Playback in Preview Window—You may get poor playback performance when previewing directly from a mounted P2 volume. The fix is to copy the card (remember to take the whole contents folder) onto a drive. Or you can also archive the volume by using the Log and Transfer window and let FCP do the work for you.

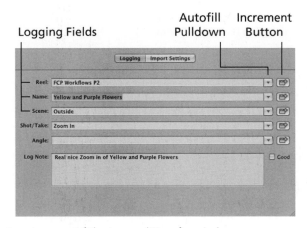

Logging Fields · Autofill Pulldown · Increment Button

Figure 7.16 The Logging area of the Log and Transfer window.

The Logging Area

Like the Preview area, the Logging area of the Log and Transfer window is almost identical to that of the Log and Capture window. The fields are the same, but there are, of course, a few differences.

Reel and Name Fields—In the Log and Transfer window, the Reel and Name fields by default take on the name of the mounted volume and the clip ID of that clip. Keep in mind that it is very important to give proper reel names in the Log and Transfer window. There are two important reasons for reel naming:

1. *Spanned Clips*—If you are using a spanned clip, you should try to name your reel something that is going to remind you to reconstitute the clip (from a folder or disk image) that it came from. So your reel might be named something like "MyShootA_B_C," indicating that three cards were used.

2. *Reconnecting Clips*—If you need to reconnect clips that have gone offline for some reason, Final Cut Pro uses the reel name you assigned—*not* the volume name of the P2 card—to help you search for clips.

Autofill Data—A very nice feature of the Log and Transfer window is the ability to autofill data. Every time you successfully ingest a clip, Final Cut Pro will add autofill information for each field in the Logging area. So, for example, if you ingest a clip from a reel called "Music Video," that name will become available in the Autofill pulldown next to the Reel field so you can use it again. Using autofill in this way speeds the logging process tremendously. Note that you can always reset autofill information by going to the Action pop-up in the Browse area, choosing Preferences, and clicking the Clear Logging Autofill Cache button.

Clip Naming—Unlike in the Log and Capture window, clip names in the Logging area are not populated using other logging information such as scene, shot/take, and so on. You can type a clip name directly into the field.

The other part of the Logging area is the Clip Settings button. This button lets you adjust whether you will be transferring both video and audio, or one or the other. In addition, you can also choose which channels of audio you wish to transfer.

Reveal Current   Transfer   Transfer
Logging Bin   Status   Progress Bar

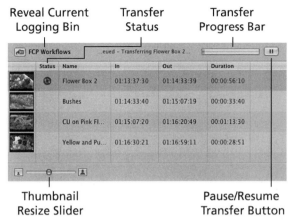

Thumbnail   Pause/Resume
Resize Slider   Transfer Button

Figure 7.17   The Transfer Queue of the Log and Transfer window.

The Transfer Queue

The Transfer Queue shows the clips that are queued for ingest.

The top bar of the Transfer Queue has a button to show the current logging bin in the Browser. Unlike in the Log and Capture window, you must set the logging bin in the Browser because you cannot set it from the Log and Transfer window. In the center is a text description of the clips in the queue. To the right is a progress bar that shows the current transfer status of a clip, as well as a Pause/Resume Transfer button.

The middle part of the Transfer Queue shows the clips that are currently queued. You can reorder the clips in this list by taking the ones you want to transfer first and dragging them to the top of the list. Also note the Status column. There are three icons that can appear here, each indicating something different:

1. *Spinning Disc*—This icon indicates that the clip is currently transferring.

2. *Still Disc*—This icon represents a clip that has been partially transferred. Such clips will be lost if you close the Log and Transfer window or close the project with the current logging bin.

3. *Exclamation Point*—This icon represents an error in transferring. Most often this is because the P2 volume or folder has been moved or unmounted prior to the transferring actually taking place.

Clips can be added to the Transfer Queue by clicking the Add Clip to Queue button in the Preview area, or the Add Selection to Queue button in the Browse area, by dragging clips and volumes from the Browse area, or by dragging clips from the Browse area to the Browser.

XDCAM Ingest

Sony's XDCAM format in recent years has gone from an SD-only format (DV and IMX) to HD with XDCAM HD. Like P2, XDCAM is based on MXF as the wrapper for its media (DV, IMX, or HDV, or what Sony calls MPEG HD). As such, there is no native support for those MXF files in FCP. Unlike P2, which uses the Log and Transfer window, there is no native interface in FCP to access an XDCAM deck or folder. With a little bit of work, however, it's quite easy to work with XDCAM and XDCAM HD footage. Final Cut Pro gives us two options:

Source List   Clip Image View   Clip Info

Player and   Import to
Transport Controls   Pulldown

Figure 7.18 Sony XDCAM Transfer window.

1. Download and install the free XDCAM Transfer Software from Sony (*https://serviceplus.us.sony.biz/sony-software.aspx?model=pdzkp1*. This is software to transfer and export via FireWire from an XDCAM deck or from a local directory that contains the XDCAM/XDCAM HD MXF files.

2. Purchase and install Telestream's Flip4Mac MXF component for XDCAM (*http://flip4mac.com/pro_xdcam.htm*). This software allows for transfer and export via Gigabit Ethernet or from a local directory that contains the XDCAM/XDCAM HD MXF files. This software is very similar to the Sony software, so we will not be covering it with a full section. However, one of its advantages is the superfast transfer via Gigabit Ethernet.

Installing the XDCAM Transfer Software from Sony installs an import and export plug-in as well as the necessary File Access Mode driver for accessing an XDCAM deck. Additionally, you will need to activate PC remote mode on the camera or deck (check the manual for the camera or deck on how to do this for your specific piece of equipment). To import footage via the XDCAM Transfer plug-in, do the following:

1. Go to File Menu > Import > Sony XDCAM.

2. This will launch the XDCAM Transfer Software. Let's look at the main interface of the software.

Source List

On the left side of this window, you will see your sources. XDCAM and XDCAM HD discs will automatically mount in this area. Additionally, you can mount local direc-

Figure 7.19   The source list of the Sony XDCAM Transfer window.

tories by using the Add button at the bottom of the source list. You can also remove a folder (Remove button) or eject a disc (Eject button). Note that this is actually the same button—the text simply changes depending on what is selected.

Clip Image View or List View

The top center part of the window contains either the Clip Image view or the List view of all the clips from the source that you have selected. Clip information such as codec, data rate, audio information, and frame rate can be overlaid on the images or listed in List view. Note that if a proxy of the clip is not available, the clip will say, "No Image Available."

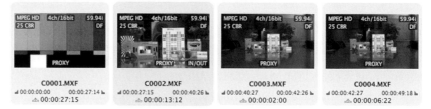

Figure 7.20   The Clip Image view in the Sony XDCAM Transfer window.

Clip Info

The Clip Info pane, located in the bottom right corner of the window, displays a bit more information about a clip than the Clip Image view or the List view does. In this window, you can also choose which audio channels to monitor and import. Lastly, you can see subclips that you have made on the media. Creating a subclip is similar to marking a clip in the Log and Capture window. In other words, you can divide one long clip into smaller parts.

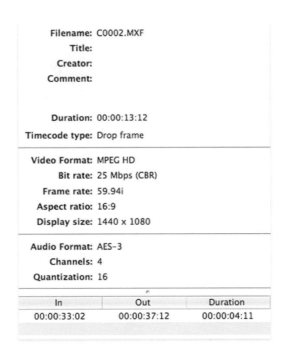

Filename: C0002.MXF
Title:
Creator:
Comment:

Duration: 00:00:13:12
Timecode type: Drop frame

Video Format: MPEG HD
Bit rate: 25 Mbps (CBR)
Frame rate: 59.94i
Aspect ratio: 16:9
Display size: 1440 x 1080

Audio Format: AES-3
Channels: 4
Quantization: 16

In	Out	Duration
00:00:33:02	00:00:37:12	00:00:04:11

Figure 7.21   The Clip Info section of the Sony XDCAM Transfer window.

Player

The player is where you can navigate a selected clip from your Clip Image view or from List view (note that you are viewing a low-resolution proxy if available, not the full-resolution media). In the player, you can also add In and Out points to create subclips, navigate essence markers (markers in the video that the camera automatically assigns based on camera events, or you can manually add them during recording), and add clips to be imported.

Figure 7.22   The player section of the Sony XDCAM Transfer window.

Import Bar

Below the player area and the Clip Info pane, there is a pulldown to choose what FCP project you want to import the file into (the pulldown defaults to the current active project). Additionally, you can also choose not to import the files into a project, but to simply transfer the files to your selected import location (see the next section for details on import preferences).

Preferences

Because the Sony XDCAM Transfer Software is a separate application from Final Cut Pro, it has its own set of preferences. To launch these, go to File Menu > Preferences from within the XDCAM Transfer Software.

General—In the General tab of Preferences, you can choose to have imported files open up in Final Cut Pro or in another application. You can also choose to automatically add discs when mounted to the source list, and show offline discs. Additionally, you can choose your default image magnification in the Clip Image view, and also choose what channels of audio to monitor.

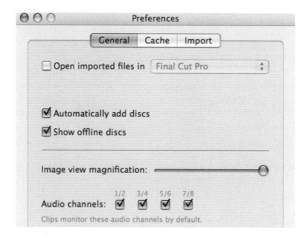

Figure 7.23 The General Preferences tab of the Sony XDCAM Transfer Software.

Cache—Here is where you can choose the location and size of the proxies and thumbnail cache.

Import—This is the most important tab in Preferences. Here, you can choose the import location of your media and choose whether to overwrite existing files. Unlike the Log and Capture and Log and Transfer windows, which use the scratch disks set up inside Final Cut Pro, the XDCAM Transfer Software uses this preference to choose where the media will be transferred to. It's often a wise idea to make this location the same as your Final Cut Pro scratch disks. There are also options here for how clips will be named, such as using the clip title as the filename. Lastly, you can choose to add handles to subclips and to import only monitored audio channels.

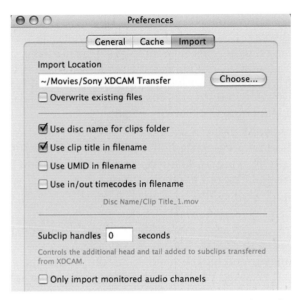

Figure 7.24 The Import Preferences tab of the Sony XDCAM Transfer Software.

XDCAM File Structure

As previously mentioned, XDCAM is based on MXF wrappers, much like P2. Although the preferred method of transferring XDCAM footage is using the XDCAM Transfer Software (or Telestream's MXF component for XDCAM), you can also transfer footage manually via the Finder to a local or remote disc, and then use the XDCAM Transfer Software to import your files from that local disc. You could do this for a variety of reasons, but one that is common in many XDCAM workflows is file backup and archiving. Just as with P2, understanding the file directory of an XDCAM disc (Sony Professional Disc) is important.

On the root level of an XDCAM disc, there are a number of XML files that refer to different metadata and instructions about clip locations and so forth. There are also four subfolders:

Clip—This directory contains the full-resolution clips wrapped as MXF files.

Name	Date Modified	Size
▶ 📁 Clip	Today, 7:59 AM	--
📄 DISCMETA.XML	Today, 7:58 AM	1 KB
▶ 📁 Edit	Today, 7:58 AM	--
▶ 📁 General	Today, 7:58 AM	--
📄 INDEX.XML	Today, 7:59 AM	5 KB
📄 MEDIAPRO.XML	Today, 7:59 AM	3 KB
▶ 📁 Sub	Today, 7:59 AM	--

Figure 7.25 Directory structure of a Sony XDCAM disc.

Sub—The proxies of your clips (the images that you see in the player and Clip Image view) are found here.

General—This can contain other documents, such as text files, scripts, and so on (up to 500MB). Some workflows use this folder extensively for keeping these documents in one place, whereas others do not use it at all. Final Cut Pro and the XDCAM Transfer Software do not interact with this folder, so you would add or extract information from this folder manually.

Edit—EDLs from Sony's proprietary logging application are stored here. This is a Windows-only application, and is not used in most FCP workflows.

When manually backing up XDCAM discs, it is important to maintain this directory structure and also not to rename files.

File Importing

We have discussed three ways to get footage into Final Cut Pro: Log and Capture, Log and Transfer, and Sony's XDCAM Transfer Software. Frequently for a video project, you also need to use files that are already saved on a hard drive somewhere. These files include still images, graphics (animated and still), and audio files (music, narration recording, etc.). Final Cut Pro refers to this type of ingestion as importing, and it is easy to do.

In general, to import these files, go to the File Menu -> Import and choose a specific file, or choose to import files or folders. Files and entire folders can also be dragged and dropped directly into the FCP Browser from the Finder. A Finder folder dropped into the Browser becomes a bin, meaning that in the Browser, you can maintain directory structures that were created in the Finder. Technically, a file can be saved anywhere that a user has access to, and can then be imported into FCP. However, it is a good idea to have these files on your scratch disk (or on a different disk that is designated and organized for this purpose).

As discussed in the previous chapter, many file types also need some preparation to be optimized for FCP. If you try to import into FCP a file that it cannot recognize, you will get an error message. If you import a file that is recognized but not optimal, there is no message.

Next Steps

In the past few chapters, we have explored the technical aspects of video and compression and have taken a look at preparing for the edit session and ingesting media into Final Cut Pro. We are now ready to embark on the rough cut, an exciting and creative part of the process.

8 The Rough Cut

There is an old saying that carving a statue out of rock is easy: just cut away all of the rock that doesn't look good.

We teach our students to think of nonlinear editing in the same way. In both cases, the process is about refinement. When carving rock, you progress through a series of tools. You may begin with a large sledgehammer, good for knocking away large chunks of rock. When you have chipped away the largest chunks, you switch to a large but crude chisel, good for chiseling away to the next layer of detail—and so on through finer and finer tools, until you are using sandpaper and finally a polishing cloth.

Nonlinear editing is really very similar. The rough-cut phase and the techniques discussed in this chapter are like your favorite large chisel. If the process is all about eliminating what you don't want, this really starts in the shooting phase, when the shooter is selective about the footage they capture. The next major cutting of material is in the ingest phase, when you decide what, out of all of your acquired material, needs to go into Final Cut Pro for editing. The ingest stage is something like the big sledgehammer—good for eliminating big chunks of unusable stuff, but not good for detailed work.

This chapter picks up when you have all of your material nicely organized as clips in the FCP Browser, and it is time to start cutting. This is an exciting moment, because the initial goal is to string together for the first time the actual clips that will make up your program. Don't worry about the fine details and the polish when you are rough cutting. There will be time and different tools for that later. The idea at this stage is to take your statue from a blocky chunk of stone to something that begins to resemble your final piece.

Those who already have some understanding of editing in FCP will get the most from this chapter. We assume, for example, that you already know how to mark a clip and place it on the Timeline. This chapter is not a basic tutorial, but rather a collection of intermediate techniques and workflow-related concepts.

Defining the Objectives of a Rough Cut

Unfortunately, not everyone means exactly the same thing when they say "rough cut." When you are involved in this stage of a project, it is a good idea to define the objectives for the cut, and to understand how a particular cut fits into the process and how the team will use it.

There is a world of difference between a "rough cut" that is intended for the internal team to see how the story flows, and a "rough cut" that is intended to get the client's approval on a project. If you are a sculptor, and your benefactor comes to the studio expecting to see an almost finished statue of himself or herself, and instead sees a roughly shaped piece of rock, you might have some explaining to do.

Part of this is called managing expectations. This is particularly important when working with rough cuts, because they are often intended to focus on certain aspects of a project and to ignore others.

So, you may explain to your reviewers (clients, teammates, collaborators) that a cut is intended to focus on story, and that the mix is not done and the titles are only temporary. However, it is often hard for people to focus on what they are supposed to, so you may still get a lot of comments about how the music was too low at spots and the titles didn't look good. There is a lot more on reviews in the next chapter.

It is important to see the rough-cut stage as a larger phase of the project, a phase that in itself has some constituent subphases. Each project is unique in regard to its need for rough cuts and revisions. It is important to manage expectations for each cut along the way, but still to be prepared for comments that are out of order. It is important to realize that even though there are some gray areas in this terminology, the rough-cut phase must have a clear process to completion.

The following concepts and terms are useful in conceptualizing and defining the rough-cut phase of a workflow.

Assembly Edit

This type of edit implies the initial assembly of clips on the Timeline for any scene or project. We use this term to mean going from nothing to something. We talk about "just getting from beginning to end." Assembly editing is something like doing the edges of the puzzle before you tackle the interior.

In most workflows, we find it very useful to assemble the Timeline as a first priority. Even if not all of the media assets are available yet, it is still a useful building block to place the material you do have on a Timeline in the proper order with gaps for what is missing.

There are also exceptions to this beginning-to-end philosophy. Sometimes you will need to take a single scene, and edit it through several phases of postproduction as a proof of concept before even beginning the rest of the piece.

First assemblies are often not pretty. Generally only the core team sees these cuts, and sometimes the cuts are too rough to be interpreted by anyone who is not familiar with the postproduction process. For those of us who are editors and producers, this is an exciting moment. In an assembly edit, we can start to really see the full potential of a piece. Sometimes this is also the moment when you get the first inkling of a problem (or a full-on disaster).

For this reason if none other, we recommend making a raw assembly cut a major milestone in most workflows.

Review and Approval Cuts

Most rough cuts are intended for some sort of specific review, and it is good to define this and communicate it to everyone working on the cut. Who is the review group for this cut? What will they be commenting on, and what have they seen previously on the piece? The next chapter is about how to facilitate the actual review process.

Sometimes a cut is meant for more than just review. It may represent completion of some aspect of the project, or even the final project itself. It is good to make it clear to everyone involved what, if anything, you are looking for in the way of approval in a cut.

Picture Lock

The point in the process where all of the shots are in place and all timings are correct is known as picture lock. This is an important technical milestone because many of the tasks in finishing (such as music composition, color correction, and mix) depend on having final timings. Therefore, once picture lock is established, many of these tasks can go forward simultaneously. If picture lock is declared and these tasks commence, and then, for any reason, there is the need to change the timing of the shots, these changes will affect the work of a lot of people.

The picture lock should be the culmination of the rough-cutting process, and a major milestone in any workflow.

Rough-Cutting Concepts

Here are a few terms that refer to common concepts used during the rough-cut stage, helping to further define the objectives of a cut and the purpose of a particular edit session.

Trimming

Adjustments to timing once an initial assembly has been created are called trimming. Later in this chapter, we have a large section on trimming techniques. Keep in mind that although assembly and trimming are two different modes of editing, we often use them together, not as wholly different phases. In other words, we inevitably do a little bit of trimming as we place shots on the Timeline, but then we often need to go back and do finer trimming later.

A-Roll / B-Roll Editing

This terminology refers to the basic structure used in most nonfiction editing. The A-roll is generally an interview, or someone on-camera saying something. B-roll means the shots that illustrate what the person in the A-roll is saying. Of course, there are lots of variations on this theme. In the news, the A-roll might include the correspondent's stand-up. On MTV, you might see A-roll placed on-screen simultaneously with B-roll using a *24*-like style (or, for you old-schoolers, the *Woodstock* style). In fiction filmmaking, the difference is not always as clear-cut, but we still refer to beauty shots as B-roll.

Editorial Work

Editorial means storytelling. Generally you will want to focus on editorial concerns first, before moving into more aesthetic concerns, although, in editing, it would be a mistake to try to completely separate these two. One quickly comes to realize that the emotive tone you can create with "aesthetic" techniques is not really separate from the meaning of the content. Anyone who doubts the old adage that editorial technique can affect meaning has never practiced nonlinear editing.

Still, it often pays to focus on the editorial first. For instance, when cutting a piece in the a traditional A-roll/B-roll style, often we will start by stringing out all of the interview bites first. Then we'll do a second pass to add the B-roll.

Pre-Editing with Subclips and Markers

If you have been intimately involved in a project through the production and ingestion of the media, you may be sufficiently familiar with the footage at this point to just sit down and start editing. Just as often, however, you will come to a project at the rough-cut stage, with little familiarity with the source media. In this case, before you actually cut, some review of the material and some further preparation are needed.

It is important to recognize that there is some overlap in the tools you can use for various levels of review and refinement. Choices that you make during the ingest phase have a large effect on what you do during (or if you even need) the pre-editing stage. Sometimes it will be more efficient to use the Log and Capture process to break your clips up into discrete shots, but what if this is not your workflow? Sometimes it is better to capture a whole tape, and deal with breaking it up into shots with subclips and markers later.

That is the idea of pre-editing. Subclips and markers are particularly useful in workflows where:

1. The editor or editors cutting the rough cut are not already familiar with the material. Pre-editing is an opportunity to review the material and make notes that will help in the editing process.

2. The ingest process was done less precisely (it was more convenient to capture whole tapes than to break them up into individual clips during ingest).

3. Anytime you want to make detailed notations about your clips.

Subclips

Sublclips are just what they sound like: clips that are subsections of other clips.

Creating a subclip is simple:

1. Open any clip in the Viewer.

2. Mark that clip with an In and an Out point.

3. Choose Modify > Make Subclip.

You will observe at this point that a new clip appears in the Browser. This clip has a special icon in the Browser (Figure 8.1). The icon with rip marks denotes a subclip—as if it were torn from the middle of a larger clip, which in essence it was. You'll notice that when you create the subclip, it comes into the Browser with a name, but the name is already selected for you to change. Final Cut Pro assumes that if you are bothering to make a subclip, you probably want to name it something.

Indeed, naming subclips is a good idea. Inside Final Cut Pro, subclips operate much like other clips. The reason you are probably wanting to make them in the first place is that during ingest, you did not break down your footage into precise enough clips to be convenient to work with while editing. To stay organized, it is a good idea to carefully name your subclips and, in some cases, to organize them in bins. Subclipping is a second opportunity (after ingest, but before you start actually editing) to organize your footage in the Browser.

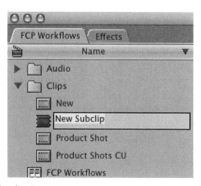

Figure 8.1 A new subclip in the Browser.

Here are a few final things to remember about subclips:

1. *A subclip references the same media file as the clip it was created from.* No new or duplicate media is being created. The subclip exists inside your FCP project as a reference only.

2. *It is a good idea to put "pad" on your subclips.* There is no reason to try to set your subclip's limits to the exact frames that you want to use. Just as with Log and Capture, it is actually better to purposely leave some pad, or handles (extra footage on either side of your subclip), for use in fine adjustments and to make transitions.

3. *Subclip limits can be removed.* Unlike with a normal clip, if you are editing with a subclip and you reach a media limit, this is likely not a true media limit—it is just the end of what you designated in the subclip. In this case, subclips allow you to remove their limits.

This is done by selecting the subclip and going to Modify > Remove Subclip Limits. The result of removing a subclip's limits is that the clip now has access to the full length of the original media clip. You will notice in the Browser that the rip marks on the icon disappear when subclip limits are removed. However, the subclip retains the name that you gave it.

Markers

In some ways, markers are like subclips, but really, they are much more flexible. Useful for pre-editing, they can also be used for many other tasks during the editing process. (They also provide hooks to carry information to other programs.)

Markers are something like "sticky notes"—little flags that you can place on any frame of video to leave a note for yourself, for someone else, or for a piece of software. Markers can be placed on clips in the Viewer, in the Timeline, or directly onto an open Timeline (sequence). For the purposes of pre-editing, it is going to be useful to make markers on clips in the Viewer, so this is the technique we will focus on.

There are a number of ways to make markers in FCP. Here are three:

1. *With a menu:* Mark > Markers > Add.

2. *With a button:* Located on both the Viewer and the Canvas (Figure 8.2).

3. *With a keyboard shortcut:* Just hit M.

The process when engaged in pre-editing, or familiarizing yourself with the footage, is:

1. Open a clip in the Viewer and position your playhead on a spot that you want to use later.

2. Create a marker with one of the previous methods.

3. Just as with subclips, when using markers for pre-editing, it is often a good idea to name them. To name a marker, with your playhead still on the same frame as

Figure 8.2 Add Marker button.

Figure 8.3 Edit Marker window.

the marker, hit M again, and you will open the Edit Marker window (Figure 8.3). This window will let you name the marker, and will also provide some other features that we will describe later.

When you make a marker in the Viewer, as described here, you will notice a couple of things:

1. There is a small mark (it looks like a little house) in the scrubber bar to represent the marker. This marker is pink most of the time, but it turns yellow when the playhead is on the exact frame of the marker (Figure 8.4).
2. In the Browser, the clip itself now has its own disclosure arrow, which is what we are used to seeing with bins. Twirl this arrow down—the clip itself is now functioning like a bin to hold the markers (Figure 8.5).

You can see already that markers have the powerful function of taking specific notes on your media. There are a few more marker functions that are valuable in the pre-editing stage.

If you take one of those markers as it manifests itself in the Browser, notice that you can drag the marker directly to the Timeline as if the marker were a clip. By default, editing a marker into a Timeline using this method will cause all of the media from the marker until the next marker on the clip (or, if there were no other markers, until the end of the clip) to be edited onto the Timeline.

What if you want to edit with markers, but you don't want to use all of the footage through the next marker—what if you just want a second or two? Did you notice the Duration field in the Edit Marker window where you were about to name the marker?

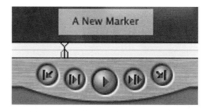

Figure 8.4 Marker on scrubber bar.

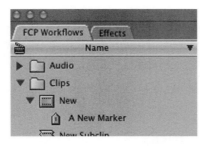

Figure 8.5 Marker in Browser.

Go ahead, put in a duration and click OK. You will notice two things different about a marker with a duration:

1. The marker as it appears on the scrubber bar has a "tail"—an extension that shows its length (Figure 8.6).
2. In the Browser, the marker now has a value in the Duration column.

And, as intended, if you drag the marker from the Browser to the Timeline, you will get only the set duration. This technique is great when you are cutting something with a bunch of shots that are all the same length. Say you have a long clip of jungle scenes and want to cut a montage where you see each animal for one second. You could go through, putting a marker with a one-second duration on the best shot of each kind of animal—puma, monkey, snake, and so forth. Now you can use these markers with duration to quickly edit a sequence of shots, each of which is one second long. Remember, once the clips are in the Timeline, they act just like any other clips. You can change their position, duration, and so on.

For pre-editing purposes, markers do many of the same things as subclips. Depending on your needs, either one (or some of both) might be appropriate. Probably the biggest difference between the two is the sense in which a marker stays with its clip, and a subclip (for all intents and purposes) represents a clip of its own. If your initial organization of clips is pretty good, and you just want to add some notes, think about markers. On the other hand, if you want to reorganize more deeply, think about subclips. As mentioned earlier, there is no reason not to use both in the same project. (Indeed, you can even place markers on subclips if necessary).

Markers are good for pre-editing, but really, they are much more versatile than that. For some great tutorials on different ways to use markers, check out Diana Weynend's *Final Cut Pro 6* from the Apple Pro Training Series. Also, in Chapter 11, there is further discussion on markers used to pass information along to other programs in Final Cut Studio.

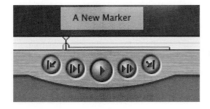

Figure 8.6 Marker with duration in the scrubber bar.

Pre-Editing and Workflows

Not every workflow requires an extensive pre-editing stage. Many workflows get a lot of this naming and organizing out of the way during ingest, but this is not always practical. Also, these tools are not strictly used at the beginning of editing, then forgotten. Sometimes you realize later on that you are going to use a certain type of shot a lot in a piece—say, the main character smiling—so you go back to put markers on all the good smile shots you can find.

Organizing Your Tracks

One mark of an experienced editor is organized use of the audio and video tracks. There are no set rules for what goes on what track, but an experienced editor tends to keep things fairly neat. Exactly how he or she organizes the tracks is dependent on the particulars of the project and on the editor's personal style.

There are different approaches to organizing audio and video tracks. All in all, it is not very complicated, but let's look at a few ideas in both audio and video.

Organizing Audio Tracks

Because of the way that audio tracks work, they are actually more important to keep organized than are video tracks on most projects. For one thing, most Timelines will have more audio tracks than video tracks. Also, it is likely that the audio tracks will need to be worked on by another operator (a mixer), and possibly outside Final Cut Pro. Making these audio handoffs is discussed in Chapter 12, but whatever the workflow is for your audio, it is going to be easier if the tracks are organized.

What do we mean by this? Basically, that you keep similar audio content together on the same track.

So, music on one track, voice-over on another, and natural sound on its own track. As you can see from Figure 8.7, it is actually a bit more complicated than that. Stereo pairs require two tracks, and the same type of audio sometimes needs to overlap in order to transition properly. It is easy to wind up with quite a few tracks pretty quickly.

Notice that in figure 8.8, the music (in stereo pairs) alternates from being on tracks 8 and 9 to being on tracks 10 and 11. If you alternate tracks in this way, the audio transitions are more clearly visible on the Timeline, and will be easier to work with. We call this style of alternating tracks "checkerboarding." Although it means using more tracks in total, checkerboarding works well for enabling you to see the organization of audio tracks at a glance.

Figure 8.7   Organizing audio tracks.

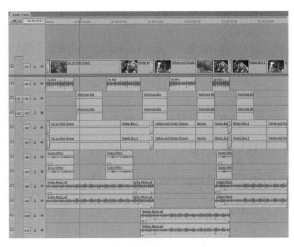

Figure 8.8 Organizing audio tracks on a complex project.

Track Selection Tools

When you are doing this sort of organizing, you will find that the Track Selection tools are often useful. And once you diligently organize your tracks, they will be even more useful, and actually will become even more powerful.

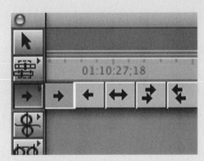

Figure 8.9 The Track Selection tools.

Each of the tools works by selecting a specific track (or tracks) in the direction (or directions) that the arrow points. So, ➡ selects one track going forward, ↔ selects one track in both directions, and so on.

The keyboard shortcut for the Track Selection tools is T. Hit T once, and you will get the Select Track Forward tool, a second T will get you the Select Track Backward tool, and so on with successive T's down the line of Track Selection tools.

Admittedly, these tools are very limited in their use, but they do come in handy sometimes, especially when working with track organization.

Organizing Video Tracks

Track organization is also useful for video tracks, although because the layering order is more important with video tracks, there is a lot less leeway in how these tracks can be organized. What we mean by this is that your titling is always going to be on a track that is above your video image (or else you wouldn't see the titles!).

A more strategic use of video tracks is to separate A-roll and B-roll. This is a convention that works well in a number of projects, but it is a convention only, not a rule. The idea is to dedicate separate video tracks to A-roll and B-roll material. Literally placing the B-roll on top of the A-roll visually represents on the Timeline the way the B-roll "covers" the A-roll.

Notice in Figure 8.10 that the two sequences look exactly the same when played back, but the second sequence is easier to look at in the Timeline (Figure 8.11). To be very clear, we are going to repeat that: there is NO DIFFERENCE to the program in using this technique—it is purely a matter of organization and preference.

Advantages of working with A-roll and B-roll in this way include:

- *The ability to "see" your piece more clearly.* When you organize your Timeline like this, it becomes a more useful visual representation of your piece. For instance, you can see the overall distribution of screen time between the type of shots and how this plays out over the whole Timeline.

- *The ability to more easily trim and manipulate the B-roll clips.* By putting your B-Roll clips on track 2, you separate them from the A-roll clips, and leave nothing on either side of them to interfere with trimming or moving them. In effect, the result of this is that you can freely move and adjust those clips without needing to change from the Selection tool. We discuss using the other tools below, but play with this a little bit. You can see how good organization can streamline the process and ultimately benefit your creativity.

One disadvantage to this method is that it limits some trimming techniques such as ripple.

Organizing video layers is nice for simple A-roll/B-roll projects, but we see more and more projects these days that involve heavy graphics and compositing with background layers, extensive titling, and video content created from animated stills. On these kinds of complicated projects, it is even more important to keep your tracks organized.

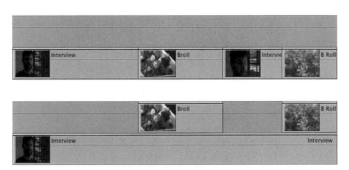

Figure 8.10 A-roll and B-roll clips are placed together on the same track *(top)*; on the bottom, they are organized on separate tracks. The sequence that plays back is exactly the same in either case, but by organizing tracks, it is easier to see the structure of your piece on the Timeline.

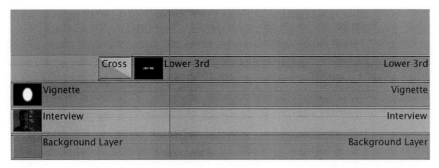

Figure 8.11 This Timeline organized not only A-roll and B-roll, but also background and overlaid graphics layers.

Customizing Your Timeline

Final Cut Pro allows you some options to customize your Timeline. Along with organizing your tracks, customizing your Timeline can help you "see" your piece on the Timeline. Many of these options are activated in the Timeline Layout pop-up (Figure 8.12).

Figure 8.12 The Timeline Layout pop-up has many helpful customizations.

There are actually many things that can be turned on or off in the Timeline, so here are some of our favorites for rough cutting:

- *Show Audio Waveforms*—A visual reference of the sounds in your audio clips. This is incredibly useful when editing audio. (See Figure 8.13.)

Figure 8.13 Audio waveforms on the Timeline.

- *Show Duplicate Frames*—This puts a colored bar on the bottom of a clip for any frames that appear more than once in the same sequence (Figure 8.14). In some projects, reusing shots is really frowned upon. When that issue comes up, this is a handy tool.

Duplicate Frame Indicator

Figure 8.14   Duplicate-frame detection.

- *Clip Overlays*—This very useful Timeline feature is actually not on the Timeline Layout pop-up menu. It has its own button (Figure 8.15).

The clip overlays (Figure 8.16) are black lines on video tracks and pink lines on audio tracks. The black and pink overlays represent the opacity level and audio level, respectively. This feature is so useful because the clip overlays not only show you the levels, they also allow you to adjust them. This is definitely a quick way to rough mix while you are cutting, and you can even keyframe levels on the Timeline by using the Pen tool on the overlays.

Figure 8.15   The Clip Overlays button.

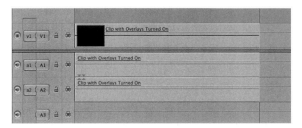

Figure 8.16   Clip overlays.

Assembling the Sequence

For us, the first assembly of a sequence is one of the most exciting parts of the process. It is also one of the most challenging. We have no secret potion for making original editorial and visual decisions in the edit room. Even if we did, the approach will differ for every project.

Assembling the first cut is going to be part of any workflow, but it is planned as just one task. When experienced in real life in the edit room, the first assembly can be a dramatic roller coaster for the team. The tips that follow are intended to help you focus on this crucial part of the process. A successful assembly edit is dependent largely on the work that has come before it. For this reason, it should not be a surprise that we have seen some of these themes in other places.

1. *Focus on getting from beginning to end.* More than anything else, that is the point of the first assembly. If you cannot find the perfect B-roll shot, put in a less than perfect one, or leave a hole to address later. A lot of times, in the process of doing the first assembly, we are also becoming more intimately familiar with the footage. Often we find that perfect B-roll shot later, when we are looking for something different. This is why it is important to keep pushing forward.

2. *Don't be afraid to work out of order.* Sometimes it is the narration that pulls you through a project; sometimes it is the music. If there is an aspect of the piece that is easy to work with, and especially if it can lend structure, by all means work with that part first. The assembly edit is like putting together a jigsaw puzzle. Just as you work on the corners and edges first, and the puzzle parts with the most recognizable details, this is a good way to approach the first assembly of your project.

3. *Be prepared.* This means a lot of things (see Chapter 6). Important preparation for the first assembly includes being familiar with your footage, having it organized, and having a clear editing script as a guide. Simply watching and aggressively annotating your footage with markers is one of the best ways to be prepared.

Storyboard and Multicam Editing

Storyboard editing and multicam editing represent alternate ways of making an initial assembly edit in Final Cut Pro. This is why it is logical to group them together, although the processes are different. In essence, these techniques represent two completely different approaches to the initial assembly of a sequence. Another nice thing about these techniques is that if you choose to use one for your initial assembly, you can still go back and make trims and adjustments to that sequence as if you had constructed it in the traditional way.

Storyboard Editing

As with many features of Final Cut Pro, the choice to use these techniques can be driven by personal preference, or by the needs of a particular project, or (most often) by a combination of both. In the case of storyboard editing, we have found it to be generally popular with people who have experience in other creative visual roles—for example, art directors and creative directors. Perhaps this is because of the similarity of storyboard editing to traditional activities in these disciplines, such as using a lightbox to view slides or (of course) using traditional storyboards. Projects (or individual scenes) that lend themselves to this style of editing include content that is very rich in visual imagery and where audio or dialogue is less important.

The basic idea behind storyboard editing is to use the thumbnails in the Browser to put your clips into a visual order, and then to use this visual arrangement in the Browser to quickly put the clips in time order in the sequence. The best way to learn how this is done is to try it. The following steps will give you the general idea. Some more tips to help you get the most from this style of editing follow.

1. Start with a project that has about six clips. It is best if they are visually diverse. You should also have an empty sequence.

2. Change the Browser to show large icons. This can be done with View > Browser Items > as Large Icons, or by right-clicking in the Browser.

Figure 8.17   Arrange your clips in a stair-step grid to place them in order when using storyboard editing.

Figure 8.18   Storyboard editing bases the editing order on the height of the top edge of the thumbnail. If we edit the arrangement in this image, the clip called B-roll would be first.

3. Arrange your clips in a grid, but allow the rows to consistently move down as they go from left to right (Figure 8.17).

   The reason for the stair-step is that FCP is going to order your clips based on their position from top to bottom first, and then left to right second. So if you make a grid with perfect rows, this will be correctly read one row at a time (clips on exactly the same level will be read from left to right). However, as soon as you slip by just a little bit, and one of the clips in your row is higher than the others, that clip will be the first taken from that row.

   Consequently, it is recommended that you not try to line up your storyboard in a perfect grid but rather in a stair-step pattern so that it is easier to be sure about the order of each row.

4. Using a marquee (or drag) selection, select all of the clips that you have arranged, and drag these clips to the Timeline. Before you release the mouse button, notice the brown outlines that show you where the clips are going to land. You can see that all of the clips are coming together. The result is a sequence in the order of the storyboard, assembled very quickly.

You can see how storyboard editing is a completely different spin on the assembly edit. Choosing the storyboard approach has a substantial effect on the workflow and the creative process. Which is not to say that a storyboard edit needs to be totally planned ahead. An editor may decide to use storyboard editing to play with a scene that is giving him or her problems. For one thing, it allows you to try out a lot of ideas quickly.

Here are a few more ideas of ways to use storyboard editing in a workflow:

In and Out Points—In the preceding example, all of the media in each of the clips in the Browser would be edited onto the Timeline—something that is usually not desirable. But storyboard editing can also utilize the marks (In and Out points) on your clips. So, one workflow with storyboard editing is to first go through your clips, marking the sections that you want to use. Think again of the example of assembling a montage of animals in the jungle. You would first go through, marking the best shot of each type of animal. Then storyboard your montage in the Browser and drag it to the Timeline for a fairly clean first assembly.

Poster Frames—The image that appears in the thumbnail is called the poster frame. By default, the poster frame is the first frame of the clip—or the In point, if there is one. However, you can set the poster frame to be anything you want it to be. If the tiger shot that you want to use starts on the jungle, before the tiger enters, that generic jungle shot might not suit you as a poster frame for storyboard editing.

    The technique for this is easy. With the clip open in the Viewer, place the playhead on the frame that you want to be the poster frame. Then do Mark > Set Poster Frame, or the keyboard shortcut Control-P.

The Scrub Tool—This tool can be found in the Tool palette, grouped with the Zoom tools (Figure 8.19). The keyboard shortcut for the Scrub Tool is HH (or Control-H), and it looks like a hand with two arrows. The Scrub Tool allows you to view the footage in a clip by dragging the tool over the thumbnail. If you haven't done this before, try this out—it's pretty cool.

    The other neat trick with the Scrub Tool is that you can also use it to set the poster frame on a clip directly on the thumbnail in the Browser. Just hold the Control key before you release the mouse when you drag to scrub. Whatever frame you release on becomes the new poster frame.

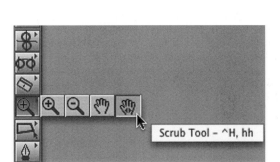

Figure 8.19 Location of the Scrub Tool.

Tweak and Trim—As with any kind of assembly, don't expect the storyboard edit to be anywhere close to your final product. It is only a starting point. Once on the Timeline, the tweaking, trimming, and revisions begin. This is the heart of the process.

Multicam Editing

Like storyboard editing, multicam editing provides an alternate way to assemble your first cut of the piece. The idea of multicam editing is to work with multiple synchronized camera angles of the same event (known as "synced sources") in a real-time way that mimics the experience of directing the broadcast of a live multicamera shoot. Multicam editing tends to work well with live events such as concerts, sports, and speeches. It is also sometimes used for scripted programs—for example, sitcoms.

    The choice to use multicam editing will have something to do with the preference of the editor, but more so than other techniques, it is going to depend on the project. Only a certain type of project lends itself to this method.

Again, the best way to understand this is a bare-bones, step-by-step explanation, followed by additional methods and tips to incorporate what we have learned into professional workflows.

1. To use multicam editing, you need to have synced sources. This simply will not work with just any footage. There are two ways for FCP to work with synced sources: based on timecode or based on the content of the clip, as designated by In or Out points.

2. If you are using the second method (in other words, the actual timecode on your source tapes is not synchronized), the next step is to find a sync point in all of the camera angles. This is a visual or audio event that happens on all of the synced source clips. One traditional way to do this is with a clapper slate. When filming a live event, you can look for distinct moments—for example, when the house lights go down. Whatever sync point you find, mark it with an In point in each of the clips you want to use (or you can use an Out point if the event is toward the end of the clips—the house lights coming back up, for instance).

3. Select all of the synchronized clips in the Browser, and create the multiclip with the menu command Modify > Make Multiclip. When you do this, you will get the Make Multiclip window. The Make Multiclip window will give you some controls over the multiclip, and also allows you to preview the clip graphically before you make it. (See Figure 8.20)

4. In the Synchronizing menu, choose In Points. This means that all of the clips will sync based on the In points that you created. Now click OK.

5. Your new multiclip will be in your Browser with a unique icon, and a name that changes based on the active angle—something you will see when you start to play with the multiclip. (See Figure 8.21.)

6. If you open the multiclip in the viewer, you can play back all of the angles simultaneously, and start to manipulate the clip. But to really edit with the multiclip, you will need a new sequence. Go ahead and create one and edit your new multiclip into it.

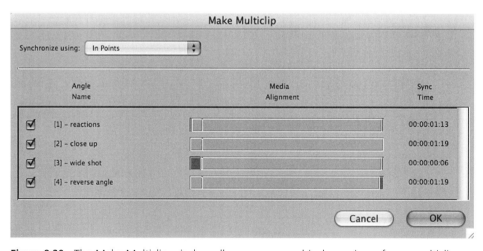

Figure 8.20 The Make Multiclip window allows you a graphical overview of your multiclip before you make it.

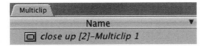

Figure 8.21 A new multiclip in the Browser window.

7. If you want to be able to cut between angles in real time during playback using the viewer, make sure you set the playhead sync pulldown (the middle pulldown in the Viewer) to Open. Now, as you play back in the Timeline the multiclip plays in sync with it. As you chose new angles in the viewer, markers are placed on the Timeline, and when you stop playback, cuts to the new angle are placed at each marker.

This all takes some practice, and there is a bit more to it (some of which is described later), but these steps should get you started on working with multiclips. Once you have committed to this path, there are some additional things to keep in mind when planning the details of the workflow.

Plan Ahead—Yeah, we know, that is a theme around here. When it comes to multicam editing, preparation is extremely important. Ideally, all of the shooters in the field should know that their material is going to be used in this way, and they should plan accordingly. If a visual cue such as a clapper board is used, everyone needs to shoot this together.

If timecode is going to be synchronized by another method—for example, using time of day—this needs to be set up on all of the cameras. If the program is long, there needs to be a plan for tape changes and/or media changes to stay in sync. Reel-naming conventions and metadata entered during ingest are all the more important with multicam.

Multicam editing allows a spontaneous style of editing, but that doesn't mean you don't want to plan ahead before you cut something. Say you are cutting a music video (a classic use of this technique). You probably want to spend some time just listening to the song before you start cutting, thinking about the parts of the song, it's rhythm, the different instruments and voices (literal and figurative). Then you are going to spend some time just looking at your camera angles—what are the best visual aspects of each? By the time you technically set up your multiclip, you should already be living and breathing the material.

Be Patient—Multicam editing is one of those things that take some patience to set up right. The reward is that once you have it working, this technique can make cutting quick and fun. Take your time in setting up the multiclip, and in preparing, as mentioned before. Also, when you actually start cutting in the style, don't be afraid to try different things. Part of the beauty of multicam editing (like storyboard editing) is that it makes it easy to quickly try out an idea.

Get comfortable—There are a lot of different ways to make the cuts when multicam editing. You can make your cuts with mouse clicks or with keyboard shortcuts, and FCP includes prebuilt keyboard setups and button bars to facilitate multicam editing. If you like this style of editing, it is worth doing some experimenting and customizing to figure out what works best for you.

Cut to the Beat—There is something inherently rhythmic in this style of cutting. For the music video example, that seems pretty obvious, but even if you were cutting sports, you might want to try cutting to the beat of a music track. It's not even necessary that you ultimately use the music in the piece. You might even try cutting to the beat of music that is just playing on your stereo.

Tweak and Trim—Just as with storyboard editing, multicam editing can be merely a starting point. All of the trimming techniques that follow can be done on multiclips.

Audio and Video—When working with a multiclip, you are able to switch or cut video angles separately from working on the audio angles. This is useful because frequently there is one source for good audio, and you want to use the multicam to cut the video to that audio. There are several ways to accomplish cutting video only. One simple method is to load only the video track back into your Viewer from the Timeline. When working with a multicam in the Viewer, the blue box represents the current video angle, and the green box represents the current audio angle. You will notice that if you load only the video track into the Viewer, there is only a blue box to manipulate—you'll be cutting video only.

Collapsing Multiclips—Once used to create a sequence, multiclips can be collapsed. This means that the editorial choices you made with the multiclip can be turned into standard cuts. It is not difficult to collapse a multiclip. Just select the multiclips in your sequence and then Modify > Collapse Multiclip(s). This is useful if you are finished using this feature and wish to minimize confusion in later stages of the postproduction process. For instance, your online editor has no need to work with multiclips—it's more convenient at the online stage for the Timeline to be set up in the traditional fashion. You do not need to collapse a multiclip in order to trim or adjust it, although that is recommended. It is definitely a good final step. Also, you can uncollapse the multiclip later on if needed: Modify > Uncollapse > Multiclip(s).

Trimming Techniques

The process of refining or making small adjustments to edit points on the Timeline is referred to as trimming. If we were carving our statue, the basic form has taken shape; now it is time to work into the details. At this stage, a lot comes down to timing.

It should be emphasized that assembling and trimming are not really discrete tasks. Instruction books always make them seem that way (and we have done this here: first assemble, then trim). However, the reality is that you are constantly changing between the tools in Final Cut Pro and the modes of editing. There could be some debate as to whether trimming can properly be called part of rough cutting at all. Some might call the techniques in this section fine cutting (and that's fine with us).

There are tools in FCP that are either exclusively or primarily used for trimming. Most FCP users realize quickly that one of the easiest ways to trim is with the Selection tool, simply by dragging on edit points in the Timeline. It doesn't take too long to realize that there are also limitations to that technique. In this section, we are not so concerned with the very basic sense of trimming, nor are we concerned with detailing every single trimming tool in FCP. Lots of great FCP books cover the basics. We like *Focal's Easy Guide to Final Cut Pro* by Rick Young. Our goal is to look at some techniques and concepts that help strengthen workflows and efficiency.

Roll or Ripple?

Any trim has one of two objectives. Do you want to make an adjustment that will affect the overall length of your sequence, or an adjustment that doesn't? In Final Cut Pro, adjustments that affect the overall length of the sequence are generally called ripple edits, and adjustments that don't are generally called roll edits. (See Figure 8.22.)

Figure 8.22 The Roll tool *(left)* and Ripple tool *(right)* on the Timeline.

Roll and ripple are tools (and in a moment we will discuss how to use them), but they are also powerful concepts. We will see throughout the rest of this section how the concepts of roll and ripple are at work even when you are not actually using the tools.

Using the tools, however, is not very complicated. They are grouped together midway down the Tool palette, and their shortcuts are *R* for Roll and *RR* for Ripple. The icons of these two tools telegraph their function nicely. Notice how the Ripple tool has one tail, but the Roll tool has two. The tails represent pieces of film (or media), and the circles represent film rolls. The Ripple tool lets out or takes in media from one side of an edit only. The difference is not made up anywhere else; thus the length of the sequence needs to change. The Roll tool conversely has two rolls and two tails, implying that both sides of an edit are adjusted simultaneously—one side losing what the other gains. This is why overall sequence length is maintained when using the Roll tool.

Notice how if you take the Ripple tool and you mouse over a cut on the Timeline, the tail will actually switch direction depending on which side of the edit point you are on. This is an indicator of which side of the edit point will be adjusted. Because the Ripple tool is the only tool that acts on only one side of an edit point in this way, this is a useful contextual indicator.

When using the Roll or the Ripple tool (as well as others), there are several indicators (we call them clues) that FCP gives you as to what the resulting edit will look like:

1. The yellow box on the Timeline gives you your delta, or change value (Figure 8.23). This is a measurement in minutes, seconds, and frames of how much you will be trimming when using either the Roll or Ripple tool. When using the Ripple tool, this is also a measurement of how much the length of the Timeline will be changing.

Figure 8.23 The delta, or change value—one of several contextual clues that appear while you are doing a drag trim on the Timeline.

Figure 8.24 During a ripple or roll edit, the canvas dynamically shows you a preview of the new In and Out points.

2. The brown outline on the clips in the Timeline gives an indication of what that part of the Timeline will look like once the adjustment is made.

3. The Canvas shows a side-by-side preview of what the new edit is going to look like. The new Out point (of the previous clip) is on the left, and the In point (of the following clip) is on the right in the two-up view (see Figure 8.24). In the case of the Ripple tool, you will notice that one side always stays the same. This is because only one side of the edit is being adjusted. This view is particularly useful for making detailed visual comparisons between frames before committing to an exact frame of an edit.

Useful Keyboard Shortcuts

Most people who work with software agree that one of the marks of advancement in any particular program is using keyboard shortcuts. There is no doubt that Final Cut Pro falls into this category, and that the creative and flowing techniques of the rough-cut phase are particularly good shortcuts to learn.

Shortcuts are called shortcuts because they get you where you want to go quickly, and because you need to already have a good knowledge of the territory to feel comfortable using them. There are several distinct ways to use keyboard shortcuts in FCP. To gain a better understanding, it is worth discussing these here, though they apply to much more than rough cutting.

Shortcuts for Actions—The first shortcut a lot of people learn is Command-Z (Undo). Unless you always do everything right the first time, this is certainly a useful shortcut. Command-Z falls into a group of shortcuts that are both useful and easy to understand: those that cause a specific action in the software. Along with Command-Z, these include:

Command-S (Save Project)—Save early, save often. Make Command-S a habit.

Control-U (Standard Window Arrangement)—It is a great benefit that Final Cut Pro's interface can be arranged to taste, putting windows wherever they are most convenient at the moment. However, sometimes the screen just gets to looking sloppy. In that case, use Control-U for the standard window arrangement to put everything back where it belongs by default.

Command-R (Render Selection) and Option-R (Render All)—Perhaps these shortcuts become habit because they come after doing intense work, but right before taking a break. There is something satisfying about pushing back from the computer, punching Option-R, and knowing that the computer has to think while you rest your eyes or get some coffee.

Shortcuts for Transport Controls—Most FCP users learn these quickly because these shortcuts are very convenient and so much better than the other options. Just in case you have been using Final Cut Pro under a rock, the following keyboard shortcuts work for playback of video in the Viewer or Canvas (and thus also on the Timeline):

Space Bar—Play/Stop

J, K, and L for Playback Control—The *L* and *J* keys work much like the traditional shuttle control on a deck. Hitting *J* once will play the video, again will go to double speed, and faster still for four successive taps. *L* goes in reverse, which means that if you hit *L* when the video is stopped, it will go backward, but if you are already going at 2× speed, it will just slow down to 1× (and so on). *K* will always stop playback.

Standard Software Shortcuts—You'll be happy to know that many keyboard shortcuts that are standard in other programs also work in FCP, including:

Command-C (Copy)

Command-X (Cut)

Command-V (Paste)—Remember, FCP will paste a copied clip or clips starting at the playhead position and on the same tracks from which the material was copied.

Command-A (Select All)

Shortcuts for Tools—As we have already seen with some tools, every tool in the Tool palette has a keyboard shortcut. Moreover, almost every grouping in the palette (a tool and all the tools that are "under" it) has a single-letter shortcut, with an additional tap of that letter going to the next tool in this group. We are not going to run through all of these shortcuts, because it is much easier to look at the tool pallet with tool tips turned on.

Using keyboard shortcuts to change tools starts to point the way toward more advanced habits and workflows. For instance, you can use the keyboard to toggle between the Selection tool (A) and the Pen tool (P) when doing fine work on keyframes.

Shortcuts to Navigate the Interface—As you start to work with Final Cut Pro more, you begin to realize the importance of the active window. The shortcuts for transport controls, for instance, can work in either the Viewer or the Canvas, depending on which one is active. To switch between windows, many FCP users would just grab the mouse and click the window they want to work on, then switch back to JKL (if that's what they were doing). However, you can also use the keyboard to navigate between the windows. The shortcuts are:

Command-1 (Viewer)

Command-2 (Canvas)

Command-3 (Timeline)

Command-4 (Browser)

Using shortcuts to move between windows is nice because it helps you to link your shortcuts more. The fact that you don't have to go to the mouse to switch to controlling the Viewer means that that you can keep your hand on the keyboard. Sure, it is a small efficiency if taken once, but as you learn more shortcuts—and begin to link them together, thinking a few steps ahead—the efficiencies compound.

Shortcuts for trimming—Getting back more specifically to trimming, several shortcuts are particularly useful. With enough keyboard shortcuts at your disposal, it is possible to do almost everything you need to do in terms of trimming, without even touching the mouse. Next, there is a list of useful trimming shortcuts with explanations. Learning these, and combining and linking them with the preceding ideas, will lead to smooth keyboard trimming workflows.

I and O for Mark In and Mark Out—Marking with the keyboard is something that comes early on the learning curve because marking is an important early task in learning nonlinear editing. Also, the letter associations are very clear. Because I and O sit on the keyboard directly above J, K, and L, it is very natural to start using these shortcuts.

V to Select an Edit Point—A less known but very useful shortcut is V to select the nearest edit point on the Timeline. V selects the edit point that is closest to the current playhead and moves the playhead to that point.

Figure 8.25   A selected edit point.

Figure 8.26   Out point only selected *(left)*; In point only selected *(right)*.

U to Toggle Sides of the Edit—When an edit point is selected, the U key will toggle between having both sides of the edit selected, the In point only, and the Out point only. If we are really trying to do the most possible with the keyboard only, this is very useful because it means that we can switch very quickly from doing a roll or ripple edit. (Remember, anytime we are working on both sides of the edit point at the same time, this is a roll, whereas working on only one side is a ripple.)

Arrow Keys to Navigate the Timeline—The Right Arrow and Left Arrow keys are used to move the playhead a single frame in either direction. Shift with the arrow keys will move a full second in either direction. The Up Arrow and Down Arrow keys move one edit point in either direction on the Timeline. If the playhead is already on an edit point that is selected (by using V, for instance), the selection also moves with the up and down arrows.

Brackets for Nudging—You can nudge either a clip or an edit point one frame forward or backward using the bracket keys. When nudging an edit point, you will be doing a ripple edit if only one side of the edit point is selected, and you will be doing a roll edit if both sides are selected (and you can toggle between these with U).

When combined with V and U for selecting edit points, and up and down arrows for moving between edit points, using brackets starts to approach an all-keyboard trimming solution.

If you combine the Shift key with the brackets, this will give you a multiframe edit. This is a ten-frame nudge by default, but the amount of the multiframe edit can be changed in the User Preferences window. Doing so will make the change not only in the bracket shortcut, but also anyplace you are making a multiframe adjustment with a button or shortcut.

Numerical Edits—Many Timeline adjustments that can be done with a drag or a nudge can also be accomplished by typing a number that corresponds to hours, minutes, seconds, and frames. This works just by typing a number when a clip or an edit point is selected in the Timeline. (Like nudging, when a clip is selected in the Timeline, this clip will be moved numerically; when both sides of an edit point are selected in the Timeline, the edit point will be rolled based on the number typed in; and if only one side of the edit point is selected, this will be a ripple edit.)

As soon as you hit the first number, you will get a dynamic pop-up on the Timeline (Figure 8.27). This indicates the type of edit you will be making, and has a field that the numbers continue to get typed into. By typing in one or two num-

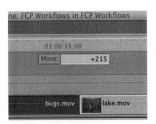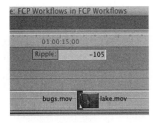

Figure 8.27 A dynamic pop-up shows you numerically what type of edit you will be making.

bers, you'll be trimming (or moving if the whole clip is selected) by frames, three to four numbers, seconds and frames, and so on in this format (hh:mm:ss:ff). The neat thing is that by typing a period after a number you enter, FCP assumes you are navigating by a whole second (the period equals 00 frames). You can further control this navigation by entering a minus sign prior to typing in numbers. By doing this FCP will trim (or move) backward.

E to Extend—Just one more, and it may seem like a one-trick pony, but this shortcut actually comes in handy. The idea is that just hitting E will extend a selected edit point to the playhead. You can also select multiple edit points (by holding down the Command key) and extend multiple edit points to the playhead simultaneously. Of course, if there is not enough media to extend the edit, then nothing will happen.

As you move further into keyboard shortcuts, you begin to combine the keystrokes and become more fluid with them. Using keyboard shortcuts actually helps you see the steps in advance, and you find yourself thinking through things more quickly. It is not that using the keyboard instead of the mouse makes you a better editor; it is just that these two things seem to happen simultaneously.

The Trim Edit Window

This window allows you to look very closely at a single edit point and make fine adjustments as you watch a loop around that edit point. This is the most up-close way to deal with an edit point. Using the Trim Edit window is pretty straightforward. In fact, a lot of the things we have just learned about roll and ripple and keyboard shortcuts also work here.

Figure 8.28 The Trim Edit window.

To open the Trim Edit window, just double-click on any edit point in the Timeline. You need to be right on an edit point and not a clip; otherwise, the clip will open in the Viewer instead. When it first opens, the Trim Edit window looks a bit like the Viewer and Browser window—but look closely, and you will see that the controls at the bottom of the window are actually different.

There are some important things to notice in the way this window works. The two video frames represent the media on either side of the edit point, similar to what you see in the Canvas when doing a roll or ripple edit. The transport controls in the center play a loop around the edit point, rather than a single clip. The buttons in the gray area below the transport controls allow you to actually trim the edit point.

Notice that there is a green bar across the top of both video images. This is the indicator for which side of the edit is going to be trimmed, or whether both sides are going to be trimmed. When the green bar goes across both images, as it does when the Trim Edit window is first opened, this indicates that both sides of the edit will be adjusted—in other words, that a roll edit will be performed. When the green line is over only one of the video frames, this indicates that only that side of the edit will be adjusted—in other words, a ripple edit.

Next, mouse over the window, particularly in the center of the window, where the two video frames touch. Notice the mouse pointer when it is over the video frames. When it is over the right frame, the mouse pointer becomes the Ripple tool with the tail to the right. When over the left frame, it becomes the Ripple tool with the tail to the left. And when the mouse pointer is over the line between the video frames, the pointer becomes the Roll tool. Click when you see any of these pointers, and you will set the Trim Edit window to edit that side (or sides) of the edit. This is how you move the green bar, by clicking on the side of the edit that you want to ripple (or in the center, if you want to roll the edit).

If this tool is new to you, you may just want to try combining switching sides of the edit, and making single-frame and multiframe edits with the buttons without playing the loop. This is an alternate way of making these edits, but really, the beauty of the Trim Edit window is to make the adjustment on the fly, while continuously watching a loop of the edit. This is useful for making a very detailed edit that needs to be perfect.

To make edits while looping in the Trim Edit window (called dynamic trimming), the small check box (Dynamic) on the bottom of the window must be checked. Now, using JKL on the keyboard, you can to trim dynamically. Depending which side you're editing or both (the green bar), each time you hit K the edit will update. In addition the side you place the cursor on (*place*, not click) is the one you will preview prior to making the new edit. Combine all of this with the loop functionality of the Trim Edit window and you have one of the best ways to fine-tune an edit.

It should now be clear how ripple and role as concepts are intrinsic to the function of the Trim Edit window. You'll be glad to know that the keyboard shortcuts that we just learned for trimming also operate in this environment. So, tapping U still toggles through Ripple In Point, Ripple Out Point, and Roll. If you have the Trim Edit window open, you will see the green bar change, as well as the selected edit point on the Timeline.

Rough Cuts, Workflows, and the Future

The rough-cut stage is one area where a lot of tensions have been felt during the democratization of the medium. We can recall seeing the rolling eyes of salespeople at postproduction houses when their clients first started bringing in their own rough cuts (as well as the sad faces of the employees who were let go when these same companies failed to adapt to the changing postproduction environment). Offline editing, the old name for many of the general techniques discussed in this chapter, used to be a lucrative service for post houses to provide. This is rarely the case anymore.

From a business and technical perspective, due largely to Final Cut Pro, this work has clearly shifted to less expensive, less dedicated machines. Things have also fundamentally changed from a creative and editorial standpoint. Because so many individuals and small production companies can now do their own nonlinear editing on the desktop, the range of people who now have the opportunity of having the creative experience of actually cutting has increased tremendously.

In Chapter 6: Preparation, we made a big deal over editing scripts and paper edits. This is all part of the same theme. The creative freedom of nonlinear editing is powerful. It allows new ideas to be tried out quickly, and fosters an intense collaborative environment. If this freedom is not tempered by some knowledge of the process and workflow planning, the result will be less than professional. With great power comes great responsibility.

This all has to do with one of the central themes of this book, which is how traditional roles and processes have been changed (in both good and bad ways) by new technologies, especially FCP. There is no topic more central to this discussion than where the rough cut is done, who does it, by how many people, and how they collaborate.

Here is the kicker—we are now only at the middle of the beginning of this revolution. The ways in which "producers" and "editors" (and lots of other people, which is a big part of the point) will collaborate to create their video projects will continue to change rapidly. For instance, one of the features of Final Cut Server is that producers will be able to cut rudimentary sequences in a simple cuts-only environment outside Final Cut Pro. This is now considered part of media-management solutions. We have no doubt that in the future, people will be logging on to web sites that let them rough cut their wedding videos, and journalists will be rough cutting on handheld devices (if not color correcting, mixing, and broadcasting with them as well).

There are two additional chapters on Final Cut Server workflows on the Web at *http://booksite.focalpress.com/Osder/finalcut/*.

9 The Review Process

They say that writing is really rewriting.

Editing is very much the same; it's all about review and revision. We cannot over-emphasize the importance of feedback and adjustment. It is the nature of any creative activity, but in postproduction especially, that the closer you are to something, the harder it is to see.

This is not meant to be some Zen koan. It's just that when you have spent days in the editing room with the same material, you are so focused on the details, and you know the footage so well, that it is literally hard to see it for what it is. In postproduction, we talk about "fresh eyes." This simply means bringing in new people to review cuts of your piece at strategic milestones.

Sometimes the review process is with clients and stakeholders, and the goal is approval. Other times, reviews are with collaborators or members of your creative community. In this case, you may be looking for creative input and new ways of seeing challenging issues.

The review process exists as a feedback loop in most workflows. Sometimes this is an iterative process, where the same team members review and adjust until all parties are happy. Sometimes reviews need to progress up a corporate ladder—one boss must approve before the next one can see.

Some projects specify the number of reviews and exactly where they fall in the workflow and schedule. This sort of structure is useful when a project is on a very tight schedule. It is also used by some vendors to help define the scope of a project. A project-scope document might specify two rounds of review, and that any others will be charged extra.

A review can take place at any point in the project. It is best to plan several reviews at different milestones to focus on different aspects. Communicating with your reviewers about what you are trying to get out of a review is crucial.

The mechanics of the review process are the topic of this chapter. It is also understood that the feedback needs to be acted on back in the editing room. Obvious, we know, but it brings up an important point: make sure to put time in your schedule for review *AND REVISION*. Don't give your client their first look at the piece only two days before the final deadline!

Our discussion of the review process has two parts:

1. Some general thoughts and tips on getting the most from the review process
2. Detailed instruction about using the Web to facilitate the review process

Tips on the Review Process

The following is a collection of ideas that help the review process go smoothly. Like building almost any other part of the workflow, the review process has no strict rules. It is better to suit the process around the needs of the project and the team.

1. *Have specific reviews for specific purposes—be strategic.* As mentioned above, you should plan major reviews at key milestones in the workflow. Although it may be good from time to time to bring in fresh eyes spontaneously, it is also good to include in your workflow specific times for reviews, what team members will participate, and what the goals are. Major review sessions could be held after the first assembly and before committing to the picture lock, for instance.

2. *Prepare the review cut so that it best suits the purpose of the review.* When you are reviewing the rough cut, content and flow are the most important things. Therefore, online review with a low-quality web file might be the perfect solution to review a rough cut (visual quality is not important at this stage). Conversely, if the reviewers need to comment on graphics or titling, you need to provide a high-quality review copy. (This could still be web based, but at a higher quality.) If you need your client to approve a DVD, you must provide a working proof with menus, compression, and everything—not just a copy of the video that goes on the DVD. The point is: for each review, prepare your review screener in a way that makes it easy for your reviewers to focus on the things you want them to.

3. *Communicate with your reviewers about the goals of the review (and communicate with your reviewers about everything else too).* Communication is key to all parts of this process. The more that you are able to explain the purpose of the review, the better notes you will get on your piece. Review and feedback can be an intimate process, and it is good to keep lines of communication as open as possible. Maybe during the review, a reviewer has additional questions about your audience. Don't let this opportunity to expand the discussion pass you by. There is probably some worthwhile feedback behind the questions. You should strive for an environment where any and all questions organically bubble up to the top with as little friction as possible. Deep and careful communication throughout will yield the best results.

4. *Take detailed notes using timecode reference.* Anyone involved in the review should take notes, and base those notes on the timecode of the piece. Depending on the size and style of review, different reviewers might compare and consolidate notes, you may use those notes to brief the editor, or sometimes the notes themselves will just get used as a hit list for changes to the piece. There are two elements to this— they are pretty straightforward, but we want to make them abundantly clear:

   a. Use notes so that you can remember what you were thinking. Thoughts and ideas come quickly during a review session. Sometimes we have trouble even getting them all written down. Without notes, it would be impossible.

   b. Use timecode so that it is easy to find the part of the piece that your note is about. Timecode is always going to work better than trying to describe a shot in your notes. Depending on the review format, the timecode might be burned right into the image, or you may need to look at a separate readout. Chapter 6 has instructions for adding timecode using the timecode reader filter.

5. *If possible, watch the piece together with the whole team.* The best way to do a review is all sitting together watching the piece and discussing. Notwithstanding that much of the rest of this chapter is about online reviews, there is no substitute for sitting together and watching a piece. This discussion does not remove the need for notes. You get the purest most direct feedback when you can see people's initial reaction to viewing a piece. The drawback to this is that some ideas take some time to percolate. If you begin your review with a group viewing session, it is also good to allow your reviewers to digest and then offer follow-up comments.

6. *Be gentle.* When you are reviewing someone's work, remember that no matter what you think is wrong with it, someone has already put in a lot of time and effort up to this point. We discussed above how editing is no different from other creative activities in the need for fresh eyes. It is also no different when it comes to the thin skin of the creators. Remember to be gentle and diplomatic when delivering a critique. It is not uncommon for people to be initially resistant or defensive when receiving feedback. Sometimes you will need to work into more difficult issues slowly, or come back around to something later in the review once the communication has warmed. Remember this especially if you are writing your review in an email. Email has that special way of sometimes reading more harshly than intended.

Online Reviews

Using the Internet to facilitate the postproduction process is one of the most exciting and money-saving innovations of the past decade. Whereas the previous section was about the review process in general, this section focuses on using the Internet and web video to streamline the process of reviewing cuts with clients and team members. Although we may prefer to do our review sessions in person, the convenience, ease, and economy of moving the process online are all very compelling. Online reviews have become ubiquitous.

The advantages of online review are numerous, but the biggest one is the savings of time and money. This is particularly apparent on a project when there are a large number of reviewers, and when they are geographically distant.

For one of the last projects we did before online review became prevalent, about half a dozen executives needed to see a cut at the end of each editing day. These executives were scattered around the country, and the cost to make the VHS tapes and FedEx them ran easily into thousands of dollars.

They key to saving time and money with online reviews is providing the video files in a way that anyone (even those who are not particularly technical) can access them easily. This means taking into account many of the same factors that are considered when creating web video for a general audience, as well as concerns particular to the process on a specific project.

You don't want to force your client to get a plug-in or wait an overly long time for a download. It is also very important to communicate with your client about these things in advance so that you know how to best prepare their video for review, and so that they know what to expect. A question such as "Does everyone in your office have QuickTime installed?" can be a big help later on.

This section briefly covers some of the fundamental concepts and issues of web video in general. This discussion is tailored to the needs of facilitating online reviews

of works in progress, but many of the ideas are applicable to consumer applications of web video as well. Also, Final Cut Server is a new product from Apple that will facilitate and streamline this process further. This is discussed some at the end of this chapter, and even more in two new web chapters available at *http://booksite.focalpress.com/ Osder/finalcut/.*

Web-Video Variables

The thing that makes the Web most challenging for creators of traditional media (print and television) is the lack of control. One has to come to accept the fact that when working on the Web, your final product is produced on the user's machine, and therefore is slightly (or sometimes not so slightly) different almost every time. Unfortunately, web video has always been one of the trickier parts of the web landscape because the content is played by an additional piece of software (a plug-in) in addition to your Internet browser, and this means even more variables that can have an effect on performance.

The basic methodology in planning for a web-video project is to analyze your audience, and then choose parameters to accommodate what you know about the audience and the content. Luckily, when preparing video for online review, your audience is smaller, and you can usually get a pretty good idea what equipment your users will be using in order to view. For instance, does everyone in the office have a broadband connection?

The key variables that you want to account for in web-video projects are:

Connection Speed—This is still a factor in any web-based project. Now that broadband has become more prevalent, however, file size is not as big a concern as it once was. Often in web video produced for a wide audience, you will still see different-sized versions to accommodate different connection speeds. This is generally not a solution for online reviews because making alternate versions takes time, and image quality is often too important for a low-bandwidth review.

Operating System (OS) and Hardware—These are the next two things you should consider for any web-video project because web-video applications work differently on different platforms. Again, for online reviews, this is less of a concern, because you can find out if your client is all Mac or all PC.

Different Browsers—A central issue in designing anything for the Web is that different browsers will do slightly different things with various web-video file types. For the most part, though, if you plan for the OS and the plug-in, you will probably be okay with the browser. In the case of online reviews, it may be appropriate to tell your review group which browser to use (you can't really do this with a public web site).

Video Architecture—What architecture (or, from the user side, what plug-in)? That is the final question. Apple and Microsoft, the two major makers of operating systems, also each have a media player (QuickTime and Windows Media Player, respectively). Because each software company ships its media player with its OS, you can count on Windows users having Windows Media Player, and Mac users having QuickTime. However, both companies also make versions of their players for the rival operating systems. Also, there are RealPlayer, Flash, and other browser plug-ins. Lastly, each playback architecture works with its own proprietary file types (for example, .wmv for Windows Media Player and .mov for QuickTime), but many plug-ins are also capable of playing back generic file types. For instance, Windows Media Player, QuickTime, and RealPlayer are all capable of playing .mpg video files and .mp3 audio files.

If this seems like a big mess, well, it can be. However, we can continue to consider ourselves lucky that we are using web video for online reviews with a small and defined audience. When preparing web video for a general audience, it is a real challenge to set all of these variables in a way that will work with most users without compromising quality. This is why many web sites end up offering the user different choices for web video.

When preparing video for online review, the task is relatively simple because you can know much more about your audience. On the other hand, the consequences of failure can be much worse when using the Web for online reviews. Consider, if a video for a general audience fails to play on a specific machine, the only harm is that a particular user misses out on some content. If a video posted for online review fails for a reviewer, it can affect the whole postproduction schedule and even affect your client's confidence in your ability to deliver.

Downloads, Streaming, and Progressive Download

Before we move into specific techniques for online reviews, it is worth defining some terms that are often confused.

- *Streaming* is a term that is often used incorrectly. True streaming video on the Internet actually works much like a traditional broadcast medium—the video plays simultaneously as it is being received on the client computer. This type of streaming requires special server software, and is transferred via a special protocol (Real Time Streaming Protocol, or RTSP). This is generally overkill for an online review, and not something we cover here.

- *Video download* is the opposite of streaming. The idea here is that an entire video program is downloaded to a local machine and stored before it can be played. Some organizations use an FTP server for this type of file transfer. (More on the FTP protocol in the sidebar, FTP and HTTP Protocols). Video downloads have some

---

FTP and HTTP Protocols

FTP (File Transfer Protocol) and HTTP (Hypertext Transfer Protocol) are two common transfer protocols for the Internet. A protocol is a set of rules governing communication within and between computing endpoints.

- HTTP is the protocol that allows browsers to receive web pages (hypertext documents) to be viewed in a browser.

- FTP is a common protocol for transferring files from a local computer and a server, but it is transfer only. There is nothing in the protocol that supports display (like HTTP does).

  FTP transfers can be done in a few ways:

  1. A dedicated FTP program such as Fetch, Transmit, or Coffee Cup (there are many of these, and some are free).

  2. A secure web site. Many production companies have an area of their web site that uses FTP for client transfers and reviews.

  3. Natively in the OS. Most operating systems support FTP access to servers right in the OS.

  Just remember, FTP is only about file transfer. Its only purpose is moving something to or from the server

advantages for online review. Reviewers may appreciate having the file saved on their hard drive so they can easily go back to it without needing to go online.

- *Progressive download* is somewhat of a compromise between true streaming video and video download. The idea is that the video starts downloading and begins playing when enough of it has downloaded to play to the end without interruption. This requires the computer to make an estimate based on the download speed and the file size. The video playback is controlled by the plug-in, and the data is transferred through the common HTTP protocol. No special server software is required. (When you view a QuickTime on the Web and in the playback bar, you see a gray loading bar extend, and then you see the playhead "chase" it to the end—this is a representation of the progressive download.)

Exporting from FCP

We have discussed some of the considerations and parameters of making video files appropriate for the Web. The next two sections give detailed instructions on how to make these exports from FCP, as well as some recommended settings to use.

When exporting files from FCP for review, there are three choices under File > Export that will be particularly useful: QuickTime Movie, using QuickTime Conversion, and using Compressor. (There is more about some of the other choices in the Export menu in Chapter 13.)

Each one of these choices is a different variation on the same theme: making an export to create a new file for displaying video and audio, and controlling the codec and parameters of that export. The three tools each have a different level of robustness, control, and complexity.

QuickTime Movie

The simplest of these export features is QuickTime Movie. Because we know that Final Cut Pro is based on the QuickTime video architecture, and we know that most of FCP's native media files are QuickTime files (.mov), it stands to reason that exporting a QuickTime file should be easy, quick, and painless—and in fact, it is.

Export QuickTime Movie is not particularly useful for creating files for web review, but it is useful for creating the native QuickTime files that are commonly used in Final Cut Pro. When you choose this option, the window that you get looks a lot like a Save As window you might see in any program. This is accurate—you are saving your sequence as a new QuickTime file.

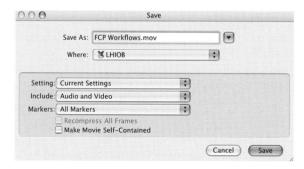

Figure 9.1 The window that you get when you choose File > Export > QuickTime Movie looks much like a familiar Save As dialogue box.

The Save window has familiar controls to name your file and place it in the proper directory on the proper drive. The pulldowns at the bottom of the window give you a small amount of control over the export you are about to make.

Settings—By default, the Settings pulldown is set to Current Settings. This means that the export that you make will have the same settings as the sequence you are exporting from. The other choices under Settings are the same as the sequence presets list. This means that what Export QuickTime is really good at is kicking out new QuickTime movies in any of the flavors that Final Cut Pro normally uses. If you are working on an HD sequence, and you want to export a DV QuickTime (fairly good quality, not as large as your HD project), Export QuickTime is a good way to go, but for web outputs, the other two choices (discussed next) will be better.

Include—A quick place to make an export of audio only or video only (Audio and Video is the default). This is handy for lots of reasons—for example, you can choose the Video Only option to give footage to a motion-graphics artist.

Markers—As discussed further in Chapter 11, this pulldown lets you include certain types of markers that can be read by other software in Final Cut Studio. You can also export all of your markers to QuickTime. This means that you will see your marker names come up in the QuickTime player as you play that part of a clip. That can be handy for reviews.

There is one more thing worth noting in this Save window, and that is the two small check boxes under the pulldown menus:

Recompress All Frames—This check box tells FCP to analyze every frame for the new file. This is recommended only as a troubleshooting measure if you are having a problem getting something to export.

Make Movie Self-Contained—This check box tells FCP to include the actual media in the new QuickTime file. If left unchecked, the new QuickTime file will be just a reference movie—in other words, a small file with instructions telling which media clips to play for the sequence exported. This makes for a small file, but it will play back only on the computer that has access to the associated media.

This can by useful for certain kinds of reviews. For example, perhaps you are working the night shift, and you want your producer, who comes in in the morning, to view your work. Because your producer doesn't know how to use FCP, you need to make things simple. You can put a reference movie on the desktop for your producer. You can even name it "Double-Click to Play." It doesn't get any more foolproof than that!

Export Using QuickTime Conversion

As we already know, QuickTime is an architecture that can play more than its own file type. Along with .mov files, QuickTime can play .mp3, .wav, and .aiff audio files; .mpg and .mp4 video files; .jpg and .png still-image files; and many, many more.

The idea of QuickTime Conversion is that you can make an export to one of these other file types that QuickTime supports, but one that is not necessarily native to FCP. One place, besides reviews, where this comes in handy is when you need an export for a different medium—say, some still exports for the Web, or some audio exports for the radio. A number of the choices available with QuickTime Conversion are useful for web reviews also.

When you choose File > Export > Using QuickTime Conversion, the Save window that comes up looks a lot like the one we just saw using Export QuickTime Movie. The

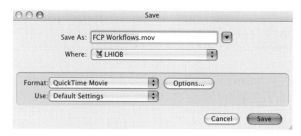

Figure 9.2 The window that you get when you choose File > Export > Using QuickTime Conversion lets you choose different options for your exported file.

only real differences are at the bottom of the window where the pulldown menus are. The options here are different—we now have pulldown menus for Format and Use, as well as an Options button.

By default, the Format menu is set to QuickTime. Without changing this, if you take a look at the Use menu, you see that the choices are presets based on connection speeds: Broadband High, Broadband Low, and so on.

Now take a look at the choices in the Format menu. These are a mixed bag of video and audio formats, along with some options for still images. For those of us who have used the program for years, this list is an interesting topic of discussion. The choices on it have changed a lot. For instance, for a long time, MP3 (MPEG-1 Layer 3) was on this list, and this was an easy way to make web audio directly out of FCP. However, MP3 is no longer on the list, and now you need to use other conversion software if you want to make that file type.

For other formats, this export technique has become more robust. For instance, the workflow to make Flash Video used to require additional software. Now, if you have the Flash authoring software installed on your computer, this export is available right on this menu. Other additions to the list over the years have included 3G (a mobile standard), iPod video, and recently Apple TV. We can only ponder the myriad of reasons (technical, political, and marketing) that led to the decisions on what export options to include and what to leave off.

The next important thing to realize is that what you pick in the Format menu determines the options you see in the Use menu. For instance, try changing Format to Wave (an audio format used for CDs). With Format set to Wave, pull down Use. You can see that this list has now become a selection of presets of audio sample rates and stereo/mono options. If you try different things on the Format menu, you will see that some choices come with their own set of presets, but for others, the Use menu (and also the Options button) are grayed out.

There is one more piece to this, which is the Options button. Click this, and you will get a separate Settings window. What is in this new window is dependent on what you have selected in the two pulldowns (Format and Use). The Format menu determines the options that you have in the Settings window, and the Use menu determines the presets these options are initially set to.

The process of making a QuickTime Conversion export goes like this:

1. *Choose your format.* This should be based on the needs of your export. If you are exporting video for an online review, you probably want either QuickTime or MP4. (The QuickTime presets in QuickTime Conversion all use the H.264 codec at the time this is written. More on this codec later.)

2. *Choose the setting to use.* Remember, these are presets that can be tweaked if necessary. It is usually a good idea to start with a preset that is close to your needs. Broadband Medium might be a good compromise between size and quality for web reviews.

3. *Tweak the options.* If none of the presets in the Use menu are exactly what you are looking for (maybe you want a small frame size but a high bitrate), use the Options button to change the setting on your chosen preset.

QuickTime Conversion is convenient for making a wide range of file types directly out of Final Cut Pro, but to have the most robust control over exports, there is another solution.

Export Using Compressor

Compressor is part of the Final Cut Studio and is a very robust standalone compression program. When you choose Export Using Compressor, Compressor will launch with a number of different windows and controls. This can be a little intimidating to some, but Compressor follows the same principles as any compression program or exporting function; it just has more controls and choices.

When you launch Compressor from Final Cut Pro, the sequence from the Timeline will already be in the Batch window. Below the Batch window is the Settings window. From here, you can drag various settings (organized by format and function) to your sequence listed in the Batch window to apply them. Additionally, you can drag output destinations from the Settings window to apply an output destination.

Compressor also excels at various types of automation. Saving presets is one of these features. When we have a client with whom we work a lot, we will save presets that work well for their reviews. Compressor can also use Apple Script so, for example, you can automate the uploading process to an FTP server. It will even email you to confirm!

Don't think that Compressor is all about presets, though. We can create or augment existing presets by using tools that can be found in the Inspector window. We can also

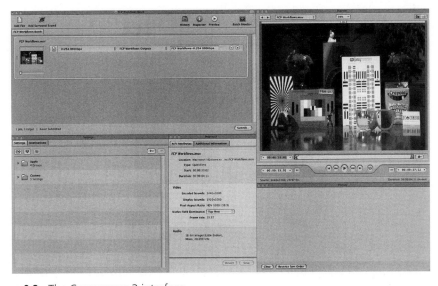

Figure 9.3 The Compressor 3 interface.

preview our compression settings, add markers, and add In and Out points for our compression in the Preview window. Although there is a lot more to Compressor, these choices are really not fundamentally different from the Format and Use menus we saw with QuickTime Conversion. Across the board, the process is similar, but Compressor is often much more versatile.

For a great guide to using Compressor, we recommend the Apple Pro Training Series: *Compressor 3 Quick Reference Guide* by Brian Gary (Peachpit Press).

Choosing a Solution

We now understand that there are variables in web video, and that communication with our reviewers is key. We understand the mechanics of making an export from FCP. So, how do we go about actually picking the codecs and settings for our online review files?

As you should realize by now, this is ultimately going to depend on your project and your reviewers, but from experience, there are some good things to try first. The following is a list of our three favorite specific solutions, including what we like them for and why.

MPEG-1—This kind of video has been around for over ten years. It creates relatively large files with relatively poor quality and little control over parameters, including size. Why, then, would we put it on this list of useful formats for web reviews? MPEG-1 does have some benefits:

- It is probably the web-video file type that will play without technical problems on the widest range of computers. Because this format has been around so long, it is recognized and playable by most video architectures.

- It encodes quickly compared to other web-video codecs.

- For early reviews such as rough cuts, it provides a good amount of detail, but small image size and poor quality discourage nitpicking.

We find that when considering these kinds of technological questions, there is a tendency to either go with the latest and greatest solution, or stick with an old workhorse. MPEG-1 is the old workhorse of web video. We still like it because we can quickly make an output, and can have confidence that any user with a web connection will be able to view it.

Now let's look at the latest and greatest.

QuickTime H.264—The H.264 codec is an MPEG-4 variant that is the latest in a long line of codecs that Apple has introduced to provide the best possible image quality at the smallest file size. The main advantage of using H.264 for online reviews is that you can provide your client with a file that approaches full broadcast size and quality on the Web. The disadvantages of H.264 include:

- It takes a LONG time to encode.

- Reviewers need to have an up-to-date version of the QuickTime software. This is free, but it may need to be downloaded and installed.

- Although H.264 makes a great size-to-quality ratio, when using it to produce large high-quality videos, those files are still very large.

Using this codec tends to be great when you have strong communications with your reviewers and they are fairly technically savvy. If they have the proper software (or can get it), and they understand that the reason for the slow download is the large size and high quality (which is to say, they realize that it is worth the wait), clients tend to be very happy with this solution for reviews.

One thing that we like to do is use MPEG-1 early in the review process. This format is quick, and it gets reviewers to focus on the content, which is what we want in the earlier stages. Later, we use H.264 to show off detail work, such as graphics. When near-final pieces need to be circulated to a wider group, we often provide both an H.264 file and an MPEG-1 file as backup to cover our bases.

Of course, it is our preference to have clients come into the studio and approve a final deliverable at its highest possible quality. We have found that when using high-quality H.264 compressions for review, clients often prefer to just do their final approval online.

Windows Media Video—Whoa! Where did that one come from? Might be one of the few times you see the *W*-word in this book, but Windows Media is the third format that we find particularly useful for the review process.

Why?

- These files will play on most any Windows machine, and many Mac users can play them also.

- The quality-to-size ratio for Windows Media is comparable to H.264, if not better.

- Windows Media is particularly good at playing web videos that are at full broadcast size.

- It is much quicker to encode these files than to encode H.264 files.

Of course, to encode .wmv files, you will need some more software beyond FCP or Compressor. There are several solutions available, but we happen to like the ones from Telestream (*www.flip4mac.com*). These are a suite of utilities that allow the Mac to get along better with Windows Media. There are several levels to the software, from a free play-only plug-in to several levels of supported encoding, including hi def.

Posting to the Web

Once you have prepared these files, putting them on the Web should not be complicated. Most of the important concepts for this are covered at the beginning of this chapter. When you place any of the file types above on an HTTP server, and link directly to it (e.g., *www.yoursite.com/reviews/rough-cut.mov*), this file will play on most computers. To keep things simple, this is what we most often do to post cuts for reviewers. We put the file on the server, and send an email with the link and any technical or reviewing instructions.

Of course, there are all kinds of extra things you can do on the Web. Mentioned before was a secure client web site for review. This may support commenting on cuts through the site as well. Depending on your needs, a fully implemented web system might be overkill, but you might still code a quick HTML page to keep track of different cuts. (We tend to do this for certain types of reviews, such as casting screeners. We code a quick page with the names of all of the actors who auditioned as links to the clips. That way, we can send just one link to the page in the client email.)

There are virtually unlimited variations on this theme, from one quick page to a huge investment in web-based media-management software. Apple has just recently jumped into this game with Final Cut Server.

Final Cut Server and the Review Process

You may have noticed that this new software, just on the horizon, keeps popping into lots of the chapters in this book. Indeed, Final Cut Server is likely to have an effect on many, if not all, aspects of Final Cut Pro workflows: review of footage, media management, scripting, and rough cuts (to name a few biggies).

Using Final Cut Server for the review process may be one of the most enticing promises of the new software. The real potential of Final Cut Server is not only for the review process, or any single aspect of the process that it can facilitate. The real promise is about integration. Final Cut Studio has already started to change the way we think about the process, especially finishing. In the next chapter, there is much more about the integration possible in this area. The ultimate promise of Final Cut Server is that it will bring similar integration to the entirety of the postproduction process, and more importantly, to all members of the team.

Some of these goals have been accomplished to a degree in the past with custom solutions (we look at one of these in the case study in Chapter 16). As this chapter shows, the principles are not at all new. Many of the ideas in this chapter would apply if you were reviewing a cut over a high-speed Internet connection or sitting around a Steenbeck with a bottle of Chianti.

Still, if you take the innovations of Final Cut Studio as an indication of the potential of Final Cut Server, it is an exciting prospect.

Learn more about Final Cut server by accessing two web chapters at *http://booksite. focalpress.com/Osder/finalcut/*.

10 Final Cut Pro Finishing

We have seen a lot to this point on preparing projects, getting them into FCP, doing editorial or storytelling editing, and sharing works in progress for review and feedback. This chapter is one of three that pick up from here with instructions on how to finish a piece and get it out of Final Cut Pro.

This chapter covers finishing concepts in general, and techniques that are done from inside the FCP interface. Chapter 11 discusses integrating Final Cut Pro with other software included in Final Cut Studio. Finally, Chapter 13: Working with External Resources covers workflows that leave the Final Cut Studio environment entirely. Finishing techniques are an important part of workflows because they are highly technical, they tend to be expensive, and they often involve various handoffs from one machine or operator to another.

If we go back to the rock sculpture idea, finishing is the sandpaper and polishing cloth. A good sculptor realizes that there is a level of work that might go unnoticed by a lot of people who see the piece. However, their overall impression of the piece will benefit if all of the detail work and the polishing are done carefully.

Postproduction finishing is much the same. You will rarely get a comment that the color correction or the mix is exceptionally good (unless maybe these issues were particularly bad when you started). In fact, in a way, you don't really want those kinds of comments—they indicate that the viewer is watching the technique and not the content. The cumulative effect of finishing work should be video pieces that look and sound great, and don't draw attention to any technical aspects.

In these three chapters, we have taken a broad view of finishing as a way to bring in a wide range of activities such as DVD creation and music composition. The modern producer or editor needs to be aware of these things. DVD creation used to be a specialty; today, editors are almost expected to know how to do it. Music composition was once considered a very, very specialized skill; today, a surprising number of editors are offering some level of music-creation service. Even if you are not interested in taking on all of these skill sets, it is important to know how to interface with the people who do this work.

The choices that are made in a workflow regarding finishing have serious financial consequences. Going to an audio house or post house to do a mix or color correction session in a dedicated suite can easily run into tens of thousands of dollars. Keeping this work in-house within Final Cut Studio will save money, but will quality be sacrificed? And how long will it take? This is the same old quality-vs.-cost question that came up when talking about formats in Chapter 4.

Every project is going to be different in this regard, but planning for what finishing steps will be done where, and by whom, is an important part of any workflow. The goal of this chapter, along with Chapters 11 and 13, is to better prepare you to make and execute these decisions.

Before we look at specific techniques for finishing, it is important to understand some of the general goals and methods for this stage of postproduction. The sections that follow define these ideas in ways that will be useful regardless of whether you use the tools inside Final Cut Pro (this chapter), in Final Cut Studio (the next chapter), or even if you choose to use additional external resources (Chapter 13). The ideas are grouped here by concept, for easy reference.

Conforming and Online Editing Concepts

As mentioned in Chapter 1, the meaning of the term "online editing" has changed with the evolution of technology. One way to understand these changes is through comparison to a related term: "conform."

To conform a show means to assemble the show at its highest-quality uncompressed format, regardless of whether this task is performed in a linear or nonlinear fashion. Different ways of conforming have led to different processes for the online phase:

- When the online editing concept was first invented, it referred to using a linear editing system to conform a show at full resolution using an EDL (edit decision list) to reference the editorial decisions made in an offline editing session.

- With the advent of uncompressed nonlinear editing, onlines could now be performed in a nonlinear environment. The process still involved conforming (now also referred to as recapturing or redigitizing) to ingest the footage at the highest possible digital quality.

- Lastly, as more projects are initially captured at full uncompressed quality, there is no longer a need to conform footage. Conforming is necessary only if the footage was previously compressed for offline editing.

When the term "online" enters the workflow conversation (or when you are being hired or hiring someone to do an online), it is a good opportunity to have some deep communication about exactly what the online process is for the particular project.

Currently in the film and video world, we see the term "online" used to mean three different, related, and all totally relevant things (and the word is used for a totally different set of concepts in the web world!):

1. To conform a sequence to its highest possible quality. Today, this may involve either the linear or nonlinear methods mentioned above, or a totally digital process of moving and relinking files (think tapeless workflow).

2. To check all elements of a sequence for quality and technical issues. This usually refers to footage, stills, and motion graphics, and may even refer to audio in some cases.

3. As a catchall for any steps involved in finishing. So, many people refer to the online stage to include color correction, compositing, mix, and any other step that takes

place between completing the editorial process and delivering the show. In this sense, it is used like a phase of the process, not to mean any specific technical task.

Of course, these are not mutually exclusive, and people often mean more than one of the above when they say online. The bottom line is that online always refers to finishing and polishing a piece, and not to editorial or storytelling.

In the final meaning listed above, all of the concepts below could be said to be part of the online phase, and we could have called this chapter Online Editing with FCP. We prefer the word "finishing" because it is more descriptive, and it reserves online for its more technical sense.

Color Correction and Color Grading Concepts

One of our favorite parts of the finishing process is color correction and grading. For us, this process is where we can make a good piece shine. Good color correction and grading are subtle arts, but done well, they can drastically improve your images.

Arguably, this aspect of postproduction has seen more growth in the desktop market in recent years than any other area of finishing. Final Cut Pro and Final Cut Studio have not been exempt from this growth. FCP boasts an impressive set of real-time color correction tools inside the interface. Additionally, with Final Cut Studio 2, Apple introduced a full-fledged color program: Color.

We've been amazed recently by how many people understand the basic goals of correction and grading. We can remember just a few years ago that color correction and grading were considered only for higher-end projects. Now they have become a standard part of most workflows.

Before we discuss the color correction and color grading toolset inside Final Cut Pro and Color, we need to look at few basics.

Color Correction

The term "color correction" is often used globally to describe the process of correction and grading. Although understood by most, we like to think of correction and grading as separate concepts. Color correction, as its name implies, is all about correction, or fixing bad color and brightness issues. Examples of color correction include correcting for color casts from improper white balance and lighting, fixing over- or undersaturation of colors, fixing under- or overexposed footage, and correcting for broadcast legality (all discussed below). Many videographers and directors of photography would like to think that the images they record are perfect. The truth is that almost every shot can benefit from some color correction.

Color Grading

Color grading shares some of the same goals as correction (broadcast legality being one), and often occurs in conjunction with correction. However, it is really a wholly different concept. Grading refers to the process of giving footage a look and style. This could be done on a shot-by-shot basis, or, more commonly, grading has a goal of giving a distinctive look to the entire piece. A number of famous instances of grading in movies and television come to mind. *Traffic, The Matrix, O Brother, Where Art Thou?* and *Pleasantville* are classic examples of grading in film, *CSI, Carnival,* and *The Shield* are great modern examples of grading for television. Grading is often used to elicit an emotional response from the audience, to create a mood, or, in extreme cases, to bend reality. Because it is subjective, grading is often a much more involved process than is correction. Often the decisions that are made during grading involve many members of the postproduction team. It's common for editors, colorists, DPs (directors of photography), producers, and directors to all work together to come up with a look and feel for the piece.

Broadcast Legality

One area that color correction and grading share in common is the idea of legality. Believe it or not, broadcasters have technical rules about the video signal. These rules dictate how bright and dark an image can be, as well as the maximum saturation of the colors. Failure to comply with these standards can possibly cause your show to be rejected by a broadcaster. If you're thinking to yourself, "My show will never be broadcast" (it is going to DVD, or the Web, or cell phones), adhering to broadcast safety standards ensures greater consistency over a larger range of display devices.

Although it's always best to check with your particular broadcaster, there are a few rules to follow to meet basic requirements.

Luma—Typically, luma should be less than 100 percent on a digital scale, or 100 IRE (a unit of measurement named after the Institute of Radio Engineers) on analog scopes. Most broadcasters will, however, allow for short peaks up to 105 percent digital, or 105 IRE. Additionally, most broadcasters require that black not be below 0 percent, or 0 IRE—what is known as superblack.

Chroma—On a digital scale, chroma levels should be less than 100 percent, and less than 100 IRE on an analog scale. Most broadcasters will allow for peaks up to about 110 percent IRE. RGB saturation should also be less than 100 percent, although some broadcasters will allow for slightly higher levels. Although most video is encoded $Y'C_BC_R$, it's a safe bet that at some point during distribution, the video will be displayed on an RGB device. Therefore, monitoring these levels is very important.

Scopes

The video scopes are your primary tool for measuring and analyzing your video. They provide you a way of seeing color casts, over- or underexposure, contrast, and so on. Video scopes existed long before Final Cut Pro, and it is worth noting generally the kinds of scopes that are available.

Hardware Scopes—These are the boxes with CRT monitors that we are used to seeing in editing rooms of all kinds.

Rasterizers—These are a newer kind of scope—one that uses hardware components to analyze the video, but then runs the information through a PC, and displays (or rasterizes) it on a dedicated RGB monitor. This is basically an updated version of the hardware scopes that run through a dedicated PC.

Software Scopes—These are virtual scopes available inside software applications. In particular, both Final Cut Pro and Color have software scopes contained in them.

Let's take a look at the various scopes available to us in FCP and in Color.

Waveform Monitor—The Waveform Monitor is your primary tool to analyze luma information in your image. In Final Cut Pro, this scale ranges from –10 to 110 percent; in Color, from –20 to 110 percent. The higher the percentage, the brighter the image. In FCP, you can also view saturation on the Waveform Monitor by right-clicking and choosing Saturation. Color has a more robust set of Waveform Monitor tools allowing you to view your signal in a variety of ways.

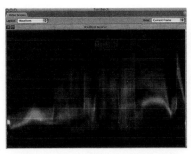
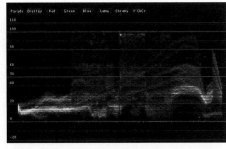

Figure 10.1 The Waveform Monitor in Final Cut Pro *(left)* and in Color *(right)*.

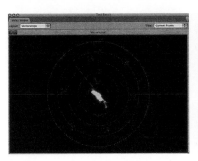
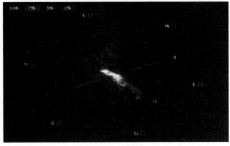

Figure 10.2 The Vectorscope in Final Cut Pro *(left)* and in Color *(right)*.

Vectorscope—The Vectorscope is your primary tool to analyze the chroma portion of your image. The center of the scale represents zero saturation; the farther out toward the edges of the scale, the greater the saturation. The direction out from center represents hue. The outside edges of the scale in both Final Cut Pro and Color represent 100 IRE. The color targets make it easy to see the hue the signal is pushing toward, and often are used as boundaries for saturation (although this a conservative approach). The Vectorscope also has additional markings for measurement. The first marking goes from the center of the scope, and shoots between the yellow and the red targets. This is known as the Flesh Tone line in Final Cut Pro. In Color, this is known as the –I bar (Inphase), and it appears in the same place. If someone appears on-screen, their skin tone, regardless of complexion, should fall somewhere on or around this line. The other marking on the Vectorscope that appears only on the Color Vectorscope is the Q bar (+Quadrature), and it's used in combination with the –I bar for troubleshooting the video signal.

3D Color Space Scope—This is a unique tool, exclusive to Color, that allows you to view luma and chroma portions of your signal in different color gamuts (RGB, HSL, $Y'C_BC_R$, IPT) in 3-D space.

Histogram—The Histogram shows the distribution of brightness values in your image. In Final Cut Pro, the Histogram shows a combination of RGB values. Color allows for further control in the Histogram—you can display RGB, red only, green only, blue only, or luma alone.

RGB Parade Scope—Parade scopes are separate waveform monitors for the red, green, and blue parts of the video signal. Because most video is not encoded as R'G'B',

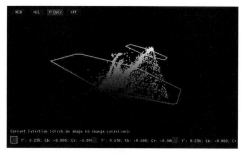

Figure 10.3 The 3D Color Space Scope in Color.

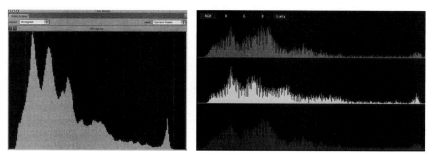

Figure 10.4 The Histogram in Final Cut Pro *(left)* and in Color *(right)*.

these scopes will show you a representation of that gamut even if the video was encoded as $Y'C_BC_R$.

Although the video scopes in Final Cut Pro and in Color are accurate to a certain degree, they should not be thought of as total replacements for hardware scopes or rasterizers (hardware-based scopes displayed on a computer monitor). Hardware scopes and rasterizers are often more accurate, and in some cases provide additional monitoring. Options such as the diamond display, which allows one to measure how $Y'C_BC_R$ fits into legal R'G'B color space, and the arrowhead display, which measures legal composite signals, are primary examples.

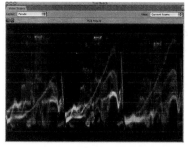 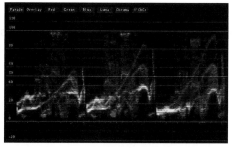

Figure 10.5 The RGB Parade Scope in Final Cut Pro *(left)* and in Color *(right)*. Note that in Color, this is not a separate scope; it appears as an option for the Waveform Monitor.

Audio-Finishing Concepts

Audio finishing goes perhaps more unnoticed than color correction and grading, but arguably contributes more to the final product. Whether it's a door slamming closed with a big thud or music swelling in just the right spot, audio finishing is much like color correction and grading—when done well, it's intangible, but, subconsciously, all these things add up to the impression of a quality piece. Fortunately, we have a strong toolset for audio finishing, both with Final Cut Pro and with Soundtrack Pro. Let's take a look at several key concepts about audio finishing.

Mixing

Mixing is a broad term that often refers more to a process than to any one particular action (much like editing). In this broad sense, mixing refers to balancing levels and making things sound good. Depending on the workflow, this might also include placing final music and/or narration. To some degree, mixing is literally about blending all of the disparate audio elements together—as they say, it's all in the mix. Mixing can be broken down further into more specific terms:

Levels, Panning, and Groupings—A large part of the audio-finishing process is balancing levels (volume) between the various pieces of audio. One often overlooked aspect of levels is broadcasters' requirements. For example, some broadcasters require that audio must average 20 decibels below full scale (–20dBFS), with peaks at –10dBFS. Adjusting panning is another large part of the mixing process. This has become increasingly important as more and more projects are being finished in surround sound, not just stereo. Audio grouping also becomes an issue for audio finishing. Today, most broadcasters have requirements for what audio should be on what channels on a master tape—for example, stereo mix of the show on channels 1 and 2; VO, sync on channel 3; music, effects , and nat sound on channel 4.

Equalization and Processing—One way to allow separate elements to blend together further is with equalization (EQ) and processing. Equalization means the boosting or cutting of frequencies; processing refers to additional processing, such as limiting, multiband compression, reverb, and special effects.

Restoration and Fixing Problems—Like video, audio material has its own unique challenges. Many of these present themselves during audio finishing. Issues such as low or superhigh levels often have to be addressed at this stage. Such problems as noise from an air conditioner or power hum can often dominate audio finishing.

Sound Design

We've always been amazed by good sound design, perhaps more than by the cumulative effect of color correction/grading and mixing. Good sound design is an incredible thing because it relies heavily on attention to the physical world, and often on the exaggeration of it. If you think about it, those creaky footsteps across a wood floor in your favorite horror movie or the boom of a massive explosion in the latest spy television drama—taken together with other aspects of the mix—really add a lot to the final product. Sound design relies heavily on the following:

Sound Libraries—Software programs such as Soundtrack Pro contain sound libraries that are at the heart of the toolset for sound design. These libraries are often chock-full of prerecorded sounds such as crashes, screams, noises found in nature, and so on. A good sound designer will develop his or her own library of favorite sounds from different sources over years of work.

Foley—When the desired sound cannot be emulated with a prerecorded sound from a library, oftentimes the only option is to record that sound. These recordings are typically done using a process known as Foley (named after the American sound technician Jack D. Foley). In this process, Foley artists employ various props and actions to create the desired sounds.

Music Creation

So you're finishing your soon-to-be-award-winning documentary—and realize that you forgot to budget for an original score for the project. Have no fear! There are quick and inexpensive ways to get a score for your film. Increasingly, part of the audio-finishing process is music "creation." That being said, the techniques below should not be thought of as a substitute for original composition and recording a score. They are approximations only, and the highest-quality original content still uses original music.

Here are two things you can try if you lack the money or the time for original music:

Music Libraries—There are a plethora of music libraries on the market. The biggest factor when choosing a library is that it should provide you the variety that you need. We are big fans of Pump Audio (*www.pumpaudio.com*).

Creation via Loops—Applications such as Soundtrack Pro and GarageBand (part of iLife '08) allow you to use modular pieces of music and sound to make original new compositions. Of course, these are not original in the sense that a real composition would be, but they are more original than what would come from a library. Composing with loops is somewhat of a compromise in that way.

Motion Graphics and Compositing Concepts

Chances are, even if you don't consider yourself a motion graphics artist or compositor, you're often called on to do these tasks. The terms "motion graphics" and "compositing" are broad concepts that today include text design and animation, simulated camera movement and lighting, greenscreen and bluescreen keying, masking, and even stabilization and tracking. Final Cut Pro and Motion together provide a robust set of tools for creating motion graphics and compositing. Let's take a look at some key concepts.

Text Effects—Creating interesting and captivating text effects is at the heart of most motion graphics and compositing workflows. These effects can be as simple as text fading up and then down for a lower third, or can be a complex set of animations of text flying about for a show open. Compositing of text also plays into the overall effect. We've all probably seen text with images or video placed inside of it (think flowing water). This combination of animation and compositing can create some pretty cool looks.

Masking and Keying—Two other areas of motion graphics and compositing that have a lot of time dedicated to them are masking and keying. Masking refers to using predefined or user-created shapes to show or hide certain areas of an image. A classic use of a mask is to create a spyglass or binocular outline for a point-of-view shot. Keying is a related subject, and is a way of removing specific chroma or luma values from an image. Keying is often used to remove subjects from a greenscreen or bluescreen background for the purpose of placing them on a different background.

Figure 10.6   The original clip *(left)* and with a mask applied *(right)*.

Figure 10.7   The original clip prior to the key *(left)* and after the key *(middle)*, composited on a background *(right)*.

Keyframing—Whether it's having a filter change properties over time or having a piece of text animate on-screen, keyframes are what make this possible. Keyframes are the way you tell Final Cut Pro to change a value over time. Almost every desktop video or motion graphics program allows keyframing. Of course, the complexity of your keyframing is dependent largely on the complexity of the effect that you are trying to create.

Stabilization and Tracking—Have you ever had the experience of having to deal with shaky footage that was so bad you wondered if the camera operator had had a few drinks before starting to shoot? Luckily, we can stabilize those shots! Stabilization is relatively new to desktop motion graphics and compositing applications, but we can now save plenty of shots that would have been discarded in the past. We can do this with stabilization tools in Final Cut Pro, Motion 3, and Shake. Additionally, we can now track masks and color corrections and other elements as they move through a shot, a process that, until recently, either had to be done manually or required additional tools.

Blending—One goal of most motion graphics and compositing tasks is to get disparate items to blend together. There is a variety of techniques that can be applied to do this, but common methods include using opacity and blend modes (sometimes called composite modes). Opacity means the relative transparency of an image. If an image has an opacity of 100 percent, it is completely opaque; if its opacity is 50 percent, the image is semitransparent. Blend modes and composite modes use different mathematical computations to combine pixels of multiple images together.

Lights, Camera, Particles—One of the more exciting aspects of motion graphics design and compositing is using virtual lights, cameras, and particle systems. By using lights and cameras, we are able to simulate and sometimes embellish real-world shooting and lighting situations. Particle systems take this simulation a step further. Using particle systems, we can create lifelike weather systems (for example, rain, snow, fire, explosions), and more abstract particle systems to create interesting effects and textures that can be used for a multitude of purposes such as lower thirds, background, and so forth.

Finishing Techniques inside Final Cut Pro

Now that we have an overview of some common techniques and concepts in the realm of finishing, let's get to the heart of this chapter: the finishing tools that are available right inside Final Cut Pro.

When the program was first introduced, many saw FCP's main strength as an offline edit solution. As desktop computers have become more powerful, and as the FCP toolset has expanded, Final Cut Pro is now being seen as a more reasonable tool for professional finishing work. Many people at all levels of postproduction use FCP for their first, last, and only step on a project.

The main advantage of doing finishing work inside the FCP interface is that all of your work is conveniently accessible to you. Most of this gets done on clips in the Viewer or even directly on the Timeline. It is definitely convenient to tweak an audio filter or color correction setting in the same place that you can make a trim.

The main disadvantage to working this way is that you are stretching outside the core functionality of the program. FCP's core strength is editing. Sure, it has some audio, color correction, and motion graphics tools, but we should not expect these toolsets to be as robust as the ones inside a program that is dedicated to a specific finishing task. In general, we like to see people use software for its core capabilities, but sometimes this is not practical or economical. As with so many new and inexpensive methods, one can get very acceptable, even exceptional, finishing work out of the FCP interface if it is used with knowledge, care, and skill.

Lastly, we don't want to imply that this is an all-or-nothing proposition—that finishing is done either inside FCP or outside. These methods are combined in many different ways for different projects. A good workflow is strategic about what finishing steps are done where, and especially about how the transfers between these steps happen.

Online Editing and Conforming within Final Cut Pro

The resolution-independent nature of Final Cut Pro and the inherent flexibility FCP brings with it really shine when doing any kind of online process. As described in Chapter 1: What Makes Final Cut Pro Special? conforming a show originally cut with Final Cut Pro does not require any sort of EDL. It is simple to perform a conform, all from within the FCP project.

Here are general instructions for a conform. Of course, the specifics may vary depending on your exact workflow, the format(s) you are using, and especially if you are working with more than one frame rate or video standard. The steps below assume that you are using a tape-based workflow. The steps start with the use of the Media Manager tool, which is covered in depth in the next chapter.

1. Select the final picture-locked sequence from the offline version of the project.
2. Go to File > Media Manager.

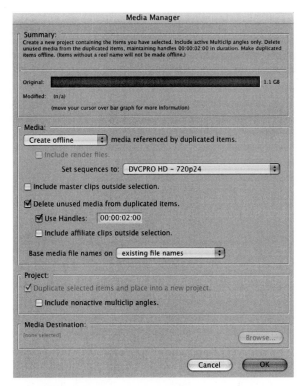

Figure 10.8 The Media Manager window with the described settings.

3. Choose Create offline from the Media pulldown. In the Set sequences pulldown, make sure you choose the correct settings for the sequence you will be conforming to, not the one you are media managing.

4. UNCHECK the "Include master clips outside selection" option—you want only the media from the clips on the Timeline.

5. Next, check "Delete unused media from duplicated clips," and add a few seconds of handles in case you need to adjust edit points in the online edit. Usually one to two seconds is enough. UNCHECK "Include affiliate clips outside selection."

6. Choose how you want to base media file names. Generally the best option is to use existing file names. Click OK. This will prompt you to save a new project file. Give the project a name and save it. After you have saved, FCP will process your clips. This might take some time as the program calculates media usage.

7. Once processing is complete, the project you just saved will open in FCP. You will notice two things: your sequence and a bin called Master Clips. The sequence name will always be the name of the original sequence you media managed.

8. Open the Master Clips bin. You'll notice that all of the clips are offline—exactly what you wanted! Select all of the clips, right-click, and choose Batch Capture.

9. Final Cut Pro will open up the Log and Capture window with the Batch Capture dialogue box on top. Using the Batch Capture dialogue box, make sure you choose to capture all the items in the logging bin. Check Use Logged Clip Settings, but

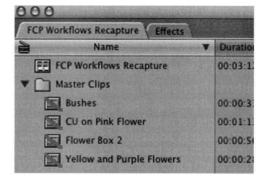

Figure 10.9 The Master Clips bin with offline clips and the sequence.

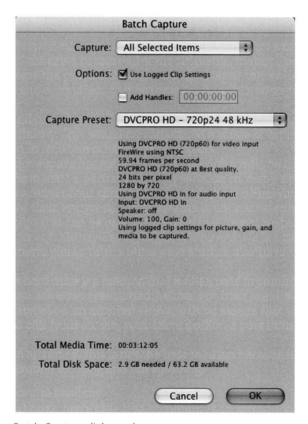

Figure 10.10 The Batch Capture dialogue box.

uncheck Add Handles because when you previously managed the offline sequence, you added handles. Make sure you are using the correct capture preset (this should match the settings for the online sequence).

10. Take a look at the media calculations and disk space needed. If these numbers are way off, you might have accidentally chosen to include master or affiliate clips outside your selection. In this case, you will need to go back to the offline version of the project and repeat the steps to create an offline version of the sequence. If these look correct, simply click OK.

11. Final Cut Pro will then present a dialogue box with all of the reels and the number of clips on each reel that will need to be captured. Insert the first tape and click OK. Repeat the process until all clips are loaded.

Keep in mind, this is capturing only footage used in the sequence that has timecode and reel references. Other items, such as stills, motion clips, or audio, will have to be moved to the online system and reconnected manually.

As mentioned above, many projects no longer need to be conformed because they are captured at uncompressed quality from the get-go. Chapter 16: 30-Second Spot for Broadcast is a case study of this sort of workflow. In such workflows, it is still important to define an online stage. This may include the workflow for color correction, or just the plan to prep the show for broadcast.

There is one more interesting Final Cut Pro finishing technique that we want to mention here: converting to an uncompressed (generally 10-bit) or a ProRes 422 sequence for finishing work in FCP. The reasons for wanting to do this are a bit technical, but the results can be undeniable.

The basic idea is that when working with footage that uses lots of compression and a low chroma subsampling ratio (DV or HDV), you up-convert this footage to uncompressed or ProRes 422 color space in the sequence (these have a better chroma subsampling ratio of 4:2:2). You then perform your color correction and compositing in this color space.

One place where this will be the most noticeable is when you are compositing text or graphics over moving footage. Have you ever noticed that when you do this on a DV Timeline, it does not always look so good? The reason is that in the compressed (4:1:1) color space of the DV codec, there are fewer colors that the compositing algorithm uses to create smooth edges. When you convert a sequence to uncompressed or ProRes 422, you will instantly see all of your graphics composite more cleanly. Of course, uncompressed or ProRes 422 color space will also give you more control in color correction due to its chroma subsampling.

Converting to a higher color space is not difficult. Here are instructions for going from HDV to uncompressed HD, but you could use similar steps for going from DV to uncompressed SD.

1. Create a new sequence. Name it appropriately so you can distinguish it from the original sequence.

2. Go to Sequence > Settings. This will open the Sequence Settings dialogue box. Make sure that your frame size, pixel aspect ratio, field dominance, and editing timebase are all the same as your orginal sequence.

3. Using the Compressor pulldown, choose Uncompressed 10-bit 4:2:2 (you could also choose the Apple ProRes 422 codec if your drives were not fast enough to support uncompressed playback).

4. Next, click on the Video Processing tab in the Sequence Settings dialogue box. Here, you want to choose "Render 10-bit material in high-precision YUV." This will give you the best-looking renders, although doing so will take longer. Click OK to save your settings.

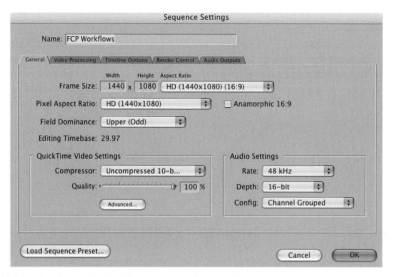

Figure 10.11 The Sequence Settings dialogue box.

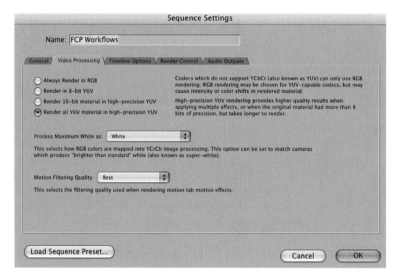

Figure 10.12 The Video Processing tab in the Sequence Settings dialogue box.

5. Find your original Timeline in the Browser. Make sure your playhead is parked on the beginning of the new empty sequence. Drag your original Timeline into the new empty Timeline, but make sure that you HOLD DOWN THE COMMAND KEY. This will bring all of the clips, NOT A NEST, into the empty Timeline. Note: you can drag the original Timeline to the Canvas window as well, and do an overwrite edit while holding down the Command key. However, using this method, you must have the same number of audio and video tracks created on the new sequence as you did on the original before performing the edit.

6. Finally, render the new sequence.

It's important to note that you could have also simply opened and changed the sequence settings on the original Timeline. However, using the method described above, you did two things: (1) your original was untouched, and (2) because you started with a blank sequence, you avoided having links to bad render files. We have seen problems with FCP linking to old render files when simply switching over a sequence to uncompressed. Making a new sequence and editing the original seems to fix these types of problems.

Color Correction and Grading within Final Cut Pro

Over the years, we have been fortunate enough to participate in quite a few large (read: expensive) and complicated postproduction projects. Almost always, a large portion of the expense and complexity of those projects has to do with color correction and grading. These projects were for the most part corrected in dedicated suites with *very* expensive hardware.

We can remember the first time we suggested to a client that we color-correct their show using the Final Cut Pro toolset. Let's just say our client gave us one of those looks that said, "You're joking, right?" Well, after successfully completing that project, we have been color-correcting corporate and broadcast shows ever since. Using FCP's toolset to color-correct is often the fastest and most straightforward way to correct a show.

We have also used Final Cut Pro to grade shows to create unique looks, although, for many broadcast programs, this type of stylizing is generally subtle and straightforward. For documentary, feature, and music video projects, Final Cut Pro can be a perfect tool to grade, especially if you combine several techniques in the application.

Perhaps no part of color correcting and grading is as important as proper monitoring. Although computer monitors have gotten much better over the years, they are still no substitute for a calibrated NTSC, PAL, or HD monitor. These monitors do cost a lot, but there is a reason for the price: they provide consistent reproducible color and brightness. Your corrections and grades can really be trusted only if seen on a properly calibrated and maintained monitor that will allow you to get the most from your toolset. At the very least, you should set up your system to be able to view images on regular plain-vanilla TV (although the color temperature and black levels may be suspect).

This section is intended to give you a good understanding of color correction and grading; however, it is not a complete guide. For a lot more information about correcting and grading in Final Cut Pro, check out Alexis Van Hurkman's excellent *Encyclopedia of Color Correction: Field Techniques Using Final Cut Pro* (Peachpit Press).

The toolset for color correction and grading in Final Cut Pro is found in several places.

Range Checking

One of the first ways that people are introduced to color correction in Final Cut Pro is by trying to figure out what the big green circle with a check in the middle of it (or a yellow triangle with an exclamation point) is doing in the Viewer or the Canvas!

This is known as range checking, and can be enabled in more than one way. The first method is by going to View > Range Check. Here, we can choose from the following options: Excess Luma, Excess Chroma, or Both.

The second method is in the View pulldown in both the Viewer and the Canvas window. In this pulldown, there is an option for Show Excess Luma. Note that there is not an option for chroma; you have to enable that in the View menu.

With Show Excess Luma enabled, areas in the image that are above 100 percent on the Waveform Monitor will be marked with red zebra stripes in the viewer or on the canvas. Areas of the image that are between 90 percent and 100 percent on the

Figure 10.13   Footage with illegal luma shown by the red zebra stripes and yellow triangle with exclamation point *(left)*. Footage with luma between 90 and 100 percent shown by a green circle with a check and an upward-facing arrow *(right)*.

Figure 10.14   Footage with illegal chroma shown by the red zebra stripes and yellow triangle with exclamation point.

Waveform Monitor will be marked with green zebra stripes. Additionally, when a portion of the image exceeds 100 percent, a yellow triangle with an exclamation point in the middle of it will be displayed, indicating illegal luma values. When a portion of the image falls between 90 and 100 percent, a green circle with a check and an upward-facing arrow will appear. If no portion of the image is above 90 percent, a green circle with a check mark will appear.

With Show Excess Chroma enabled, areas that are greater than 120 percent IRE saturation will be marked with red zebra stripes (although the exact point that this warning is enabled will depend on the luma levels of the clip). If the portions of the image contain illegal chroma values, a yellow triangle with an exclamation point in the middle of it will be displayed. If there are no illegal chroma values in the image, a green circle with a check mark will appear.

With Show Both enabled, portions of the image that have either illegal luma or chroma values will be marked with red zebra stripes, and a yellow triangle with an exclamation point in the middle of it will be displayed.

Note: for zebra stripes and other marks to show up in the Viewer or Canvas, Show Overlays must be enabled in the View pulldown of those windows.

Video Scopes

Let's first take a look at launching and using the scopes. To access the scopes, go to Choose Tools > Video Scopes (or press Option-9).

The default view is to have all four scopes up (Vectorscope, Waveform Monitor, Histogram, RGB Parade). We can control which scope or combination of scopes is displayed by using the Layout pulldown. Below this pulldown are two small buttons where we can control the brightness of the video lines, or traces (the white one on the left), and the brightness of the grid lines, or graticule lines (the orange one on the right). Additionally, we can control what the scopes are looking at by using the View pulldown menu.

The video scopes also provide a few additional features to help us. By positioning your cursor over any of the scopes, you will get a measurement percentage. In other words, with your cursor on the Waveform Monitor, for example, as you move your cursor up and down the scale, you will get a yellow line and a percentage, letting you know where you are on the scale. This is useful to pinpoint where exactly the trace is occurring on the scale.

By right-clicking in each monitor, you will also get additional options:

- Right-clicking in any of the monitors will let you change the color of the trace from white to green.
- Right-clicking in the Waveform Monitor will let you toggle saturation on or off.
- Right-clicking in the Vectorscope will allow you to magnify or zoom in to the center portion of the display.
- Right-clicking in the Histogram will allow you to choose whether black is included in the display.
- Right-clicking in the RGB Parade will let you choose if the traces of the separate colors are bright or pale.

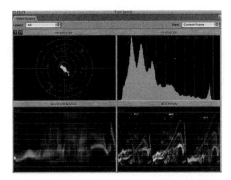

Figure 10.15 The Final Cut Pro scopes.

Frame Viewer

This is a simple and accurate comparison tool. To launch the Frame Viewer, go to Tools > Frame Viewer (or press Option-7). When the Frame Viewer launches, you may notice that it becomes a tab on something called the Tool Bench. This is a window that can contain any of the following tools when opened: Frame Viewers, Scopes, Voice Over, Audio Mixer, and QuickView (a way to preview clips you have to render).

Figure 10.16 The Frame Viewer.

The top bar of the Frame Viewer has two sides—one with a green square and one with a blue square—that tell you your sequence timecode of the clips that you are comparing. The main window is the preview area where you can see the compared clips. What's neat here is that the green and blue squares are in this area as well. Grabbing and dragging the squares will let you change the relative sizes of the two sides that you're comparing.

Below the preview are controls for what the Frame Viewer will be looking at to make the comparison. One side has the green box and the other the blue. Each side has a pulldown where you can choose from Current Frame, 2nd Edit Back, Previous Edit, Current Frame w/o Filters, Next Edit, 2nd Edit Forward, In Point, or Out Point.

Finally, the lower bar has presets for vertical and horizontal splits, as well as a button that lets you swap the position of the clips you're comparing. All in all, the Frame Viewer is a great way to compare clips, but this view is not outputted to your external monitor (which, of course, is your most accurate display of color).

Color correction Filters

The last location for color correction and grading tools in Final Cut Pro is in the color correction category of video filters. These filters can be accessed in two ways. The first is the Effects tab of Browser > Video Filters > Color Correction. The second way to access these filters is to go to Effects > Video Filters > Color Correction.

Specific color correction filters available in Final Cut Pro are covered in an appendix with color pictures available at *http://booksite.focalpress.com/Osder/finalcut/*. We've tucked all the nuts and bolts on the color correction filters into this web appendix. You may need this info to follow some of the instructions below if you are not familiar with these tools.

Common Corrections and Grades

The more pieces that you correct and grade, the more you realize that you often find yourself doing the same type of corrections and grades. There are many books written on this subject, so we will keep it brief by looking at a few simple corrections and looks inside Final Cut Pro. All of the corrections below assume that you have already done three things:

1. Applied the Color Corrector 3-way filter.

2. Opened the clip in the Viewer and activated the Visual Color Corrector tab.

3. Opened the scopes (press Option-9 or choose the Color Correction window layout).

Underexposed—Dark, or underexposed, footage is a very common issue to deal with, and most of the time is correctable.

1. Using the Black Level slider, first adjust your black levels so that the darkest part of your image rests just at 0 percent on the Waveform Monitor.

2. Next, use the Midtones slider to raise the levels of the midtones of the footage. You should see immediate improvement in the exposure of the footage (the trace in the Waveform Monitor expands upward toward 100 percent), but you will probably also see two additional problems. The first is that the apparent saturation of footage has decreased drastically. The second is that depending on the footage, you may have increased noise in the image. Don't worry—we can fix these issues.

3. Let's first fix the noise issue. By dramatically raising midtone levels, we increased the noise in the footage. Let's back off a bit on the midtone level, and use the White Level slider to expand the top end of the footage toward 100 percent. As you do so, you should notice that the exposure increases, but noise does not increase as drastically as it did with the aggressive adjustment using only the Midtones slider. Be careful not to push the white level too far—you might possibly make your footage illegal.

4. Next, use the Saturation slider to increase saturation in the footage. Depending on how much you stretched the levels, you may have to increase this quite a bit to get your footage to look natural.

Overexposed—Footage that is overexposed is too bright, and is generally harder to deal with because a lot of detail has been lost due to levels being pushed to extremes. Overexposed footage tends to be illegal, so one goal of correcting this footage is to bring it back into legal range.

1. Using the Black Level slider, first adjust your black levels so that the darkest part of your image rests just at 0 percent on the Waveform Monitor. Depending on how overexposed the footage is, you may need to drag this down quite a bit to bring back definition in the image.

2. Next, use the White Level slider to bring highlights that are over 100 percent back into the legal range. Next, using the Midtones slider, adjust the overall exposure of the image.

Improper White Balance—This is one of those annoying issues that everyone faces from time to time. The problem might be from a shooter who forgot to white-balance or from a shot that quickly goes from inside to outside. Correcting for improper white balance is easy:

1. Balance the contrast of the image using the level sliders for blacks, mids, and whites.

2. Looking at the Vectorscope and the RGB Parade will allow you to identify the color cast in the image. For example, if the blue channel in the Parade Scope is drastically elevated, and most of the trace in the Vectorscope pushes toward blue, you can be pretty sure that you have a strong blue cast in your image.

3. As a general rule of thumb, to correct for improper white balance, you first identify the color cast in the image, then drag the color-balance controls in the opposite direction of the cast. If you identified a blue color cast in the image, then dragging the color-balance controls to yellow/red will eliminate that cast.

4. Most of the time, you can use the Whites color wheel to correct for white-balance issues. So, in this case, drag the Whites color wheel toward yellow/red on the wheel.

5. You may also have to use the Mids color wheel to further adjust the color cast.

Cool, Desaturated Look—Cool looks (no, not cool as in "that's cool"—we mean color temperature) are often used to express seriousness or sadness. Often cool looks are desaturated slightly to give a flatter, duller feeling. There are many ways to create this look. We'll examine the most basic. As with any technique, the severity of the cool look is up to you.

1. Cool looks are often very contrasty, so balance your contrast by using the level sliders for blacks, mids, and whites—paying special attention to crush the blacks a bit and extend the midtones. Check the Waveform Monitor to see how much you are crushing the blacks and extending the mid range. Remember not to crush the blacks too much, or you'll just end up getting a muddy picture.

2. Using the color-balance controls, push the whites and mids toward blue, while at the same time keeping an eye on the RGB Parade and the Vectorscope to make sure you're not pushing toward illegal values.

3. After you have a color that you like, use the Saturation slider to desaturate the image. As you do so, you may have to go back to the color-balance controls to adjust the look of the image.

Warm, Saturated Look—This is a great way to show warmth (as in the emotion), excitement, anger, and other feelings. These looks are also used to heighten reality—think extra-blue sky or lush green forests. From a technical standpoint, the most dangerous thing about warm, saturated looks is that it's very, very easy to make them illegal. Let's take a look at a simple example.

1. Balance your contrast in the image, paying special attention to the midtones. Often lowering the level of the midtones (and, to a lesser degree, the blacks) can give the appearance of a slightly more saturated look.

2. Next, use the color-balance controls for the whites and mids, and push them toward yellow/red. You will need to do this only a little bit.

3. Using the Saturation slider, raise the saturation for image (how much is your preference). Keep an eye on the Vectorscope as well as the RGB Parade to make sure you have not created illegal chroma levels. It is also very helpful when creating saturated looks to right-click on the Waveform Monitor and turn on saturation to make sure you are not producing illegal saturation.

Audio Finishing within Final Cut Pro

Although not as sophisticated a toolset for audio finishing as Soundtrack Pro, Final Cut Pro does have quite a few tools for helping us finish our audio. These tools are found in a few places in FCP, but before we explore those tools, let's first discuss the importance of monitoring.

Just as with color correction and grading, having audio monitors that have been properly set up is very important for being able to really hear what's going on with your audio. You are unlikely to pick up subtle details in your audio if you're listening on your laptop speakers. There are, of course, hundreds of different speaker and headphone manufacturers out there—the only way to find the right set is by auditioning some yourself. In addition, we find that by monitoring our audio in different ways, we are able to get a true picture of what's going on. What we mean by this is that it's a good idea to listen to your audio both on your main speakers and by using a set of headphones.

The tools to help us with audio finishing can be found in quite a few places.

Audio Meters

The audio meters in Final Cut Pro are, well . . . small. They are not the only way to view your levels, but they are a convenient way to do so. The audio meters range from –96dBFS to 0dBFS. (*dBF*S stands for "decibels full scale" and is the standard unit of measurement for digital audio; *–96dBFS* means 96 decibels below full scale.) On this scale, if audio reaches 0dBFS, there is a good chance that there will be noticeable peaking and distortion.

Of course, distortion and peaking should be concerns for you, but the audio meters also allow you to monitor your average and peak levels. In other words, many broadcasters dictate that average levels occur between –20dBFS and –15dBFS, with peaks around –10dBFS. For nonbroadcast projects, these levels are typically a bit higher: –12dBFS for average levels, with peaks around –3dBFS.

There is an easy way to mark audio peaks as well to ensure that you are not violating a broadcasting requirement for peak levels. By going to Mark > Audio Peaks > Mark, Final Cut Pro will automatically place markers on frames where the audio is peaking above 0dB. If the clip was in the Timeline when you marked it, the markers will appear on the clip. If the clip was in the Browser when you marked it, the marks will appear much like subclips listed sequentially under a clip. After these points have been marked, you can adjust levels at that point. You can also clear all audio-peak markers by once again going to Mark > Audio Peaks > Clear.

---

dB vs. dBFS

You're not likely to get in a heated debate about dB versus dBFS, but understanding the difference is a good thing. Likewise, understanding how these scales relate to VU meters (yes, we still see them from time to time) is important. Like many other technical aspects of video and audio, these terms are often used interchangeably, or simply used under the moniker *dB*. Although this is generally accepted, let's take a look at the difference.

There are actually three common ways to measure analog audio: dBm, dBu, and dBV. We don't need to get into the technical details of these—just know that dBu is the most common scale for analog audio, whereas dBFS is the standard way to measure digital audio. VU (which stands for "volume units") is an older way of measuring volume on analog equipment. The important thing here is to understand the relationship of the scales.

Let's look a reference level for each of the scales: 0VU equals –20dBFS and +4dBu. We already know that 0dBFS is the top end of a digital scale, and can represent clipped audio if levels are above this. Additionally, this number equals +24dBu. With properly calibrated VU meters, this would equal maximum level.

Figure 10.17 The Final Cut Pro audio meters.

Audio Mixer

Although many users have become comfortable with keyframing audio levels directly in the Timeline using the Pen tool, some don't know about—or are intimidated by–the Audio Mixer in Final Cut Pro. The Audio Mixer can be accessed by Tools > Audio Mixer (or by pressing Option-6).

When the Audio Mixer launches, you are presented with a window that is just about full. Let's break it down.

The top bar lets you choose up to four separate views. By using the Track Visibility controls on the left-hand side of your window, you can select or deselect which tracks will be visible for each of the four views. It's common to have all of your tracks in View 1, your dialogue tracks in View 2, natural sound and effects in View 3, and music in View 4. You can, however, make any combination that you want.

The top bar also has a button bar with a default button. This button is called Record Audio Keyframes. We'll get back to this shortly.

The Source pulldown lets you choose if the Audio Mixer is looking at the Viewer or at the Canvas, or whether it automatically switches between them.

The Track Strips area contains a strip for each audio track in your view. You can manipulate the level faders by either dragging them up or down or by entering a value (from +12dBFS to –inf). If you have stereo pairs on your sequence, these are treated as such in the Audio Mixer, and both channels of a stereo pair will be adjusted at the same time.

Next to each level fader are large level meters, a unique Audio Mixer feature that helps further the mix process. Above the level faders are pan controls, which you can manipulate by dragging or entering in a value. Just as with the level meters, if you have a stereo pair, the pan controls will move in tandem. Finally, above the pan controls, there are mute and solo buttons for each track.

The Master area looks much like an individual track; however, it operates a bit differently. At the top of the Master area is a small disclosure triangle that lets you show or hide the Master area. Below that is a Master mute button that mutes all tracks. This control, however, mutes tracks only on playback, not on output.

Next, there is there is the Downmix control. When you have multiple audio outputs assigned in your sequence settings, activating this button will output all of your audio tracks down to stereo for playback, output, and exporting to a QuickTime file. This control is very useful when you have multiple outputs, but have only stereo monitoring capability.

Below the Downmix control is the Master fader, which controls overall level. Next to the Master fader are the Master audio meters. Each audio output that you've

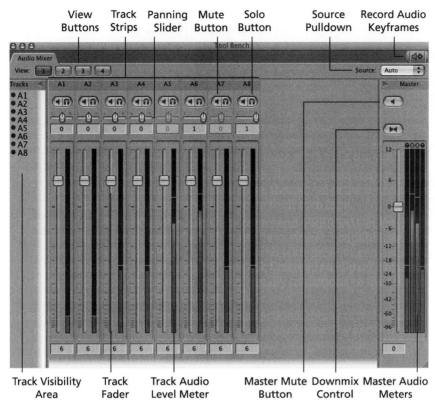

View Buttons Track Strips Panning Slider Mute Button Solo Button Source Pulldown Record Audio Keyframes

Track Visibility Area Track Fader Track Audio Level Meter Master Mute Button Downmix Control Master Audio Meters

Figure 10.18 The Final Cut Pro Audio Mixer.

defined for your sequence will have its own meter. These meters will show only the audio assigned to that output. So, in other words, if you assign only your VO track to output 1, the Master meter for output 1 will show only that VO. If you add nat sound and, say, interviews to that output, the Master meter for output 1 will show you the cumulative effect of all of those separate pieces of audio.

For those of you who crave the tactile control of a real hardware audio mixer, don't fret. Using a MIDI interface and compatible mixer, you can control the Final Cut Pro Audio Mixer by using the hardware mixer. It's pretty cool! For more information on how to set this up, consult the Final Cut Pro User Manual.

Now that we've taken a look at the basic controls of the Audio Mixer, let's take a closer look at the Record Audio Keyframes button. By using this control, Final Cut Pro will automatically place level and pan keyframes on the clips for each track we adjust, in real time. You might be thinking: "What's the big deal? I can adjust levels in pan already on the Timeline or in the Viewer." Well, think of this as another tool to add to your arsenal. In the following example, we assume that you have interview footage on channels 1 and 2, and music on tracks 3 and 4.

1. Back your playhead up to the start of the sequence.
2. Launch the Audio Mixer (Option-6).
3. Make sure that the Record Audio Keyframes button is active.

Multiple Outputs

Many projects have audio-assignment requirements. For example, stereo mix of the show on channels 1 and 2, primary audio (VO and sync) on channel 3, and nat sound, music, and effects on channel 4. It's easy to make these assignments. With your sequence active, go to Sequence > Settings, and click on the last tab, labeled Audio Outputs. Here, you can choose a preset (you can create presets in the Audio Outputs tab of Final Cut Pro > User Preferences) or create up to 24 outputs. The number of outputs you create and/or need will depend on the hardware you are using.

You can choose whether the output is stereo or dual mono, as well as selecting the amount of downmix. The downmix controls allow you to compensate for volume change as you combine multiple mono tracks.

For our previous example, we would have four audio assignments. Channels 1 and 2 would be stereo with 0 downmix (remember, channels 1 and 2 are the stereo mix of the show). Channels 3 and 4 would be dual mono with –3dB of downmix applied to compensate for adding multiple mono tracks together.

After we've set up our audio outputs, another thing to consider is creating *submixes*. These mixes allow you to group the audio necessary for specific outputs. In other words, you can export a stereo mix, all of the primary audio as a mono file, and effects, nat sound, and music as a mono file. Then import those back into FCP, and place them in your sequence.

Now we need to assign those submixes to the four audio outputs we created earlier. This can be done in two different places:

- Right-click in the track-control area in the Timeline and choose Audio Outputs. From here, you can assign that track to an output.
- Right-click in the Track Visibility area in the Audio Mixer and choose Audio Outputs. From here, you can assign that track to an output.

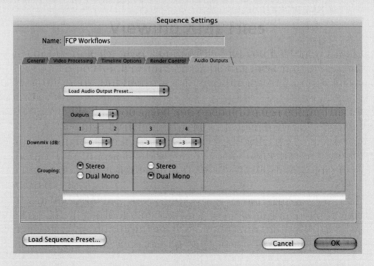

Figure 10.19 Audio-output controls.

4. Start playing your sequence. As you do so, adjust your music on tracks 3 and 4 so that their levels are not competing with the levels of your interview bites. Notice how both faders on 3 and 4 move in tandem. This is because they are a stereo pair.

5. In between interview bites, raise the Level slider of your music tracks. This swell in music will help keep the pace in the piece.

6. Stop playback, and you will notice that Final Cut Pro automatically has placed keyframes based on your movements on each Level slider (make sure to turn on the Toggle Clip Overlays button in the Timeline).

7. If you messed up, though, don't fret. One of the nice things about the Audio Mixer is that you can simply back up and do it again. The new pass will over-write existing keyframe information.

8. You can also use the Pen tool to help you fine-tune the keyframes in the Time-line or Viewer.

You can control how many keyframes Final Cut Pro creates by selecting Final Cut Pro > User Preferences, and then clicking on the Editing tab. On the left-hand side, there is an option to choose how audio keyframes will be recorded. The default is Reduced, which will average your movements on the level controls and pan controls. The Peaks Only option will record only the keyframes at the defining point of each movement, and will record a new keyframe for every minuscule movement of the controls. The All option will record any and all movements.

Audio Filters

If you've ever taken a peek at this section of the Effects tab or Effects menu, you will have noticed that there are a lot of filters. Audio filters are broken down into two categories: Final Cut Pro and Apple. The Apple filters use Apple's Audio Units specification (meant to help standardize plug-ins across multiple applications). The Final Cut Pro audio filters are ones that are native to FCP. In many cases, similar results can be obtained by using a filter from either category, but the Audio Units filters sometimes offer finer control and can be used across multiple applications such as Soundtrack Pro. We could spend a whole chapter just describing all these filters in detail. Instead, we have chosen to take a look at the different categories of filters, and then highlight a few of the most helpful ones.

EQ Filters—Put simply, an EQ (equalization) filter is a way of manipulating certain frequencies. You might want to do this for several reasons. Perhaps you're trying to match VO recorded at two different times. The first recording doesn't sound nearly as full as the second, so you might apply a three-band EQ to adjust the low end of the first recording. In a lot of cases, there are both Final Cut Pro and Audio Units equivalents, which we denote with (AU). The EQ filters include 3 Band Equalizer, Parametric Equalizer (AU), AU Graphic EQ, Low Pass Filter (AU), High Pass Filter (AU), Low Shelf Filter (AU), High Shelf Filter (AU), Band Pass Filter(AU), Notch Filter, and DC Notch.

Noise-Reduction Filters—These filters allow us to correct for problems in the audio. Issues such as hum or sibilance can be reduced or completely fixed with noise-reduction filters. These filters include Hum Remover, Vocal DeEsser, and Vocal DePopper.

Ambience Filters—Filters that provide delay, echo, or reverb to the audio are called ambience filters. For example, you might apply the Reverberation filter to the nar-ration track to give it slightly more "breathing" room. Filters that allow us to create ambience include AU Delay, AU SampleDelay, Echo, and Reverberation.

Compression and Dynamics Filters—These filters work by controlling in some way the volume of your audio. For example, by applying the AU PeakLimiter filter to multiple clips, you can control their volume so that none of them peak above a certain level; this is very handy. You could also apply the Gain filter to quiet clips to raise their levels without having to raise their levels manually. Compression and dynamics filters include AU DynamicsProcessor, AU MultibandCompressor, AU PeakLimiter, Compressor/Limiter, Expander/Noise Gate, and Gain.

Audio Options in the Modify Menu

There is a surprising amount of control for your audio under the Modify menu.

Modify > Levels (or pressing Command-Option-L) allows you to change the levels of your selection in a sequence (single clips or multiple clips). There are two options here: relative and absolute. When you choose to alter the levels of your selection using relative, your levels will change up or down from their current position. In other words, if you had two clips selected—one at –12dBFS and the other at –20dBFS—and you entered –3dBFS, your result would be –15dBFS and –23dBFS. Using the absolute method, on the other hand, sets the selected clips level at the value you enter. So, for two clips—one at –12dBFS and the other at –20dBFS—if you were to enter –10dBFS, the result would be both clips having a level of –10dBFS. This is a great method for altering a large group of clips all at once.

Modify > Audio gives you several additional options for adjusting your audio. The keyboard shortcuts listed on this menu are even more useful than the menu itself. Using the shortcuts here, it is very easy (perhaps even easier than with the mixer) to raise and lower the levels and pan of selected clips.

Also located in this menu is a new feature in Final Cut Pro 6 called Normalization Gain. The Apply Normalization Gain command will nondestructively sample the audio to find peaks, and then raise or lower the peaks to the level that you set. This is also a great way to average peaks between multiple clips so that no one particular clip stands out.

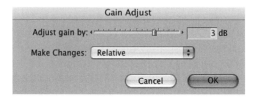

Figure 10.20 Audio Levels dialogue box.

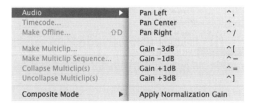

Figure 10.21 Audio options and their keyboard shortcuts.

Motion Graphics and Compositing within Final Cut Pro

Increasingly, editors are being called on to perform ever more complicated motion graphics and compositing tasks. Oftentimes these editors are not familiar with or are not quite comfortable with applications—such as Motion and Shake—that specialize in this kind of work. Final Cut Pro, however, provides a robust set of tools for motion graphics and compositing directly inside the application. With that said, if you do have access to tools outside Final Cut Pro, it might be more efficient to use them. Let's take a look at the tools in FCP.

Text

Final Cut Pro offers a number of tools to create and adjust text. The neat thing about text in FCP is that it is treated just like any other clip. Thus, it can be color-corrected, keyframed, or have filters applied to it. Although applications such as Motion and LiveType excel at text creation, oftentimes you don't have time or don't need to use those applications to create your text. The text tools in Final Cut Pro can be found in two places:

- The Generator pop-up menu (bottom right corner of the Viewer)
- The Video Generators bin in the Effects tab of the Browser

Each location contains the built-in generators for Final Cut Pro. Among these are two categories that have text tools: Text and Boris.

The Text category contains a number of preset text generators. They include Crawl, Lower third, Outline Text, Scrolling Text, Text, and Typewriter. After you have selected the generator you'd like to use, a new tab called Controls will appear in the Viewer. Using the controls on this tab, you change and input your text. It's important to note that all of the generators have a built-in alpha channel (transparency), which makes it easy to composite over video.

The second category that contains text generators is Boris. Boris is a third-party company that has partnered with Apple to provide a robust set of vector text tools. These tools include Text Scrambler, Title 3D, and Title Crawl. Choosing one of these generators will also add a Controls tab to the Viewer. In the Controls tab, you have controls for different aspects of your text, but to be able to format (color, spacing, etc.), you must click the Text Entry and Style Button, which will launch a new window. From here, you have a lot of control over the formatting of your text, including the ability to save presets. All of the Boris generators also have a built-in alpha channel.

Keyframing

This is a way to have properties of a clip change over time. These changes could be to the attributes of a filter, animating the position of the clip, or making a piece of text fly on-screen. Although we can apply static effects with no keyframes, at least two keyframes are needed in order to have something change. There are quite a few places where we can keyframe inside Final Cut Pro. Let's briefly take a look at each.

Motion Tab—This tab gives control over motion properties of our clip. There are numerous parameters we can control here, including scale, rotation, center, anchor point, crop, distort, opacity, drop shadow, motion blur, and time remap. You can keyframe some of these parameters directly in the Video tab of the Viewer with wireframe turned on; the Motion tab, however, gives you greater control of those parameters.

Every parameter has either a slider, rotation clock, pulldown, or entry box to change its value. To the right of the parameters, there are keyframe controls (the

Parameters   Keyframe Controls   Keyframe Graph

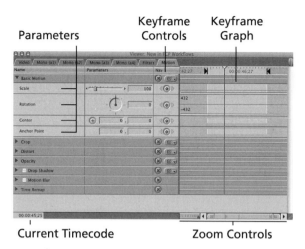

Current Timecode   Zoom Controls

Figure 10.22 The Motion tab and keyframe controls.

diamond inside the circle) where you can add or remove keyframes as well as navigate between keyframes or, if you mess up, reset the parameter (using the red x).

To the right of the keyframe controls is the keyframe graph area. This area can be a little confusing, but it's really quite simple if you look at the details. When you load a clip into the Viewer, you'll notice on the keyframe graph that the clip is represented by the light gray area, whereas the rest of the Timeline is represented by the dark gray area. This area acts like the Timeline, where time increases from left to right. Note that if you load a clip directly from the Browser, this dark gray area will be the handles of your clip, not the rest of the Timeline.

Below the parameters and keyframe graph area is a timecode box that denotes the current timecode (of your clip or Timeline, depending on where the clip was loaded from). There is a Zoom control and Zoom slider to help you expand or contract the keyframe graph so it is easier to look at.

As you apply keyframes, they will appear in the keyframe graph in the position you specified. After you've applied keyframes, you change them further by navigating to the keyframe and using the parameter controls to adjust the value of the parameter, or you can use the cursor to reposition the keyframes in time (left and right) or change their value (up and down).

Filters Tab—Many times, motion graphics looks can be accomplished by simply animating a filter. For example, by animating the Light Rays filter on a piece of text, you can create a unique look. Keyframing in the Filters tab works just like it does in the Motion tab. The parameters that you can keyframe depend on the individual filter, but any attribute that has a numerical value is generally keyframable.

Timeline—One of the easiest places to keyframe is on the Timeline. This functionality, however, is not immediately obvious. To be able to keyframe on the Timeline, you must first do the following:

- Turn on the Toggle Clip Keyframes button (the green and blue parallel lines).
- With Toggle Clip Keyframes on, you'll notice that a gray box appears under your video and audio clips. This area is known as the Timeline keyframe editor. By right-clicking in this gray area, you can choose the specific motion or filter parameter you want to keyframe.

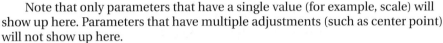

Figure 10.23 The Timeline keyframe editor.

Note that only parameters that have a single value (for example, scale) will show up here. Parameters that have multiple adjustments (such as center point) will not show up here.

You'll notice that at the top of the keyframe editor, there is either a green line or a blue line. The blue line represents motion keyframes; the green line represents filter keyframes. From here, you can use the cursor or the Pen tool to further adjust the position and values of keyframes directly on the Timeline, without having to load the clips into the Viewer. You can exert more control over what appears in the keyframe editor by going to Sequence Settings (for the current sequence) and User Preferences (to set the default settings for new sequences you create).

Keying and Masking

These are relatively easy ways to be able to separate a foreground subject from a background subject or vice versa. There are many reasons that you might want to mask or key footage. For example, you might mask out the top and bottom portions of 4×3 footage to create a widescreen look, or you might apply a chroma key to separate a subject from a greenscreen or bluescreen background.

Masking—Most of Final Cut Pro's masking tools are located under Effects > Video Filters > Matte. Each of these filters works slightly differently, but all contribute to the same goal of making part of the image transparent for the purpose of compositing or "masking" out a portion of the image.

Keying—Perhaps you've seen those small independent films *The Lord of the Rings, Star Wars,* and *Spider-Man*? All kidding aside, these films take advantage of keying to place characters on surreal cityscapes—or, in the case of *Star Wars,* spacescapes! Keying involves eliminating a color or luma range (or a combination) to make those areas transparent.

Just as with the matte category, there are several filters that allow us to pull and or assist in creating keys. All of them are located in Effects > Video Filters > Key.

Specific masking and keying filters available in Final Cut Pro are covered in an appendix with color pictures available at *http://booksite.focalpress.com/Osder/final-cut/*.

Stabilization

Stabilization tools, such as the new SmoothCam filter found in FCP, can really help you save shaky shots that were previously unusable. That is not so say, of course, that every shot can be saved by stabilization. The SmoothCam filter excels at fixing shots that have a minimal to moderate amount of shakiness. Don't expect the shot you got riding down a bumpy desert road on the back of a motorcycle to look like it was shot on a Steadicam (unless, of course, it actually was!). Stabilization in Final Cut Pro is

Figure 10.24 The Background Processes pop-up and the analysis overlay in the Canvas.

the duty of the SmoothCam filter. Using this filter, you can analyze selected clips, an In point to an Out point, or whole sequences. SmoothCam first has to analyze your clip for motion changes before you can tweak how much stabilization will occur. The neat thing is that this happens in the background (called a background process), so you can continue working in FCP. You can control the background processes by choosing Tools > Background Processes. The window that pops up will allow you to stop (cancel), pause, or resume analyzing the clip. You will also notice that the Canvas (or the Viewer if the clip is loaded into it) has an overlay that indicates the status of the background process.

After the analysis has finished, you can use the controls for the SmoothCam filter in the Filters tab of the Viewer for the selected clip. For more information about these specific controls, check out the Final Cut Pro user manual, page 1240 (III-445), found by choosing Help > Final Cut Pro User Manual from within FCP.

Opacity, Composite Modes, and Layering
Three additional tools to build composites and motion graphics in Final Cut Pro are pretty straightforward to apply. They are not mutually exclusive, though; almost always, they are used together. Let's take a look at each.

Opacity—Refers to the overall transparency of the footage. A clip that has an opacity of 100 percent is completely opaque, and therefore cannot be seen through. On the other hand, a clip with an opacity value of 50 percent is 50 percent transparent. There are several places where we can adjust clip opacity:

- The Motion tab in the Viewer using the Opacity parameter.
- By turning on the Toggle Clip Overlays button in the Timeline. This places a black line on the top of each video clip in the sequence. Here, we can use the cursor or the Pen tool to adjust opacity.
- By turning on the Toggle Clip Keyframes button and right-clicking in the Timeline keyframe editor and choosing Opacity. From there, we can use the cursor or the Pen tool to adjust opacity.

Composite Modes—Also known as blending modes or transfer modes in other applications, composite modes are a way to have pixels of two or more layers interact. There is a variety to choose from—each applies a different mathematical calculation to pixels of the combined images. These calculations can work with luma, chroma, alpha, or a combination of the three. For example, the Add composite mode adds together the brightness values of pixels. For a full explanation of how each composite mode works, consult the Final Cut Pro user manual, starting on page 1182 (III-397), by going to Help > Final Cut Pro user manual.

The way most editors and designers we know use composite modes has little to do with the math. They just get a feel for the different looks each mode makes. They also might try a few combinations of composite modes and opacity levels to get their desired effect.

Composite modes work in a top-down manner. So you apply the composite mode to the clip that is higher in the track order. The easiest way to apply a composite mode is to right-click on a clip and choose from the Composite Mode submenu.

Two examples of effects that involve composite modes are a vignette, which can be created with a Feathered Shape generator on the top layer, and compositing it to the footage below with a combination of multiply and opacity, and a "silk," or "gauze," effect that can be achieved by making a duplicate layer of a clip, then blurring that layer a little bit, and compositing it back on top of the original at a low opacity and with a Screen composite mode.

Layering—In its most basic sense, layering is placing one piece of footage on top of another (video on top of video, text on top of video, etc.). As a general rule of thumb, Final Cut Pro works with a top-down approach. By default, when video layers overlap, 100 percent of the topmost layer of video is visible. As we have seen, there are lots of things that can change this and allow the video layers to mix together—including motion effects such as scaling or cropping, opacity changes, keys, masks, and composite modes. In fact, most video effects are created by multiple clips interacting with each other in a composite.

Motion Templates

A new and exciting feature of Final Cut Pro 6 is the integration of Motion templates directly inside FCP. Although this does provide an amazing amount of flexibility, we should note that it is not the same as working with a template directly inside Motion. Many parameters and adjustments are available only directly inside Motion. Depending on the template, there will be more or fewer options that you can control. However, you can at any point open the template in Motion for further editing and adjustment. You can make changes that will affect all instances of the template on the Final Cut Pro Timeline, or changes to an individual instance.

Motion templates can be found in three places within Final Cut Pro:

- The Generator pop-up menu (bottom right-hand corner of the Viewer) > Master Templates
- The Master Templates bin in the Effects tab of the Browser
- By choosing Sequence > Add Master Template

From any of these locations, you can choose the template of your choice. This will load the template into the Viewer and add a new tab called Controls. From the Controls tab, you can adjust the parameters for that template. This is limited text entry and size adjustment along with applying footage to Drop Zone placeholders. You can make your own original templates inside the Motion application and save them to be used in Final Cut Pro.

Mark Spencer and Jem Schofield's *Motion Graphics and Effects in Final Cut Studio 2: Field Techniques for Editors and Designers* (Peachpit Press) is an excellent resource for learning more about creating your own templates, and in general about Motion graphics in Final Cut Pro and Final Cut Studio 2.

Motion templates are a way to access some of the power of Motion inside FCP, but they are just the tip of the iceberg when it comes to the bigger topic of integration with Final Cut Studio. The next chapter introduces us to this greater concept. However, the concepts in finishing—what you are trying to get out of your color correction or mix, titling, or sound design—are much the same whether you are working inside Final Cut Pro, integrating with Final Cut Studio, or extending your workflow into other postproduction platforms, as is covered in Chapter 13.

11 The Power of Final Cut Studio

One of the most exciting things to happen to desktop postproduction since the introduction of Final Cut Pro is the movement toward bundling software. Apple's name for its bundled software package is Final Cut Studio, and in version 2, the program contains eight powerful applications:

Final Cut Pro 6—Ingest, editorial, media management, and transitions and effects

Cinema Tools 4—Film and 24p video conversion tools and database

LiveType 2—Text creation and design

Motion 3—2-D and 3-D motion graphics design

Soundtrack Pro 2—Sound design, mixing, audio analysis, and repair

Color—Color correction, grading, and effects

Compressor 3—Compression for web, DVD, and other devices; media transcoding

DVD Studio Pro 4—DVD design and authoring

The whole idea of the suite is to streamline workflows and to provide small shops with a complete toolkit for postproduction. The goal of this chapter is to give you an idea of how to start thinking about workflows that involve different Studio programs. It is outside the scope of this book to describe how to use each individual program. When planning detailed workflows with the Studio applications, it is a good idea to really bone up on each piece of software you plan to use. There are books on each of the Studio applications, and more coming out all the time. Don't expect your Final Cut Pro knowledge (or reading this book) to give you everything you need to know about the whole Final Cut Studio. Make no mistake: each one of these programs merits its own deep exploration.

Integration among the Studio programs is something that is always being improved and enhanced, so although there are a lot of specific techniques discussed later, we can expect there to be more in the future. However, many of the goals and concepts of these processes—such as round-tripping and using markers to pass information—

we expect to remain the same, at least in principle. These two general techniques are discussed next, followed by a brief discussion of some things to be aware of when planning workflows for each of the applications in the Studio.

Using Markers to Pass Information

Markers are a wonderful thing! In their most basic sense, markers can be used simply to mark an important spot in a clip, but they are so much more powerful than that.

Almost every application within Final Cut Studio uses markers. We will be limiting our discussion, however, to markers that you create within Final Cut Pro. These markers can serve a variety of purposes, such as passing information to different applications in the Studio.

As we saw in Chapter 8, creating a marker is easy to do in Final Cut Pro. The easiest way to add a marker is by using the M key. You can add a marker to a clip loaded in your Viewer, a selected clip in a sequence, or a sequence itself when no clips are selected in the sequence. Although markers on clips are very useful for creating subclips or aligning different events, sequence markers allow information to flow between applications.

So you've added markers. We now need to be able to adjust the marker and define what type it is. Adjusting these parameters is relatively easy to do. Once you have added a marker, hitting M again when your playhead is on that marker will open the Edit Marker dialogue box. Here, you can edit the marker's properties.

Our first option is to name the marker. This might seem straightforward, but you should pay special consideration to naming. The name that you apply here will show up in other applications—Compressor, DVD Studio Pro, Soundtrack Pro, QuickTime Player—so make sure you name your markers something meaningful.

Next, we can add comments. These might be notes to yourself or references to issues that need to be worked on in other Studio applications. Below the Comments field, we can adjust the starting point of the marker, as well as its duration, using timecode. Additionally, if you've made a mistake, you can choose to delete the marker from here.

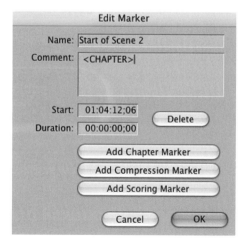

Figure 11.1 The Edit Marker dialogue box.

Lastly, there are three buttons at the bottom of the Edit Marker dialogue box. Clicking on these will make the marker a chapter marker, a compression marker, or a scoring marker. As you add these markers, you will notice that they show up in the Comments field as <CHAPTER>,<COMPRESSION>, or <SCORING>, respectively. Let's take a look at what each type of marker does.

Chapter Marker

Adding a chapter marker in Final Cut Pro means that the marker can be used as a DVD chapter marker in DVD Studio Pro, and is visible and editable in Compressor. The nice thing about adding chapter markers in FCP, as opposed to inside DVD Studio Pro, is that we can place the marker exactly where we want (frame accurate). In DVD Studio Pro, after the video has been encoded, we would be limited to placing a chapter marker only on an I-frame or the first frame of a GOP (see Chapter 5). Another way of saying this is that adding a chapter marker in Final Cut Pro can force an I-frame at the chapter marker's location. Chapter and compression markers must be in the Timeline, not in individual clips.

Compression Marker

A compression marker is a way for you to help the MPEG compression process—this is known as a manual compression marker. By adding compression markers, you are telling DVD Studio Pro or Compressor (whichever program is doing the actual MPEG compression in your workflow) to add an I-frame at that location. Unlike chapter markers, these compression markers will have no effect on navigation on your DVD. As we discussed in Chapter 5, we know that very fast moving parts of video are particularly difficult for MPEG encoders. Therefore, by adding I-frames manually, we can ensure that during these fast-moving sections, there are enough complete frames of video (the I-frames) to make the video look acceptable. Using the Duration field in the Edit Marker dialogue box is an easy way to extend the duration of a compression marker for several frames. Don't overdo it, though—the more I-frames you mark, the bigger the compressed file will be. Note: Final Cut Pro automatically assigns an I-frame at each cut point in the show (this is known as an automatic compression marker).

Scoring Marker

A scoring marker is a way to mark places in your sequence where you want audio events to happen, and places that you need audio sync. When we export these scoring markers (discussed later in this chapter) they will show up as visual cues in Soundtrack Pro. You can use these cues to help you build your music composition, sound design, and mix.

Exporting Markers

After you have created all of your chapter, compression, and scoring markers for a given sequence, you need to be able to pass them on to the next application in your workflow. Doing so is straightforward.

For example, when you export your sequence via File > Export > Using Compressor, all chapter markers and compression markers that you have defined will make their way into Compressor. From there, you can choose to add, delete, or edit existing markers. Similarly, when you send your work to various programs in the Studio, the appropriate markers are maintained.

If you choose to export your movie as a QuickTime (either referenced or self-contained) using File > Export > QuickTime Movie, besides the options already discussed in Chapter 9, you will have the option to choose which markers you want to include.

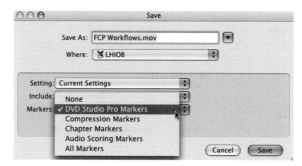

Figure 11.2 The different types of markers you can include in a QuickTime Movie.

Let's look at the options.

None—This option is self-explanatory: no markers will be included.

DVD Studio Pro Markers—Chapter markers, as well as automatic and manual compression markers, will be exported as metadata in the QuickTime file.

Compression Markers—This option will include only automatic and manual compression markers.

Chapter Markers—Only chapter markers that you've added will be included in the QuickTime Movie.

Audio Scoring Markers—Only scoring markers that you've added will be included in the QuickTime file.

All Markers—This will include all of the various markers in the exported Quick-Time file.

Markers are just one way that Final Cut Pro is able to pass information to other programs in Final Cut Studio. There are also other methods of integration and work-flows that are possible. Each program is somewhat different in this regard, but another concept that is shared by several of the programs is round-tripping.

Round-Tripping

One of the most powerful workflow aspects of Final Cut Studio is the ability to send clips to and from Final Cut Pro to various applications inside the Studio for additional work, and then automate how those clips are updated in the FCP Timeline. For example, one might send a piece of video to Motion to have a nifty lower third applied, send a whole sequence to Color to be color-corrected and graded, and send clips and sequences to Soundtrack Pro to be mixed and to add music.

Whatever your particular application, the concept of round-tripping is powerful. You're not simply sending the information to an application; you can actually get your work seamlessly back into Final Cut Pro!

Although this method clearly has great potential for efficiency in workflows, we have gotten uneven results with it. Round-tripping is quite elegant, but it puts a lot of complicated software processes behind the curtain (FCP and Motion have to talk to each other in a really complex way). The result is that sometimes things get messed up.

Our advice is this: by all means, give round-tripping a shot if it seems that it would benefit your project. However, all of the applications within the Studio have the capabil-ity of exporting self-contained files (AIFFs, QuickTimes, etc.) to be imported into FCP manually. If you start having problems with round-tripping, it is easy to troubleshoot by doing it the old-fashioned way.

Not every application in the Studio is capable of round-tripping, nor do they all need to be. For example, from Final Cut Pro, you can only send to Compressor—you cannot receive from it. Thus, in the case of DVD creation, it is a one-way trip.

Studio Integration

As we've discussed, one way to look at FCP is as the hub of the Final Cut Studio, with projects flowing out to the Studio applications and then back to the center. The processes by which each one of these programs talks to FCP is slightly different (and this is logical because each program has its own unique function). Briefly, let's look at integration for each application in the Studio.

Color

This is a new application for color correction and grading. When round-tripping with Color, one important factor is that you can send only whole sequences to Color, not individual clips (unless they are on their own sequence). To get your footage into Color, simply select your sequence, then go to File > Send To > Color. A dialogue box will open, describing your selection as well as letting you name the Color project. The name defaults to the name of the selected sequence. After correcting and grading your footage, you will need to render the clips in Color. Then, from inside Color, go to File > Send To > Final Cut Pro. This will generate an XML file that FCP will use to reconnect to the rendered clips from Color.

In general, Color provides you with more ways to evaluate, correct, and grade your footage. For example, as we saw in the previous chapter, both Final Cut Pro and Color have built-in video scopes to evaluate your video image in different quantitative ways, but Color has more scopes with more features.

Other features of Color include:

- Color correction with curves
- Four primary grades, each with up to eight secondary color corrections
- Powerful prebuilt color effects (you can make your own too)
- Geometry controls such as Pan & Scan tracking (interchangeable with FCP's Motion tab settings) and Shapes

These powerful features are some of the reasons to consider using Color for your workflow.

It is important to know that when you send a sequence to Color, there are limitations. And depending on your project, some of these limitations can be important.

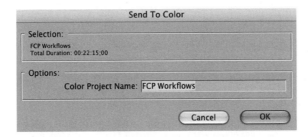

Figure 11.3 The Send To Color dialogue box.

- Most filters that you have applied in Final Cut Pro will not be previewed or rendered by Color. The one exception is the Color Corrector 3-Way filter, which is translated as a correction in the Primary Room in Color. Once you have rendered and sent your project back to FCP from Color, the filters you've applied will once again take effect. This is especially important for color correction or image-control filters. Prior to sending to Color, it's a good idea to remove those filters—otherwise you might get weird results when your project has returned to Final Cut Pro and those filters are again active. In general, you want to choose either Color or Final Cut Pro to do your color correction and grading work, and not mix the two.

- Track layering will be maintained in Color; however, opacity and composite modes will not be previewed or rendered out of Color. Instead, this information is maintained and rendered in Final Cut Pro.

- Like filters, transitions are not previewed or rendered by Color. Instead, the transitions are rendered when the project returns to FCP.

- Speed effects are maintained and previewed by Color. They aren't, however, rendered by Color. Instead, they are rendered by Final Cut Pro.

- Generators such as text and shapes, still frames, Motion files, and LiveType project files that are in your sequence are ignored by Color, and will not be previewed. Their position on the Timeline is maintained, however. When the project is sent back to Final Cut Pro, these items will relink and be displayed again. If you do need to color-correct or grade these items, you will have to render them out of Final Cut Pro as self-contained QuickTime files, and then re-edit them back into your sequence.

One conundrum that Color poses is that you now have another Studio choice besides Final Cut Pro for color correction and grading. So how do you decide which one you should use? Unfortunately, there is no simple answer. In general, though, we have found that projects that require more grading than simple correction benefit immensely from Color, whereas many corporate communication and lower-budget broadcast pieces can be corrected more efficiently using Final Cut Pro. With that said, however, the choice is ultimately dependent on your workflow. Here is some food for thought.

Consider using Color for color correction and grading if:

- Your primary role is that of a colorist, or there is a dedicated colorist in your workflow. Color will provide you or the colorist with most of the tools required to excel in that role.

- You require much finer control over your image using features exclusive to Color—for example, curves, multiple secondary color corrections, and pan and scan.

- You must meet strict broadcast standards. We have found Color's Broadcast Safe controls to be more exact than Final Cut Pro's.

Consider using Final Cut Pro for color correction and grading if:

- Color correction and grading are among many tasks that you need to complete. Final Cut Pro is multifaceted, whereas Color pretty much excels only at correction and grading.

- If speed is your primary concern, then use Final Cut Pro. Because you never have to leave the FCP interface, your workflow should be faster than going to Color, where you will have to render and possibly render again when coming back to Final Cut Pro.

- The project is still in an intensive editing phase, but for some reason you want to do some color correction now. Because the color correction filters travel with the clip inside FCP, minimal effort is required for adjustments.

- You need to color-correct and grade stills, Motion and LiveType projects, text, and other generators. These items will not appear in Color.
- You don't have the time to learn Color, you are already proficient with the color correction and grading toolset inside Final Cut Pro, and that toolset meets your needs.

Finally, if you do plan a Color workflow, it is a good idea to consider at what point you should send the project to Color. It can be very frustrating and sometimes technically complex if you've started correcting a project, and then half of the show gets reordered. For that reason, it's generally a good idea to wait until the picture lock has been achieved on the project before sending it to Color for correction and grading.

Motion
As we saw in the previous chapter, Motion templates provide one powerful way to use Motion inside the Final Cut Pro interface. However, this is just one way that Motion and FCP interact.

A more common scenario is sending footage to Motion from the Final Cut Pro Timeline to add particles, 3-D space effects, animated text effects, and so forth. You then send the project back to FCP, where it is rendered for inclusion in the show. A Motion project on a Final Cut Pro Timeline is known as a Motion clip.

To send items to Motion, select the ones you wish to send from your sequence. Next, go to File > Send To > Motion Project. This will bring up a dialogue box where you can choose the Launch Motion and Embed Motion Content options. When you choose Embed Motion Content, Final Cut Pro will replace your footage on the Timeline with a Motion project file, what is known as a Motion clip (as well as create a new sequence with your original footage). It's important to note that when you send clips to Motion using this method, the clips and their layering will occupy the same positions in the Motion Timeline.

After you have worked on your footage in Motion, simply saving the project will update the embedded Motion clip on your Timeline. If you need to make fixes, you can right-click on the Motion clip in the Timeline and choose Open in Editor, which will launch Motion. Simply make your changes, save, and the file in FCP once again will update.

Note that you can send sequences and clips directly from the Browser to Motion, but the option to embed Motion content will not be available in the Send to Motion dialogue box. This means that simply saving the Motion project will have no effect back in Final Cut Pro. You would need to import the Motion project file back into FCP manually.

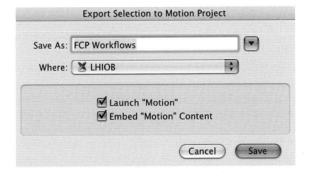

Figure 11.4 The Send To Motion dialogue box.

> # Motion Project File vs. Motion Clip
>
> One thing that causes some confusion when dealing with Final Cut Pro and Motion is the use of Motion project file versus Motion clip. As a general rule of thumb, the names can be used interchangeably, but here is how it works.
>
> A Motion project file is the file that contains all the instructions to create your award-winning design. When the Motion project is imported into Final Cut Pro, it becomes a Motion clip. It can then be used just like any other clip. The Motion clip, just like other media files, refers to a file on disk. In this case, the file on disk is the Motion project.

If you do choose to send sequences and clips from the Browser to Motion, there are a few things to be aware of. If you send a clip or a group of clips directly from the Browser to Motion, a new Motion project is created, and the clips are loaded into the Media tab of Motion. The Motion Timeline, however, will be blank. If you send a sequence from the Browser to Motion, a new Motion project is created, and the Motion Timeline is populated with all the clips, with their layering and positions the same as from the FCP sequence.

Just as with Color, it is important to understand what is maintained between FCP and Motion, as well as other limitations.

- All timings, and most Motion tab attributes—including keyframes, composite modes, and clip and sequence markers from clips—in Final Cut Pro will be maintained in Motion.
- Audio, including levels and pan information, will go to Motion.
- Filters, generators, and transitions are not sent to Motion (the one exception is the SmoothCam filter, which is translated into the Stabilize behavior in Motion).
- Audio in Motion projects does not come back to Final Cut Pro.
- Properties of a Motion clip (duration and frame size) are set by the Motion project, not by FCP.
- Objects and layers in Motion are flattened into a single layer in Final Cut Pro. To work with these objects and layers again, you can choose to edit the Motion clip in its editor (Motion). In this sense, working with a Motion clip is something like working with a nest: all of the separate layers are represented as one clip on the Timeline, but you can open up this package and work on it directly in Motion.
- The Media Manager in Final Cut Pro does not manage the files used to create a Motion clip. You will have to manage those files manually! This is important because if you forget to include those files—say, when copying a project to another drive—the embedded Motion clip will come up as offline next time you open the project.

One thing to keep in mind when planning workflows with Motion is that it makes sense to plan what tasks are going to be done in Motion. Some things—such as particle effects, camera moves, and certain behaviors—cannot be done in FCP. Other things—for example, basic animations, text creation, masking, and keying—can be done by either application. The issues that follow are by no means the only things to consider. Every workflow is different, but the following list is a good starting point for deciding whether to use Motion in your workflow.

Consider using Motion if:

- Your primary role is that of motion graphics designer or there is a dedicated motion graphics designer in your workflow. The toolset in Motion will provide most of the tools needed for that role.
- The task can be completed only in Motion: particles, camera moves, 3-D space, and certain behaviors.
- Your project could benefit from more sophisticated motion graphics.

Consider Using Final Cut Pro if:

- You don't have time to learn Motion, and you are already proficient with the toolset in Final Cut Pro for motion graphics and compositing.
- Your motion graphics and compositing tasks are straightforward and can be handled by Final Cut Pro.

Other ways to integrate Motion into your workflow are designing templates to be used in DVD Studio Pro and transitions that can be used in Final Cut Pro or DVD Studio Pro.

Soundtrack Pro

Now in version 2, Soundtrack Pro represents a powerful resource for working with audio. In Chapter 10, we detailed many of the tools available for working with audio inside Final Cut Pro. Although these instruments on their own can be powerful, Soundtrack Pro is a more comprehensive tool. That doesn't mean it is necessary for every workflow, however. Below are some considerations for choosing between Soundtrack Pro and Final Cut Pro.

Consider using Soundtrack Pro if:

- The primary role of you or a member of your team is that of audio mixer and sound designer. Soundtrack Pro will provide most of the tools needed for that role.
- You require advanced mixing capabilities, such as multiple buses and sends, surround sound, panning, and fader/slider automation.
- You require powerful filtering and effects, as well as restorative options such as noise reduction, click and pop, power-line hum, and clipping detection and fixing.
- You require music creation and sound design. Using Soundtrack Pro's audio library (more than 20GB), you can create your own scores and add in sound effects, many of which are in surround sound.

Consider using Final Cut Pro if:

- You don't have time to learn Soundtrack Pro, and you are already proficient with the toolset in Final Cut Pro for mixing.
- Your mixing needs are straightforward and can be accomplished using the tools inside FCP.
- Ultimately, your mix will be done by a vendor, so any audio adjustments that you make in Final Cut Pro are only temporary.

There are several workflows to use in Soundtrack Pro for further adjustment. Which method you use depends on what you're attempting to do. All of the methods for moving audio from FCP to Soundtrack Pro are found by going to File > Send To.

Soundtrack Pro Audio File Project—Using this option, each item in your selection will be sent to Soundtrack Pro as a separate audio file project. When you choose

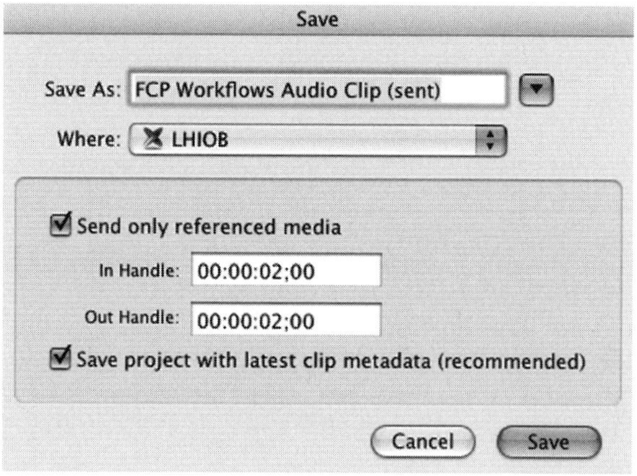

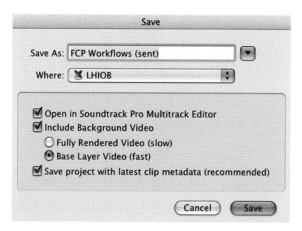

Figure 11.5 The Send To Soundtrack Pro Audio File Project dialogue box.

this option, a dialogue box will appear. Here, you can choose to limit the audio sent to Soundtrack Pro by sending only the media referenced by your selection. You can also add handles—extra media on either side of the selection. In addition, you can choose to save the project with the latest clip metadata. Clicking *OK* will automatically create a new file in your Browser (in the same directory), with the word "sent" in parentheses. *Note:* if you sent the clips from the Timeline, those clips also have "sent" added on to the end of the name. The beauty about this process is that it allows you to adjust your audio nondestructively. Now, in Soundtrack Pro, you can process your files by adding effects, reducing noise, and so forth. Once done, simply save the Soundtrack Pro file. This will bring up a dialogue box that asks whether you want to include or reference the original audio. If you choose to reference, Final Cut Pro will connect back to the Soundtrack Pro audio file.

Soundtrack Pro Multitrack Project—Whereas the Audio File Project option is great for fixing and adjusting a single clip or a few clips at a time, the Multitrack Project option allows you to take your entire sequence, including video, into Soundtrack for purposes of mixing (stereo or surround), adding music, sound effects, VO,

Figure 11.6 The Send To Soundtrack Pro Multitrack Project dialogue box.

and so on. When you choose this option from Final Cut Pro, a dialogue box pops up, allowing you to choose if you want to automatically open up Soundtrack Pro, include your video (referenced or self-contained), and save the project with the latest clip metadata.

Once in Soundtrack Pro, you can mix and design your show. When done, you have several options. The easiest option is to have your mix automatically update back in Final Cut Pro. To do this in Soundtrack Pro, go to File > Export. There are several options here, including if you want to export a master mix, individual tracks, and so forth. After you've chosen the appropriate options, you'll notice there is a pulldown box on the bottom of the Export dialogue that is labeled After Export. There are quite a few options here, but the one that is very useful is "Send files to Final Cut Pro sequence." After you click Export, Soundtrack Pro will process the files and open Final Cut Pro.

Back in FCP, you will be presented with an Import XML dialogue (XML is how Soundtrack Pro and FCP communicate about timing and location of files). Here, you can choose the destination project along with several other options. After clicking OK, you'll notice on the imported sequence that FCP automatically pushes your original audio down and disables those tracks. This is a nice feature if you ever need to go back to the original audio.

Soundtrack Pro Script—A Soundtrack Pro script is a great way to perform repetitive audio tasks. In Soundtrack Pro, you can set up a list of actions (noise reduction, normalization, etc.), and then save those actions in AppleScript. In Final Cut Pro, you can then send your audio to the script. A dialogue box will appear, warning that if you are using ordinary audio/video files, the script will destructively edit these files. If you do not want that to happen, you can choose to convert the file to a Soundtrack Pro project file.

Soundtrack Pro is a flexible tool that continues to evolve and improve. Once you have made adjustments, you can bring audio back into Final Cut Pro as individual clips or as a whole sequence. Version 2 of the software added the Conform feature for automatically updating your audio project to match editorial changes made inside FCP. This is an immensely powerful feature for workflows where picture changes have to happen concurrently with sound changes.

For more on Soundtrack Pro 2 integration, see *Soundtrack Pro 2: Audio Editing and Sound Design in Final Cut Studio* by Martin Sitter (Peachpit Press).

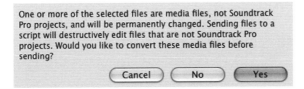

Figure 11.7 The Send To Soundtrack Pro Script dialogue box.

LiveType
Integration with LiveType is straightforward. You can send a sequence to LiveType by going to File > Export > For LiveType. The dialogue box that appears is identical to the one you see when you export to a QuickTime Movie. Note that exporting does not automatically open LiveType. Inside LiveType, you will have to go to File > Place

Background Movie in order to import the file. After adding text to your project, you can either render out a new QuickTime file to import into Final Cut Pro, or simply save the LiveType project. By saving the LiveType project file (.ipr), you import the file directly into Final Cut Pro without having to first render from LiveType. Whichever method you choose, just make sure to disable the background layer in LiveType so that your text can be properly composited back in Final Cut Pro.

Another interesting aspect of LiveType is that all of the program's LiveFonts can also be used inside the Motion interface, which is another aspect of Studio integration.

Cinema Tools

This program never gets a lot of attention, because—let's face it—it's just not sexy. Yet Cinema Tools provides a valuable set of instruments for working with film and 24p video projects. Final Cut Pro and Cinema Tools integrate in a number of ways. By going to File > Export, you can choose to create a Cinema Tools audio EDL, change list, film list, or XML film list. Additionally, you can use Cinema Tools to reverse telecine and to synchronize your project with a Cinema Tools database—options that are found in the Tools menu.

For a full discussion of Cinema Tools and all aspects of Final Cut Pro film workflows, see *The Filmmaker's Guide to Final Cut Pro Workflow* by Dale Angell (Focal Press).

Compressor

Although there is no round-tripping per se, it is easy to send clips and sequences directly to Compressor. Simply select your clips or sequences, then go to File > Export > Using Compressor. As noted earlier, markers that you designate as compression and chapter markers inside Final Cut Pro will carry through to Compressor.

DVD Studio Pro

There is no direct export or integration from Final Cut Pro to DVD Studio Pro. However, that doesn't mean that things you do inside FCP don't impact results in DVD Studio Pro. Adding chapter markers and compression markers are two examples.

As briefly noted before, you can also integrate Motion and DVD Studio Pro to make Motion menu templates.

Shake

Although technically not part of Final Cut Studio, Shake is often the best way to perform complex compositing tasks. You can export clips or whole sequences to Shake. To do so, select your clips or sequences, then go to File > Send To > Shake. This will bring up a dialogue box where you can choose the name of the resulting new sequence in FCP,

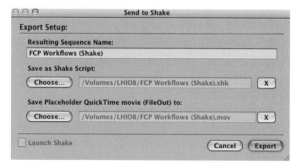

Figure 11.8   The Send To Shake dialogue box.

the name of the Shake script (synonymous with a project file), and the name of the FileOut node in Shake. Finally, you can also choose to automatically launch Shake if you have it installed. This process does a few things. It creates a new Shake script, a placeholder QuickTime File is created on disk and in your FCP project, and the file will ultimately be populated by the render from Shake (the FileOut node).

FCP Studio and Professional Roles

There is much more to be said about each of the pieces of software in the Studio. One thing that is interesting from a workflow perspective is how the integration of Final Cut Studio reflects back on the discussion of professional roles begun in Chapter 3.

Is Color the software that will allow the specialized colorist to more readily move out on his or her own without the financial and technical infrastructure of a larger company?

Will the next generation of editors/producers/designers all be hybrids, expected to be able to deliver not just edited video but original motion graphics, color correction, audio work, and the final DVD?

Will the key to success be the integration and workflows discussed here—how you move your project through Final Cut Studio, getting the most out of each piece of software and each team member?

These are all possibilities, and the one thing we can be sure of is that workflows will continue to evolve. We expect the movement toward integration to continue, maybe even to the point where it eclipses the current trend of separate bundled programs. In the future, we may see some of the programs collapsed into feature sets of others.

In the last two chapters, we have seen finishing techniques inside Final Cut Studio. A related topic is how media can be organized and shared between team members, especially on a larger team. This is the topic of the next chapter. However, we are not totally done with finishing, because Chapter 13 discusses transferring projects outside Final Cut Studio for additional finishing options.

12 Sharing and Managing Media

Recently, I mentioned to a colleague that I was working on a book about Final Cut Pro workflows.

"What's the big deal?" he said. "All I hear about is workflow this and workflow that, but you shoot, then edit, then output. So what's the big deal?"

For a moment, I bristled, but then I realized that he had a point. For many people, postproduction workflows do not need to be all that complicated, and we don't mean to make them complicated. When I recovered my composure, I gave him what I thought was a reasonable and not-too-defensive answer.

I told him that he was right, for a lot of people, especially students of the craft and those working exclusively in the DV environment. I went on to say that if it all ended there, he would be missing one of the truly revolutionary aspects of Final Cut Pro: scalability. Although the super-simple workflow is going to be adequate for a lot of prosumers, it is not a solution if you are producing 26 episodes in hi def, shooting on seven different formats, or running a television network. Final Cut Pro has been making headway into all of these areas—in fact, into all areas of postproduction, period—largely because of its scalability.

Part of working on a larger, more complicated project—or in a more sophisticated postproduction environment—is working with more people. When we introduced the concept of media management in Chapter 6, and when we discussed logging and entering metadata in Chapter 7, we mentioned that more care was needed in these areas when working with larger teams or on larger projects. The topic of this chapter is methods and strategies for managing your media to work on these more complex postproduction projects.

This is often referred to as media management or digital asset management, though both of these terms are sometimes used more broadly, referring not only to postproduction. Our focus is on concepts and techniques that are particularly useful in designing and implementing Final Cut Pro workflows. Although it is true that these methods tend to be most needed on larger projects, many of them are applicable to smaller projects and/or organizing on a small-studio level as well. In general with postproduction, it is difficult to have too much organization, but easy and dangerous to not have enough.

These topics touch many other aspects of workflows:

Preparation—The stage in which a lot of this thinking needs to be implemented

Storage and Compression—The technical aspects underpinning media management

Ingest—When most media and metadata are put into the system

Rough Cutting—When editors need access to raw but organized media

Finishing—When media may need to move to other machines or operators

The goal of this chapter is to mesh the ideas we have already discussed with advanced media-management techniques toward an understanding of workflow strategies for scaling Final Cut Pro to meet the needs of the most complex projects.

Scratch-Disk Organization

The traditional media-drive setup for nonlinear editing is a dedicated drive or drives, or a RAID attached directly to the NLE system through a high-throughput connection. Whether a single-drive or RAID solution (discussed in Chapter 5), the traditional setup has only one NLE accessing the media.

In the early days of nonlinear editing, this looked like a large RAID unit tethered to the computer by a thick SCSI cable, or sometimes the drives were inside the CPU enclosure, or in an extended enclosure. The introduction of FireWire (see Chapter 1) meant a simpler external cabling solution that had a high enough throughput to capture and play video (DV anyway). It became more common to see traditional setups that now relied on external FireWire drives.

High-speed external FireWire drives brought a lot of flexibility to media management, in the form of what we call a "sneakernet." A bit more on that later, but first, we want to explore some strategies of organizing your media in the traditional paradigm.

We learned about scratch drives in Chapter 7, including how Final Cut Pro automatically creates folders on the scratch disk (Figure 12.1):

- A folder is created for each type of media that FCP saves to the scratch drive: capture scratch, render files, audio render files, and so on.

- Within each one of these folders, Final Cut Pro automatically creates a folder based on the name of the project.

So, any scratch disk is automatically separated into directories based on the types of media it contains. Then each one of these directories is organized by the project that created the media.

This last part is important. The second level of project-based organization that FCP does automatically on scratch drives is based on the project that *originally created the media*. This is important, because the organization of the scratch disk does not affect the organization of clips in FCP. You can also have two or more clips (in the same or separate projects) that reference the same media file. However, the media file that is referenced will always be in the scratch-disk directory associated with the project that created it.

Building on what we know about scratch disks, there are two approaches to media management worth discussing at this point. These are building-block concepts that can be augmented or customized. Rather than complete solutions, they are basic examples meant to get us more into the media-management mind-set.

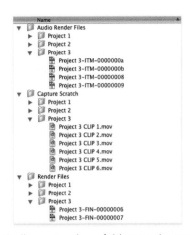

Figure 12.1 FCP automatically creates these folders on the scratch disk.

Dedicated Media Drives

Using a drive (or drives) for media and nothing but media is probably the most traditional, even the original, approach to media management. With Final Cut Pro, a good
way to do this is to set the scratch disk to be the root level of a large dedicated media
drive, never change it, and ideally not use the drive for anything else.

There are really two parts to this idea:

1. The media drive will contain nothing but media. In and of itself, this is an organizational boon. Projects (and everything else) will be located on a different drive.

2. The organizational system inherent in how FCP sets up scratch disks will be
   utilized fully for the organization of the drive.

This idea is both straightforward and easy to execute. Here are some of the advantages:

1. It is exceedingly simple. The basic instruction for a new editor working in this
   system is: don't change anything.

2. It is easy for anyone to go onto the media drive and find the types of files they
   want (at the root level) and what project they are associated with (the next level
   down in each directory). Because this is the traditional setup, it is probably the
   first place they will look.

3. It is easy to expand the system. For instance, because still images are not
   imported through Log and Capture, FCP does not create a folder for them on
   the scratch disk. No problem—you can just go ahead and make that folder to
   keep these organized in the Finder. To stay consistent with this organizational
   scheme, you would make a new directory (call it "Still Images") at the root level
   of the scratch drive. Then organize this directory with folders that are based
   on project names. Using this method, the organization of your still images (or
   other media assets) will work exactly the same as with the rest of your media.

4. Putting the media on a separate hard drive from the project has certain technical advantages. As hard-drive speeds have increased, this has become much less
   of an issue.

This traditional approach works as an example of a media-management principle that we introduced earlier: having a system (any system at all) and sticking to

that system are the most important things in media management. The traditional dedicated-media-drive solution might seem so simple that it is not even like organizing, but that is just fine. It still works well for a lot of shops, particularly where one system is used by a lot of different people on a lot of different projects.

Because the solution is traditional, it requires little or no instruction. It is helpful when using this method to have someone who periodically cleans up the media drive and erases old media. Because this person can see the project-named directories, this is a fairly simple task.

Project-Based Directories

A different approach to media management is creating a directory on your media drive for each project to contain all project files and assets. The big difference here is that all of the files associated with the project, including the FCP project itself, are stored at the same location.

Here is how it works:

- On the root level of your media drive (or in an area designated to you for this work), create a folder, and name it based on the name of the project.

- Save your FCP project to this directory. If you are going to have multiple project files as part of a larger project, you may want to create a subdirectory called "Project Files." (If you are wondering why you would want multiple project files for one project, see the case study in Chapter 17.)

- Before capturing, also set your scratch disk to this directory. Once you have done this, the directory will look something like Figure 12.2.

- Proceed to capture media and work on your project. When you need to import anything at all to your project—still images, music, motion graphics—make sure to save them within the top-level project directory.

- As mentioned earlier, don't be afraid to add additional organizational folders at the first level of the project directory. You could wind up with additional folders: Photos, Music, VO, gfx, and so on.

- And just as before, remember that this stuff can be organized differently in your project(s). This is only the organization of the actual media files as they exist on the media drive.

The big benefit of this method is that it keeps ALL of the files associated with a project in one place. It also allows editors and producers more organizational freedom for individual projects. (You can basically make your own rules inside the project directory,

Figure 12.2 A project-based directory.

whereas, with the traditional approach, everyone needs to play the same tune.) If, at any point, you need to copy or move or delete your entire project, this is as simple as dragging and dropping the project folder.

The disadvantages of this approach include:

- May not be as effective with multiple editors, because the system needs to be explained, and there is more room for variation.

- Ignores certain conventions of the traditional approach. Although this is unlikely to cause any technical problems, it might confuse someone new coming into the project.

- May be more difficult for an administrator who is unfamiliar with the material to clean up the drives (but if everyone follows the same system, this should not be a big deal).

- Putting the project file on the same drive as the media means that if the media drive fails, you could also lose your project. Of course, any drive can fail, so you should always back up your projects anyway.

All in all, we often find this to be a good starting point on media management for many projects and setups.

Remember, scratch-disk organization is one part of the larger media-management puzzle in most workflows. The way you set up your drives needs to make sense in terms of the other decisions you make when setting up your system and your project.

The Sneakernet

In the days before FireWire, managing media in the post house could be a real pain. For instance, if one client needed to take a break from a project, but a different client needed to use the system in between, there was a real hassle over what to do with the media. (Remember that drive space was also much more expensive back then.) Even something simple, such as switching edit rooms, usually meant an overnight network transfer.

Using external FireWire drives as media drives changed all that. Now moving to a different edit system became as simple as unplugging the drive and plugging it in in a different room. (Okay, there was some sneakernetting prior to FireWire, but FireWire made it easy and ubiquitous.) This method was given the tongue-in-cheek name "sneakernet" for the technology that moved the media around the facility (the feet walking down a hallway).

Jokey though it may be, the sneakernet is a real part of the digital video revolution. We still use it ALL THE TIME. We could have called this book "Preditors on the Sneakernet," but we also wanted some nongeeks to buy it. The case study in Chapter 14, and two of the the additional case studies on the Web, all use variations on the sneakernet principle.

The Master-Project Approach

The master-project approach to media management works well for larger projects and organizations with ongoing media-management needs. It also starts to hint at the more sophisticated solutions later in this chapter, although it can still be done with a traditional media-drive configuration and Final Cut Pro as the only necessary software.

The idea is to create a master, or archive, project into which you import all of your media into Final Cut Pro. This can be done on a project level or on a larger, multi-

project or multifacility level. Several of the case studies in Part 3 use a take on this idea. In essence, you are designating an FCP project—the "master," or "archive," project, depending on the application—to be primarily a media database.

Creating a master project is something you will want to do only if your project has some degree of complexity, multiple pieces, a substantial amount of media, or some long-term archiving need. It might be helpful to imagine an example. Let's say we are a company that shoots a lot of political speeches, and then cuts those into a number of pieces for various clients. We can choose to keep all of those speeches in a tape library and capture them when we need them, but if we do enough of this work over a short span of time (such as an election cycle), that is going to get very inefficient.

Instead, we could manage these media by setting up a master FCP project. In this case, we might call the master project Speeches. Every time a new speech is shot, we'd ingest it into this project. We would also use a consistent system for the metadata, so it would be easy to find a speech by the politician's name, the date, or keywords based on the topic of the speech. We might want to do some bin organization as well, organizing the speeches by party, let's say.

Now, anytime a producer needs to access the political speeches, they use this Speeches FCP project like a library, searching for the material they need, and then pulling it into a different project to do their work.

We have seen this basic method used with great success in a lot of situations. We have clients who also use these same basic ideas to create a rolling archive that continues to collect evergreen material over the course of years. Although the master project is not meant for individual cuts, you can also archive sequences back to it to be recycled later. Several of our clients have built up something of a video template archive that they cost-effectively update to keep their video presentations fresh.

Working with Media on a SAN

As discussed in Chapter 5, SAN (shared area network) storage is a solution that allows multiple users to access the media simultaneously. Essentially, it is a video network. As with any network, a key feature is control over permissions and access. These are very powerful tools for organizing media, and they really move this discussion to a higher plane entirely: SAN network administration for video.

As stressed earlier, the level of complexity here can get very, very high. If you are contemplating creating an Xsan environment, strongly consider bringing in an expert to design this and get it off the ground. Best to keep this person's phone number handy after the initial installation as well, and you might even want to put them on retainer. You are probably going to have questions to ask and troubleshooting to be done.

If our biggest recommendation with SAN solutions is that you hire an expert, you have probably realized that we don't intend to provide a whole lot of instruction on setting these up. We do want to offer a few ideas to get you started thinking about media management in a SAN environment. If nothing else, this will give you a feel for just how different these setups are from your traditional media drives.

Remember, you can find technical information about SANs in Chapter 5, and the case study in Chapter 17 uses a SAN environment extensively. The following are only some basics for how to think about working with a SAN.

Organization on the Network Level

Working on a SAN provides a higher overall level of organization for machines and drives on the network. You already have an idea of what I mean if you have ever worked in a (nonvideo) network environment where you could log in with your identity on different machines on the network, and have access to the same features and files regardless of where you physically were on the network.

Setting this up requires a lot of work on the back end, but the experience to users on the network can be seamless. A good example is a large SAN developed to support the FCP labs and classrooms of a large university. In this case, a system of logins and permissions was created so that every student who accessed the network had a login that allowed them to access their own media—and no one else's. There was a system for assigning and retiring logins and disk space as the students cycled through. There were special logins for the instructors, so they could access all of their students' media and could grade projects right from their offices.

You can see that sophisticated setups to fit particular needs are quite achievable with SAN systems. But again, setting up these systems is not simple. These solutions do not come out of a box—they take a lot of expert configuration.

Organization on the Media Level

Once you have set up this higher level of access and organization on your SAN, there is another set of questions regarding where media are stored. Combining your media organization with your network organization leads the way to powerful collaborative work environments in the SAN.

One simple benefit is that often used graphics, IDs, and stock footage can be put onto the SAN in a place that allows access for all users. Now, even if most of the media is separated based on logins and permissions, you can also have an area of media that is accessible to all.

As you might expect, organizing media on the SAN has certain things in common with strategies you would use in a traditional drive setup. However, with the SAN, there are even more possibilities and options.

There are a number of great resources for learning Xsan. They include *Xsan Quick-Reference Guide, Second Edition: A Comprehensive Guide to Xsan Setup and Administration* by Adam Green and Matthew Geller (Peachpit Press); *Optimizing Your Final Cut Pro System: A Technical Guide to Real-World Post-Production* by Sean Cullen, Matthew Geller, Charles Roberts, and Adam Wilt (Peachpit Press); and *Mac OS X v10.4 System Administration Reference, Volume 2: Directory Services, Security and Networking and File Services* by Schoun Regan (Peachpit Press). The Web provides some great resources as well:

- *http://www.xsanity.com*—a great site specifically about working with XSAN
- *http://www.afp548.com*—a great resource for OS X server administration

Using the Media Manager Tool

The Media Manager is a powerful but underutilized tool in Final Cut Pro. We think that probably many editors either don't know that it exists, don't know what it does, or just don't think they have any use for it. The idea behind the Media Manager is that it is a tool used for manipulating your media files by executing the decisions that you've made inside the project, as filtered by the choices you make with the tool.

Sounds a bit complicated, but if we break the Media Manager down and really understand how it works, we can unlock its power. Before we get to the technical details, however, it is important to illustrate why the Media Manager is so powerful for workflows.

You know from all of your experience with FCP that it is a nondestructive program. Media files are saved on a hard drive, and the project contains decisions for playing back those media in sequences. Basically, no matter what you do inside Final Cut Pro, the media files on your drive remain unchanged. This is what makes it a nondestructive program. The one exception is the Media Manager.

Make no mistake: the Media Manager has the power to mess with your media files as they exist on your scratch disk or anywhere else they are stored. In older versions of the software, we used to call this tool the Media Mangler, because we had such difficult experiences with it. The tool has gotten somewhat better, but it is still something to be careful with. Before you execute a media-manage (and especially before you permanently wipe out any media), always double-check that you have what you need and are doing what you intend to do. The Media Manager is less forgiving than are other parts of Final Cut Pro. There is no undo here, so you definitely want to measure twice, cut once.

Why Use the Media Manager?

Before we go any further into how to actually use the Media Manager, it is useful to mention some real-world scenarios in which we would employ this resource. The Media Manager is a flexible tool, but all of its functions have a central theme: manipulating media based on project decisions. Keeping in mind some specific instances where this resource is useful will be helpful in understanding how it works.

- You are working on a hi-def film at the studio where you are employed. It is nearing the end of the day on Friday, and the scene you are working on is not coming together. Your boss asks if you would mind taking it home to work on it over the weekend on your laptop.

    It means some overtime for you, so you are game, but your laptop can't handle uncompressed hi def. You need to package up the work-in-progress sequence(s), along with any of the media you are using for the scene, and down-convert those media to a codec that will work well on your laptop, such as DVCPRO HD, DV, or OfflineRT.

- You have used your home machine to offline at DV resolution some footage that was originally shot in HD. For finishing, you wish to reconform the piece using the full-resolution HD footage. We know from Chapter 1 that one of the things that makes FCP special is resolution independence. You should be able to move from the DV to the HD environment by taking your project—no need for an EDL or other transfer medium. You just need a project containing the final sequence with clips that are offline and ready to be recaptured.

- You have a large project that is still in progress, but you have already determined that you don't need a lot of the media you originally captured. You want to keep working, but to clear drive space based on what you now know you're not going to need.

- You have captured a number of full tapes of interview material, and have then broken them up into separately named bites using subclips. Now you want to make new media files with your descriptive subclip names and, based on the subclip limits, throw out all of the excess media that contain the unusable material.

Although some of these objectives could be achieved by other means, the Media Manager is particularly useful in tasks like these that involve manipulations of media files and FCP projects based on the workflow needs of a project.

Master, Affiliate, and Independent Clips

Before we break down the different controls in the Media Manager, it would be a good idea to look at one area that causes a lot of confusion about media management: the difference between master, affiliate, and independent clips, and how they relate to the Media Manager.

Master Clip—This is what is created the first time a clip appears in the Browser. The master clip also controls the relationship of the affiliate clips to the media on disk.

Affiliate Clip—This is a clip that refers back to the master clip (and therefore back to the original media). There are two good ways to understand this relationship: (1) If you duplicate a master clip in the Browser and then rename the master, the duplicate (the affiliate) will also have its name changed; and (2) if you a bring a master clip into the sequence (creating an affiliate), and then use the Reveal Master Clip command (Shift-F), the master clip will be revealed. Here are the ways of creating an affiliate clip:

- Edit a master clip into a sequence.
- Duplicate a clip in the Browser or in a sequence (Option-drag, copy and paste).
- Drag a clip back into the Browser from the sequence (if a master is already in the Browser).

Note: you can make an affiliate clip its own master clip (Modify > Make Master Clip), therefore breaking its relationship to the original master clip and allowing you to give the clip its own name and attributes. Additionally, duplicating an affiliate clip will always create another affiliate clip, and subclips are automatically master clips when they are created.

Independent Clip—This is a clip that severs the relationship between an affiliate in the Timeline and its master. All properties of the clip are independent, and independent clips reference the media directly rather than linking back through the master clip. This means that unlike affiliate clips, any changes you make to a master do not affect an independent clip. Remember, independent clips live only in sequences. Dragging an independent clip into the Browser creates a new master clip, and the formerly independent clip becomes an affiliate of that new master.

To make an instance of a clip on the Timeline an independent clip, simply right-click on the clip and choose Make Independent Clip.

Knowledge of these clips is important in understanding what and how much media are going to be included in a media-manage operation.

Controls in the Media Manager

The Media Manager is a fairly complex tool. However, it is divided into several sections for the different kinds of controls you have when you use it. Taking these one at a time will help us understand the different ways in which the tool can be used, depending on your objectives.

You can launch the tool with File > Media Manager, but notice that this option is grayed out unless either the Timeline or the Browser is active. For now, unless otherwise noted, let's just assume that the Timeline is active. In this case, the Media Manager will be acting on the open sequence. When you choose this menu option, the Media Manager window launches (Figure 12.3).

Now let's look at each section of the tool individually. The result of the media-management action will depend on all of the settings together, so they are all related.

Summary—The top section of the Media Manager tool is itself divided into two sections: a text summary and an interactive graph. These are both considered part

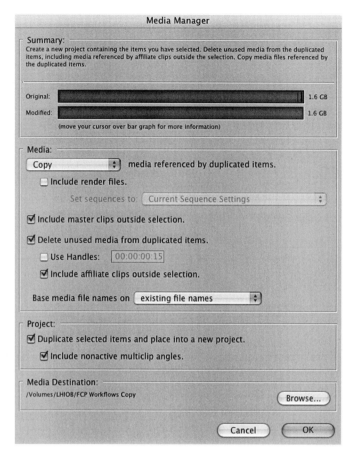

Figure 12.3 The Media Manager.

of the Summary section because they each offer a different way to summarize the results of the Media Manager action if taken with the current settings

Text Summary—This is a narrative description of what will happen if you press the OK button at the bottom of the window. Let's take the Summary paragraph as it comes up when the Media Manager is in its default setting. If we break the paragraph down into parts, then we can see how this will change if we change the settings.

Create a new project containing the items you have selected. We said for this example that the Timeline would be active, and thus the "items selected" means the current sequence. So a new project will be created containing the current sequence in the Timeline.

Delete unused media from the duplicated items, including media referenced by affiliate clips outside the selection. This means that by default whatever media are not used in the current sequence will be not be included in our media-manage action. However, the affiliate clip language means that the action will include media of clips affiliated with the clips in your sequence—for example, affiliates in other sequences.

Copy media files referenced by the duplicated items. This is key. What will happen to the media that we have chosen to use in (and now to manage based on) our sequence? In this case, it will be copied to a new location.

Interactive Graph—Located directly below the text summary, the interactive graph gives both numerical data about the media-manage action indicated by the settings, and a visual representation of this action. Like the text summary, the graph will adjust depending on the settings below.

The two bars represent the amount of media referenced by the selection in the existing project, and the amount of media that will be referenced by the resulting project. The green bars represent regular media files. Sometimes you will see gray extensions to the green bars; the gray extensions represent render files.

To get numerical information, mouse over various sections of the graph. As each section of the graph is highlighted, you will see below the graphs some information regarding the amount of data, the location, and the duration of the media.

It is important to realize that the purpose of the Summary sections is to give you a conceptual preview of the result of the actions planned by the current Media Manager settings. Therefore, as you change the parameters in these other sections, you will see the Summary dynamically adjust.

Media—The choices here determine exactly what the Media Manager is going to do with your media files if you hit the OK button below. Let's take the choices here one at a time. Many decisions that you make in this section will affect the other choices available to you. All of them will change something about the preceding text summary, and some will also have an effect on the graph.

Media Pulldown Menu—This choice is key to the action that the Media Manager takes on your media. Let's take a look at what each one of the choices does.

Copy—A duplicate of the media used in the sequence will be made in a new location.

Move—The original media file referred to by the sequence will be moved to a new location. Let's pause here for a second. Remember how we said that the Media Manager can be destructive? Consider that if you use the Move function, the files that you manage will no longer be in the location where they used to be. If the original project, or any project or any person, needs to reference those files in the future, the originals will not be there. Be very careful when using Move in the Media Manager.

Recompress—This allows you to compress the indicated media files and save them in a different format for a different use. This is what you would use in the case of making a DV version of all the media used in a scene to take home.

Use Existing—This means that no files will be moved, but the new project will have references (or links) to the original media on the drive. Use Existing never increases the total amount of media, but this option can decrease the amount when used in combination with the Delete Unused Media check box described later. This is a way of removing unused media from a project, or "trimming down the fat." Again, this is destructive because it is altering your media files as they exist on the scratch drive. When you are executing a media-manage action that will remove original media, you get a special warning—and indeed, you should be very careful with this. Consider, does anyone else use these media? Could there be references to it in any other projects? And most of all, do you have the corresponding source tapes safe and organized? To that point, this is particularly perilous in tapeless workflows where there are no source tapes—remember to archive your tapeless sources.

Create Offline—You would use this for preparing the project for an HD online, as mentioned earlier. Just as with Use Existing, no media is moved and no new media is made—but in this case, there are no links in the resulting project. All of the media is offline—perfect to start reconforming from HD tapes.

Include Render Files—This determines whether or not to use any render files that are associated with the sequence. Depending on the project, you may or may not have render files, and you may or may not want them in the media you manage. It is sometimes a good alternative to not manage the render files, and then to rerender when you get to the destination system. This option is selectable only in the Copy and Move operations.

Recompress Using—This pulldown menu is active only if you choose the Recompress option on the menu above. It is the place to set the codec that you want the new media files recompressed with. The choices here are very similar to the list of choices for native QuickTime exports and sequence-setting presets. Generally, you only want to go down in quality using this function, as in the example of taking a scene home for the weekend. To go the opposite way—from DV to HD, for example—Compressor or a hardware-standards converter is a better tool.

Include Master Clips outside Selection—This check box will choose to either include (checked) or not include (unchecked) media in master clips outside your selection. Take the following example. You are using the first 10 seconds of a 30-second clip in your sequence; however, your master clip is marked at 20 seconds. Leaving this option unchecked, only the media needed to create the 10-second clip in the sequence will be included. With this option checked, the 10 seconds *plus* any additional media needed to re-create the master clip as marked will be included. This option is selectable only in Copy, Recompress, and Create Offline operations.

Delete Unused Media from Duplicated Items—This setting determines whether the Media Manager will eliminate or keep portions of a clip that are not used in the sequence when the Media Manager moves, copies, or recompresses new clips. Normally, checking the button will cause the graphical summary on top to change noticeably. The Modified green bar will be 100 percent of the Original green bar above it if the box is unchecked. Check the box, and the Modified green bar will shrink substantially. The new relationship between the green bars is the ratio of the amount of media you imported into your project to the amount of media you actually used. This option is available for all operations.

Use Handles—This control allows you to eliminate unused media, but also to keep some extra media, or pad, around the media that are included. Use Handles is available only when Delete Unused Media from Duplicated Items is checked. This option can be useful if you are moving a rough cut to a different system for additional editing toward a picture lock. You are confident that all of the shots are roughly in the right places, but you want the new editing to have leeway to trim and adjust shots. This operation is available for all options.

Include Affiliate Clips outside Selection—This option when selected will include all media in affiliated clips in your selection. When deselected, those affiliated clips will not be included. For example, suppose you are using 20 seconds of a clip in one sequence, and 20 seconds of the same clip in another sequence. Even if you are managing only one of these sequences, that other affiliate and the media needed for it will be included in the media-manage function when this option is checked. This option is selectable only for Copy, Recompress, and Create Offline

Base Media File Names On—What will the new media files be called? This menu gives us two choices: existing filenames and clip names. This control is most easily understood if we think about the preceding example where we have made subclips, and now we want to make new media files based on them. In this case, you definitely want to choose clip names here. If you choose existing filenames, you are going to wind up with a bunch of clips with names such as "Scientist Interview Whole Tape 1_3." However, if you choose clip names, the names that you gave the subclips in Final Cut Pro will be used. So you will have informative names such as "Good Bite about Global Warming," which is much more useful. Remember, this choice has an effect only on clips that have been renamed inside the project.

Project—The Media Manager has the ability to create a new project based on the sequence you are managing. In the previous three examples, taking the scene home requires that you create a project and new media. Preparing for the HD online requires a project only (the media is recaptured from source tapes). Creating new media files based on subclips does not require a project to be created, only new media files.

The first check box simply tells the Media Manager whether to duplicate items based on the above settings, and whether or not to create a new project file. It is selectable for all operations except Create Offline. The second check box comes into play only when doing multicam editing. It allows you to also manage clips not actually used, but associated with others that are used as part of the same multiclip.

Media Destination—This lets you determine where to put the managed media.

You can see now why the Media Manager is a very powerful workflow tool. Workflows are so concerned with how media move through the postproduction process, and this flexible tool facilitates all kinds of media moves from within the FCP interface.

Archiving Media

The final aspect of media management we have to discuss is archiving: what you do with your media when you are done with a project. Like most workflow issues, this is a question that will be answered differently for each project and each studio. The need to hold onto media in a digital format is sometimes very small. Other times, archiving may be one of the main reasons for the whole project.

There is one central question that you should ask yourself when contemplating how to archive media: What is the cost of the archiving solution (in time and money) now, compared to the expected savings (again, time and money) in the future? In other words, if you invest the time and money to archive your media, what will be the payoff of that work to projects in the future? The case study in Chapter 14 illustrates how an archiving solution can be very cost effective, even for a relatively small organization.

Saving FCP Projects and Source Tapes

We consider saving FCP project files and original source tapes to be the first level of archiving. Our logic is that in almost every professional-level project, there is rarely a reason not to save these two things.

1. FCP projects are relatively small files.

2. Master source tapes represent an original record of an event. The cost that goes into documenting this event (or any kind of shot) far exceeds the cost of the actual tapes, or of storing them. Of course, things are different when working with tapeless formats such as P2. Unlike tapes, tapeless formats are meant to be reused—this is why the archiving feature described in Chapter 7 is so important.

3. For a well-constructed FCP project, just the project file and the source tapes should be enough to resurrect the entire project by recapturing.

4. When using this method, don't forget that most projects have media assets that do not originate on videotape (photographs, graphics, music, fonts, etc.). When using this archiving technique, it is a good idea to also collect these assets, burn them to a CD or DVD, and store these discs with the original source tapes.

Retaining your final FCP projects and your source tapes is so simple that it shouldn't really count as an archiving solution. You should just do it as a matter of course.

Hard-Drive Archives

When hard-drive space was more expensive, drives were used mostly to store "live" media—the stuff we were currently working with. When a project was finished, we were likely to "blow out" the drive, or erase all of the old media, to start a new project. At this point, we would save the project file and the source tapes somewhere safe. Depending on our studio and our project, maybe there were additional steps to complete the archiving process.

What we would probably NOT want to do is leave a lot of media to sit around on a hard drive indefinitely. This would be considered a waste of expensive drive space that could be used to facilitate other current projects.

However, as drive space has gotten cheaper, leaving media on a hard drive indefinitely has become at least a partial archiving solution in many situations. We have recommended to several of our clients that they purchase a FireWire drive to keep an ongoing archive of their evergreen material. This is not necessarily everything they shoot, but good clips that can be used and reused in different pieces for a reasonably long period. Chapter 14: Money-Saving Digital Video Archive is a case study describing one such scenario. Some of the other case studies also have variations on this theme.

Archiving to a hard drive is a method that is often used in combination with some of the organization schemes mentioned before. For instance, having a hard-drive archive of raw material on an external FireWire drive means that you can bring that drive anywhere to edit (your studio, your client's office, a post house). Gotta love the sneakernet!

For long-term archiving, this is not the best solution because hard drives can go bad from sitting around too long and not spinning.

Other Media-Storage Devices

Another option, though becoming less common, is to introduce a different data-storage medium, such as DVD or DLT (digital linear tape). As drive space has gotten less expensive, these secondary data-storage systems have become less necessary. Also, a disadvantage is that using these methods means an extra step of transferring media to them—and then again, when you need to reconstitute a project, the media need to be loaded back onto a hard drive. One more inconvenience is that many units of your storage device are needed to back up a whole project (think dozens of DVDs). In this case, you need to have an additional organization strategy, perhaps even additional software, to address how the media get organized onto the archiving format.

There are a lot of disadvantages to using these alternate media-storage devices, especially when hard drives are as cheap as they are now, and saving project files and master tapes is an almost automatic baseline for archiving. Still, there are occasions where archiving media to separate storage devices can be a good solution.

Database and Web-Based Archives

We touched on databases and web-video solutions previously in the discussions on preparation (Chapter 6) and the review process (Chapter 9). Many of these ideas are also applicable to archiving solutions.

We also see another theme of evolving workflows here: integration. It is likely that if you are using a sophisticated database system to log and review your source media, this same system also facilitates the archiving process. We see that the lines between these activities are also blurring. When you archive media in a way that it is easily accessible for your next project, is this really archiving, or is it starting the preparation for your next project early?

Both. And that is a good thing—that's integration.

And Once Again . . . Final Cut Server

As we know already, Final Cut Server promises to be a new keystone for integrating all of these media-management and workflow activities.

Did we say in Chapter 9 that no area of postproduction workflows has more to gain from the introduction of Final Cut Server than the review process does? Well, you could definitely make the argument that the topics covered in this chapter have the most to gain.

Actually, the argument that we want to make is about integration. The future of postproduction lies in increasingly more integrated workflows—from shooting all the way to archiving. We can see this process continuously being streamlined. Tapeless cameras remove one step of the process—we no longer need to capture from tape. SAN solutions streamline larger projects further—we no longer have to move or copy media; we can access them simultaneously.

When we look at Final Cut Server, it is easy to imagine a future when cameras not only shoot without tapes, they also upload footage automatically through wireless networks. Metadata is entered in-camera or at any location on the network. Producers are viewing footage on the Web, and editors have already begun editing while the shooter is still out in the field. . . . In the future postproduction environment, you might not have to worry about archiving much at all—by the time you are done shooting, your network will have already taken care of it. That's integration.

Like most futuristic scenarios, (at least) two caveats apply:

1. It's not going to be all integrated all the time. Sure, some workflows will always push the bleeding edge, but others will hold on to traditions. Final Cut Server is a separate piece of software, and for that reason alone, many people will continue to use FCP for archiving solutions, as discussed in most of this chapter. Final Cut Pro has always been good about supporting a wide range of workflows, from the basic to the newest and most complex. This is part of being scalable, and part of the appeal of the software, and we hope that it continues.

2. Even with the most advanced technologies and workflows, many of the same principles apply. How you record your footage or how it gets ingested makes little difference to the need for good logging and clip naming. In a sense, the need for

media management goes back to organizing clips of film in physical bins. Sure, technology has changed, but you still need to find the clip you are looking for.

When it comes to managing media, the rapid move toward integration and the real-world caveats both apply. Our archiving and organizational schemes will continue to grow in their complexity and level of integration, but many of the principles will remain immutable.

Please see two additional chapters on Final Cut Server workflows on the Web at *http://booksite.focalpress.com/Osder/finalcut/*.

13 Working with External Resources

We saw in Chapters 10 and 11 how Final Cut Studio presents an integrated system for performing virtually all of the stages of a postproduction workflow right on the desktop. For the most part, since the introduction of Final Cut Pro, the industry has been moving toward operators needing to be generalists. It is expected in many cases that an editor will also be able to do motion graphics, mixing, and DVD authoring to boot! Truly, you can be a one-man band, and more than a few people are successful with this model.

However, the process of learning all the applications in the entire Studio and developing the skill sets that they entail can be daunting, and may not be possible for all of us. Again, this raises philosophical and strategic issues about professional roles identified in Chapter 3. Just because you can be a one-man band doesn't mean it is always a good idea. Sometimes the divide-and-conquer approach is more advantageous.

There are a number of logistical reasons that you may choose to send a project out of house—for example, a time crunch or lack of resources. However, more often than not, the main reason that you reach out to outside resources is to work with a specialist. You may have some experience using Color for color correction, or Soundtrack Pro for audio mixing, but in general, a specialist (often with equipment beyond Final Cut Studio) can do the job better and faster (though probably not cheaper, which is why they say you can pick only two).

This is another example where Final Cut Pro plays well with others. This chapter is about facilitating workflows that exit the Final Cut Studio environment. This actually blends together two concepts that are related, but essentially different:

- Working with vendors. A vendor is an outside company that you hire for a task instead of using an internal resource. This chapter gives some pointers on the nature of this business relationship and how to manage it.

- Moving projects between the Final Cut Studio environment and other postproduction environments.

Often you will be doing both of these things together: hiring an outside company specifically because they have the skills outside Final Cut Studio. However, a vendor could also be an FCP specialist who is not part of your company.

This chapter is written mostly from the point of view of a studio that needs to hire and communicate with a vendor, but in truth, we are all both clients and vendors at some point. The techniques in this chapter should be easy to translate into good practices if you are on either side of the equation.

Why Work with a Vendor?

What are your needs, and why is it a good decision to delegate them to an outside resource? Like many aspects of workflow thinking, defining your needs prior to working with a vendor is critical for ensuring the success of your project.

Your needs will be based largely on the actual project on which you are working. But there are a few things that can help define these needs clearly, and thus assist you in making a good choice as to whether or not to hire a vendor.

1. *Technical Resources*—Are there technical things that prevent you from moving the project forward? For example, if the next step in a project is color correction and grading, do you know how to use Color? If you have to make your final output, do you need access to a deck that only a post house in your area has?

2. *Resource Load*—If multiple parts of your workflow need to happen simultaneously, do you have depth in your equipment and staff to make this possible?

3. *Time*—Perhaps the project you're working on has a tight schedule (don't they all?). Is there enough time for you or your team to complete all the tasks required?

4. *Budget*—Does your budget mandate that you complete all the work internally, or can you involve vendors?

It is vital to define why you want to work with a vendor. If you are unsure, keep asking these questions. Often multiple reasons will apply. It may be that you have all of the resources that you technically need, but you have the budget to hire a freelance editor based on his or her reputation. Opening up a project to vendors will not only incur cost, it will also necessitate more communication—maybe more communication than your team is prepared for. Thinking hard about these questions and defining the work you want from a vendor are the best preparation.

Poor communication with a vendor almost always leads to two problems: first, getting overcharged; second, dramatic loss of time. In our experience, poor communication is often symptomatic of larger issues. Be honest with yourself if the following areas have previously been an issue. If so, remedying them now will be time well spent.

Technical—We know plenty of editors, designers, and producers who have gotten in over their head with a project. When it came time to communicate with a vendor to complete the work, for technical reasons—such as not knowing anything about tape formats or how to produce an audio OMF (Open Media Framework) (described later)—communication with the vendor came to a standstill. Often the vendor would have to spend an inordinate amount of time educating that person and—you guessed it—charging them even more. Further examples include:

- Improper formatting of EDLs, OMFs, and XML files
- Improper formatting of tapes (timecode, slates, audio assignments)

It is always a good idea to ask your vendor for written specifications for any project or delivery. Also, you might want to provide your own written specifications for the deliverables you need.

Bad Habits—Personal habits also tend to make communication with a vendor more difficult, and often are a big reason why costs and time budgets go wild. For example, many editors we know don't have a system of what type of audio goes on what track (VO on track 1, nat sound on tracks 2 through 5, etc.). This tends to work fine for them, but when the show goes to get mixed by a vendor, the audio mixer has to spend hours reorganizing the tracks so he or she can make sense of what's going on. Further examples include:

- Video- and audio-track layout
- Inconsistent naming conventions

Bad Business Practices—Many of us in the postproduction world like to think of ourselves as fairly savvy business folks. This is perhaps truest for those of us who do freelance work. The truth is, a lot of people in this business are not particularly good at this. Behaviors such as constantly moving around bookings or not paying vendors on time are symptomatic of bad business practices. Further examples include:

- Not respecting scheduling commitments
- Unprofessional accounting practices
- Underestimating how long the project will take to complete
- Overpromising
- Underdelivering

Having a quality set of vendors to work with—and, more importantly, working with them—successfully can really benefit any project. Remember, if you have not defined your needs and analyzed potential workflow and communication problems, you may have a less than ideal experience with a vendor (or they with you, but the vendor might be too nice to tell you!).

What Kind of Vendor Should You Work With?

It may be a bit of an oversimplification, but we divide vendors into two groups: freelancers and companies. This is an oversimplification because often freelancers are actually small companies, whereas larger companies might actually be sending out employees to work much like freelancers. Here are some important distinctions:

A freelancer generally:

- Works on your equipment, in your space.
- Bills by the hour or by the day.
- Does their own booking or works within a very small business structure.

A company generally:

- Has its own facility, and you bring your project there for it to be worked on.
- Probably bills by the hour or the project, depending on the situation.
- Is a larger organization with different departments and roles for booking, billing, and actual creative work.

Over the past six or seven years, the infectious spread of Final Cut Studio has lead to a rapid growth of the freelance market. There are freelance editors, designers, colorists, DVD designers, mixers, and so forth. This is in no small part due to the affordable cost of Final Cut Studio. The tools are now accessible to a much broader group of people; therefore, many people have entered the freelance market.

The growth of this market does not mean that larger companies have disappeared from postproduction. Although, to a certain degree, the era of the mega post house is gone, many facilities have streamlined their operations and are able to offer a wide range of services.

In an interesting twist, many production and postproduction companies are hiring freelancers. In some cases, companies hire freelancers who only a short time ago were actually employees of those same companies! Often this is a simple matter of economics—by replacing employees with freelancers, the companies are no longer responsible for overhead such as health insurance, payroll taxes, and so on.

So how do you decide if your vendor should be a company or a freelancer?

Consider hiring a freelancer if:

1. You have equipment for the freelancer to work on.
2. You have a complicated schedule that you want to be able to have strong control over when the work is done.
3. Choosing the talent is more important than the equipment.

Consider hiring a company if:

1. You do not have equipment for a freelancer to work on.
2. Your schedule requirements are flexible, and as such, you can work within a system of "will-buys" and "holds" that many companies have in place.
3. You require a full-service facility.

What Kind of Terms?

One discussion that always comes up among postproduction professionals is how much to charge and how to bill your clients. In business-speak, these are the terms of a business arrangement.

How much to charge is often a loaded question because there are dozens of variables in play. Our purpose is not to discuss actual rates or specific project budgets. We do feel that it is worthwhile to discuss the "how" of charging.

When we get this question from students, we like to break it down into two fundamental ways of billing (and this applies to contract work that is much broader than just postproduction): charging for labor in increments of time versus charging a flat rate for a project. Charging for labor based on the amount of time is generally done either by the hour or by the day, and this can make a big difference in the bill.

Hourly Rate

Hourly rates from vendors often seem like a bad deal. Typically, quoted hourly rates are the highest possible rate that this work goes for—the "rate card." Hourly rates are usually quoted only for a specific service. So, for example, if it costs $200 per hour to mix your show, but then some sound design needs be done, you're looking at a separate hourly charge—probably higher.

On the other hand, with an hourly rate, you pay only for the time that you actually use. From a vendor's point of view, hourly rates are a great way to charge what a service is really worth. Additionally, hourly rates are a great way of maximizing billables; the more services that a client requests, the more you get to charge. However, your client might have a bit of sticker shock when they see the bill. This is another area where communication is important. Giving budget updates as you move through an hourly project is a good way to alleviate the stress that would otherwise result from your presenting the final bill.

Day Rate

A day rate is also an increment of time, just a larger one. More common for freelancers, working on a day rate implies that you will be spending the whole day on-site with a client, doing what they need. Because this is considered a bulk agreement, the price of a full day is generally less than what you would get by adding up the hours with a high hourly rate.

It's important to define exactly what the day covers: eight hours or ten? And what about overtime? We've had clients who seem to think that once you are booked for the day, you need to stay as long into the evening as needed. From a freelancer's point of view, those extra hours should be charged to a client, and at a premium for overtime.

Flat Rate

Working at a flat rate is a completely different principle from billing for time, and this system has its own pros and cons. The idea is that a vendor commits to a specific set of deliverables for a price, and then is responsible to deliver—regardless of how much labor it takes. Often this means that the vendor is applying a discount based on the quantity of work that the project represents—in other words, your project is a large enough chunk of work that the vendor is willing to cut you a discount in order to get the job. Maybe they are also thinking that they can do the work more quickly than you expect, so a flat rate could be designed to get more money than the vendor thinks they will get by billing for the time. When you get a flat rate from a vendor, look closely at what you have been given. How does it line up with your expectations of what the work would cost if billed by hourly or day labor?

As a vendor, remember that it is very important to define the project exactly with a flat bid. As part of your bid, it is important to document in detail all aspects of the project that you are expecting to perform. If the client then changes these parameters (we call this scope creep), this document will be key in figuring overages.

As a client, remember that if you misrepresent a project at the outset, and sign on to a flat bid based on bad information, it is probably going to come back and bite you in the form of high overage charges.

Knowing How NOT to Get Ripped Off

How not to get ripped off . . . hmmm, doesn't that seem like a good idea!

With postproduction, as with many businesses, part of the trick is to make your clients feel that you are bending over backward and experiencing real hardship to give them the fantastic deal they are getting. Of course, you don't want to actually bend over backward or experience hardships; you just want them to *think* they are putting one over on you.

Here are some tips for making sure you're getting the best deal:

1. *Research, research, research!* No other method is as important as researching your particular market. This includes—but is certainly not limited to—knowing current rates for services, day rates for various freelancers, and policies of vendors.

2. *Negotiate.* Countless times we have seen companies pay overblown fees simply because they are unwilling to negotiate. If a company quotes $200 per hour for a given service, but your budget allows for only $175, why not at least ask about getting a break? And remember, a negotiation is not a negotiation unless you are willing to walk away.

3. *Make a vendor accountable.* Holding a vendor to their deliverables, quoted time, and standards of service is mandatory. You hold a lot of leverage in the sense that you control payment.

Although it is outside the scope of this book, having your commitments on paper in the form of a contract is also an important part of not getting ripped of. If you don't want to hire a lawyer for a small project, check the Web for boilerplate contracts—it's better than nothing.

Booking a Vendor

It is a fact of postproduction that schedules shift. When working within your own studio, you handle this internally, shuffling resources to other projects, but when you are working with vendors, it can become a much bigger issue. We see a lot of problems in the area of scheduling vendors.

Many vendors have a booking system in place, based on the concepts of "hold" and "will-buy." Although understanding that system is nowhere near as difficult as understanding chroma subsampling, it can be just as important to your project.

Hold—A hold is simply a way of reserving a day, an edit room, talent, or some other item with no hard commitment. Holds are generally stacked in the order in which they are received. For example, if you call your favorite audio post house to book a mix session, and they tell you there is already a hold on that day, you will become a second hold. Another way of looking at this is that you are next in line if the first hold should drop out.

Will-Buy—A will-buy is a commitment to a day, an edit room, talent, or some other item. By making this commitment, you are in most cases financially obligated to that vendor. For example, if changes in the project schedule now dictate that the mix day you bought for Monday now needs to be moved to Friday, you will have to pay for the Monday session regardless of whether you actually used the time. Therefore, it is extremely important that prior to making will-buys, you are sure of your schedule.

Challenge—In most cases, a hold can be challenged. What this means is that if you had a hold on a particular day, but someone else came along and committed to a "will-buy" for that same day, the vendor would ask you to either respond with your own will-buy commitment or else release the day. The hold is, in essence, a right of first refusal.

Although not every vendor works with a will-buy and hold system, *smart* vendors do. It is a way of protecting their interests and making sure that if and when they turn away work, they are compensated. We have all learned by this point that "time *is* money."

Paying a Vendor

Have you ever been stiffed by a client? This happens for a variety of reasons—such as "We're waiting for our client to pay us first," or (our favorite) "Oh yeah, that check is in processing"—for 110 days . . . come on! Really, the rules to paying a vendor come down to the Golden Rule: Do unto others as you would have them do unto you.

1. If a vendor has lived up to their end of an agreement and performed services specified by your agreement, and they have sent you a bill, pay that bill! Pay it by any means necessary.

2. Only if—and we stress *only if*—a vendor has not provided the services required should you withhold payment. Every effort should be made to make arrangements with the vendor to remedy any existing problems and issues.

Preparing Files for Your Vendor

Now that we know a little more about workflow planning and the business aspects of working with a vendor, let's take a look at some of the technical aspects of such a relationship. It's always a good idea to go over all of the technical aspects of a handoff. Make sure to allow plenty of time for questions or concerns—ahead of the start date. Every project will have a specific set of deliverables and notes for a handoff. The following section outlines many of the key elements.

Often when working with an outside vendor, there is a need to reconstruct your sequence on your vendor's equipment. This can be for any of several reasons:

1. Moving a project to another digital postproduction environment such as Avid or Discreet for offline or an online editing session

2. Conforming a show in a linear suite

3. A color correction session

Again, getting guidelines from your vendor for this type of transfer is advisable.

There are several common methods for moving a sequence—namely, EDL, XML, and AAF.

Edit Decision List

EDLs are just what they sound like—a simple set of instructions for transferring sequences for all of the previous reasons. EDLs can take on several formats, such as CMX, Sony, and GVG. Final Cut Pro specifically supports CMX 340, CMX 3600, Sony 5000, Sony 9100, and GVG 4 Plus. Each format is named for the company that created it. Originally, these distinctions also indicated special formatting for the floppy disks on which the EDLs resided.

The difference between these formats is mainly in the formatting of the file—number of characters allowed for reel names, clip names, and even how large the spaces are between fields.

It is always best to check with your vendor about which format is appropriate for their particular equipment. That being said, CMX 3600 is the most common EDL format. The thing to remember about working with EDLs is that they are an antiquated but still widely used interchange format. Therefore, they are designed with linear edit systems in mind. Chances are, if something cannot be done in a linear edit system, you can't include it in an EDL. There are some key things to be aware of prior to exporting an EDL:

Reel Names—Generally limited to five to seven characters, depending on the format. If your reel name is longer than this, the reel name in the EDL will be abbreviated. This can cause a lot of confusion. If you know that an EDL is going to be part of your workflow, it is a good idea, for purposes of conforming a show, that you limit your reel names on ingest, or edit the reel names in the Browser prior to exporting your EDL. You should also avoid using special characters in the reel name. Use of numbers versus letters can sometimes also be an issue; it's a good idea to ask your vendor.

Number of Video Tracks—EDL formats support one video track and what's called a key track (video track 2). All other tracks are ignored. Additionally, a B-reel EDL is sometimes created as well (explained later). You can approach this limitation in more than one way. You can combine all of your video onto one track. If this is not possible, you will need to export separate EDLs for each track.

Number of Audio Tracks—EDL formats support up to four tracks of audio. If you have

more than this in your sequence, you will need to either export multiple audio-only EDLs or find another interchange method for your audio (for example, OMF).

Transitions and Effects—EDL formats support only a few standard effects, such as dissolves and wipes. Other transitions and filters that you use can be included only as a note in the EDL.

To export an EDL from Final Cut Pro, use these steps:

1. Select the sequence you wish to export. Go to File > Export > EDL.

2. Assign a title to the EDL. By default, this title will be the name of the sequence, but it may make more sense, especially if you are exporting an EDL for each track, to attach the track name in the title (for example, "MyProjectVideoTrack1").

3. Choose your EDL format. CMX 3600 is the most common.

4. Choose your sorting method: the Master, Audio Merged option will order the clips as they appear in your sequence, with audio files that start and end at the same time merged as one event in the EDL. The Source, Audio Merged option will order clips based on their original source tapes and timecode. In other words, the first item listed in the EDL will be the first shot on the lowest-numbered reel.

5. Choose whether you want to target only a single video track at a time. With this box checked, key events will not be exported. You will need to have this box checked if you are exporting multiple EDLs. Final Cut Pro uses the current destination track icon in the Timeline to determine which track will be exported. So if you want to export each track as its own EDL, you would first move the "current destination track" icon to the track you want to export, and then go to File > Export > EDL

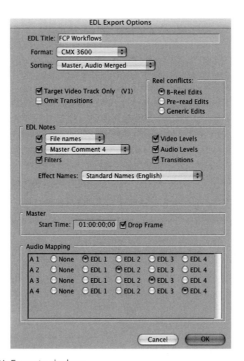

Figure 13.1 The EDL Export window.

and check the Target Video Track Only box (which, you will now notice, has in parentheses the track to which you moved the destination icon).

6. Choose whether to include or omit transitions. Remember: EDLs support only standard transitions such as wipes and dissolves. Chances are that a transition you have decided to use will not be supported. Generally, if the purpose of the EDL is for an online session, this is a really good idea—it makes the EDL pretty simple.

7. Choose what type of reel conflicts to include in the EDL. A reel conflict happens when a transition needs two clips from the same reel (something that normally is not possible to do in a linear suite). This actually becomes an issue only when a show is being reassembled in a linear suite. Here are three ways to fix the conflicts:

B-Reel Edits—Final Cut Pro creates a separate EDL that contains only the conflicts. To properly conform this in the linear suite, though, all of the B-reel shots (the second shots in the transition) must be on their own tape.

Preread Edits—Final Cut Pro adds the command PREREAD in the EDL and requires two decks, one of which must have preread capabilities. Preread is sort of a technical sleight of hand. A deck with preread can act as both a playback deck and a record deck. The deck first reads a clip off a master tape, then lays it back on the same tape, and finally transitions to the second clip, which is played back from another VTR.

Generic Edits—Final Cut Pro takes no special action if there are reel conflicts. This is the option to use if the show is going to be conformed by another nonlinear edit system—there are no limitations about using two clips from the same reel to form transitions.

8. Choose what information you want to be included as notes in the EDL. You can choose to include either the filenames (as they exist on disk) or the clip names (what you've named them in FCP). You can choose which Comment fields from the Browser to include. Lastly, you can choose whether to include video levels (opacity), audio levels (volume), transitions as notes.

9. Choose the starting timecode and timecode format of the EDL. This should match your sequence.

10. Lastly, choose how tracks are mapped. Remember, in most EDL formats, you are limited to four tracks.

XML

XML stands for eXtensible Markup Language. Unlike EDLs (described before) and OMF files (described later), XML is much more flexible. In fact, it is designed to be a lingua franca for the whole world of computing. Since version 4, Final Cut Pro has been an XML-compliant program. Almost every aspect of a clip, sequence, or project can be exported as part of an XML file.

XML is farther-reaching than just simple file interchange. In Part 3, we detail a project where XML was used to create a custom media-management solution on the Web. Applications such as Final Cut Server also have XML at their core. Widely used inside the Final Cut Studio, XML is a way of sending information to and from applications (more on this in Chapter 11: The Power of Final Cut Studio).

XML is also a great way of getting around project-file-version limitations (described later). This is because XML is not tied to a specific application version—only to the version of the standard. So, in other words, if you needed to take an FCP 6 project and open it on an FCP 5 system, you could export an XML file using the correct version of the interchange.

Figure 13.2 The XML Export window.

Not every postproduction tool works with XML, but more and more are becoming compatible. Without getting totally computer science about it, the thing to understand about XML is that it is an open-markup language—it can relate any data for which there is a definitions document. Anything that is defined in XML can be processed in various ways, most notably by being "translated" to a different XML definition. The actual XML definition for FCP can be found at *http://developer.apple.com/documentation/ AppleApplications/Reference/FinalCutPro_XML/index.html*.

So any software that has an XML definition can now work with Final Cut Pro in some capacity.

To export an XML file, use these steps:

1. Select the sequence, project, or clip(s) you wish to export. Pay special attention to what you have selected—all of the items that are selected will be exported.

2. Choose which version of the XML interchange you want to use. Typically, this will be the latest one (version 4 for FCP 6) but if you need to export for older versions of FCP or for other software that supports only older versions of the interchange, you can choose the correct one here.

Viewing XML Files

If you are curious to learn more about XML, and you have never looked at an actual XML file, it is pretty interesting. Manipulating these raw files is a bit outside the scope of this book, but here are some simple instructions to just see what they look like.

Take the XML file that you saved and open it in a text editor. This file has an XML extension. Because, by default, this file will open back in FCP, you will need to tell your system to open it as a text file by right-clicking and choosing Open With (you can then choose TextEdit, or any other text editor or web-authoring program that is on your system), or by dragging the file icon to the icon of your text editor in the dock.

Once you open the file, you will see a lot of code. This is your FCP project described in XML. If you look closely, you will see some language familiar to you from FCP in this code: duration, rate, in and out, and things such as description and log note (these are the same fields that you fill in during logging). Essentially all of the data contained in your FCP project has been written out in this XML code, and can now be read by other software (as well as, to a certain extent, by humans).

3. Choose to include master clips outside the selection. With this checked, the XML file will include master clips assoiciated with a given sequence from the in point to the out point that are set on the master clip.

4. Choose whether you want to save the project at the same time you export the XML file with the "Save project with latest clip metadata (recommended)" check box.

5. Choose a destination for the file.

AAF

As discussed in Chapter 5, AAF (Advanced Authoring Format) is a new format that promises to be a universal method of transferring assets to varying software applications. It contains both media and metadata "wrapped up" together in a package that should be highly transferable. Currently, Soundtrack Pro is the only application within the Studio that supports AAF import and export. Final Cut Pro does not natively support AAF interchange. However, Automatic Duck's Pro Export FCP 3.0, an export plug-in for Final Cut Pro, can be used to support the AAF interchange directly from Final Cut Pro.

OMF

Introduced by Avid in 1991, OMF stands for Open Media Framework. OMF has become the standard way that audio is passed on to a vendor for sound design and mixing. In a nutshell, when you export an OMF file from Final Cut Pro, all of your audio (media) and their timings (In points and Out points, as well as position on the Timeline) are combined into a single OMF file. When the file is opened up by your vendor, all of your tracks and their timings are reconstructed in the software that your vendor is using.

Although OMF can be used for transferring video files via OMFI (Open Media Framework Interchange), Final Cut Pro supports only the export of OMF audio files. There are also several things that you should be aware of with OMF:

1. OMF files are limited to 2GB in size. Therefore, if you are exporting a very long show, you might need to export multiple OMFs. This can be accomplished easily by splitting up your export. To do this, turn off some audio tracks by using the green Audio Controls button in the track-control area of the Timeline. Final Cut Pro will respect this, and export only the tracks that are on. For example, OMF #1 might be tracks 1-6, and OMF #2 tracks 7-12.

2. OMF files from Final Cut Pro 6 (not previous versions) can contain volume, pan, and cross-fade (but not filter) information. Always check with your vendor to find out if they want this information embedded in the file. Some mixers like to start with a blank slate, whereas others like to have your volume and pan keyframes included so they can use them as a reference.

3. Nested-sequence audio will be exported as one file, not as the separate files that make up the nest. Also, any clips that have a speed change or have been reversed will be embedded in the OMF file that way.

4. OMF files embed timecode from your sequence into the file. This means that if your sequence starts at 01:00:00;00, that will be the starting timecode of your OMF file. This is particularly important if your audio vendor is mixing to picture using a reference master (discussed later). The timecode of your OMF must match that of the reference master in order to ensure sync.

To export an OMF from Final Cut Pro, follow these steps:

1. Select the sequence you want to export.

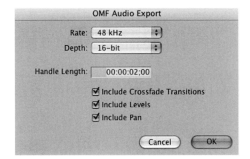

Figure 13.3 The OMF Export window.

2. Go to File > Export > Audio to OMF, or right-click on a sequence in the Browser and choose Export > Audio to OMF.

3. When the dialogue box pops up, choose your appropriate sample rate (32kHz, 44.1kHz, 48kHz, 88.2kHz, 96kHz) and bit depth (16 bit, 24 bit). Generally this should match your current Timeline settings.

4. Choose your handle length. Handles will add extra media to your clips on both the In point and Out point sides. By adding handles, you give your vendor "wiggle" room for things such as cross-fades and slipping. Two to three seconds is standard. Be aware that handles add media to the OMF file. On long projects, this can easily contribute to files being larger than 2GB, thus requiring multiple OMFs.

5. Choose whether you want to include cross-fade, level, and pan information in the file.

6. Save the file to your selected destination.

7. Burn the file onto a CD or DVD, label it, and deliver it to your vendor—or, if bandwidth will allow, upload the file to an FTP server that you and your vendor can access.

Reference Masters

Video references often accompany OMF files going to audio mix when picture lock has been reached. The audio mixer uses the reference tape so they can mix to picture. This reference is usually on a videotape with matching timecode, but other methods—such as using a QuickTime file with embedded or burned-in timecode—are acceptable and are starting to be popular for exchange.

The important thing to understand about reference masters is that they don't necessarily have to have the final images, text, graphics, and so on, but they do have to be picture locked. Often, after an OMF and reference tape have been delivered and mixing is taking place, stock imagery is replaced, final graphics are placed, and other visual problems are fixed. What cannot change, however, are timings. If you lengthen or shorten visuals, especially items that have sync sound, you will have to re-export your OMF file to match. This is why picture lock is so important.

Project Files and Media Files

Although EDLs, XMLs, AAFs, and OMFs are great for interchange between different software applications, sometimes the vendors that you will be working with are using the same software that you are.

If this is the case, consider yourself very lucky! Final Cut Studio project files contain vastly greater amounts of information than any interchange file format can. With that said, if you are exchanging project files with a vendor, there are some issues to pay attention to.

Versions—Final Cut Studio applications can read previous-version project files, but (for obvious reasons) cannot read newer versions. This can be important if you're on the latest and greatest versions of the applications, but your vendor is working on old versions.

Media Files—By itself, exchanging a project file doesn't do a whole lot. Remember, a project file is everything about your project *except* the media. Your vendor will require the media. The media can reside on disk as previously captured or created files, or—as is the case for many offline/online workflows—on the original tapes, which your vendor can then recapture.

Documentation

With all the wonderful ways of exchanging media project files with vendors, one of the most overlooked aspects of these workflows is documentation. More mistakes and problems arise from improper documentation than you'd probably think. It never hurts to document things more than you need to. Let's take a look at some things you should document.

Tapes—Any tape that goes to a vendor (this should be a rule in-house too) should be properly labeled, both on the box and on the actual tape. Additionally, master tapes should also include a printout of slate information—such as segment in/ outs, durations, and clean scenes. Original footage tapes should include a log of shots and or scenes included on that tape.

CDs/DVDs—Like tapes, CDs and DVDs should be properly labeled, both on the actual disc and on the packaging for the disc. It is also very helpful if, just as with a tape, a printout of the disc's contents accompanies the disc.

Comments/Notes—Many vendors and freelancers are really good at what they do; however, they are not mind readers (at least the ones we know), so documenting comments and providing notes are very important. Examples of the type of notes and comments you would want to provide are:

- Mix and sound-design ideas and/or problems.
- Color correction/grading ideas and/or problems.
- Rough-cut or edit-version notes.
- Media-related issues such as rights and licensing, and technical issues such as frame rate, progressive/interlaced, and pulldown patterns.

Next Steps

This chapter concludes Part 2. We've now covered a full range of activities expected in most Final Cut Pro workflows. In Part 3, these building blocks are put into context in a series of real-world case studies.

Moving forward into your own workflow planning, you can count on two things:

1. Postproduction will continue to change. The stages and general structure of this section will hold for a little while, but the techniques and specifics will need to be

updated relatively soon. It is best to remain flexible and open-minded about even what seem like the most secure aspects of workflow thinking.

2. Your own experience will inform the choices you make, and will hone your sense of style for producing, editing, and managing workflows.

Part 2 shows us the conceptual and technical building blocks needed to construct effective workflows. Part 3 will give us some examples of interesting workflows that you can study and adapt. They are not always perfectly planned projects—there are plenty of examples here of thinking on the fly, and things we would have done differently.

PART 3

Real-World Workflows

14 Money-Saving Digital Video Archive

This project was developed in response to the unique archiving needs of a nonprofit client. The organization accumulates a lot video material, and edits a moderate number of pieces with it each year. However, it lacks the budget or internal resources for a full-blown media-management system. Important aspects of the solution are media management at the ingest stage and using an FCP project file as a master archive (also discussed in Chapter 12).

Highlighted Concepts and Techniques

- ⊗ FCP project-based media management
- ⊗ The sneakernet
- ⊗ Digitally screening footage as QuickTime

Challenges

- ⊛ Disorganized source tapes
- ⊛ Limited budget

Overview

This workflow developed organically when the talented and thoughtful staff at an innovative independent studio recognized the long-terms needs of a new client. Their first project together led to a simple archiving solution and an ongoing business relationship.

The idea for the archive solution is the concept of a Final Cut Pro project used as a master project, described in Chapter 12. Some media management applied at the ingest stage and taking advantage of Final Cut Pro's resolution independence (particularly using the DV codec and the ProRes 422 codec as near-full-quality archiving formats), make for a robust and flexible solution.

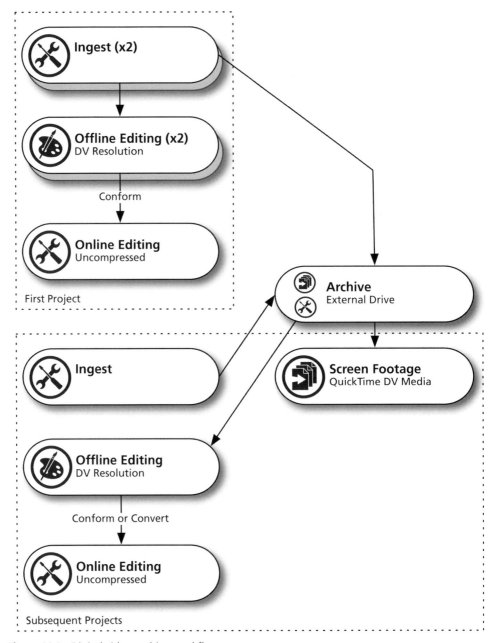

Figure 14.1 Digital video archive workflow.

Project Roles and Responsibilities

The important roles in this project are fairly typical for a corporate (read: nontelevision industry) client working with an independent studio.

Communications Director—Jill is the communications director (client point of contact) for the nonprofit organization. Her organization works on global health issues and uses celebrities to spread their message worldwide.

Frequently, they tour foreign countries with their celebrity spokespeople, and film these trips (as well as other domestic events) to be used for fund-raising and general communications. However, the organization's video experience is minimal, and their small staff is stretched thin managing all aspects of these trips and programs. Not much time or money is dedicated to producing their video content in the field.

As the communications director, the job of supervising postproduction for the organization's videos falls to Jill. She is responsible for hiring the studio, communicating the organization's goals to them, and supervising the work. In a sense, she is the executive producer (EP) of the project. The studio is working to make her happy, and she is the one responsible for getting them paid. However, this should not imply that she has much experience in this area, and Jill is counting on the studio to do good work and to look for opportunities for improvement that she is not aware of. This kind of client/EP relationship is the norm in corporate video.

Producer—Charles is the producer assigned to the project by the independent studio. In the business model of this small studio, this means that he has both creative and management responsibilities. He is the main point of contact with the client, and also works closely with the editors to develop the piece, and to think of solutions for the studio's clients.

Editor—Tommy is the senior editor at the studio. He runs the Final Cut Pro workstation, especially during supervised client sessions. He also works with junior and assistant editors, interpreting the clients' and producers' goals for his subordinates, and supervising their execution toward those goals. Although his main focus is creative, Tommy is very technically knowledgeable, and also participates in designing and executing media-management solutions.

Assistant Editor—Cindy is an assistant editor at the studio. She works under Tommy and supports him, especially in time-consuming tasks such as Log and Capture. Cindy is creative and talented, and she often does original creative work with Tommy's guidance.

Required Equipment

The following list describes the equipment for the specific needs of this project. However, the real keys to this basic workflow are the FCP system and the external FireWire drive. So many, many FCP users can take advantage of these concepts on some scale.

BetaSP Playback Deck—Most of the shooting that this client commissions is in BetaSP. Although this format is quickly becoming antiquated, remember that this client shoots all around the globe with local crews, making BetaSP more common, and it is still their default shooting format.

Uncompressed Final Cut Pro System with Analog Capture Card—The FCP systems used in this project have high-speed drives rated for uncompressed video playback along with analog capture cards to capture uncompressed video. It is also possible to capture at DV resolution through these cards.

External FireWire Drive—A common piece of equipment, but it is really the heart of this project. As mentioned in Chapter 1, the introduction of FireWire and the

ever-dropping price of disk space are two factors that have driven the changes in the industry. This solution takes advantage of both these things.

Execution

The First Project

When Jill initially contacted Charles at the studio, she was in rush to create a video retrospective for a celebrity who had given a lot to their cause. The star's birthday was in ten days, and the nonprofit wanted to give the video to her on a DVD so she could watch it with her family as a special birthday celebration.

In the past year, the celebrity had done two major trips abroad with the organization (one to Africa and one to Asia). There was a lot of footage from these trips, but it had not been organized, or even viewed by anyone. The nonprofit also had plenty of other video material with the star in it from her ongoing participation with the charity. There was hour upon hour of good footage to work with, but none of it was organized.

So Jill showed up at the studio with an ungainly box of source tapes. After some discussion with Charles, they established that the studio would take the creative reigns of the project, and present her with ideas and cuts to review. Jill left in a rush, making it pretty clear that she had other things to do and did not intend to be looking over their shoulder during the process.

With the tight time frame, there was not a whole lot of time to make a workflow plan or do a complete review of the tapes before ingest. However, Charles and Tommy had a brief meeting, and made some decisions about media management, roles, and process:

1. They decided to split the project onto two separate workstations. Tommy would handle the Africa footage on one FCP system, and Cindy would take care of the Asia footage on a separate workstation. The team felt that this would work because the footage from the different trips would be used in two separate parts of the final video. Of course, the two halves of the piece would have to be put together sometime, but a lot could be accomplished concurrently with this approach.

2. They decided to capture at DV resolution. They wanted to save time by reviewing footage at the same time that they captured it, but this would likely mean capturing more than they needed. So the compromise to capture at DV meant they would not have to be too careful about how much they captured (DV footage takes up much less drive space than uncompressed does), but they would have reasonably good quality to edit with. For finishing, they could reconform from the source tapes, or up-convert to uncompressed color space in FCP if they ran short on time. (The second method would mean some quality loss, but it might be an acceptable compromise for this project.)

3. They set up naming conventions for everything captured on both systems, so that regardless of which station the material was captured on, all of the metadata would follow a consistent scheme. Specifically:

   a. All reel names would be exactly the same as what was written on tape.

   b. The initial bins in the Browser would also be based on tape name, so that the root level in the Browser would have bins that matched the tape and reel names.

   c. A simple controlled vocabulary was created for the other metadata and clip naming. When the star was on camera, it was decided to always use her ini-

tials in the description field rather than her first or last name, for instance. Similarly, it was decided that the scene field would always contain the name of the country that the clip was shot in.

As we saw in Chapter 7, the check boxes in the Logging tab allowed the metadata information to be included as part of the filename. This turned out to be an important aspect of the workflow.

These choices, though made in a hurry, constitute a basic workflow to get started. Charles and the team did not try to lock down the endgame precisely. Rather, on the tight schedule, they decided on some workflow aspects that would get them moving in a hurry—and (they hoped) not paint themselves into any corners.

As we will see, these decisions turned out to be good ones, because the client was happy with the final product—but also because they opened doors to a long-term media-management solution and, in turn, to a long-term client relationship.

The rest of that first project went very smoothly, especially considering the short amount of time and the large amount of disorganized sources. Cindy did some amazing creative work on the Asia material. When it was time to put the two pieces back together, the two sequences were joined together on Tommy's workstation, and he recaptured only the footage that was used in the piece at full uncompressed quality for the online and DVD output. The celebrity and her family loved the video, and it was an appropriate thank-you.

The Archive

By the time the project was done, the studio had logged and captured over six hours of video at DV resolution for a piece that was only about six minutes long. Of course, this was necessary because they had started with so many disorganized tapes. Of the budget on the project, roughly a third of it had gone toward this logging and capturing work.

More to the point, this was unlikely to be the last video that the organization would need to cut with this footage. They have the need to make new videos for events and fund-raising every year, and they pull from the same collection of footage. The footage that the studio (mostly Cindy) had logged and captured at DV resolution would be very useful for these future projects. However, if the studio now erased that media from the drives (as they needed to do to start new projects), much of the work would be lost. (Of course, by maintaining the FCP project, the process of recapturing the media from the tapes could be automated, but that would still take time and require that the tapes be maintained and available.)

Having learned quite a bit about the needs of the organization during the first project, Charles brought the issue of archiving up to Jill. She readily agreed that maintaining an archive of digitized footage would be useful to the organization, but she had no desire to make an investment in their own editing system. Charles then suggested that the organization purchase their own FireWire drive to use as an archive. The studio would set it up for them (for a fee), and then they could use this archive for all of their future video projects.

Because this project was not the first time that Jill had spent the organization's money on video, she understood how much of each project budget goes toward organizing and capturing the material. Working together, Jill and Charles came up with some basic goals for a video-archiving solution for the organization:

1. Avoid the expense of repeating the ingest stage for the same footage on different projects.

2. Organize material at the ingest stage because it is likely to remain unorganized in the field due to the way the organization does their shooting.

3. Maintain an external drive with footage that can be used in a wide range of postproduction environments, and that can also allow people to view the footage on a desktop system without nonlinear editing software.

4. Archive the piece that was cut in the initial project, and continue to archive the new projects so that there is a record of these pieces, and they can be dissected and modularly reused.

Charles assured Jill that this could all be accomplished quickly and painlessly. He pointed out that the full cost of setting this up now—including buying the new drive—would be less than the amount spent on Log and Capture for the initial project. Logically, then, if the organization was going to need to do just one more project with the same footage, and they could avoid the expensive Log and Capture stage with the archive, it would pay for itself right there.

Jill agreed with this logic, but Charles stressed that the real benefit of the archive would be realized over time, as more and more footage was added and new projects were cut and also saved as part of the archive.

From having completed the piece, and with all of the captured DV footage on two separate FCP systems, it was fairly easy to create an archive that fit the goals. Mostly this was a matter of consolidating the media onto the FireWire drive and creating a master FCP project to reference those media. This was helped by the media-management decisions they had made at the outset.

Here are the steps they took to create the archive:

1. Purchased a large FireWire drive.

2. Used the Media Manager to move all of the media in the project that was on Cindy's machine over to the new drive. The selection for the Media Manager was all of the original bins in the project that were based on the tape names. The FireWire drive now had an FCP project with organized clips and bins and all of the media that the project refers to. This new FCP project would be the master archive project once they also added the media from Tommy's system.

3. Now this drive was mounted on Tommy's computer, where the online had taken place.

4. Because the decision was made to make the archive at DV resolution, all of the uncompressed footage that had been recaptured for the online could be discarded (they did, however, make a tape output of the final online piece).

5. All of the DV media from Tommy's workstation were now copied onto the FireWire drive, to the same directory where they had put Cindy's media.

6. With both projects open—the one from Tommy's machine and the one that had been created by the Media Manager on the FireWire drive—all of the clips in the Browser on Tommy's machine, as well as the final online sequence, were copied into the new project. Now all of the clips had been consolidated into the new master project.

7. The archive was almost complete, but there was one more important step. The new FireWire drive now contained an FCP project with all of the proper clips and sequences, and a media folder with all of the required media. However, these two elements—the project and the media—were not yet properly linked together. Currently, the clips that had been captured on Tommy's workstation would still be linked to the original files, not to the ones that they had copied onto the FireWire

drive. The last issue was to properly link all of the clips in the new project to the correct media residing on the FireWire drive.

There are several good ways to accomplish this task, but Tommy suggested something that was foolproof. He took the new archive drive and mounted it on a third FCP system that had never done any work on the project. Then, he relinked everything in the project. When it all linked up, with no media missing, Tommy knew that it would be safe to erase the media on the other two systems.

Jill was given the archive drive and went on her way, but for the next several years—and, in fact, long after Jill had left the organization—the nonprofit kept coming back to the studio to do video work. And the studio kept adding to the DV archive—both new video footage and the sequences they made.

The procedure for a new project using the archive was simple:

1 Open the master project and capture any new media directly into it, using the same naming conventions and the media folder on the FireWire drive as the scratch disk. (In this manner, all new media content would be added to the archive.)

2 Create a new FCP project for the new project. Copy any media that you want to use from the archive project to the new project, or browse and use media in the master file by leaving both projects open.

3 As with the first project, work at DV and then recapture or up-convert for the final output.

4 At the end of the project, make a copy of the final sequence, and move it to the master project for safekeeping.

All of the goals that Charles and Jill had initially discussed were achieved:

- Employees at the organization used the archive to view footage nonlinearly using QuickTime Player. Without Final Cut Pro, they had to access the media directly from where it was saved on the drive. This meant looking through a long list of clips because all of the media are saved into one directory. (As the studio continued to add footage to the archive, this single directory was used as the scratch disk.) However, because of the naming conventions implemented at the beginning, even this long list of files was not hard to look at because each one had an informative and consistent name (initials for the celebrities, name of the country where the footage was taken, etc.).

- Log and Capture time was minimized, because only new material needed to be dealt with as it came in with a new project. The waste of time and money of repeated logging and capturing was eliminated. In this way, the archive paid for itself many times over.

- The organization continued to shoot in a fairly haphazard way, but they worried less about this because they had the archive system to tame this footage once they returned home with it.

- The archive of sequences became a modular library for video pieces. So the organization could call the studio and say that they wanted to try one of their standard corporate opens to lead into new footage of a new celebrity volunteer. It was easy to tailor their video pieces for different presentations. On at least one occasion, they resurrected the original birthday piece, repurposing it when another video they had planned for a big presentation fell through at the last minute. Just having the archive made the organization much more agile in all of their video work.

Discussion

This was a simple solution that came about organically. It turned out to be a win-win for both the nonprofit and the studio. The charity saved money and executed better video pieces. The vendor earned a long-term client.

Although this was a workflow solution, it was not a case where a complete plan was made and then executed. Rather, things evolved, from early media-management decisions made to deal with a tight turnaround and disorganized source tapes, to the suggestion of the archive, and finally to the integrated relationship that developed between the studio and the nonprofit.

The initial decisions by Tommy and Charles were made quickly and out of necessity on the first project. The way these decisions played out is educational, because it led to consistent media naming for the archive and easy browsing of the media files in the Finder (among other benefits). Tommy and Charles didn't know when they made these conventions exactly how things would play out, but they were basing their decisions on sound workflow principles:

- They knew that they were working on a project with a lot of disorganized media.
- They knew because of the time crunch that they needed to have two editors working concurrently.

These two things both indicated that strong attention to media management would be a good idea. And:

- They knew that it is easier to throw out organizing conventions later than it is to add them.

So they began with a fairly tight media-management setup. This had some effect on the smoothness of the first piece, but it had a larger effect in setting the stage for the archive and getting it started quickly and efficiently.

The decision to archive at DV quality is an interesting one, and some may question it. DV is good enough to view the footage and make effective cuts, and it can be your final output in a pinch. All of these things, combined with the small file size, made it a reasonable decision at the time, but there is a loss of color depth from an uncompressed capture of the BetaSP sources.

Final Cut Pro 6 added the ProRes 422 codec, which became a preferable format for the archive. The benefits of using ProRes 422 instead of DV include:

- Higher image quality largely removes the need to ever recapture or up-convert. ProRes 422 is considered a mastering format.
- The ProRes 422 codec works with both SD and HD video.
- The multiformat Timeline feature of FCP 6 allows this new ProRes 422 material to be mixed in real time on the Timeline with the older DV material.

In the final analysis, this solution is an example of how the democratization of the medium allowed a nonprofit to do more for less, to overcome some of their limitations, and to improve their video communications across the board.

15 Web-Based Viewing and Ordering System

This innovative use of Final Cut Pro was designed for a national political campaign. The goal was to streamline the process they used to cut campaign spots with different consultancies around the country. The idea was to replace the traditional process of reviewing footage on videotape (which had to be shipped to different locations) with a web-based viewing and ordering system that integrated smoothly with Final Cut Pro.

Highlighted Concepts and Techniques

- Database media-management solution
- XML integration
- Online review screeners

Challenges

- Developing a custom solution from scratch

Overview

On September 26, 1960, John F. Kennedy and Richard Nixon participated in the first-ever televised presidential debate. It is said that those who listened on the radio felt that Nixon had won, but those who watched on TV felt that the winner was Kennedy. Of course, Kennedy won the election, and experts see the debate as a sea change in presidential politics.

Today, there can be no doubt that television is one of the most powerful tools in political campaigns (possibly the most powerful). In each campaign cycle, hundreds of millions of dollars are spent to produce and air campaign commercials (also called spots).

This project began when the executive producer for a national campaign approached a small but innovative postproduction and new-media company to create a system to streamline their postproduction process.

The campaign would be working with several dozen political consultancies in different parts of the country to cut spots appropriate to their regions and specialties. The source footage they would all be using would be stored centrally in Washington, D.C. In

past campaigns, the screening process involved a lot of phone calls to discuss what footage was available. This was followed by a VHS screener being made and shipped to the consultancy. Then another conversation about that footage, perhaps another VHS tape with more footage, and finally a high-quality master tape being created and shipped.

Each time a consultancy needed footage for a spot, it involved several phone discussions and several tapes being made and shipped. With many consultancies all around the country, cutting many, many spots, all of this talking and dubbing and shipping added up to a lot of time and money.

The executive producer for the campaign had been working with the studio and with FCP for a while, and she approached the studio with an idea. Could they use Final Cut Pro and the Web to create a system that would replace the screening process of dubbing and shipping with a web site that would allow the consultancies to browse available footage and order it from the central library of footage?

The result was an innovative and cost-effective custom web database. During the campaign, this system paid for itself many times over in the savings on dubbing and shipping, Moreover, the system led to the whole campaign being more agile in its postproduction, enabling it to communicate much more efficiently internally and to respond with new television spots more quickly than they previously could.

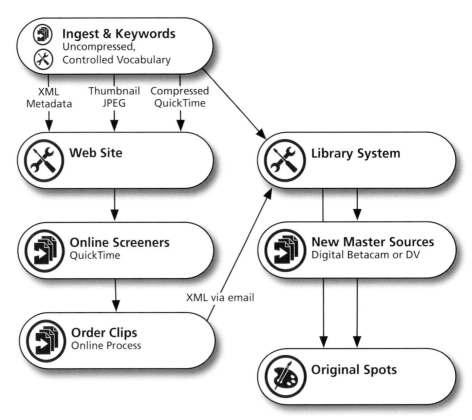

Figure 15.1   Web-based viewing and ordering workflow.

Project Roles and Responsibilities

This project required a "hybrid" team, combining elements of a traditional postproduction team with web programmers and a flexible "librarian" role that turned into much more.

Executive Producer—Allison was the executive producer who first conceived the idea. Her position was high in the overall campaign staff, and she was responsible for all of the television production for the campaign, including managing all of the consultancies and the crews who shot the footage. Allison's role was management, and she was always focused on the big picture. She rarely needed to get involved in the production of a specific spot (except maybe to assign it to a particular consultancy and review it when nearly finished). Allison's job was to keep the whole machine functioning efficiently, and she saw a major opportunity for efficiency in the web-based archive.

Postproduction Consultant—Jacob was Allison's main contact at the studio, and the person she first told about her idea for the new system. As an experienced editor on political campaigns, Jacob was familiar with the challenges. In his role as a consultant on the project, Jacob synthesized the needs of the editors, the campaign, and the web programmer. Essentially, he was the glue of the project, understanding the goals at all levels and acting as a communications hub. It would be accurate to call Jacob the producer or project manager; however, it was his deep knowledge of Final Cut Pro and the postproduction process and his ability to communicate this knowledge to all those who needed it that were Jacob's main contributions.

Web Programmer—Max was a web programmer, and led the web team at the studio. He had a lot of experience with web sites and databases, but very little with video at the outset of the project.

Assistant Editor / Librarian / Editor—Yoshi was hired by the studio to do all of the Log and Capture of tapes into the archive, and to run the system once it was set up to facilitate the distribution of footage. The logging and capturing tasks were typical of the assistant editor role. Because his main responsibility was to maintain the footage archive, his initial role was as a "librarian." As we will see, Yoshi's role evolved. At the end of the campaign, he was also playing the role of a full-fledged editor.

Required Equipment

The equipment listed here (except for the web server) was purchased by the campaign for the sole purpose of this project. A substantial investment, but a cost-effective one, because it saved a lot of money in the long run.

Uncompressed Final Cut Pro System—This was the "library" system, where Yoshi did all of the Log and Capture, received orders from consultancies, and made the uncompressed outputs for final delivery.

Large External High-Speed RAID—An Xserve RAID rated for uncompressed SD video playback was used for uncompressed storage of all the footage in the archive. About midway through the campaign, a second RAID was purchased for more storage space.

Digital Betacam and DV Play/Record Decks—All of the footage arrived as Digital Betacam (D-Beta). For outputs, the consultancies had the choice of D-Beta or DV.

Hosting Space on a Secure Web Server—This was provided by the studio as part of the package, and was necessary in order to host the web site that allowed the consultancies to view and order footage.

Execution

Initial Setup

Essentially, this project was a custom software and hardware solution. The solution was created to support a unique postproduction workflow, but the process of building the system itself resembled software development more than postproduction.

The first step was to bring together all of the key team members and stakeholders in a series of meetings meant to define the project technically. This was an interesting process, because unlike most of the studio's projects, it involved both the video and web teams. In general, these two groups did not understand each other's work particularly well.

As mentioned above, Jacob was a key player in this project because of his deep understanding of the editing process for political campaigns. It also helped that Allison was a true executive who knew how to delegate. She understood that Jacob's knowledge of the campaign's technical needs for postproduction was far superior to her own.

The process of defining the solution quickly became a two-person conversation between Jacob and Max. It was Jacob's job to describe the postproduction needs of the client, and the technical workings of FCP, to Max. It was Max's job to figure out what would be possible with the web-archive system, and how to accomplish it.

Their work together produced a scope document for Allison to review and sign off on. This document defined all of the specific objectives of the project, as well as, on a basic level, how it would function for the users. This was divided into two basic sections: the functionality for the librarian and the functionality for the web user. The specifications included:

Library system functional requirements:

- System can capture and store uncompressed video.
- Process includes a controlled vocabulary for logging and metadata. This is a strict system that will be used for searching keywords in the web-based archive.
- The process of compressing and uploading video, thumbnails, and metadata to the web system will be automated.
- The system will receive orders for footage by email, and the process for fulfilling these orders on tape will be as automated as possible.

Web user functional requirements:

- Users can search for clips based on a defined set of keywords.
- Users can view clips online as low-resolution QuickTime files.
- Users can fill a shopping cart and order the clips they want as full-quality sources from the library.
- The final uncompressed footage will not be transferred via the Internet; it will be shipped to a location of the user's choice on the format (D-Beta or DV) that they request.
- The system has no e-commerce functionality. Although it utilizes a "shopping cart," no money changes hands—all users are working for the same campaign.

- Users gain access to the secure web site by creating a login profile that is authorized at the library location.

Once these parameters were defined, Max and Jacob really got to work. Max needed to create the software to power the web system and integrate with Final Cut Pro, and Jacob needed to purchase the equipment (on behalf of the campaign) and set up the hardware for the library FCP system.

Most of Jacob's job at this stage was pretty straightforward. He had set up uncompressed FCP systems before, and there was nothing terribly special about this one. They did decide to use an Xserve RAID for media storage. (RAIDs are discussed in detail in Chapter 5.) This was important in order to have plenty of drive space to store the uncompressed version of all of the archive footage.

Max's job was a little more complex. He had worked on a lot of data-driven web sites before, including search and shopping cart functionality, but a lot of the video and Final Cut Pro stuff was new to him. Final Cut Pro's XML compatibility was the key to the work that Max needed to do.

XML is discussed some in Chapter 13; however, it may be easier to get a grasp on its power in the context of this project. Max was already familiar with XML as a key technology underlying the movement toward standards-based web programming. He understood that XML is fundamentally about structuring data. In his own web-programming world, XML-based languages such as XHTML (a new version of HTML, based on an XML foundation) and SMIL (Synchronous Multimedia Interchange Language) were already helping to standardize the wild world of the Web. (XHTML has since become the main standard for web pages; SMIL has not really caught on for multimedia applications.)

The meaning of extensibility (remember, XML stands for eXtensible Markup Language) is that XML can be customized to represent virtually any type of data. In FCP version 4, Apple made the program XML compliant, meaning that the data contained in an FCP project could be written as and read as an XML document.

Max knows just what this XML compliance means—he can manipulate FCP projects (in XML form) with the same programming languages that he uses to work with any other data and incorporate it into web sites. His software needs to take an XML document exported from FCP and extract the relevant data (the keywords entered during Log and Capture and timecode information), and then use that data in the web application for searching for clips. As we will see, Max's software is also able to create FCP projects in XML to facilitate the fulfillment of orders.

So, Jacob builds an editing system, and Max builds some software, but there is still the step of integrating these two things. This process involves a few elements:

- Defining a controlled vocabulary for the metadata (what words to put in the logging fields for the librarian, and what the search terms will be for the web user).

- Designing the procedure that the librarian will follow to place new content on the web site (exporting XML, exporting video and image files, and uploading).

- Designing the procedure for the librarian to fulfill orders.

Of course, this integration is based largely on how Max designed the new software. Designing these procedures, properly documenting them, and training the librarian are also important. We are going to discuss each of these aspects briefly.

The Controlled Vocabulary

We have discussed controlled vocabularies before, and the basic idea is to define the way in which a project will use language as metadata. For this project, the controlled vocabulary is all the more important, because it will become the keywords that users will search with on the Web. It is decided that the web system will not support an open search with a search box. All searching will be done via a pulldown with the predefined keywords.

It is very important to have these words telegraph the content of the footage well. If not, it will be hard to find the desired footage on the web site. It is even more important that the librarian be totally consistent with the use of these keywords in the logging fields. A typo in the logging field might mean that the clip does not show up on a web search.

For this particular controlled vocabulary, recognizable keywords were chosen to represent large areas of content. So, "education" would be used for anything having to do with schools and teachers, or anything even metaphorical for education, such as footage of a child's ABC blocks. All of the central issues of the campaign, and the types of footage used, were given keywords. (Shots with the candidate in them used his last name as the keyword, not initials.)

A clip could have up to three keywords to describe it. So footage of the candidate reading to schoolchildren would have both the "education" and his last name keywords and would show up on a search for either.

Ultimately, a list of only about 100 words was developed to describe all of the footage in broad strokes, and a glossary page was added to the web site. That way, users could read what each keyword included, in case they were having trouble finding what they were looking for.

The Export Process

The way this process was designed, each day the librarian would start a new project on the FCP system. The name of this project would be based on the date. Throughout the day, he would add footage to the library, logging it with the words from the controlled vocabulary, and making new video files on the RAID at uncompressed quality.

At the end of each Log and Capture day, there were only a few steps needed to upload new footage to the library:

1. Export the daily project as XML.
2. Batch export all of the clips captured into the project with a web preset in Compressor.
3. Do a second batch export of JPEG still images to be used as thumbnails; this was done using a QuickTime Conversion preset.
4. Place the XML file into the folder with all of the compressed QuickTime and JPEG images and create an archive of the entire folder.
5. Upload this archive to the server, where the software would take over, open the archive, and add the new footage and metadata to the system.

Fulfilling Orders

The procedure for fulfilling orders was perhaps the slickest part of the whole system. When a web user placed an order, the system would send an email to the librarian with a new XML project file attached. The email contained two pieces of information: the shipping address of the user placing the order, and their preferred tape format (D-Beta or DV). The XML file contained the information on the clips that the user was ordering.

When the librarian received the email, he opened the XML file in FCP. This FCP project (created by the web system based on the items in the user's shopping cart) had

a sequence with all of the clips on it with five seconds of black between each one. The media clips were already linked to the uncompressed files that resided on the RAID. All the librarian needed to do was output this sequence to the desired tape format and ship it.

Using the System

Once the system was set up, there were several days of testing and debugging in a testing environment with a limited amount of footage. Once all of the kinks were worked out, it was time to start ingesting massive amounts of footage, adding it both to the RAID as uncompressed video files and to the web system as compressed QuickTime files so they could be browsed and ordered.

Yoshi was hired at this point, and it was especially important to get someone doing the ingest work who was particularly diligent and careful. Small mistakes in the Log and Capture process could essentially ruin the carefully planned functionality of the system.

There were several months of acquisition and ingest before any of the consultancies signed up and started actually using the system to browse footage. Once they started to use the system, everyone saw its benefit immediately. A process that used to take several days could now be done overnight. The system was saving the campaign money, but more importantly, it was saving them time.

Because he had done all of the Log and Capture, Yoshi was very familiar with all of the footage, and his role in the campaign started to evolve. Although Allison did not originally plan to get involved in the editing of individual spots, she now found that having Yoshi and the edit system at her disposal had some unexpected benefits.

She started going to him to work out ideas for new spots without even working with any of the consultancies. Pretty soon, along with maintaining the archive and fulfilling orders, Yoshi was also cutting original spots. This was an organic evolution of roles, and now Allison had even more flexibility in getting spots produced. She could work with her nationwide team of consultants—who were now cutting spots more efficiently than ever before—or she could turn to Yoshi, who had deep knowledge of the footage available and was quickly proving himself as a talented and creative editor.

Discussion

This project was a staggering success. The campaign won the election, based largely on the power of the spots. The studio had a groundbreaking and profitable project. Yoshi started an exciting career as an editor.

At the time of this project, there were other solutions available, but they were expensive and proprietary. The benefit of a custom solution was that it did exactly what the client wanted, nothing more and nothing less. It is unlikely that any of the proprietary systems would have worked as well, and they definitely would have been more expensive.

In the time since, similar systems have become more common, but mostly they are either still high end, proprietary and expensive, or custom solutions utilizing XML extensibility like this one. However, Final Cut Server is poised to change all of that.

At the time of this writing, Final Cut Server software was not yet available, but it promises to be a solution from Apple to do exactly this kind of thing inexpensively and fully integrated with Final Cut Pro. It seems likely that if faced with the same challenge today, Final Cut Server would be part of the solution. For a case study using Final Cut Server, please go to *http://booksite.focalpress.com/Osder/finalcut/*.

In general, the power of XML compliance has probably not been as fully exploited as it could be. It is used primarily as an interchange format between software platforms both within and outside Final Cut Studio. However, additional innovative web applications are certainly possible.

Lastly, Yoshi's evolving role is a great example of a happy accident. The editing system and Yoshi's position were both created for the sole purpose of supporting the consultancies that were supposed to cut all of the spots. However, once all of the pieces were in place, and especially because Yoshi was already familiar with the footage, it was an easy jump to have him start editing.

There is a saying that good luck is the residue of good planning, and we feel this can be applied to many workflow situations, including this one. Creative success is built on the foundation of a well-planned workflow. Happy accidents often occur in the context of a good plan and a well-integrated team.

16 30-Second Spot for Broadcast

The idea of this project is a simple uncompressed (1:1) editing process for a high-quality short piece on a very fast schedule. Relatively few people and a streamlined workflow accomplish the goal quickly and efficiently. Advances such as Xsan and Motion round-tripping add additional efficiencies and creative options.

Highlighted Concepts and Techniques

- ⊗ Uncompressed editing
- ⊗ Xsan
- ⊗ ⊗ Integration with Motion
- ⊗ Audio finishing with an external resource

Challenges

- ⊗ Very tight schedule for a professional product

Overview

The key to this workflow is using footage at its full uncompressed quality throughout the editing process to save time. As discussed in Chapter 1, there was a time when this was not even possible, and there was a time after that when it was prohibitively expensive for anything but the shortest pieces. Today, 1:1 editing is used in many workflows. This still means an investment in more drive space than would be needed for a traditional offline/online workflow, but as drive space has gotten cheaper, this has become a worthwhile investment in many cases.

To use this method to get a project done in a hurry, the traditional offline stage can be skipped entirely in favor of initially capturing all sources at their highest possible quality. In this way, editorial work can move seamlessly into effects and finishing work with no need to recapture at full quality. In this example, the Xsan (Apple's storage area network) provides added convenience because the motion graphics elements are easily accessible and kept up-to-date.

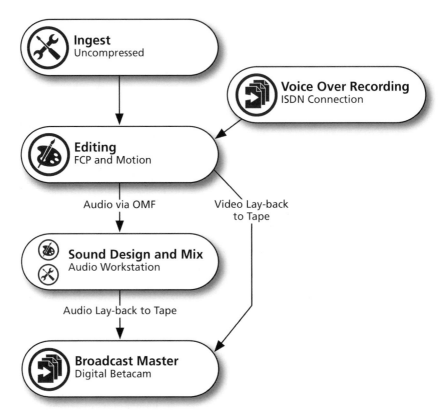

Figure 16.1 30-second spot workflow.

In the specific workflow that follows, the final audio mix was done in a dedicated mixing suite. However, it is also very possible to do the final audio work within Final Cut Studio. Similarly, this specific example was done at standard definition, but as we will see, the evolution in thinking about codecs and workflows continues in the high-definition age.

Project Roles and Responsibilities

One of the interesting things about this project is that a lot of the traditional roles have been collapsed, so there are really only three key people (plus support staff) in the whole postproduction process.

Executive Producer—Diane is an executive producer of promotions at a major cable network. She has a team of producers who work under her. Usually she assigns a producer to specific promos, with some direction, and then reviews and approves work at various stages.

In this case, however, Diane needs her spot in a hurry, so she is skipping the middleman. She is playing the producer and writer, and supervising the editing session herself. (But she does not have time to waste!)

Account Manager—Jessica is an account manager at a postproduction house. It is her job to communicate with the client (Diane and her network) and to help manage the scheduling at her facility.

Editor—Dave is an experienced offline and online editor. He is both technical and creative. In this project, it is Dave's responsibility to do all of the Final Cut Pro work, from the initial Log and Capture through editorial, compositing, and preparing the project for the audio specialist.

Required Equipment

This workflow happens to take place in a professional post house, and some of the equipment choices reflect this high-end (and expensive) environment. However, the central idea of working with uncompressed media files can be used in many ways and with many combinations of equipment. The decreasing price of equipment is making variations on the uncompressed workflow viable for more projects all the time.

The following list of equipment adheres to what we used in the original project, but alternatives are also noted.

Digital Betacam Play/Record Deck—To make a spot for broadcast, you need to have access to a broadcast-quality deck that plays and records. For standard-definition delivery, this probably means Digital Betacam. This is needed to do the initial Log and Capture, as well as the final output.

To follow a similar workflow in high definition, the equivalent would probably be an HDCAM or D-5 deck. However, with the proliferation of digital formats, it is always good to check on delivery specifications with the broadcaster.

The deck is usually the most expensive single piece of equipment in any workflow. In a post house, this is no big deal, but it can be a major investment for a small production company. Remember that the deck is needed only at the beginning and end of the workflow, so renting—or going to a facility solely for ingest, and then again for final output—is an option.

Final Cut Pro System with Uncompressed SDI Capture Card—As noted at the beginning, not every system that runs FCP can do this workflow. These days, most CPUs are fast enough to work with uncompressed video, so the keys are the video RAID and the capture card.

SDI capture cards are available from several vendors. The recommended speed for a video RAID to work in standard-definition uncompressed is 60MBps sustained read (assuming multiple tracks). Here again, the cost of this equipment continues to plummet. And again, everything needs to be bumped up a notch to work in high definition.

Digital Audio Workstation—Today, it is most common to see audio suites using Pro Tools, Logic, and Soundtrack Pro. The digital audio workstation (DAW) receives audio and metadata from FCP as an OMF, AAF, or XML file.

Storage Area Network—Working in a storage area network (Xsan) environment means that media is stored on high-speed drives that reside on a high-speed network (Fibre Channel). All of the Final Cut Pro workstations on the network can access the media. In this case, the network motion graphics are kept updated on the Xsan—very convenient when you need to cut a spot in a hurry! In the Xsan environment, Xserve RAIDs serve as the media drives.

Execution

Day 1

Diane's network is about to air the sequel to their biggest hit special of all time. This event has been hyped on the network for almost a year. Now we are six days out, and the network is hoping to see another phenomenal ratings night due to more hype and more spectacular 3-D graphics than the original show.

On the morning of Day 1, Diane sees a preview of the final show, and decides that there should be one more spot, one more promo, to put it over the top. Now that the show is finished, she can use the very best clips for a real teaser, something that screams: YOU CAN'T MISS THIS!

She can see the whole thing in her head, and while it is still hot in her mind, she hits speed dial on her cell phone for the direct line of her account manager at her favorite post house. "Jessica: I need to cut a spot ASAP!"

Jessica has not had as much coffee as Diane on the morning of Day 1. She needs to slow things down. "Diane, wait a minute. Let's look at the schedule and see what we have. . . . When do you want to do the offline?"

"No time for offline, I need to get this done in the next two days to make my deadline. . . ."

Jessica thinks for a second, staring at an overpacked schedule on her computer screen. "Dave has tomorrow open. Do you want to work with him?" Diane is enthused, and begins to see a plan come together.

She jumps in: "Jessica, can I work with Dave tomorrow in an uncompressed non-linear room, and then schedule a mix for the next morning?"

Jessica pauses for a second, looks again at the schedule. "Yeah, I can work that out. But Diane, where are your sources? Do you have a script? Because that room is booked the next day, so you have only one—"

"I've got all the sources I need on this one tape, and you guys have the latest graphics package on the Xsan. We're doing one 30-second spot; I know exactly how I want it to work! Thanks, Jessica. You're the best. See you tomorrow!"

Jessica looks at the phone and wonders what just happened. She shrugs, types the booking into her schedule, and resolves to get in to work early the next day—and to make sure to have a cup of coffee before Diane arrives.

Day 2

Diane and Jessica have both had their coffee on the morning of Day 2, but Dave is just now getting his first briefing on the project.

"We're gonna do WHAT?"

"We're going to cut this spot today," repeats Diane. Dave looks dubious, but Diane is unfazed and reassuring. She is not unreasonable, but she is brutally efficient. Also—and this is a big thing—she is approving her own work.

Diane is the head of the department, so whatever she says is final—there will be no waiting for approval. Dave and Jessica both breathe a sigh of relief when they learn that final approval is in Diane's hands. They have experienced plenty of projects where time and money are wasted because of differences of opinion among different stakeholders at a client company.

The work begins with capturing the footage. Diane has only one tape, the show master that she got yesterday. The latest network graphics are ready to use on the Xsan. Dave is familiar with the graphics package, but cringes when he sees that they have an hour-long source tape on this tight schedule.

But Diane is on point, and she has four specific shots that he needs, and gives Dave the timecode for each. He captures a bit of additional show footage because the 3-D animation really is extraordinary.

Next, Diane reads her script for scratch track using the Voice Over tool in Final Cut Pro. With this tool, a recording is made at mediocre quality right in the editing suite. It is just temporary ("scratch"). In this case, there are only a few lines, reinforcing the YOU CAN'T MISS THIS! feeling.

Before lunch, Dave has all of the pieces ready for editing and has started to place them on the Timeline, but the spot has not yet taken shape. They've made a lot of progress so far, but Dave is starting to get nervous about getting everything done today.

After a quick lunch, Diane leaves Dave in the editing room while she goes to record the final narration. The network has their signature voice on retainer, and she quickly scheduled a time with him yesterday after she talked to Jessica. Bill lives in a different city, so they record using a remote ISDN connection. The audio engineer places the narration track on the Xsan where it will be easy for Dave to access it.

Before leaving the edit room, Diane tells Dave to "see what works" with the footage and scratch track. Dave thinks that he can see the spot coming together, but he is very aware of the time. He reminds Diane that he will need time at the end of the session to make the tape and OMF output. She agrees, but also adds that it is one 30-second spot, and thus should not take very long.

By mid-afternoon, Diane is back in the edit suite, and Dave is placing the real narration under a good-looking spot that Diane seems pleased with. (It was easy to grab the narration off the Xsan.) In the hour or so that Dave worked on his own, he was able to put the shots in order, roughly place graphics, and was working to make the spot flow smoothly.

The addition of the narration instantly makes the spot feel more complete. However, the lack of polish on the video track is now more apparent in comparison. Dave and Diane watch the spot through several times. Dave asks Diane to approve the basic ordering and timing of the shots and graphics with the final narration. After a few small adjustments, she does.

Now Dave goes to work on the transitions and compositing, getting each shot to go into the next with perfect smoothness. This spot is made up of two things: 3-D shots from the film, and animated motion graphics. These two sources need to be carefully massaged to meld together.

Somehow, the next few hours go by very quickly. The spot is looking better, but something is missing. Diane feels that it has her message, but is not SCREAMING.

The end of the day is bearing down on Dave, and he is aware that he is supposed to make outputs before he finishes. As an editor, he wants to please this important client. Deep down, Dave agrees that the spot needs something more, but it is the end of the day, and he is out of good ideas for the moment. On top of that, people are starting to filter out early for a weekly happy hour.

Diane dials Jessica's office. "I think we are going to need another half day tomorrow." Jessica doesn't answer immediately. She knows without looking at her schedule that the room and the editor are booked tomorrow.

After a pause, and without going into detail, eventually Jessica responds: "Let me see what I can do." After a few minutes, she calls back, "Okay, I've moved things around to free up Dave and the suite tomorrow morning. And I pushed your mix back to the afternoon. Will that work?"

Diane and Dave exchange a look. "Definitely. Thanks, Jessica. You are the best!" With that, Dave and Diane break for the day, and head out to meet with coworkers at that happy hour. Jessica still has paperwork to finish.

Day 3

Dave is the first to arrive. With a full night of sleep, things are looking fresh again, and he has had some new ideas for making the spot work. As he is implementing some new transitions, Dave reflects that he has never worked on something quite like this, and how time away from the material (and sleep) are necessary for the creative process.

By the time Diane gets to the edit suite, he has a new cut to show her. Diane is very pleased, and the solution turns out to be oh so simple. "All it needed was a white flash in some of the transitions," Dave explains.

Several of the graphics pieces have lightning elements in them, and sometime between going to bed and waking up, Dave realized that it was a simple white flash that would work with the lightning, add drama and visual interest, and bring the piece together.

Dave and Diane are very happy with the spot, but a moment later, Bill, the senior motion graphics artist, walks by the suite. Because they have a few minutes to spare, Dave calls Bill in to take a look at the spot. Bill likes it, is impressed by how quickly it came together. He agrees that the white flashes pull it together, but he has a suggestion to take it further.

"You could use Motion to make a custom transition. That way, it wouldn't just be a white flash—it could have a lightning element right in the transition."

Dave is hesitant at first. "I don't know, Bill we have to make outputs before our deadline. . . ." The truth is that Dave is not an expert in Motion, and he is not a designer. He does not want to get out of his comfort zone and embarrass himself with the client.

But Bill has worked with Diane for a long time, and he can see by the look on her face that she is sold on his idea. Bill has no intention of hanging Dave out to dry. Bill has been doing a lot of work in Motion recently, and he knows that he can execute his idea quickly. "Dave, do you have a few minutes to spend on this? I can walk you through it. I think it will really work, and I promise it will be quick."

Dave can see he is both outnumbered and outranked. He quickly relents, inviting Bill to help him, but he is not going to lose control of the delivery. "Okay, but a few things first: we do have to output these before noon, so you need to give me a half hour to do that. And Diane, before we go down this path, is there anything else besides the transitions that you want to work on?"

Diane says that it is just icing (and in fact, she was perfectly happy to sign off on the spot as is before Bill walked in, but she also believes in Bill and likes his idea). She thanks Dave for watching the deadline, and truly appreciates his professionalism.

Bill sits down with Dave, and both Diane and Dave are amazed at how quickly Bill is able to coax a custom lightning transition out of Motion. In almost no time at all, Diane approves the transition, and Bill is giving Dave some simple instructions for how to apply the transition to other edits in the spot. ". . . and there is no need to render in Motion. You can render inside FCP, just like a regular transition."

After this brief detour, Dave and Diane are both happier with the spot. Diane feels that the lightning transition really makes it SCREAM. It is exactly how she envisioned it. They watch the spot a few more times together, and agree that it is perfect. They discuss adding a sound effect on the new transition in the audio session that afternoon.

It is roughly 48 hours since Diane decided to make the spot.

Dave makes a Digital Betacam output and OMF output with time to spare. The video on the tape is the final video for air, and the OMF contains all of the audio. Diane takes him out for lunch while they are loading the material into the audio suite.

Later that afternoon, Diane has plenty of time for sound design and mix on her 30-second spot. The master tape is sent out to the broadcast facility that evening.

One more thing happens in this process: Jessica pulls Bill aside to ask him: "Hey, are we going to bill Diane for your time?" Bill thinks about this for a second. As a senior creative at the post house, he is certainly aware of the need to keep billables up. On the other hand, he didn't spend much time at all working on the piece, and Diane is an important client and deserves a perk once in a while . . .

Ultimately, he pushes the issue back to Jessica: "Why don't you raise this with Diane? I don't think she will mind paying for an hour of my time, but I kinda walked in on them. It was not really booked, and I don't think we should catch her off guard with the billing." (Although Bill is a creative, and technically part of the client management team, he has worked in postproduction long enough to have a good feel for how to deal with these issues.)

In the end, Diane is happy to pay for an hour of Bill's time, and she appreciated the respect of being asked by Jessica, rather than just seeing the charge show up on a bill. Diane leaves at the end of the day very happy: she has made the spot she set out to make, more or less on schedule, and the professionalism and teamwork of the post house staff has really shown through on this project.

Discussion

As mentioned, there was a time when this workflow was not possible, and also a time when it was possible and very expensive. Today, working at uncompressed quality from the beginning to the end is a realistic choice for many projects.

In the final analysis of this project, the lessons learned were more about communications and creativity than technology, although one could also argue that the sound technological base at the post house provided the foundation for great execution on the fly. In any case, dedicated people, all understanding their roles and contributing their best work, achieved success.

By curtailing the number of steps and people involved in the postproduction, time can be saved. However, with fewer people in the process, everyone needs to be very good at their work—and very careful. Also, there are times when "fresh eyes" can be helpful.

This workflow can be deceptive when it comes to time, because many of the traditional steps (editorial, online, and compositing) have been collapsed into a single session. It is almost like magic . . . but it's not. Be sure to budget time for all of the things that will need to be done, even if the same person on the same machine is doing them all. As we saw, this workflow reached a point where Dave and Diane really needed Bill's input in order to take the spot to the next level.

For this project, only a single day was budgeted for all of the editing, from ingesting the footage all the way to outputting the OMF. In fact, we ran over—and needed an extra half day to get this all done. This pushed the rest of the schedule along, and pushed the deadline to its very limit.

In the end, the extra half day was a blessing in disguise. It allowed Dave to rest and digest creatively, and then there was the happy coincidence of Bill showing up with a great quick improvement.

Diane envisioned the spot in a flash of creativity. Technically, it was quite possible to complete the spot in one day, and with Dave only. Creatively, to execute her true vision required a bit of extra time, and the help of an additional artist who was not on the initial roster.

Remember that postproduction technologies are always changing. The all-uncompressed workflow represents one stage in the evolution. The proliferation of

digital formats and the resolution-independent nature of Final Cut Pro mean that there are constantly new formats, codecs, and workflow options. In particular, new HD formats and compressed but high-quality codecs are pushing the envelope in this area. For example, the case study in the next chapter uses DVCPRO HD as an offline format for a show shot and finishes at uncompressed HD quality. This is another example of taking the traditional offline/online process and bending the rules to take advantage of new technologies in order to meet the particular needs of a project.

17 Multipart TV Series with Multiple Editors

A large Xsan and Final Cut Pro deployment were installed in a large production company to facilitate working on a ten-part, big-budget, high-definition network series. This chapter focuses on the technical setup and management of that system, as well as the online stage for the series. One unique aspect of this project was that the editorial phase on all ten episodes happened simultaneously, with multiple producer/editor teams all working through the Xsan. Challenges arose in terms of team coordination and the changing demands of the network, but good planning and a robust technical foundation enabled improvements and adjustments along the way.

Highlighted Concepts and Techniques

- Xsan and Final Cut Pro integration
- Final Cut Pro media and project management
- QuickTime review screeners
- Conform, online, and color correction all performed inside Final Cut Studio

Challenges

- Coordinating a large postproduction crew working on different episodes simultaneously
- Managing a large amount of HD footage
- Maintaining data integrity in a real-world SAN environment
- Adapting to the changing will of the client

Overview

A major network has commissioned a successful production/postproduction company to create a new series. After years of success in the international market, this is the first major U.S. network project the company has been awarded. Prior to this commission, the company had relied exclusively on vendors for their productions. This project will be their first in-house production. After many months of pitching the piece to the network, the company is excited to finally be executing the project. This excitement quickly turns to dread as they realize the resources that are required for postproduction of a high-definition series.

The company is aware of the Final Cut Pro movement, and, after careful study, has decided to use Final Cut Pro and Final Cut Studio as their postproduction solution. To gear up, they hire a local Apple Video reseller and systems integrator to build and design their facility to complete the project—and, they hope, many more like it. After many informative meetings, the company and the reseller determine the following requirements:

- Design a centrally located machine room for decks and other video hardware. Install two ingest stations in the machine room for an assistant editor to ingest footage.
- Equip ten edit suites, each capable of compressed high-definition ingest, monitoring, and editing.

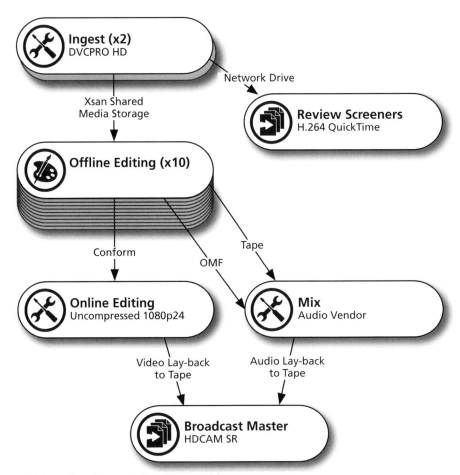

Figure 17.1 Series with multiple editors workflow.

- Equip an online edit suite with dedicated online storage capable of uncompressed HD. Equip the suite with evaluation tools so that all projects can be finished in-house, including final color correction and grading.

- Install and set up an Xsan for the ability to share all media and projects, with special consideration for dedicated storage for the online edit suite.

After negotiating the terms of the series with the broadcaster, it is determined that editorial on all ten episodes of the series will have to happen concurrently in order to have the series air during a major promotional push for the network. Because of this, the company devises an internal plan for working on the various episodes concurrently:

- A media-management plan will be designed to take advantage of the facility described above and to support the needs of the project.

- Editorial for each episode will be assigned to a single freelance editor and producer.

- All episodes will be color-corrected and color graded by an online editor, using Final Cut Pro and Color to ensure consistency across all episodes.

- All episodes will be mixed and sound designed by an audio vendor. This vendor will also be responsible for layback to the master and final audio deliverables.

- Creative control falls to an accomplished and respected internal executive producer.

Project Roles and Responsibilities

This project has many roles and responsibilities to cover both the editorial and technical aspects.

Executive Producer—Catherine is an exceptionally talented executive producer. She has won numerous industry awards, including a broadcast Emmy. She has the added benefit of having worked for the network for over ten years. She excels in quick and meaningful decision making and understands the power of concise delegation.

In the project workflow, Catherine will be responsible for approving an episode before it goes to the network for their review, interpreting any feedback from the network, and communicating that feedback as action items for the whole team.

In general, Catherine's responsibilities to the series and to the new facility are great. She also hires all of the episode producers and the director of postproduction—who, in turn, is responsible for more technical hiring and a lot of decisions about execution.

Director of Postproduction—Bob has worked for the company for quite some time; however, every project prior to this one has relied on external vendors. Additionally, all of the projects that Bob has overseen in the past have been Avid-based, and he is worried about how Final Cut Pro will change the role he has established for himself. Bob will design and oversee all aspects of postproduction, including designing workflow documents, hiring freelance editors, and dealing with day-to-day technical problems.

In the past, Bob has also had the responsibility of being a video engineer in facilities that are the same size or larger than the one they are building. However, Bob has never worked with an Xsan, and he considers himself more of a video guy, not a network guy. He understands the power of shared media storage, and he is excited to learn more, but Bob knows he will need some help, so he takes his time in selecting people for other key postproduction roles.

Assistant Editor and Media Manager—Sam is a young but technically proficient assistant editor. Although never having worked for this company before, he has a

few years of assistant editor experience under his belt. On this project, Sam's main role will be to ingest and organize all footage in master projects, to assist editors with technical issues, and to provide media management for the Xsan. Also, last year, in a smart career move, Sam was certified by Apple as an Xsan expert after he took a number of classes from Apple about OS X Server and Xsan. This is probably the top reason that Bob has hired Sam.

Online Editor—Jorge is a talented online editor and colorist. His main role will be to conform the shows in their final HD resolution, to place network graphics, to provide broadcast packaging, and to color-correct the show. He will also do final video outputs of the shows (audio layback will be done by an audio vendor). His main duties will commence once offline editorial has been completed. The schedule calls for him to do one show a week for ten weeks. Additionally, Jorge is an Apple-certified instructor who teaches regularly when he is not doing online work. Because of this, Bob has asked Jorge to come in for a day prior to the start of editing on the project to give himself and the editors a refresher course on best practices for FCP and Studio.

Editors—Bob has hired a talented group of ten Final Cut Pro editors to work on the project. Each editor will be assigned one episode, and will work directly with his or her producer to see the shows through to completion. All of the editors use Final Cut Pro, but none have experience with SAN technology, so this will require additional training.

Producers—Catherine, in her role as executive producer, has hired ten producers. Each has extensive experience with broadcast-television series, although this is the first time they have dealt with shared storage and FCP workflows. Each producer will work directly with his or her editor to see the shows through to completion.

Required Equipment

Much went into designing the company's facility, from power concerns to cabling. It was an immense project that took three months prior to the start of editing on the series. The FCP and Xsan integrator and his team spent many long days building the central machine room and edit suites and wiring the entire facility. The choice to build a central machine room is not key for this project to work. Decks and such could just have easily been attached to one edit system with access to the Xsan. The advantage of the dedicated machine room is that it provides easy access to all of the decks and hardware for every room in the facility. There are, however, a few key pieces of equipment that made this project/facility a success:

- Each edit suite was equipped with a Mac Pro with KONA LHe HD/SD capture card, 23-inch Cinema Display for computer display, 23-inch Cinema Display with SDI-to-DVI converter for monitoring.
- The online edit suite is equipped with a Mac Pro with KONA 3 HD/SD capture card, two 23-inch Cinema Displays for computer display, 20-inch calibrated HD CRT monitor for critical evaluation, and hardware scopes (rasterizer).
- 42TB Xsan system.

Execution

Because this project took place over months, it is easiest to look at it in various places in time.

Week 1: Media-Management Planning

The systems integrator has done a fantastic job equipping and designing the facility. All during the design and building process, Bob has supervised the vendors to build out the facility. At the end of the day, Bob is very happy with how the facility has turned out. He is also pleased with the hard work he has done documenting the machine room. He even created an internal web site so that editors and producers can find documentation about the facility.

Another benefit of this internal web site, Bob thinks, is that he can use it as a blog to keep everyone in the facility updated about repairs and maintenance and other technical issues. This gets him to thinking that if he is going to put technical information up on this site, that will be a good place to also put workflow documents for their upcoming series. That way, everybody on the team can be on the same page. Bob realizes that forward-thinking workflows are not just a matter of fancy equipment (though he does like the new equipment)—they are also about facilitating communication and the sharing of information.

A big part of these workflow documents will be information about how clips and other media are going to be organized on the Xsan, and managing Final Cut Pro project files. It will also be a place for editors to share information about prepping their shows for online. Bob has some good ideas about this, but considers himself more of a video engineer and manager than an Xsan and Final Cut Pro expert. Although he is getting more savvy with the tools every day, Bob's lack of expertise is one of the main reasons that he hired Sam. Sam is a talented young guy, and clearly part of the upcoming generation of video geeks. He is quickly becoming an Xsan expert. In fact, Sam was instrumental in helping Bob communicate with the Apple Video reseller and systems integrator on the design of the Xsan.

Bob knows it will be a top priority to set up some guidelines with Sam about media management, so he meets with Sam to discuss it.

". . . Thanks again, Sam, for coming to this project. I think having you on board will help us keep the project on pace. The thing I want to get out of the way, though, before any editorial happens is coming up with a system for how media are organized on the Xsan. Also, we have to keep things like projects, screeners, and anything else you can think of organized."

"Well, you know me, Bob. I always geek out on these workflow things, so I've already been putting some thought into it. To be blunt, the biggest part of this is going to be making sure all of the editors and producers are on the same page as us. It's going to be important that everyone stick to the system of media management and logins. If not, things could get messy, you know?"

"I know exactly what you mean, and I've been thinking about that too. I think once we're done loading the footage, audio, graphics, and whatever else, and before we actually start editing, I'd like to have you, me, and the online editor, Jorge, brief the editors about the system and prepping projects for online."

"Agreed!" (Sam is beginning to feel good that although Bob is not an expert on SAN systems, he gets the big concepts, and he is really listening and starting to trust Sam.) "I think it is time well spent. So, do you want to dive into this and make a plan?"

After a few hours of discussion, Bob and Sam come up with a good game plan. But it is just that: only a game plan. Both of them—especially Bob, with all his years of experience—realize that although it is important to have a workflow going in, no project ever goes exactly as planned. Therefore, workflows have to be flexible. Here is what they've decided:

- All of the original source footage (HDCAM SR) will be digitized at DVCPRO HD for offline. This will provide great-looking video (often used for mastering), but

at a fraction of the space required for uncompressed 10 bit, which will be used for the online.

- QuickTime screeners with burn-in timecode will be created for each tape so that producers can use them to write scripts and review footage. These screeners will be saved to a network drive that everyone can access. Compressor will be used to make the compressions and add the timecode burn-in in one step.

- The media will all be stored on the Xsan, but the editors will access it through FCP projects that reference it. These will be referred to as master projects. This will be the same for audio and graphics.

- In the interest of time, Sam will log and capture tapes as whole chunks. Additionally, he will provide only basic metadata. Information about the footage on a particular reel will be provided to the editors and producers as a paper log that was created on the shoots.

- Project files will live on a separate network drive, not on the Xsan. This is for safety (not having media and projects on the same volume) as well as for technical reasons. Because project files (as well as FCP cache files and, to a lesser degree, render files) are written so often, they have the potential to fragment the Xsan quickly.

Weeks 2 through 4: Ingest and Screeners

Now it has come time for Sam to start the hard part of the project for him, ingest. Although all episodes of the show have to be worked on concurrently, the company was very lucky to be able to shoot all of the footage for the episodes prior to post starting. If it were necessary for shooting to happen at the same time as post, things would be frantic for sure.

So Sam stares at quite a few large boxes of tapes and lets out a big sigh, knowing that there is a lot of work ahead of him. Because he and Bob have worked out a detailed media-management plan before even the first frame of video has been captured, Sam is confident that everything should go smoothly.

All of the footage was acquired 1080p24 using Sony's HDCAM SR tape format. This is the latest and greatest HD format from Sony. Although the production company has not yet shot anything at 4:4:4 R'G'B' (which this format is capable of), if they decide to do so in the future, they already have the equipment. HDCAM SR is capable of working in 4:4:4 or 4:2:2 chroma subsampling—4:2:2 was chosen as an improvement over HDCAM's 3:1:1. This will allow for much more latitude in color correction and grading. The company has two of these decks—one to match up with each ingest station in the machine room.

Although the company has a large amount of storage, there are roughly 30 hours of raw footage per episode. Ingesting all 300 hours of uncompressed HD is out of the question.

As a compromise, last week Sam and Bob decided to digitize all of the footage as DVCPRO HD. This is not a traditional choice for an offline codec. The quality is high enough for it to be considered a mastering format in some places. DVCPRO HD is a good compromise for this project, however, because it is a heavily compressed codec with a very low data rate, but still very good looking. The system integrator has designed the Xsan to support this bandwidth, and they have plenty of storage. Sam and Bob do the math to figure out how much space it will take to capture all of the footage at the DVCPRO HD codec, and they decide that it is their best bet. Again, the way in which

FCP works with different formats and codecs means that you can tailor an offline/online workflow to meet the exact needs of your project and your equipment.

Once all of the episodes are complete, only the footage that is used in each show will be recaptured by Jorge, the online editor, at full quality using the uncompressed 10-bit codec at HD resolution.

Because time is tight already, having to log individual clips for each tape would be too time consuming for Sam at this stage. Using the plan they devised last week, Sam will provide basic logging information (reel number, episode, etc.) for each tape. Each editor will be provided with a paper log of the footage that was made in the field.

Sam works for three weeks (plus some extra-long days and weekends) capturing all of the footage. He captures footage into master projects for each episode. These master projects live on a separate network drive called FCP Projects, inside a folder called Master Projects. Meanwhile, the media live on the Xsan, so Sam's scratch-disk preferences are set to the Xsan. This creates a folder on the Xsan called Capture Scratch. Inside the Capture Scratch folder are subfolders for each episode master project. Inside each of these subfolders is the footage.

There are other items that Sam has to ingest—namely, audio (music and sound effects). The company has a blanket license for a popular library. Sam loads the whole library onto the Xsan using iTunes. He knows that iTunes is an easy way to batch ingest audio tracks while at the same time converting them to 48kHz. He also knows that he can use iTunes to load the music to a specific location—in this case, the Xsan. So he creates a folder on the Xsan called Audio. Then, using iTunes, he proceeds to ingest all of the music and sound effects to that location. After he has gone through the entire library, Sam imports the whole thing into a new master project called Audio.

He has a problem, though. Sam knows that creating a master project for the audio is a good idea so that editors don't have to go searching around the Xsan for music, but he also knows what can go wrong. One person having a project file open at the same time another person has that same file open can cause problems. So after Sam has loaded the audio library into a master project, he decides to duplicate that master project ten times: one for each edit suite. This should avoid problems. At the end of this process, Sam now has all of the audio on the Xsan in a folder called Audio, and he has the master projects on the FCP Projects drive in the Master Projects folder.

The graphics for the series will be arriving shortly from the network. When they do, Sam will follow the same procedure for creating master projects as he did for the audio. The graphics themselves will live on the Xsan in a folder called Graphics; meanwhile, the master projects (one for each suite) will exist on the FCP Projects drive in the Master Projects folder.

Because of the need for the producers to have screeners of all the raw footage, part of Sam's workflow is to set up a batch encode from Final Cut Pro to Compressor with all of the footage captured that day. As he and Bob discussed last week, these screeners will be small but high-quality QuickTimes at half-raster size. They will use the H.264 codec and have burn-in timecode.

Normally, encoding a huge amount of footage like Sam has on one machine would take quite a long time. One advantage that he has, though, is that there are no editors yet on the project. Thus, Sam can use Compressor and its clustering services to network render the screeners. This means he can now use the 2 ingest stations in the machine room, the 10 edit suites, and the online room—for a total of 13 machines to encode the files! He has to consult the FCP user manual on how to set this up, but it takes only a half hour to do so—and boy, is he happy!

Sam sets up these batches at the end of each workday. When he returns the next morning, the screeners are done. All of the files are saved onto a separate network drive that the producers can access.

Once Sam gets his workflow down, it is a model of efficiency. He is taking full advantage of all of the equipment that is available to him. He spends each day alternating between the two HD decks to do the capturing. At night, he harnesses all of the FCP workstations (and the network) to do massive amounts of media compression. In a few short weeks, he is able to prep the system for the simultaneous editing of all ten shows.

By the time the ingest stage is done, Sam is happy with himself, but worn out. He also knows this is just the beginning.

Week 5: Training

Bob has hired a group of talented (in some cases, award-winning) editors to edit each episode. Likewise, the producers are very talented and experienced. There are some limitations to the team, however:

- None of them has worked on a project before that used an Xsan.
- Each of them has their own "style" for media management and project organization.

Having your own media-management style is fine when working by yourself, but everyone needs to follow the same rules when collaborating on the Xsan. If the series is going to be done fast, it is important that the whole team get on the same page about how the Xsan works and best practices for prepping a show for online. So, on Monday morning of Week 5, Bob and Sam, along with all the editors and producers, gather in the company conference room for some training.

Bob has also asked Jorge (who will serve as the online editor for the show, but who is also an Apple-certified Final Cut Pro instructor) to come in and give everyone some tips and tricks for prepping the shows for online. Additionally, Bob has asked Sam to brief the team on the media management of the Xsan.

"Okay. . . . Now that I've given you my little pep talk as your director of post, and you have all had a chance to suck down your coffee, let me hand the floor over to Sam and Jorge for some technical need-to-know information . . . Sam?"

"Hi guys. For those of you who don't know me, I'm Sam. I'm the assistant editor on the series. Of course, I'm here for whatever you need, but I want to talk about how footage is organized on the Xsan and some things to be aware of. I know that many of you might yawn at all this technical information, but believe me, understanding how we've set up the Xsan and how to work with projects and media is vital to the success of the project. Let's start by taking a look at how our system is set up, and logging on to your computers."

Logging In—The network is governed using OS X and Open Directory. This means that each editor is assigned a user name and password. By logging in using this name and password, proper access and permissions to files on the Xsan are maintained. It's vital that editors log in to only one machine at a time. Otherwise, file and or Xsan corruption could happen.

Project Organization—Project files will not live on the Xsan, but on another network volume. This network volume, called FCP Projects, will mount automatically each time the editor logs in. This volume contains a folder called Master Projects. This folder, in turn, contains master projects for each episode, as well as master audio and graphics projects for each suite.

All these master projects link to media on the Xsan. Sam explains that these master projects should *never* be altered by anyone but him. He adds that a good way to think of these is as libraries. Each editor will have their own project(s) for the actual editing of the episode. These will also reside on the FCP Projects drive, but in a folder labeled Episode Projects. Because editors will undoubtedly need to grab footage and or sequences from other episodes, Sam explains that the easiest way to do this is by opening up that episode master project or episode project, and pulling the media into their specific episode project. However, Sam warns that each editor should check before opening one of these projects. It is important to check to see whether a project is open in another suite because, by having the project open in two places, when one saves it will overwrite the save from another edit suite, creating project file complications. To aid in this process, Sam has set up Bonjour messaging using iChat on all of the edit suite computers.

The Xsan—On each editor's machine, the Xsan shows up just like any other volume. Inside this volume are a number of folders: Capture Scratch, Audio, Graphics, Online. The Capture Scratch folder contains subfolders for each master project (each episode). This is where the media for each show was ingested to. The Audio folder contains the entire music and sound effects library for the entire series. Sam has already loaded these songs into a master project called Audio 1, 2, 3, and so on (one for each suite), so that editors may quickly preview and then add music and sound effects to their episode project. The Graphics folder contains all of the graphics that the network has provided for the series. Just as with the audio, Sam has added these graphics to a master project called Graphics 1, 2, 3, and so forth (again, one for each editor). Finally, the Online folder is specifically for online sessions. Sam explains that although it is possible for one to go directly onto the Xsan to find media files and pull them into a particular episode project, both he and Bob have agreed that rather than having to navigate the Xsan every time an editor needs a clip, it is easiest to set up master projects.

Screeners—Sam explains that when he spent three straight weeks digitizing footage for the various episodes, one of the things he did was create small QuickTimes of each tape with burn-in timecode. His purpose was to provide producers with screeners of all the footage so they could write scripts and do whatever else they needed to do. These small QuickTimes use the H.264 codec, so they still provide very good visual quality. All of these files are located on a shared network drive that the producers can access from their laptops.

Approval Cuts—Sam explains that the network requires that all approval cuts be delivered to them via a secure web site. In addition, he explains that because the network uses mainly Windows-based PCs, they require that the approval cuts be delivered as Windows Media 9 files. This is okay, though—the systems integrator that the company hired installed Telestream's Flip4Mac in each edit suite. This installed QuickTime components so that Compressor can be used to make the .wmv files. The cool thing, Sam explains, is that because they use a high-speed network and everyone is using the same software, they can leverage the power of all the edit suite computers to encode these files, saving valuable time. The downside, he explains is that this will tie up each edit suite machine. This means that he will have to do this encoding at night, after the editors leave.

After lunch, the group reconvenes. Bob now introduces Jorge, the online editor and Apple-certified instructor. Jorge is going to brief the group on best practices for preparing their projects for online.

"... So my job, then, is to make sure the shows are technically sound, as well as to color-correct and color grade them. I'm also responsible for slates, inserting credits, prepping OMFs for audio mix and sound design—and, of course, for outputting the

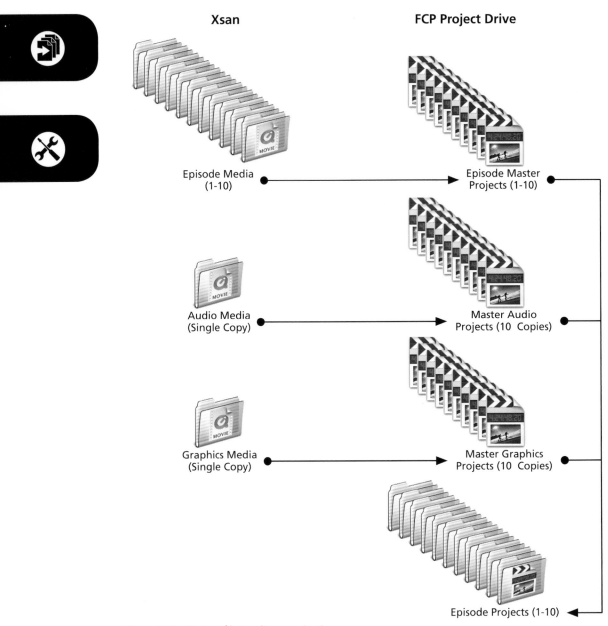

Figure 17.2   Project file/media organization.

shows. Because our onlines for this series have to happen one right after the other, any backup or delay could be a big problem. So, to ensure we don't run into any problems, I want to briefly give you some tips that will make the onlines go easier."

Track Organization—Jorge asks all of the editors to please follow a few simple rules. The first is to make sure that all audio is organized in a logical fashion. He explains that this will make the mix and sound-design process go faster. For this series, he explains that everyone should use the following audio-track layout:

- Narration on audio track 1
- Interviews and other on-camera sync audio on tracks 2-6
- Nat and ambient sound on 7-10
- Sound effects on 11-12
- Music on 13-16

Jorge also describes the importance of video-track organization. This means that although it is okay to have clips on lots of tracks, if they don't technically need to be organized that way (for purposes of an effect, etc.), then, where possible, the editors should try to organize clips onto a single track. This will make it much easier for Jorge to color-correct and color grade the show.

Nested Sequences—The next thing Jorge describes is the importance of making sure that items are not nested on the final Timeline. Later, when he goes back to the original master tapes to conform, any nesting could cause problems.

Documenting Problems and Their Correction—Jorge is a big believer in strong communication. He describes to the team the importance of keeping paper records of problems and places for specific corrections in the show. The editors should not assume he will catch all of the problems. Where possible, they should point them out for him. One example would be noting that at a certain timecode, there is a tape hit ("So please check this frame again after conforming the show"). Or the problem might be more aesthetic—making sure a look that the producer or editor envisioned is realized in the final show ("Can you make sure that the blue in the sky of these few shots is really saturated?").

After a lengthy day, all of the producers and editors leave feeling that even though it is going to be tough, they are now armed with the knowledge to complete the editorial on the project in a fast and efficient manner.

Weeks 6 through 14: Editorial and Approval

Editing begins on each of the ten episodes simultaneously. Like most edit projects, this starts slowly as producers and editors get acquainted with each other and with the material. The first few weeks go well, and a few episodes are quickly ready for network review.

Catherine, the executive producer for the company, has been working very closely with each edit team to polish each episode. Normally, she doesn't like to micromanage her teams like this, but Catherine is aware of something that they are not.

Recently, the network had a major personnel overhaul. After years of airing trendy, fluffy shows, the network now wants to return to solid, meaningful programming—something that this series represents. With that said, though, management—specifically Meg, the network executive producer with whom Catherine has been working—has been sending signals that the network really wants something else out of the series.

Catherine and her team submit the first few episodes of the series for approval to the network. Technically, this goes great—the system of encoding that Bob and Sam set up works flawlessly. The problem is that the network executive producer wants to talk. . . .

So Catherine sets up a phone call with Meg.

"I think the show works great, Catherine. Don't get me wrong, but I think the addition of a host will really help. I would really like to swap some of the segments from this first episode to the third episode. I get the feeling I'll probably want to do that quite a bit, you know?"

"I understand, Meg, but when we originally pitched the show, we did have a host. At that time, you decided that a host wasn't needed, and that the show worked better

without one. In addition, we have only a few more weeks before all of the episodes need to be delivered to you. This means that adding the host and reordering the segments is going to be extremely tight. I'm not sure we can do it."

"Oh, it's not that complicated. The host can be shot standalone—think of using the host as connective tissue between the segments. I have just the person in mind. And as far as reordering the segments, I thought you guys just set up some fancy edit suites. That should make moving things between episodes easy, right?"

Catherine has worked with networks for years, and she can see that there is no way of avoiding Meg's requests. "We did. I tell you what: I think we can do this, but it will be tight. Can you send me the info for the host you have in mind? I'll get it set up."

"Sure. Thanks again, Catherine. This will be a piece of cake! Talk soon. *Ciao!*"

Catherine, of course, is concerned about the budget. Making changes like the ones Meg wants is going to cost money. So Catherine's next call is to the line producer of the series (the line producer is the keeper of the budget). After 20 minutes of discussion, they are able to work out many budget implications. However, Catherine still feels uneasy. There are still some questions to answer. The next person she needs to talk to is Bob. Before she even goes to look for him, Bob walks into her office.

"Umm, did I come at a bad time?"

"No . . . Bob . . . umm . . . I mean yes. I was just talking to Meg over at the network, and she has some pretty substantial changes to the series and to some of the episodes we just submitted for approval."

Catherine goes on to brief Bob about the conversation. He understands the frustration in her voice, but he really isn't worried about these changes.

"Listen, Catherine, the moving around footage is the easy part! Our Xsan will really facilitate that whole process, and with Sam and all the editors being really technically savvy, I'm not worried about that at all. It will, of course, require the producers to be clever with the writing, but that should be okay too. As far as the host, how quickly do you think his lines can be written, and how much of it do you think there is?"

"I think there are probably five or six places in each episode where we will need to place the host. In terms of how much, probably a few hours altogether."

"Well, that sounds pretty straightforward. As soon as you get the host on board, I can coordinate with the camera crew to get this set up. The second the tapes come back here, we'll load them onto the Xsan and be good to go."

Over the next week or so, the show segments are reordered per Meg's request after she sees versions of each episode. During this time, the host is shot, and Sam loads that footage onto the SAN and into the appropriate master projects. The benefit of the Xsan implementation in this case is that editors can keep working on parts of the episode the whole time that Sam is loading footage for them.

After weeks of editing, the shows, one by one, are getting approved and heading to the next part of the process: online.

Weeks 10 through 20: Online and Finishing

Jorge likes online. Many parts of onlining a show are technical, and he considers himself a technical guy. Also, he loves doing color correction and grading. No other part of the process is as exciting to him as seeing footage really come alive after he has corrected or graded a clip.

This series is one of dozens that he has worked on for this network, so Jorge is very familiar with the technical aspects of delivery. He knows how slates need to be organized and notated, the requirements for duration of segments and for the show in general (called the network clock), how credits should be formatted, and any other broadcast packaging requirement.

The first thing for Jorge to do as he starts the online for each episode is to make outputs for the audio facility that is mixing the pieces. Each output consists of an OMF and a reference tape. To make the OMF, Jorge selects the sequence and chooses File > Export > Audio to OMF. Here, he adds three seconds of handles, and chooses to include level and pan information in the clip so that the mixer can get an idea of how the editor and producer want to mix the show. After this is exported, he burns the file to a DVD and labels it. Next, he outputs the reference tape, making sure that the timecode on the tape matches that of the OMF.

Of course, Jorge has not yet done his online work, so the reference tape he makes for the audio vendor is not final. The reference tape is of the offline picture-lock cut. This is all that the audio vendor needs as a video reference for the mix, as long as Jorge does not make any changes in the timing of the sequence.

The next step is media managing and conforming. To prep the finished offline segments for online, Jorge will simply open up the final version of the project that the offline editor has made for him. Then, selecting the final sequence, he will make an offline version of the sequence using the Media Manager. One big thing that Jorge often has to remind himself of, though, is to make sure that when he makes the offline version of the project, he *unchecks* the "Include master clips outside selection" option. He also must remember to uncheck the "Include affiliate clips outside selection" option. He wants only what is on the final Timeline, plus a second or so of handles. Jorge also makes sure to set the sequence to 10-bit uncompressed 1080p24. This will ensure that when he recaptures the footage, the sequence will be set up properly.

After creating the offline version of each project, Jorge begins the task of conforming the show. This process is made a little easier due to the fact that all graphics, stills, and audio (music and sound effects) are already on the Xsan and do not need to be captured but simply reconnected to the files on the XSAN. Jorge selects all of the offline clips that he has just created. Then he right-clicks and chooses Batch Capture. This prompts Final Cut Pro to open the Log and Capture window and present Jorge with the Batch Capture window. Here, he chooses to capture the clips, again double-checking that he is capturing 10-bit uncompressed 1080p24.

Jorge clicks OK on the Batch Capture dialogue box, and Final Cut Pro prompts him with a list of the tapes he needs and how many clips will be captured from each tape. He clicks OK, and proceeds to feed FCP the tapes that it requests.

After the entire show has been conformed, the fun part starts for Jorge. Finally, it's time for color correction!

For this series, Bob and Jorge have decided to use Color to correct and grade the show. Jorge is well versed in Color and is excited to be using it. However, he will not be able to use Color exclusively for this show because there are a ton of stills as well as motion clips in the sequence, and Jorge knows these elements will not go to Color. So, for the stills and motion clips, he will use the color correction tools in Final Cut Pro. To send the final sequence to Color, Jorge uses the Send to Color command in the File menu in Final Cut Pro.

Jorge considers himself an accomplished colorist and online editor, but he also appreciates the power of collaboration. Therefore, he sits with each producer as their shows go through the online process, and corrects and grades the shows with them. For Jorge, this is a good creative process—but also it is a bit of a safety net that he has learned over the years. By watching and working together, Jorge *and* the producer are responsible for the final product, not just Jorge alone.

In the past, he has been burned by not having a broadcast-legal master. He has learned his lesson, though. During his correction and grading, Jorge pays special atten-

tion to broadcast legality. Luckily, Color has a strong set of broadcast-safe controls, and the facility has a hardware legalizer. So Jorge can be confident the show is legal.

After correcting and grading a show and checking that it is broadcast safe, Jorge renders the clips. From the File menu in Color, he chooses Send To > Final Cut Pro. This reconnects FCP to the newly rendered clips. Jorge now also completes color correction on the remaining stills and motion clips.

The last step in the online and finishing process is broadcast packaging. This means that Jorge builds slates and credits along with clean covers (clean covers are shots sans text or other graphics; these shots can be used by the network should re-editing or changes be required). Luckily, for this series Jorge does not need to produce a separate graphics reel because all of the show graphics were provided by the network.

After watching the show several times to ensure that he has not missed anything, Jorge outputs each show. As he finishes each show, the master tape is sent to the audio vendor. This is now the broadcast master tape, and the final step is for the audio vendor to lay back just the mixed audio tracks (the vendor will not affect the video tracks at all) to the master tape.

Discussion

This project was a success for both the network and the production company, but it was also a high-wire act, and it could have very easily gone bad in a hurry. In many ways, this was an aggressive workflow that required innovative thinking at all stages and levels, and pushed the envelope on postproduction technology. Stretching the boundaries and breaking new ground are high-risk/high-reward chances. Here are several areas where the production company gambled and won:

- By investing in Xsan technology (an investment in both time and money), they enabled innovative and very efficient workflows through the entire process.

- By setting up and hiring a large and complex postproduction team (many producers and editors, plus support staff), they were able to harness the purchased equipment for maximum concurrent creative work.

- By choosing to work in a modified offline/online workflow and choosing specific codecs and formats to fit their needs (H.264 for review screeners and DVCPRO HD for offlining—neither one a traditional choice), they were able to always work at the best quality at every stage and to ensure complete timecode consistency.

Pretty much every gamble paid off. Which is not to say that everything was always perfect. For instance, we did not discuss Xsan administration and network problems very much, but they were factors. There were some mornings that the network was down, and it was an hour or two of hustling to figure it out and get it back up. Of course, unlike with traditional FCP systems that are not networked, when the network goes down, ALL of the editing stations go down with it. This is just an example of why the points above were risks. If the network problems had persisted, the people involved might have regretted their choice to go with newer technology.

Of course, workflows are not a blind gamble. There were plenty of choices along the way that made for a relatively smooth outcome. It is never just the quality of your plan that determines success—it is the team's collective talent and their ability to communicate with each other that make all the difference.

Here are some important factors that helped the risk/benefit scenarios turn out in a positive way:

- Bob's recognition of his limitations in the area of Xsan administration, and his decision to bring in Sam as an expert, and to delegate important decisions to him
- Sam's enthusiasm and flair for the technology, and his desire to raise technical efficiency to an art form
- The emphasis placed on education of the editors when they came onto a project that had elements that were unfamiliar to them
- Catherine's communication skills and leadership of the team, working at the hub between the client and the senior management on the project (including hiring them in the first place)

In the final analysis, the lesson learned is a classic: when a team is well organized and people really understand their roles, they can achieve the best possible work, and they can adapt nimbly when changes occur.

18 Music Video with Multicam Editing and Multiple Outputs

A talented young director/producer has been hired by a small music label to produce a music video for one of their promising fledgling acts. The record company, however, does not want to invest a hundred thousand dollars on the video because they are not sure this band will ever achieve mainstream popularity.

It is an important element of the project that the video work well—not just on television but also in all of the popular new-media channels: online, cell phones, and video iPods. The director/producer is known for his creativity—and, more importantly, for his ability to stretch a dollar. After discussing the project with the band and the label, a decision is made to shoot the video in high definition using Panasonic's AG-HVX200, a P2 HD camera. Often music videos are shot on 35mm film, but shooting HD will save a lot of money. This will allow them to shoot with multiple cameras and to put a lot of time and money into postproduction.

Highlighted Concepts and Techniques

- Multicam editing
- Working with a solid-state format (P2)
- Green-screen compositing
- Review process with multiple stakeholders (who have egos)

Challenges

- Delivering a high-end product on a budget
- Managing the review process on a complex special effects-driven piece

Overview

A small music label has signed an emerging young band called Run Scooby Run. The record company has much to gain from the success of the band. This act has the potential to get noticed. It could help their little label get purchased by a major company . . . well, maybe.

One of the things about being a small label is that you don't have a lot of money to make mistakes. The label can invest in only a few acts per year—and frankly, they are not totally sure about Run Scooby Run. They are willing to take a chance, but not a big one.

A major aspect of marketability is getting the band known to the public. One of the principal methods available to the record company, besides traditional distribution and sales on iTunes, is to produce a music video. Simply having this video on television

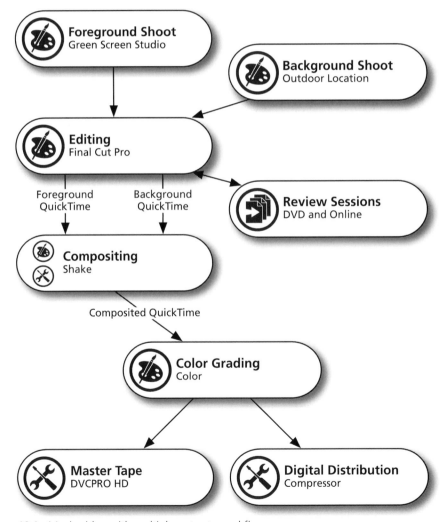

Figure 18.1 Music video with multiple outputs workflow.

won't cut it, though. The label knows that in the mediated world—one dependent on numerous forms of communication—in which we live, distribution to other outlets such as the Web and portable devices (iPods, smart phones, etc.) is essential to getting this band known—and, at the same time, growing the company.

The label hires a respected and creative music-video director/producer. His reputation has earned the trust of the record company, especially because he is known for his ability to get the most value out of what's spent, something that is especially important in this case. The label doesn't want to risk a lot of money on this band—but they don't want it to *look* that way.

After a few meetings with the producer/director and the band, the label has a good plan and, more importantly, a solid budget to produce the music video.

- The video will be shot HD instead of film, like many of their productions in the past.

- The director/producer will come up with a concept that both the record company and the band will approve. Then there will be a screening of a picture-lock cut with rough effects only. Both the label and the band will approve this screening before the final finishing work is done.

- To get the maximum coverage and the most flexibility for postproduction, they will shoot with four Panasonic AG-HVX200 HD cameras. These relatively inexpensive cameras will allow them to save money and put more of the budget into post.

- The postproduction will take advantage of desktop technologies such as FCP, Shake, and Color, but it will also rely on talented specialists in these areas.

- The video will be delivered on DVCPRO HD tape for broadcast and as separate files for Web, video iPods, and cell phones.

The producer/director has come up with a creative way to shoot the video. He will shoot the band on green screen, and then composite them over a cityscape background. The whole look will be enhanced by the fact that he is using four cameras for different creative angles on the band in the green-screen studio. He also plans to push color grading to the extreme to create a surreal look. Lastly, he has put a lot of thought into working for the "small screen" of handheld devices, and he has lots of ideas for creative styles that will work well within these confines.

Project Roles and Responsibilities

The director/producer on this project is far from a one-man band. During the postproduction, he relies heavily on an editor and colorist with whom he has worked for years, as well as a compositor with whom he has just recently reconnected. Together, they will see the video through postproduction and delivery.

This project was actually made up of more roles than we have detailed here. For the sake of simplicity, we do not discuss the many people required for the actual video shoot: gaffers, grips, makeup artists, and so forth. Instead, we'll focus on the roles that saw the project through postproduction and delivery.

Director/Producer—Francis has been making music videos almost exclusively for over ten years. Most of these projects have been shot using 16mm or 35mm film. His standard process requires transferring the processed film to videotape (telecine) and using these master tapes for the postproduction process.

Recently, he has also worked on several projects that took advantage of the digital intermediate process, where film was scanned and transferred to data files rather than videotape. These methods are exciting, but Francis understands that

they are *very* expensive—in fact, too expensive for this project. Francis has always considered himself a technical guy, and has followed very closely the developments in the world of HD video production and postproduction.

During this study of HD production and postproduction, he realized that for some projects, HD is the way go, especially when trying to pinch pennies (as is the case with this project). His primary role is to direct and produce the entire music video. He will shepherd this process from planning all the way through to delivery.

Francis has an interesting philosophy when it comes to his work. He fuses the traditional modes of creative, technical, and managerial in favor of concentrating on his overall vision, with all of its implications.

"When I sit down to do a budget, I am thinking about equipment and formats, but also how I am going to do something different, as well as the team I will use, and how I will communicate with and inspire them. . . . So you tell me, then: is this a management activity, creative, or technical?"

Editor and Colorist—Annie is a talented editor and colorist who has also been working almost exclusively on music-video projects during her career. She has had the good fortune of working with Francis quite a few times on various music videos, and really communicates well with him. Established relationships and patterns of communication are very helpful in any creative process.

Annie has her own small postproduction company that consists of her and her best friend, Bubba, the fearless postproduction watchdog! One reason that Francis likes working with Annie and her small shop is that he is very comfortable there and can really push the bounds of creativity. In this project, Annie's main role is to edit and color-grade the piece. She will also be responsible for final tape and file output.

Compositor—Paulo loves a challenge—and, in many ways, compositing provides the challenges that he needs. The bulk of his work these days involves compositing for commercials. Paulo ran into his old college buddy, Francis, at a local watering hole recently. The two got to talking, and Francis, being a gregarious artist, convinced Paulo to come on board to do some compositing for a new music video that he was shooting. Paulo was looking forward to the change from his regular advertising work. On this project, Paulo's main role would be to pull the final keys and meld the foreground (green-screen material) with the background.

The Band—Run Scooby Run is a promising new rock band. Together since high school, they have finally made some big career moves and have been signed by a respected but small label. They have already recorded their debut album, and are excited that they are making their first music video. They are even more excited that they get to work with Francis. Their arrogant lead singer, however, is worried that their "vision" will not be realized for the video, and the rest of the band seems to follow his lead.

Executive Producer at the Label—Ross is a no-nonsense kind of guy. To him, the music industry comes down to two things: (1) making money, and (2) making money. He has been the head of the record company for about five years, and has seen the label grow tremendously. It is Ross's goal in the next year or two to have the company acquired by a major label—and Run Scooby Run could be a big step toward that goal. In hopes that the first music video by the band be a success, Ross has hired Francis to direct and produce the piece. Ross's role is to approve the final version of the music video and to control the costs of the production.

Required Equipment

As described before, we'll focus on the postproduction aspects of this project. There were, of course, many more pieces of equipment used in the actual shoot—namely, Panasonic's AG-HVX200 HD camcorder. This equipment allowed Francis and the production team to shoot with four different cameras and get the maximum amount of coverage. The other wonderful thing about this camera is that it shoots HD on P2 media or hard drives such as Panasonic's P2 Store drive. This type of recording allows for much faster ingest of footage, and is capable of recording multiple frame sizes and frame rates. Other equipment included:

Final Cut Pro Edit System—A relatively fast Final Cut Pro system with plenty of RAM for multicam editing and drives fast enough to support at least 20MBps data rates (to support the DVCPRO HD footage), and an external calibrated HD monitor.

> For this project, the suite owned and operated by Annie was equipped with the latest Mac Pro and 6GB of RAM. The suite was also equipped with two 23-inch Cinema computer displays, a calibrated HD CRT monitor, and a 42-inch calibrated HD LCD monitor for Francis to view the piece. Additionally, Annie's system had a set of hardware scopes (rasterizers) that she could use to analyze the footage.

P2 Interface—To be able to capture P2 media, a P2 interface is needed. This could be the Panasonic AJ-PCD20, a P2 Store drive, or a FireStore drive. Lastly, this could also be an Apple PowerBook equipped with a CardBus slot (or a newer MacBook Pro with an adapter), or the camera itself could be used for this purpose.

> For this project, Francis and Annie will be using multiple P2 Store drives. Annie can simply mount these units to her machine via USB 2.0, and transfer the footage using the Log and Transfer tool in FCP.

Execution

Like many projects that develop over time, it is easiest to look at this project in chunks. We pick up with Francis having just been hired by the label.

Development

Walking out the door of the label's office having just gotten the gig, Francis's first thought was *What is the concept of this video going to be?* For him, this aspect of a music video was often the most fun, but also the most challenging. The problem was that he was often thinking about things that were just not possible . . . *yet*. The flexibility of video production and postproduction let him realize many of his visions, although he yearned for even more.

As he crossed the street to the coffee shop, his mind was spinning. In some ways, producing the Run Scooby Run video was going to be liberating. Many of the more established artists for whom he did videos were prima donnas. Francis also thought that this was a technically interesting project, trying out HD, multicam, and using Paulo for the compositing. . . . Even the name of the song was pretty cool: "Walking on Water" . . .

. . . *Wait a second—that's it!*

These guys need to walk on water, but how to do it? He flashed back to his conversation with his old college buddy Paulo, now a compositing specialist, at a bar near his home. Paulo was a gifted compositor and all-around artist. Francis was sure that the idea he had in his head could be realized with help from Paulo and Annie. The next step was selling this idea to the band—and, more importantly, to the label.

Francis pulled out his cell phone and called Theo, the lead singer and main voice for the band.

"Theo, my man, how you doing? Listen, I have a great idea for the video. When can we get together to break it down?"

"Francis, yo! Well it's kind of early, no?"

Francis glanced at his watch. It was 2:20 p.m. Musicians!

"Yeah . . . sorry about that, but I'm really excited about this idea. Can you assemble the guys, and I'll come over to your place?"

" Yeah, mate, that works. I just have to get these people out of my place. Late night, you know?"

"Um . . . I wish I knew. . . . Okay, I'll be at your place in an hour!"

Francis made his way across town, excited that the band was going to buy into his concept. If they did, his next step was just to pitch the idea to the label.

When Francis arrived, he knew better than to jump in. So he just hung out for a bit. Once they were feeling chummy, he worked the subject around to the video. "Ha ha ha . . . well, I slept on the sidewalk only that one time! . . . Okay guys, let me hit you up with this idea. The song is called "Walking on Water," and I thought, what better idea than having you guys actually walking on water! What I want to do is shoot you guys on a green screen in the studio, and then put you over footage of water. I'm thinking on the river where the skyline is cool with all of the skyscrapers. . . ."

"Dude! Didn't anyone ever tell you electric guitars and water don't mix?"

"Don't worry, Theo—you won't actually be near the water! Anyway, we set up the green screen in the studio. Actually, it will have to be a floor too, so we can get some shots of you guys walking and stuff. We'll have these really interesting angles and stuff. With the color treatments that we can give the sky and the city in the background, it'll look really dreamlike. My editor can do a killer job on this part. Also, the compositor . . . oh, I mean the special-effects guy . . . can work it so that water is interacting with you guys and make you look natural while 'walking on water' . . . sound good?"

There was a moment of silence. It occurred to Francis for a moment that maybe he had come on too strong. As was typical, Theo was the first to speak.

"What are we going to be wearing, mate? I want it to look epic—and most importantly, I want to look stunning. Are we wearing leather? Is this going to be like *Waterworld*? . . . I don't know, man. Kevin Costner is not my scene. . . ."

"No, no, no, it's gonna be killer! I think we can come up with something cool for the costumes. Don't worry!"

"Okay, Francis, I think we're a go—but hey, man, I want to be able to change and add to this idea as I see fit." The other band members nodded their agreement to that, although they realized that what Theo said regarded his personal opinion, not theirs. No one would mistake Run Scooby Run for a democracy.

"Umm . . . oh yeah, sure, no problem," Francis said, with more than a bit of sarcasm in his voice. He was also thinking that once money was committed in a certain direction, the label might also have something to say about the band's changes. But whatever, he was feeling more and more confident that he could make it look cool. That was his job, and he always came through.

"Let me give the label a call, and I think we can be shooting in the next two weeks."

Walking out the door of the band's loft, Francis thought that things had gone quite a bit better than he had expected. He couldn't help but feel that the band had some doubts, but wasn't that always the case?

He called the record company and got Ross's thumbs-up about the concept. Then Francis dived into the planning of the shoot. This was going to be fun!

Shooting

There were two shoots for the project:

1. The green-screen studio shoot with four HD cameras

2. A location shoot without the band, just a camera crew getting the shots that would form the background

For the green-screen work, Francis was fortunate enough to be working with a crew who did lots of this kind of work, so he was confident that things that could affect the success of this project in post (such as lighting) were being taken care of. Admittedly, the one thing he was a little worried about was using DVCPRO HD on the Panasonic cameras. Although the footage shot on these cameras was 4:2:2, it was heavily compressed. This could create some artifacts that would make it a little more difficult to composite. He accepted this limitation as a necessary evil because using these cameras was allowing him to really come in on budget with the grandeur of his idea still intact. Plus, he was confident Paulo could handle this issue when he composited the piece.

Using four AG-HVX200 cameras shooting 720p24 DVCPRO HD, with each recording to a P2 Store drive, Francis was able to get all the coverage he needed. There were two areas to which he paid special attention at the studio shoot:

1. The camera angles, which he wanted to fit with his surreal vision and his opinion of what works well on a small screen. Francis felt that meant more close-ups and more exaggeration of creative framing.

2. He wanted to get good sync points, with a clapper board for each take to be used in multicam editing.

After the studio shoot, Francis led a team down to the city to shoot all the footage of the cityscape and the water. The outdoor footage was also shot 720p24 DVCPRO HD to match the studio footage. Francis had a thorough plan going into the location shoot. It included many shot notes on the camera positions and angles used in the studio. As always, Francis was following his vision. In this case, it meant that the relationships between the foreground and the background would be slightly tweaked, in order to go with the exaggerated studio angles and contribute to the dreamlike feel.

This was the heart of Francis's special talent. It was his job to see the whole thing in his head, and then direct all of the constituent elements to achieve his vision. It was difficult, but also very rewarding. Now that everything had been shot, the next move was to get into the edit suite and start cutting all of this footage together.

Editing, Compositing, and Grading

A few days after shooting, Francis showed up at Annie's studio, greeted Bubba (the fearless postproduction watchdog), and handed off all of the P2 Store drives to Annie to ingest the footage into her system.

"You know, Francis, I love working with tapeless media like this P2 stuff. Gone are the days of having to capture from a tape!"

"I wouldn't count on tape disappearing anytime soon, Annie, but I agree that this certainly speeds up the process of ingesting the footage. How much time do you think you need to ingest all this stuff? I'd like to make a call over to the label to talk to Ross and give him an update about the project."

"Yeah, give it two hours or so to play it on the safe side. All I have to do is mount these drives and move over the footage—so do your phone call, run an errand, whatever you need to do."

After mounting each drive, Annie used the Log and Transfer utility inside Final Cut Pro to ingest all the DVCPRO HD footage for the project. Getting her first look at the

green-screen footage as well as the outdoor footage, she was pleased. Francis, as always, had managed to get some really great-looking shots. Of course, prior to transferring the footage, Annie had logged it carefully. She found that using the camera number, scene number, and each band member's name to log the clips had always helped her in the past to cut these multicamera music videos. Additionally, on some projects she was strict about setting In and Out points so she didn't capture extraneous footage. For this project, though, she decided to capture whole clips, knowing that she'd probably find some diamonds in the rough.

Normally at this stage, Annie would have also archived the drive or P2 cards using the Archive function of the Log and Transfer utility. However, because these P2 Store drives were not going to be used again until well after delivery of the final product(s), she felt confident that she didn't need to archive the footage now.

She transferred the footage quickly and without problem. The next step was syncing up the green-screen studio clips and making them multicam clips inside FCP. Better to do this now, she thought, than to have Francis waiting for her to do it.

Unlike some projects where the cameras had all been locked with the same time-code, this project hadn't used that method. This wasn't a problem, however, because Francis and his crew had used clapboards to signify the start of a given shot. With all four of the cameras pointing at the clapboard at the start of each shot, Annie could use this to sync the clips.

So she selected each of the four angles for each shot—which was easy to do because she had named the clips by angle, scene, and band member name—and found the point in each clip right where the clapboard snapped together. She marked an In point for each clip at this point. Next, she simply selected all four angles for each shot that she had just marked In points on. She right-clicked on the group and chose Make Multiclip. In the Make Multiclip dialogue box, she chose to synchronize the clips using the In Points option. Then she clicked OK. Voilà! She now had a multiclip.

Annie repeated the process for each scene, and in practically no time she was able to sync up all the angles. Almost as if on cue, she heard Bubba let out a big bark as Francis walked in.

"Yeah, I know: a couple hours turned into, like, four—but they were real productive. While I was at the coffee shop around the corner, I just really got into doing a much better storyboard for the video than the one I was going to give you. Take a look."

Francis was a pro. For editing sessions, he always showed up with storyboards, shot logs, and everything else he could think of to facilitate the process. The wrinkled piece of legal-sized paper he now handed over was a new one to Annie. He must be really feeling the creative juices flowing on this one, she thought.

"... Right. And that drawing right there is going to be tricky, but I think Paulo will be able to help with that shot."

"Actually, Francis, I was going to ask you about that. Obviously, we are going to cut together the footage, and probably do some rough compositing, but Paulo is going to do the final compositing, right?"

"Yep. I figure we can be doing some rough keys in here to see how the footage works with the background, and then we just pull off those keys after we have reached picture lock. Then we'll send a QuickTime of the video over to Paulo along with the background footage we choose, as a separate QuickTime, and Paulo can composite in Shake. After he's done, he'll send the whole thing back over to you for final grading."

Francis and Annie spent the next two weeks cutting together the green-screen footage and choosing the right background shots. Cutting together the green-screen footage was made much easier by the multicam functions in Final Cut Pro. Using the keyboard in combination with the Viewer, she was able to cut quickly between angles. The best part was that all of the angles also showed up on her nice 42-inch HD client monitor, so Francis could really play an interactive role in helping choose the shots from the different angles.

Annie had always thought of herself as musical. And so, to facilitate cutting to the beat, she first laid down some markers. As she was listening to the song, she marked the beat by simply hitting M on the keyboard with the clip selected. This placed markers on the clip that she used as reference points for cut points.

Both Francis and Annie were happy with the cut, but before they sent the footage on to Paulo, they needed to get approval of the picture-locked rough cut from both the band and the label. This brought up some challenges that Francis had already been thinking about. The cut that he was about to show didn't look very good. Because every shot in this piece was a special-effects shot, and the special effects had not yet been done, the whole thing looked unfinished. . . Well, it *was* unfinished!

Francis and Annie knew the process, knew what they were looking at, and were easily able to imagine the final product as it would look with Paulo's compositing work and the final color grading. Francis could not expect the same with the other stakeholders in this review, especially not from the band, and this worried him.

He knew from experience that it was best to prep the label and the band for what they were going to see. This was *not* the final version of the piece, and that was important for everyone to realize. Unfortunately, as with most rough cuts—or even fine cuts—it was often hard for people not intimately familiar with the process to envision the final product, especially when the whole look depended on the effects.

Francis knew that with all of his label experience, Ross would be better at this process than the band would. Therefore, it would be worth getting both Ross and the band to watch the cut together. Annie made a simple DVD for Francis by sending the sequence to Compressor and then into DVD Studio Pro.

Francis walked into the conference room to see Ross and the band already assembled.

"Gents, great to see all of you. I think we are getting pretty close to the vision we all signed off on, but I want to be clear about one thing before we watch this DVD. This is meant to be an approval cut for content and style only; none of the final effects or color grading have taken place yet.

"So this is a rough cut only, and what that means, in this case, is that you will see all of the shots—background and foreground, as they are cut together and relate to each other—but the final effects are not done.

"This means a couple of things. The edges between the background and foreground—these are not clean; that will come with the work my friend Paulo is going to do. Also, you are not seeing the final colors—we are going to do some really wild stuff with that. If you guys want, you can come over and give some input on the color; it's gonna be really cool.

"I gotta be honest, and tell you guys that reviews like this make me really nervous because the piece doesn't look that good, and it's gonna look much better when it's done. . . . You guys have a creative job, you know what I mean? Its like if you were just working on a song, and it wasn't finished, and you had to get feedback from guys who weren't even musicians. . . . Well, that's what this is like for me, so go easy on me. This is tough."

Francis popped the disc into the DVD player, and they watched the video. Everyone in the room was tapping their toes—a good sign. Then, out of the corner of his eye, he saw that Theo, the lead singer, was frowning with his arms folded across his chest.

"So what do you guys think? Ross?"

"I love it! I think I'll love it a bit more when the final effects are in place, but I think it is really the direction we were going for."

"Theo?"

"I don't get it, mate. I'm the bloody lead singer of the band, and all I see are some cool shots—but not me!"

The rest of the band looked at the floor, a sure sign that they had dealt with Theo's ego before.

"Look, Theo, we discussed the look of this shoot at length a few weeks ago at your loft . . ."

"I remember, Francis. But I also said I wanted the power to change or add to it and I'm saying add more of me, or I don't want this thing leaving this room."

Annoyed by Theo's childish attitude, Francis took a deep breath. Ross was giving him a look that said: It's your job to fix this—or else. Francis knew he had to act quickly.

"Okay, Theo, I understand. I don't think this video should be exclusively about you, but I can make some changes back in the edit suite. Is that okay?"

"Yeah, I guess, mate. Just make it good."

Francis let out a sigh, and thanked everyone for their time. As he left the review, still slightly annoyed, he realized two things, both of which qualified as good things, so he smiled.

1. After all of his worrying and blathering, no one had said a word about the effects, and no one had seemed thrown off by the rough composite. The actionable feedback had been on editorial shot selection, so the incomplete effects had not distracted them.

2. This is exactly why he had set up the review for this stage of the process. Paulo's time was expensive, so it was important to have him work on the final picture-lock cuts. Francis didn't want him working on shots that they were not going to use in the final piece.

So Francis was still confident when he sat down with Annie to do the revisions. By day's end, they had sent a cut over to Ross and the band. The cut had more shots of Theo, and was a high-quality H.264 QuickTime. After a few nervous hours, Ross called to say that he and the band were happy with the cut, so go ahead and finish up the video. But make it snappy—budget was getting smaller every hour that went by.

Relief spread over Francis as he directed Annie to prepare the cut along with background footage for Paulo. To create the files that Paulo needed, Annie had to export the foreground and background layers of the sequence separately. She did this in a few steps:

1. She turned off the key filters on the foreground layer. These were the rough keys that Annie had created for the rough cut and the review process.

2. She created a QuickTime export in the uncompressed 10-bit codec. Because she had removed the key filter, only the foreground layer was visible in this export.

3. She turned off video track 2 where the foreground layer (the green-screen material) was edited, exposing the background.

4. She made another QuickTime output (again uncompressed 10 bit)—this one of just the clean background layer.

5. Then Annie simply made a data DVD with both clips on it to send over to Paulo.

Paulo was good. In only a week, he had returned a QuickTime to Annie for color grading. Shake has some color-correcting tools, but these are designed primarily for matching layers together, and Paulo was not a color grading specialist. However, this was one of Annie's specialties. Francis had done color work with Annie before, and there was no doubt that she should be the colorist. Annie was using Color for most of her color grading work these days. She had been color-correcting for years, and she just loved having professional-quality correction and grading tools on her own desktop system.

Francis was out of town, but he had Paulo send his finished composite over to Annie to get started on. Also, he called Annie with his color-treatment ideas. Again, Francis had looked closely at the way color enhances the viewer's experience, especially on smaller mobile screens. Of course, this was not new to Annie because they had talked about it some in the offline process, and had even tried some things inside, though they never showed anyone else these quick tests. Francis wanted the piece to be very vibrant. Surreal, but not off the map—just everything turned up a notch.

Over the next two days Annie used Color to grade the video. This video was very styled, so the secondary grading and color-effects tools inside Color gave her an incredible range of options and lots of flexibility. She spent quite a bit of time doing secondary grading on the water as well as the sky in the background footage. Also, she thought that adding a slight vignette on shots with Theo in it would subtly focus the viewer's eyes on him—and, she hoped, would appease him.

When Francis got back to town, he set up a review session with Annie, Paulo, and the band. Francis had scheduled the session so that there would be time for him to work with Annie and Paulo for a few solid hours, getting the piece to where he wanted it. Then the band would show up for their final approval. Paulo, for his part, was always interested to learn new things, and Color had definitely been on his radar. So, when everyone gathered at Annie's studio, they were all in a good mood. This would be the last step in finishing the video.

"Paulo, Francis wasn't kidding about your skills. You did an incredible job with all of the compositing!"

"Hey, thanks, Annie. That means a lot, coming from you. I really admire your work. Also, it's nice to do something besides a car commercial once in a while!"

"Guys," Francis chimed in, "let's get this session started. We've got a few hours to work before the band and Ross get here, but I have some crazy stuff I want to try."

"Great, let's go," Annie responded with excitement.

"Cool," said Paulo. "Annie, let me know if there is anything technical you need to know about the composite. I totally trust your judgment on color, but I've looked closely at this footage, and worked hard to pull the keys, so I might be able to clue you in to some things along the way. Also, any wisdom that you want to throw out about Color—the software or the art form—I'm all ears."

With that, Annie gave Francis a look (she knew how important this was to him), and played the color-graded cut on the HD monitor. Francis was absolutely thrilled with the result. Annie had nailed it. Paulo and Annie geeked out a little bit about the software, but in a rare event, Francis did not have a single tweak or alternate treatment he wanted to try. It was time to call the band over.

The band arrived to a hearty greeting from Bubba (followed by an introduction to the postproduction staff). If anything, the band members were even more ecstatic than Francis when they saw the cut (which, of course, was what Francis had intended). There were hugs and high fives all around. Francis thought that this seemed to be the happiest he had seen the band during the whole process—that alone was worth a smile.

After they all shared a beer, Francis was the last to leave. "Annie, I owe you a big bottle of Bordeaux! You've done an incredible job, as always! I just got an email from Ross, and he has approved the cut from the QuickTime we posted earlier. All I have to do now is get him and the label pinned down on what they want for deliverables. They've been talking about all sorts of things—like making files for iTunes, the Web, cell phones, and, I'm guessing, probably television."

"Okay, no problem. Just get the specs from them. I have to get started on another project, but this will be safe on this machine. Once you know what's going on, I can run compressions and do outputs in the evening once you know what we need to make."

Delivery

Francis could really see the light at the end of the tunnel now. There was the usual excitement at the completion of any project, of course, but this one also had another aspect to it that was causing Francis some concern: all of the different output types.

When Francis had signed on to the project, Ross had explained to him that music videos were no longer about just television release anymore. After all, music television in general hadn't been playing just videos in years and years. The new market for music videos, Ross felt, was online, cell phones, and portable-device distribution, as well as nontraditional distributors like iTunes. Francis had to agree. Almost every piece of music or every movie he purchased these days he purchased online.

These factors had been present in Francis's mind throughout the process. They were part of the reason that the piece had its distinctive look. Now it was time for the endgame. Just a few years ago, he really had had no considerations for a project other than to make it look good, to output a tape, and to get it on TV. Now the synergy between having that piece on TV, on the Web, or on a smart phone or iPod was undeniable. These were Francis's thoughts as he went to his final big meeting with Ross.

"Great work again, Francis, on the video. I think we really have a good thing going on here with this group, and I know that this video will help them be a big success. As we've discussed, here at the label we are always looking toward the future of distribution. I've got the final specs for the formats here. Distribution will include several web versions; a version for iPods that people can download from our web site; and versions for GPRS, CDMA, GSM, and 3G cell-phone networks. We have several potential deals with cell carriers, and I want to be ready with files. I don't know whether they will want to re-encode them, but I'm trying to be proactive."

"I can do that, I think . . . To be honest with you, Ross, I'm still trying to keep up with all of the types of distribution—it seems like things are changing every day. What about iTunes distribution?"

"I think they are, Francis. And like many small companies, we're just trying to stay on top of it. As far as iTunes distribution, we are already a signed iTunes label. We can submit music for the iTunes Store using the iTunes Producer software, but we haven't yet put any of our music videos up on the store. The marketing team and I are contemplating it with your video, so we'll see."

Francis left Ross's office a little bewildered. Truly, the pace of technology was still sprinting, whereas he sometimes felt he was merely jogging. Francis smiled, though, because it was amazing: one project could literally reach millions more people than just television distribution alone. That was powerful, he thought. Maybe he'd be getting a lot more work after this project!

Francis gave Annie a call to discuss the deliverables. Annie wasn't a compressionist by trade, but using Compressor, part of Final Cut Studio, she could easily make the compressions to the specs that Francis had just emailed her from the label.

"No problem, Francis. I will set these files up to encode tonight. Actually, it's funny. I was taking a look through Compressor, and I discovered that there are actually presets for web output, video iPod output, and all the different cell-phone systems. Now that I have the specs from the label, I can simply edit the presets, and we're good to go!"

"Perfect. Oh, Annie, don't forget: we need to do the tape output too. It's kind of funny that we did this whole process tapeless, and now we have to master back to tape."

"I agree, but hey, everyone can't be as hip as us! But no problem—I have my DVCPRO HD deck right here, ready to go."

Discussion

After the final delivery, Francis was reflecting on a job well done. There were many things to smile about on this project. It had been cutting-edge throughout, from the HD P2 shooting to the multiple-distribution formats. However, the technology did not get in the way of the creative vision; it actually enhanced it.

He had been able to work with some of his favorite talent, and in a way that gave them all a lot of creative ownership in their areas. The integrated Apple postproduction workflow (Final Cut Pro, Shake, and Color) had allowed him to do everything he wanted, with exactly the artists he wanted to do it with, and still meet the budget.

He had peers who had struggled with all the radical changes in technology, but he was prospering. Some creative professionals seemed afraid that their special skill would no longer be valuable if more people could afford better equipment. Francis had never seen it that way.

The way he saw it, his special skill was the creative vision, and inspiring a team to realize that vision. After this project, he had no doubt that inexpensive, high-quality solutions such as HD P2 cameras and Final Cut Studio could be a benefit to his own creativity and to professional video workflows in general.

In Between . . .

Postproduction technology continues to change at breakneck speed.

New technologies are upon us before we have even learned to take full advantage of the previous innovations (let alone write books about them).

During the writing of this book, Apple announced (but has not yet released) the promising new software Final Cut Server "to provide media asset management and workflow automation for postproduction and broadcast professionals" (according to their web site). From everything we can gather, this new product has the potential to change the way that many large-scale Final Cut Pro implementations are conceptualized and executed.

One underlying theme of this book is to understand new technologies in the context of the technologies that preceded them. Historical context helps one to perceive underlying principles that continue to apply through generations of artists, methods, and technologies.

Our approach to Final Cut Server is no different. We look forward to using it, and expect it to be very useful in certain situations. Even if we wind up using it more often than not, the new software probably still will not fundamentally change the way we think about nonlinear editing or postproduction workflows.

One thing that the case studies in this book show is that producers of media adapt Final Cut Pro to their specific needs. Final Cut Server should enhance this flexibility but not fundamentally alter its nature.

So, we could not write an afterword to this book. We needed to write a "To Be Continued"—or, as we prefer to call it, an "In Between . . ."

Please read the two additional chapters about Final Cut Server workflows on the Web at *http://booksite.focalpress.com/Osder/finalcut/*.

Until then . . .

Jason and Robbie

Index